The Wizard of Waxahachie

The Wizard of Waxahachie

Paul Richards and the End of Baseball as We Knew It

Warren Corbett

Foreword by Brooks Robinson

Introduction by Tony La Russa

Sport in American Life

C. Paul Rogers III, series editor

SOUTHERN METHODIST UNIVERSITY PRESS

Dallas

Requests for permission to reproduce material from this work should be sent to:
  Rights and Permissions
  Southern Methodist University Press
  PO Box 750415
  Dallas, Texas 75275-0415

Cover image: Paul Richards as Orioles manager with Luman Harris. Courtesy of the *Baltimore Sun*.

Jacket and text design: Tom Dawson

Library of Congress Cataloging-in-Publication Data

Corbett, Warren, 1945-
    The Wizard of Waxahachie : Paul Richards and the end of baseball as we knew it /
Warren Corbett ; foreword by Brooks Robinson ; introduction by Tony LaRussa. — 1st ed.
        p. cm. — (Sport in American life)
    Includes bibliographical references and index.
    ISBN 978-0-87074-556-0 (alk. paper)
    1. Richards, Paul, 1908-1986. 2. Baseball managers—United States—Biography. 3.
Baseball players—United States—Biography. I. Title. II. Series: Sport in American life.
    GV865.R4278C67 2009
    796.357092—dc22
    [B]
                                                                                        2009020049

Printed in the United States of America on acid-free paper

10 9 8 7 6 5 4 3 2 1

For Wyleen Jolley Corbett and
Warren Paris Corbett Sr.

Contents

Brooks Robinson

Paul Richards was one of the best baseball people I ever knew. I feel so fortunate to have been able to sign with the Orioles and to have had Paul as my manager at the beginning of my career. He was so far ahead of everyone else. He knew every position, and he knew what made that position tick—whether it was third base, second base, first base, pitcher, catcher, or outfielder. I hung on every word he said, but he was a man of few words. Sometimes he wouldn't even acknowledge you. He always looked like he was thinking.

Seven or eight teams were scouting me when I was playing American Legion ball as a teenager in Little Rock, Arkansas. My choices came down to Baltimore and Cincinnati. Paul called my father and told him, "They lost a hundred games in Baltimore last year. We're gonna lose a hundred this year. If your boy can play, he'll get a chance to play here." The day I graduated from high school in 1955, I signed with the Orioles. The next day I took my first plane ride and went to Baltimore.

Paul signed a lot of young players and handed out huge sums of money. He gave several young men $30,000 or $40,000. I got only $4,000, and that was lucky for me. If you got more than $4,000, the rules said you had to stay with the major league club for two years, sitting on the bench most of the time. There is no doubt that spending two years in the big leagues when you are eighteen or nineteen and overmatched stunts your growth as a ballplayer. Most of the young men who got those big bonuses didn't make it. But I went to the minors where I could play every day and learn.

Cincinnati was suspicious that I had been paid some extra money under the table, so the Reds lodged a complaint with Commissioner Ford Frick. The commissioner called me up to his office in New York. He made me put my hand on the Bible and said, "Do you swear to tell the truth, the whole truth, and nothing but the truth?" And I said, "Yes, sir." I was eighteen and shaking in my shoes, but I told him I never got a penny more than $4,000.

The Orioles sent me to York, Pennsylvania, in Class B ball. I signed as a second baseman, but about fifty games into that first season my manager, George Staller, and Paul said, "We think you'll be better off at third base. You don't have enough speed to play second, but third is a reflex position, and you have good reflexes." That move made my career. And Paul upheld his part of the bargain. After York's season was over in September, he called me up to Baltimore. I was in the major leagues at eighteen years old. I batted twenty-two times and got two hits.

The next spring the Orioles brought all the young players to spring training in Arizona on February 15, two weeks ahead of everybody else. In the morning we would work out at Scottsdale Stadium. I would go over to Mesa and play a game against the Cubs and then go back to Scottsdale, where the team would work out again. A workout, a game, and then another workout—that is the way Paul operated. The coaches would throw batting practice hour after hour. We worked from daylight to dark. Paul wanted to get kids to the big leagues as soon as possible.

He was not a father figure for any of us. He would say, "Son, come here a minute." He spoke his mind and that was it. He would let you know if you did something wrong. We had to toe the line but he helped us. When you are eighteen years old, you need a lot of help.

For a couple of years I was up and down from the majors to the minors like a bouncing ball. In 1958 I stayed with Baltimore the entire season. I played 145 games but hit only .238 and never really distinguished myself. Paul kept putting me in the lineup and letting me learn on the job. I believed that 1959 was going to be my big year.

The day after the 1958 season ended, I had an army obligation of six months' active duty and five and a half years in the Arkansas National Guard. My active duty ended only three or four days before the 1959 season started. On opening day somebody was hurt, so I was put in the lineup. It was the third of twenty consecutive opening day starts I would have with the Orioles.

Just before my twenty-second birthday on May 18, Paul called me to meet him for breakfast. He told me he was going to send me down to the Orioles Triple A team in Vancouver so I could get some playing time and get the spring training that I had missed. Looking back, I think it hurt my ego more than anything else. I had been in the big leagues all of the 1958 season, I opened the 1959 season in Baltimore at third base, and now I was going back to the minor leagues? I was worried what my family and friends in Little Rock would think when they saw me back in the minor leagues. I told him I was ready to play. Paul said, "No, I want you to go to Vancouver to play every day. You go out there and get into shape and I *will* bring you back." Now, how many times has a manager said, "I will bring you back," and you never hear from him again? I thought I knew more than he did, but it turned out to be the best thing that ever happened to me.

I hit .331 in two months at Vancouver, and Paul brought me back up in July, just like he had promised. I was an entirely different player. I had more strength and confidence, and I knew I was going to play every day. I ended up hitting .284 with the Orioles. Then in 1960 I had my breakout year. The Orioles finished second to the Yankees, and I finished third in the Most Valuable Player voting behind Roger Maris and Mickey Mantle. Paul knew what was best for me as a player.

Paul and I became close later in his life when he was working for the Texas Rangers and I was broadcasting the Orioles' games. We would get together for dinner and talk more than we ever had when I was a young player. He knew things about the game of baseball that I had never even thought about.

I believe he does not get the credit he is due because he never won a World Series. But he put together the White Sox, and they got into a World Series soon after he left. He put together the Orioles, and we became consistent winners over a long period of years. Earl Weaver and Hank Bauer managed most of those great Orioles teams. Earl broke in as a minor league manager under Paul, and I am sure he would tell you that Paul taught him a lot. Earl is in the Hall of Fame, as he should be, and someday I hope that Paul will be there, too.

Paul Richards was one of the greatest influences on my career. With this book he is finally getting the respect he deserves.

Brooks Robinson won sixteen consecutive Gold Gloves as the Baltimore Orioles' third baseman and was elected to the Baseball Hall of Fame in 1983.

Introduction

Tony La Russa

I first met Paul Richards at the 1976 spring training camp of the Chicago White Sox in Sarasota, Florida. After managing the Baltimore Orioles during the 1961 season, Paul had been brought back by Bill Veeck to manage the White Sox. The next time I saw him was in the spring of 1978. This time Paul was the director of player development for the White Sox minor league system.

In 1976 I was an invited player to the major league camp after I'd had a respectable 1975 season for Chicago's AAA team in Denver. My boosters, Loren Babe and Roland Hemond, had convinced Bill and Paul to give me a look as a utility infielder. Spring training that year was disrupted by a dispute between the players' union and baseball's management. The roster players were not in camp, and the invited players had an opportunity to showcase their talents. Unfortunately the more you saw of me, the less there was to like. Those circumstances gave me an up-close experience observing two of Paul's legendary characteristics. He had a well-earned reputation for honesty and evaluating talent. It didn't take Paul long to decide that I wasn't good enough. The honesty part can be painful for a player, but it really is the best way to communicate. He explained what he saw and what I lacked.

The time I was with Paul in 1978 there were important differences. As director of player development he was responsible for the players and coaches in the minor league system. I was a first-time manager with the AA Knoxville Sox in the Southern League. By this time I had learned a lot more about Paul's storied career. It's fair to say that this knowledge was intimidating. Paul was near the end of a sixty-year run in professional baseball as a player, manager, and general manager. He had interacted with historic baseball men like Connie Mack and Bill Terry. Over the years Paul had earned a well-deserved reputation for being a master in all phases of the game. I had already become acquainted with his honesty and evaluation skills. But that was only the beginning. During the three-year period from 1978 to 1980, when I'd managed in AA, AAA, and the White Sox, Paul's influence was a career maker for me. He continually provided lessons on baseball fundamentals, strategies, and leadership.

To this day his emphasis on playing the game correctly and what that meant has been a key to my survival as a manager in baseball. His explanation of different offensive and defensive strategies has helped put my teams in a position to compete. And his leadership advice set the foundation for my contributions as a decision maker that I am expected to provide.

My favorite example of a "Paulism" was his principle that a manager should make decisions by "trusting your gut, not by trying to cover your butt." A manager's decision must avoid the temptation of taking the popular or conventional path that your bosses, fans, and media expect. Instead your responsibility as a manager is to decide what you think is your team's best shot and then take it.

My memories of Paul are mostly from the ballpark. But I also spent evenings with him that included Bill Veeck and other dedicated baseball men who loved the game. The mutual respect and trust among these men showed in their conversations about the men, not machines, trying to play baseball at the highest level. I was allowed to attend these evenings as a student. There is no institution of higher learning that could have provided a better education for me.

My exposure to Paul was limited. There is much more to be learned from the entirety of his life and career. Warren Corbett provides you a complete look at what this remarkable man accomplished. Paul's story is fascinating because his career spanned so many colorful periods of baseball history and because he was involved in many different roles in the game. If you're interested in understanding baseball at its deepest levels, then learning from Paul will get you there.

Enjoy the read!

Tony La Russa, for the past three decades one of the most successful managers in major league baseball (for the Chicago White Sox, the Oakland A's, and currently for the St. Louis Cardinals), was one of Paul Richards's last protégés.

The Wizard of Waxahachie

CHAPTER 1

"Why Can't You Forget This Guy?"

"When I managed in Baltimore, one of my players said I had the personality of a doll . . . a crocodoll." Paul Richards delighted in repeating that line, because he savored his reputation as a tough guy. Broadcaster Ernie Harwell said, "The players were scared to death of him." But this tough Texan couldn't drive a nail straight, fainted at the sight of blood, and cried when his daughter's beloved pony Ginger died.

Richards never won a pennant or a World Series as a manager and executive, but he was hailed as an innovator and as one of the game's most intelligent practitioners, as well as one of its most controversial figures. He took command of perennial losing teams in Chicago and Baltimore and turned them into winners. He built Houston's expansion team from scratch. He started Brooks Robinson, Joe Morgan, Nellie Fox, and Hal Newhouser on their way to the Hall of Fame. Two other leading stars, Minnie Minoso and Billy Pierce, owed their careers to him. Richards built the foundation for the Baltimore Orioles, baseball's most successful team over a twenty-year span from the 1960s to the 1980s.

Competition and conflict marked Richards's sixty-year career from his first week as a professional player, when the seventeen-year-old *may* have punched his manager. As a manager, Richards was thrown out of games more frequently than anyone else. In his first year as a general manager, he was threatened with suspension for cheating. He brought the first black players to the White

Sox and the first important black players to the Orioles, but several of them denounced him as a racist. In his later years his was one of the loudest and most reactionary voices opposing the rising players' union.

When his catchers couldn't handle a knuckleball, he invented a mitt as big as an elephant's ear so they could at least knock it down. He was the first manager known to enforce pitch counts to protect young arms from injury. Previously undiscovered documents reveal that Richards tracked his hitters' on-base percentages before that statistic even had a name and decades before it became a cornerstone of baseball analysis. He computed catchers' earned run averages years before the sabermetric community thought of it.

Sportswriter Leonard Koppett wrote that Richards "thought he was smarter than everyone else, which in itself is neither unusual nor necessarily unpleasant. But he gave you (or at least me) the impression that he thought you were too dumb to understand how smart he was."[1] Richards's son-in-law, Bill McQuatters, got the same treatment when he asked a question about baseball strategy. Richards replied, "It's a simple game. You throw the ball, you hit it, you catch it." Bill said, "He thought I was too dumb to understand any more."[2]

Above all, Richards was a teacher. He resurrected the careers of at least a dozen failed pitchers. He demanded that his players practice the game's fundamentals and then practice them some more. He wrote: "The simple things in baseball number into the thousands. The difficult or esoteric? There is none."[3]

Richards and the writers who covered him had a collection of stock stories about him that they repeated decade after decade. With the writers' help he created his own legend. I set out to run each of the colorful anecdotes to ground, to prove them true or false. Did he win both games of a high school doubleheader, pitching one game left-handed and the other right-handed? Did he slug his manager in his rookie year? Did he convert baseball's first Hall of Fame reliever, Hoyt Wilhelm, into a starting pitcher?

One of the most frequently cited examples of Richards's innovative genius was his stratagem, while managing Buffalo in 1949, of walking the Montreal pitcher so the next batter, speedy lead-off man Sam Jethroe, could not steal if he reached base. The story became a staple of many published profiles of Richards, and he repeated it in many forms, but Buffalo baseball historian Joseph M. Overfield attempted to debunk it decades later. As I pursued the facts, I put my notes in a file labeled "will o' the wisp," because it seemed the truth was not out there. I finally found the last word—Richards's own words. You can read about it in chapter 9.

Tito Francona, a rookie outfielder with Richards's Orioles in 1956, said nearly forty years later: "I dream of him a lot. Of Richards. He gives me nightmares. They've never been good dreams. It's always that he's getting back at me. Or I'm going up to bat, and as soon as I get to the plate he sticks a pinch hitter in for me. I've never had a dream where he said anything good to me. I don't know why.

"My wife used to get upset with me: 'Why can't you forget this guy!'

"And that's just it. He was such a great manager."[4]

"To other people, he could be cold," Richards's daughter Paula told me. "That was his persona, his mystique."[5] The child is father to the man; he was a solemn, silent boy from a small Texas town who grew a carapace of arrogance to mask his feelings. But two successful executives, one in baseball and one in business, revered him as a surrogate father. Richards did not graduate from high school, but he could recite the Gettysburg Address and the fourth verse of *The Star-Spangled Banner*. (He liked it better than the familiar first one.) He taught Sunday school in the Baptist church. At home he never used any words stronger than *damn* or *hell* and once ordered a friend out of his house when the man cursed in front of Richards's wife and daughter. But one umpire said, "He has the foulest mouth in the major leagues."[6]

Next to baseball, his passion was golf. Some believed it was the other way around. But he was a habitual cheater, so flagrant that some friends refused to play with him. His third passion was "the con"; even his daughter describes him as a con artist. He conned players, owners, sportswriters, family, friends, and golfing pigeons.

Richards's career began under Brooklyn manager Wilbert Robinson, who was born during the Civil War. Among the last men Richards mentored was Tony La Russa, one of the most successful managers since the late 1970s. La Russa told me that Richards lectured him on the need to win the respect of his players and taught him to respect "the beauty of the competition." By the time Richards died in 1986, free agency had transformed the baseball business, and the Major League Baseball Players Association had gained the whip hand in negotiations with the owners, leaving him an old-school caricature railing against the social and economic changes that destroyed baseball as he knew it.

During his sixty-year career Richards composed a more detailed record of his baseball philosophy than any other man. He published one book, wrote a 101-page manuscript of another, penned magazine and newspaper articles, left behind two oral histories, and spoke tens of thousands of words that were reported by sportswriters. With this rich record in hand I have tried to let Richards and his contemporaries tell the story, a story that traces the history of baseball from John McGraw and Ty Cobb to Joe Torre and Tony La Russa.

---

1. Leonard Koppett, *The Man in the Dugout* (New York: Crown, 1993), 196.
2. Bill McQuatters, interview by author, August 18, 2007, Fernley, Nevada.
3. The quote comes from an unfinished, untitled manuscript that apparently was typed from Richards's dictation over several years beginning no earlier than 1972 and continuing until 1978 or later, according to internal evidence. A chapter headed "A Stated Purpose" says it was intended as a manual "for high school, college and amateur managers and coaches." Richards's friend Mike Hastings provided a copy, which is in my files. Hereinafter cited as "Richards manuscript."
4. Larry Moffi, *This Side of Cooperstown* (Iowa City: University of Iowa Press, 1996), 244.
5. I spoke with Richards's only surviving child, Paula, many times by phone and at her home in Wadsworth, Nevada, from May 17 to 19, 2007. I also exchanged numerous e-mail messages with her. All those contacts are cited throughout as "Paula Richards interviews."
6. Paula Richards interviews; Mike Hastings, interview by author, August–September 2006, Waxahachie, Texas.

CHAPTER 2

Sleepy

America had a national pastime in those ancient days called baseball.
—**Eliot Asinof,** *New York Times,* **September 30, 1967**

Waxahachie is such a stereotypical small Texas town that it has played the part in at least nineteen movies; 1967's *Bonnie and Clyde* is the most famous. A turreted Romanesque 1895 courthouse and a few dozen gingerbreaded homes were planted along Waxahachie Creek in an oasis of trees, plopped down on a sun-parched prairie seared in summer by a steamy wind that robs visitors of their breath and sends locals scurrying outside the city limits in search of a cooling drink at the end of the day, because Waxahachie was, and is, a dry town.

The name, pronounced "wawx-uh-HATCH-ee," means "cow creek" or "buffalo creek" in the Tonkawa Indian language, depending on which source you believe.[1] The town is thirty miles south of Dallas.

Paul Richards was born in Waxahachie, returned there nearly every fall during a baseball career that spanned seven decades, and died there, less than two miles from his birthplace, at age seventy-seven. After Richards became a successful major league manager, a sportswriter reaching for alliteration coined the enduring nickname "The Wizard of Waxahachie." No name could be more appropriate.

The first Richards to come to America was Paul's great-grandfather, Thomas, a blacksmith who emigrated from England in the 1840s. Thomas's grandson, Jesse Thomas Richards, moved from Kentucky to Waxahachie fifty years later and taught in country schools. He was thirty-eight when he married Sarah Della McGowan Byars on December 26, 1907. Called Della, she was a thirty-seven-year-old widow with four children; she had come to Waxahachie from Mississippi to work in the cotton mill.[2] An early photograph of the couple shows Jesse with a dark, neatly trimmed beard and Della with dark hair and the prominent jaw her youngest son inherited.

Their only child, Paul Rapier Richards, was born in the family home at 814 Water Street on November 21, 1908. Sportswriters thought his middle name symbolized the sharpness of his mind, but it was a family surname that went back at least four generations on his father's side.[3] The household included Paul's half-sister, Lillie Belle Byars, and three half-brothers. One, Frank, died of tuberculosis when Paul was a child. Paul referred to the survivors, Ernest and William Byars, as his brothers. "My mother was a hard-shell Baptist [a devout evangelical Christian]," he said, "and tried to keep all of her boys in line, but she had rather a rough time."[4] She made her youngest memorize scripture, and he could quote the Bible extensively all his life. The family did not celebrate Christmas by exchanging gifts, either because they could not afford to or because Della would not sully the religious holiday with commerce.[5]

Waxahachie billed itself as the Queen City of the Cotton Belt. Cotton thrived in the rich blackland prairie soil. For two decades around the turn of the twentieth century, surrounding Ellis County produced more cotton than any other county in the nation, 106,384 bales in 1910. The Richardses' two-story frame home on the west side of town stood near company-owned houses for workers at the Waxahachie Cotton Mill, the community's largest employer.

Waxahachie's population was 6,205 in 1910. Residents got around town on mule-drawn trolleys, on horseback, or in horse-drawn buggies and wagons. Just 326 motor vehicles were registered in Ellis County, including cars, trucks, and motorcycles. Registration was voluntary, so there were certainly more. The first gravel roads were built around 1908; the county had no paved roads.[6]

In interviews during his baseball career, Richards often reminded people that his father had been a teacher, as if to imply that some erudition had rubbed off on him. By the time Paul was born, Jesse owned a grocery store—until the boy, then about seven, set it afire while playing with matches. He ran to warn his father, but Jesse was playing checkers and ignored him as the building burned to the ground. Jesse opened another grocery on Water Street, later adding a meat market.[7]

Paul's maternal grandfather, Frank McGowan, and other Confederate veterans entertained the boys with tales of the War Between the States, as southerners called it. A memorial obelisk on the courthouse lawn honored Ellis County's Confederate soldiers. Young Paul and his friends thought the war was still going on and were disappointed when they learned they would not get a chance to kill some Yankees.[8]

After Lillie Belle married, she and her husband, Lando Bolton, lived in the Richards home. Their son Stanley, born there in 1917, grew up tagging along after Paul just as Paul tagged after the Byars brothers, who were much older— Ernie by fifteen years and Bill by eleven. Paul later said, "Two of my brothers were pretty good baseball players, and from as far back as I can remember that became an obsession with me, to become a baseball player."[9] One of his father's friends suggested the boy was smart enough to become president, but Paul objected, "I'm going to be a baseball player."[10]

Jesse Richards embraced his son's ambition. Paul remembered, "My dad was determined to do whatever he could to help me in baseball. If I wanted a ball or a glove or a bat, he found some way to buy it."[11] When Jesse first noticed his little boy's interest in the game, he taught him to read the box scores. "That's how I learned to read," Paul said. "By the time I got to school I knew who was leading the league in hitting."[12] His father bought him the Rolls-Royce of baseball gloves, Rawlings's $8.50 Bill Doak model, the first one with a formed pocket. (The price is equivalent to about $105 today.) Paul said later: "My parents had no conception of what professional baseball was like. . . . But they did know that baseball was a clean, healthful sport and encouraged my participation in it. . . .The only restrictions placed upon me was that baseball was not to interfere with my school work."[13] When he wasn't playing in a game, the youngster bounced a ball off the wall of the house, teaching himself to throw left-handed and right-handed equally well. He picked up rocks off the bed of the railroad tracks and hit them with a broomstick bat. Jesse's expenses included replacing the neighbors' broken windows, a test of his dedication to his son's chosen career.[14]

"He would play baseball nine hours a day," recalled a childhood friend, Clyde Verheyden. "If enough kids didn't show up, he'd be around to your house calling you out. . . . I can't remember a day when Paul Richards thought it was too cold to play baseball. He lived the game. Year round. All day through." Whenever a carnival came to town, Paul would spend all his dimes throwing balls in the tent where he could win a prize by knocking down milk bottles.[15]

Besides following his brothers' lead, Paul had another powerful pull toward the game. In the first two decades of the twentieth century, Texas was a popular spring training site for major and minor league clubs. Baseball's most glamorous team, John McGraw's New York Giants, trained in nearby Marlin Springs (now Marlin) from 1908 through 1918. Other clubs went to San Antonio, Houston, Waco, and Mineral Wells. (Florida had not yet caught on as a spring venue because its rail system was not as well developed as Texas's.)[16]

Waxahachie business leaders craved a piece of the big league action. In

November 1915 Detroit manager Hughie Jennings was looking for a new training site after a hurricane devastated the Tigers' spring home in Gulfport, Mississippi. Jennings agreed to bring his club to Waxahachie if the town would build a satisfactory ballpark. The chamber of commerce sponsored the construction of a wooden grandstand beside Waxahachie Creek, a short walk from the Richards home, and Detroit sent its groundskeeper to lay out the field. It was named Jungle Park because it was the home of the Tigers.[17]

Like Marlin Springs and Mineral Wells, Waxahachie boasted natural hot-water wells that were believed to be healthful. The town offered comfortable accommodations at the brick Rogers Hotel on the courthouse square. Each of its sixty rooms had a sink with hot and cold water, and half had private baths. The hotel piped water from one of the wells to heat its basement swimming pool. To provide entertainment for the players, the hotel installed billiard tables and converted a nearby building to handball courts.[18]

War fever gripped Texas in 1916. The European conflict was far away, but close to home Gen. John J. Pershing led six thousand U.S. troops across the border into Mexico in a futile chase after the guerrilla leader Pancho Villa.[19]

Baseball fever gripped Waxahachie. When the Tigers came to town, fifty automobiles and two hundred people met their train and escorted them to the hotel. Their first exhibition game against the Dallas club of the Texas League drew twenty-two hundred, the largest crowd the town had seen since the heyday of its Chautauqua camp a few years earlier.[20] But the Tigers' main attraction—baseball's biggest star, Ty Cobb—was absent. Cobb habitually skipped as much of spring training as possible, and he did not join the team until it had left Waxahachie.[21]

When the Tigers returned in 1917, Cobb showed up almost four weeks late. Big crowds watched his workouts at Jungle Park, and some of the locals stalked him at the hotel. Richards said he learned his first important baseball lesson by watching Cobb:

> John McGraw's Giants were training not too far away in Marlin Springs, and they came here for an exhibition game. Naturally I went out to see the game. Well, in the very first inning Cobb dropped an easy fly ball that was right in his hands. I've never forgotten that. The greatest player in the world drops a ball. It's odd the things you remember, isn't it? If he had gone four for four, I would probably have forgotten it a long time ago because he was supposed to do that. But I can still see that easy fly ball dropping out of his hands to the grass.[22]

Richards said that experience taught him not to worry about mechanical errors, because even the great Cobb could muff the simplest chance. The story became one of Richards's staples, and he repeated it many times. It has one thing in common with many other baseball tales that have been handed down for decades: It's not exactly true. Every time Richards recounted this epiphany, he said it happened in a game at Waxahachie between the Tigers and Giants. Cobb never played against the Giants in Waxahachie.

In 1917 the Giants played their first exhibition games against the Tigers in Fort Worth and Dallas, looking for bigger crowds than Waxahachie could muster.[23] Paul may well have attended those games, and the baseball-mad eight-year-old certainly walked to Jungle Park to watch Cobb play or work out sometime between March 26 and March 29, 1917, the only time Cobb was there, and he may have seen Cobb drop a fly ball at Jungle Park. But it was not against the Giants.

Detroit trained in Waxahachie again in 1918, but Cobb did not join the Tigers until after they left town. In 1919 the team moved to Macon, Georgia.[24] The Cincinnati Reds came to Jungle Park that spring and went on to win the

National League pennant and the tainted World Series against the Chicago "Black Sox." The remnants of that Chicago team came to Waxahachie in 1921; the Series fixers had been suspended while they were awaiting trial. When twelve-year-old Paul climbed the fence to get into the ballpark, Sox manager Kid Gleason playfully chased him off the field.[25]

Paul contracted malaria in the fourth grade and missed half the school year. He was an honor roll student and a favorite of the principal, Miss Eva Grizzard, so she promoted him anyway. She appointed him captain of the school's baseball team, and by the time he reached seventh grade he was coaching younger boys. "I didn't really coach Paul," Miss Eva recalled after he became a big league manager. "He was a natural coach, himself."[26] He organized a team that hitchhiked to challenge teams in neighboring towns, with Paul pitching and playing third base.

In June 1923 Waxahachie High School's senior third baseman, Elbert Newton, got sick. Coach A. A. Scott—known as "Double-A"—reached down to the eighth grade to put the fourteen-year-old Richards in the varsity lineup for the final series against McKinney High. Batting eighth, he got no hits in the two games but "fielded the hot corner in great style."[27] He handled twelve chances with one error. Paul became the regular third baseman the next year as a freshman.

The Waxahachie Indians were a powerhouse. Double-A Scott led them to nine consecutive state championships from 1919 through 1927. There was no official state championship tournament, probably because of the difficulty of travel across Texas's vast reaches, so the top teams arranged to play for bragging rights at the end of the season. Eight of Paul's teammates from the small-town school played professional ball, and five reached the majors at least briefly: pitchers Archie Wise and Belve Bean, infielder Jimmy Adair, outfielder Gene Moore, and first baseman Art Shires. Shires was the school's star athlete, both in baseball and as a quarterback and placekicker in football.[28]

Several Waxahachie friends described Paul as "a quiet, solemn boy." Clyde Verheyden said: "He would stand for hours at a time outside Sawyer's Drug Store down on the square, and he was either eating ice cream or just had finished. And he'd stand there silent, contemplating."[29] By his freshman year he had acquired the nickname "Sleepy" because he sometimes dozed off in class. Some old friends called him by that name all his life, but he despised it. He was also a sleepwalker and was once found in his underwear several blocks from home in the middle of the night.[30] The 1924 school yearbook, *The Cotton Boll*, reported, "'Sleepy' is about the youngest man on the team, being only a 'fish,' but he is one of the nicest third basemen in the state. Good brainwork usually features his playing."[31] But Jimmy Adair would say later: "We sure never suspected he was a genius then. In fact, we all thought maybe he was kind of dumb. He never said anything. What he was doing was thinking."[32]

In 1924 the Waxahachie Indians launched a streak of sixty-five straight victories that continued for four years. By 1926 Shires had graduated and Sleepy was the team's captain as well as one of its stars as a junior, batting third or fourth and playing third base. Waxahachie allowed only one earned run in the first nine games. After charging through the regular schedule undefeated, the Indians beat Terrell High in two straight for the North Texas title as Belve Bean pitched a no-hitter in the first game.[33]

They squared off against Austin High for what was billed as the state championship series, best two out of three. Bean, the pitching ace, had been sick for several days and gave up five runs before Richards relieved him in a tie game. Lester Jordan, sports editor of the *Waxahachie Daily Light*, wrote, "After hitting Bean's fast balls for six innings the Austin players were helpless before Richards' slow curves in the final three frames and only one man reached first base."[34] The Indians scored four times in the seventh and won 9–5.

With Bean still ailing, Sleepy was the starting pitcher the next day. Staked to an eight-run lead in the eighth inning, he began alternating right-handed and left-handed pitches. An Austin hitter jumped back and forth from one batter's box to the other, so Richards dropped his glove and dared the hitter to guess which arm would deliver the ball. "Four runs were scored by Austin in the round that Richards pulled his clown baseball, but three of these were due to infield errors," Jordan reported.[35] The 12–6 victory wrapped up the championship.

That was the source of the first Richards legend. "Ripley's Believe It or Not," a popular newspaper feature, reported that the Texas schoolboy had won a doubleheader by pitching one game right-handed, the other left-handed. Richards said that was not true but that he had pitched with both arms in one other high-school game.[36]

Two days later Waxahachie met Bryan High, the Dallas city champion, at Steer Stadium before the Texas League game between Dallas and Shreveport. Playing in front of a crowd of more than five thousand, Bean surrendered four runs before Richards relieved him in the fourth. Richards gave up a run to tie the score, then shut out Bryan over the last four innings. He singled to lead off the ninth and was on third when his catcher, Neal Rabe, hit a sacrifice fly to chase him home with the go-ahead run. Richards set the opposition down in order in the bottom of the ninth, finishing it off with a strikeout, for the Indians' fiftieth straight victory.[37]

Sleepy had won three games in four days to cap his high school career. His .345 batting average was second on the team to center fielder Jack Campbell's .407. A few years later, before any of the Indians reached the majors, Double-A Scott ranked Richards as the best player he had coached, with Art Shires a close second.[38]

Professional scouts were following the powerful Waxahachie team. By the time Richards was seventeen, he had grown to be a lanky six feet one, with black hair, brown eyes, a prominent jaw, an unusually long neck, and pointed chin.[39] Photographs of him in his high school uniform show a well-built young man; he had filled out to about 170 pounds.

At least four major league clubs were interested in him. A White Sox scout told a reporter that young Richards "has more natural ability and grace in the field than any young infielder he ever saw." When Richards worked out for the Sox in Dallas, manager Eddie Collins told him to come back after he graduated.[40] One scout was not willing to wait: Nap Rucker, a former pitching star for the Dodgers who scouted for Brooklyn across the South. Richards had another year to go before graduation, but he had used up his athletic eligibility because he had played varsity ball as an eighth-grader. When Rucker offered him $1,000—a sizable bonus for that time—Richards grabbed it.[41] Because he was a minor, his father had to sign the contract, agreeing to let him drop out of school.

The fifteen-hundred-mile trip to Brooklyn at the end of May was Richards's first train ride and probably his first time outside Texas. Carrying a cardboard suitcase, he reported to manager Wilbert Robinson, a former catcher who was once John McGraw's close friend and running mate on the old Orioles of Baltimore, the rowdiest team of the rowdy 1890s. Robinson was born on June 29, 1863, just as Union and Confederate troops were massing at Gettysburg. At sixty-two he was one of baseball's fabled characters. Sportswriters portrayed "Uncle Robbie" as a fat buffoon who was beloved if somewhat bewildered. *Brooklyn Eagle* writer Harold Parrott said Robinson was "more of a habit than a manager."[42] The club was called the Robins interchangeably with the older nickname, Dodgers.

Robinson had been a successful manager in his early years, winning pennants in 1916 and 1920, but by the time Richards arrived in 1926 the team had entered its "Daffiness Boys" phase. Later that season the Robins would put three runners on base—unfortunately, all of them on third base—when Babe Herman doubled into a double play.

Richards sat on Brooklyn's bench for two weeks without getting into a game. This was the first time he had seen a regulation big league contest, but he had watched plenty of major leaguers at Jungle Park. The Robins had future Hall of Famers Dazzy Vance and Burleigh Grimes on the mound and Zach Wheat and Rabbit Maranville in the lineup, but they were headed for a second straight sixth-place finish in the eight-team National League. Richards was not impressed. He later said Robinson "put them on the field and just let them play. . . . In fact, I don't think any team in baseball did less instructing than the Dodgers in those days."[43] Veteran players, fearing for their jobs, were notoriously hard on rookies; if any Robin deigned to notice the teenager, he never mentioned it.

A young sportswriter, Tom Meany, took the boy to Brooklyn's famous Coney Island amusement park. "He rode the roller coaster so many times that I got green just watching him," Meany reported.[44] Brooklyn assigned Richards to play in semipro games around the city. Robinson had planned to let him work out with the big leaguers all season, then send him to the minors to begin his professional career the next year, when he would be eighteen. But in June the struggling Pittsfield, Massachusetts, club of the Class A Eastern League, which had a working agreement with Brooklyn, needed an infielder. Richards was sent to fill the vacancy. Uncle Robbie's wife, Mary, known as "Ma," had taken a liking to the teenager and protested: "He's such a young boy. He needs protection." According to later accounts, Robbie came home one night and told her: "That kid you were worrying about, Ma, can take care of himself pretty good. He punched his manager in the nose today."[45]

Pittsfield's manager was Neal Ball, a former shortstop who turned the first unassisted triple play in major league history in 1909. Ball put Richards in the lineup for his first professional game on June 16. The local paper reported, "Paul Richards displayed considerable class at short stop and hit a hard single to left field in the tenth inning."[46] The Pittsfield Hillies lost to Waterbury, Connecticut, that day for their fifteenth consecutive defeat. A sportswriter described Pittsfield as "the sorry team of the league."[47] It was a shock for a young man who had not played in a losing game since he was a high school freshman.

The next day Richards went hitless. In a Sunday doubleheader on June 18 he moved to third base and went 2-for-2 in the second game as the losing streak reached eighteen. By Richards's account, Pittsfield had taken the lead when he was picked off base to kill a rally. Ball barked at him and Richards snapped back. When he took his position at third, a baseball hit him in the back. He thought his teammates were being careless with the warmup ball but turned around to find his manager throwing another one at him. Richards never confessed to slugging Neal Ball; that may be a later embellishment.[48] A contemporary *Sporting News* account confirms that Ball threw a baseball at one of his players that day but does not name the player or mention a punch.[49]

After the game Richards gathered his belongings and boarded a train for Brooklyn. He didn't say whether he quit the team or was fired.[50] Robbie shipped him to Crisfield, Maryland, in the Eastern Shore League. "I came to Crisfield by train," Richards recalled, "and it was the end of the line. It could go no farther."[51]

Crisfield was close to land's end, near the Maryland-Virginia border at the bottom of the Delmarva Peninsula, which connects Delaware, Maryland, and Virginia on the eastern shore of the Chesapeake Bay. The Eastern Shore League sat on the bottom rung of professional baseball, Class D. It was a short-season league that did not begin play until late May. In his debut on June 27, 1926, in a Sunday doubleheader at Dover, Delaware, Richards led off and played first base, hitting a home run, double, and single. He shifted to second base a few days later when the manager's brother arrived to play first. The rookie hit safely in his first eleven games. After that streak ended, he started a new nine-game run the next day.

The youngest player in the league, he had left "Sleepy" behind, but his teammates gave him a new nickname, "Tex." He didn't like that one, either.[52] Those teammates included shortstop Ducky Schofield (who would become father of a big league shortstop with the same nickname, as well as grandfather of another shortstop, Dick Schofield, and great-grandfather of outfielder Jayson Werth); Clint Brown, a fifteen-year big league pitcher; and Jocko Collins, a long-time baseball scout and basketball official.[53]

Dan Pasquella, the Crisfield Crabbers' catcher and manager, remembered: "Richards was shy of girls, but finally got up enough nerve to date a girl recommended by the players. He was given warning, though, that her father, a railroad shift worker, objected to his daughter associating with ballplayers. It was important to find out when the old man was coming home before first seeing her." Richards's teammates set him up. They led him to the girl's house, where she opened the door and whispered, "Go away, my father is home and he'll shoot you." One of the players, hiding nearby, fired off a shotgun. "Richards ran for his life down the street and disappeared," Pasquella said. "He finally showed up the next morning for a bus trip for wherever we were playing.

"When told the truth, Paul took it good-naturedly."[54]

Richards's first professional season was a success. In fifty-eight games he batted .301 with eight home runs. He played primarily at second base and pitched occasionally, using both arms.[55] The Crabbers' treasurer, future Maryland governor J. Millard Tawes, paid him $37.50 every two weeks—$206.25 for his eleven weeks with the team.[56]

After Richards returned home to Waxahachie, he and his pal Jimmy Adair set out hitchhiking to California. Two cars running in a convoy answered their thumbs, and they climbed into separate cars. Richards announced to his driver, "I am a baseball player." The man introduced himself: Hollis Thurston, a right-handed pitcher who had won twenty games for the White Sox two years earlier.

"And I'm telling him *I'm* a ballplayer," Richards recalled. Adair's chauffeur was Thurston's teammate, first baseman Earl Sheely. The young Texans hoped to win jobs in the California winter league but found no takers.[57]

Less than six months after he dropped out of school, still short of his eighteenth birthday, Richards had traveled from Waxahachie to Brooklyn to Massachusetts to Maryland, Virginia, Delaware, Pennsylvania, and California. He had achieved his ambition: he was a ballplayer.

---

1. Edna Davis Hawkins, Ruth Stone, Ida M. Brookshire, and Lillie Tolleson, *History of Ellis County, Texas* (Waco: Texian Press, 1972), 55; Kelly McMichael Stott, *Waxahachie: Where Cotton Reigned King* (Charleston, S.C.: Arcadia, 2002), 21.

2. Paula Richards interviews by author, 2006–2008; Paul Richards, taped reminiscences (undated; 1983 or later, cited hereafter as Richards Waxahachie tape), in the author's files. Genealogical research provided by Paula Richards gives Della's birth date as October 10, 1868, but her marriage certificate lists her age as thirty-seven in 1907 (Ellis County Clerk's records, vol. O, p. 79). Paul Richards's birth certificate gives his mother's age as thirty-eight in 1908 (Texas State Board of Health, Bureau of Vital Statistics, file no. 1056, available in the Ellis County Clerk's office). Her death certificate says she was born August 10, 1870 (Ellis County Registrar's file no. 216 [1951]). Clearly the family accepted that date, but she may have lied to her husband about her age. (Decades later the Richards home was converted into a restaurant, The Catfish Plantation, and was said to be haunted. I visited it in 2006.)

3. Genealogical research provided by Paula Richards.

4. U.S. Census, Ellis County, Texas, 1910; Richards Waxahachie tape.

5. Paula Richards interviews.

6. Hawkins et al., *History of Ellis County*, 81, 263–64; Stott, *Waxahachie*, 66.

7. Paula Richards interviews; Richards Waxahachie tape.

8. "Stan Bolton Returns to Waxahachie," home video, November 1993, in the personal collection of Michelle Bolton-Foster; Paula Richards interviews.

9. Richards Waxahachie tape.

10. Paula Richards interviews.

11. Richards Waxahachie tape.

12. Randy Harvey, "From Waxahachie to the White Sox," *Dallas Times-Herald Sunday* magazine, August 29, 1976, 21.

13. Frank Faske, "Help from Home," *Baseball*, September 1946, 353.

14. Richards Waxahachie tape.

15. *Houston Post*, undated clipping (1961 or 1962) in the Richards scrapbooks in the personal collection of Paula Richards.

16. Frank Jackson, "Crossing Red River: Spring Training in Texas," 85–91, in Society for American Baseball Research, *The National Pastime*, vol. 26 (Cleveland, Ohio: SABR, 2006).

17. Jim Perry, "If You Build It . . . ," *W— The Magazine of Ellis County*, May 2005, 8–13; Charles C. Alexander, *Ty Cobb* (New York: Oxford University Press, 1984), 125.

18. Stott, *Waxahachie*, 53, 73; David Hudgins, interviews by author, August 16–17, 2006, Waxahachie, Texas.

19. Alexander, *Ty Cobb*, 125.
20. Perry, "If You Build It," 8–13; Stott, *Waxahachie*, 106–9.
21. Alexander, *Ty Cobb*, 126.
22. Donald Honig, *The Man in the Dugout* (Chicago: Follett, 1977), 119.
23. *New York Times*, March 31, 1917, 13, and April 1, 1917, S2.
24. Alexander, *Ty Cobb*, 138, 142.
25. Jackson, "Crossing Red River," 89; *Sporting News* (hereafter cited as *TSN*), June 12, 1951, B3.
26. Richards Waxahachie tape; *Dallas Morning News*, June 10, 1951, 5-1.
27. *Waxahachie (Texas) Daily Light*, June 2, 1923, 6. Richards sometimes said he was in the seventh grade when the varsity called him up, but he was an eighth-grader.
28. *TSN*, September 7, 1944, 3; Richards Waxahachie tape.
29. *Houston Post*, undated clipping (1962 or 1963) in the Richards family scrapbooks.
30. Paula Richards interviews; Olivia Harrington e-mail, July 19, 2006. Harrington's father knew Richards from childhood and called him "Sleepy."
31. *The Cotton Boll, 1924*. The yearbook is in the Ellis County Museum, Waxahachie, Texas.
32. Roy Terrell, "Hawkeye and His Boy Scouts," *Sports Illustrated*, April 17, 1961, 68.
33. *Waxahachie Daily Light*, May 4, 1927, 6; May 8, 1926, 6; May 10, 1926, 6; April 12, 1926, 6.
34. Ibid., May 13, 1926, 6.
35. Ibid., May 14, 1926, 6.
36. Richards Waxahachie tape. The "Believe It or Not" cartoon was cited in many published profiles. It is in the Richards scrapbooks, undated. It appeared before 1929. The archives of Ripley Entertainment, Inc., go back only that far (Edward Meyer, Ripley Entertainment, e-mail, November 12, 2007).
37. *Waxahachie Daily Light*, May 17, 1926, 6.
38. Ibid., undated clipping in the Richards scrapbooks, probably 1928.
39. Some sportswriters said he had icy blue eyes; one said they were green. His daughter says brown.
40. Billy R. Hancock, *A Story of Paul Richards Park and Waxahachie High School Baseball* (Waxahachie, Texas: Waxahachie High School RBI Club, 2008), 13; *TSN*, October 25, 1950, 4.
41. Richards Waxahachie tape.
42. Harold Parrott, *The Lords of Baseball* (1976; repr., Atlanta: Longstreet, 2001), 97.
43. Honig, *Man in the Dugout*, 127.
44. Tom Meany, "The Orioles Are Coming," *Sport*, February 1958, 27.
45. The quote is from Arthur Daley's column in the *New York Times*, September 4, 1961, 19. Tommy Holmes of the *Brooklyn Eagle* recounted the incident on October 13, 1950 (clipping in the Paul Richards file, A. Bartlett Giamatti Research Center, National Baseball Hall of Fame, Cooperstown, N.Y.).
46. Unidentified clipping (1926) in Richards scrapbooks.
47. *TSN*, June 24, 1926, 6.
48. Richards Waxahachie tape; *TSN*, August 1, 1951, 16.
49. *TSN*, June 24, 1926, 6.
50. Richards Waxahachie tape.
51. *Salisbury (Md.) Times*, January 13, 1955, 12.
52. Ibid., January 12, 1955, 10.
53. Ibid., September 22, 1954, 16; William W. Mowbray, *The Eastern Shore Baseball League* (Centreville, Md.: Tidewater, 1989), 24.
54. *Salisbury Times*, September 22, 1954, 16.
55. Ibid.
56. *Chicago Tribune*, December 18, 1975, C1.
57. Richards Waxahachie tape; *Chicago Tribune*, March 11, 1951, A2.

CHAPTER 3

Baseball as He Knew It

In history's eye the ballplayer of the Babe Ruth era was a yokel from a farm or a small town just the other side of nowhere. Hank Greenberg, a native New Yorker who began his professional career in 1930, was fascinated by his many farm-bred teammates:

> They saw the whole pattern of life in terms of animals and crops and soil, and there wasn't any situation that they couldn't describe in agricultural terms. . . . When some particularly oversexed rookie came along, they'd say he was "horny as a hound dog in heat," and this sort of remark would puzzle a Bronx boy who had never heard the word "horny" and had never seen a "hound dog" and didn't know what "heat" meant.[1]

While the South, especially Texas, was heavily represented, the Northeast produced more major leaguers than any other region—logically, since it was the most populous part of the country—with Pennsylvania the leading state.[2] Contrary to the enduring image, more than a fourth of 1927 big leaguers had attended college, though few had graduated.[3] Paul Richards of Waxahachie came close to fitting the stereotype, although he was not fleeing the danger of Pennsylvania coal mines or the drudgery of farm chores and, thanks to his parents, had an above-average education despite his lack of a high school diploma.

Fifty years before free agency, all players were chattel who had no control over their careers. Their contracts included a reserve clause that gave the club the right to renew the contract every year and gave the player no rights at all. Once he signed with his first professional team, he could be traded or sold at the team's whim. Richards learned those facts of baseball life after his rookie season. The St. Louis Browns claimed him in the draft, plucking him away from Brooklyn, the team he had agreed to play for.[4] Major league clubs did not usually draft an eighteen-year-old with only one year's experience in Class D; someone in the St. Louis organization thought the young man had promise. Richards cost St. Louis just $1,000, but the Browns had to put him on their forty-man roster and would be allowed to option him to the minors only twice before he would be exposed to the draft again.[5] That is what the rules required; in reality some major and minor league clubs conspired to hide draft-eligible players.

When the Browns called Richards's name at the draft meeting, Brooklyn manager Wilbert Robinson protested, "They can't do that." Commissioner Kenesaw Mountain Landis asked why, and Robbie blurted, "Because we had him covered up. . . . You know how it is, Judge, gentleman's agreement and all that sort of stuff."[6] Judge Landis took the matter under advisement. In February he assigned Richards's contract to St. Louis. Landis also asked the young player if he had received the $1,000 bonus promised by Brooklyn, and Richards replied that he had.[7]

Richards went to spring training with the Browns in 1927 at Tarpon Springs, on Florida's Gulf Coast, just north of St. Petersburg. St. Louis sportswriters liked what they saw. John E. Wray reported in the *Post-Dispatch*: "Richards, who is really just a small town ball player, has gained more attention than either of the others [fellow rookies, pitcher Walter Beck and first baseman Guy Sturdy]. This is due partly to the fact that he dropped out of a clear sky with little experience and shaped up like a player and hitter."[8] James M. Gould of the

St. Louis Star wrote: "He looks like a hitter, a slashing driver who puts plenty of power into his punches. . . . Right off the bat he looks like a fine prospect."[9]

The Browns sent Richards to the Class A Eastern League's Waterbury, Connecticut, club. He opened the season at second base but went 0-for-8 in two games and was replaced by a veteran. When the Eastern Shore League began play in May, he was back in Crisfield. In his second crack at Class D pitchers he batted .323/.417/.653 with a league-leading twenty-four home runs and 198 total bases in eighty-seven games. (The "slash stat" method of presenting batting statistics shows batting average/on-base percentage/slugging percentage.)[10] At the end of the season the pennant-winning Parksley, Virginia, club borrowed Richards to play in the Five State Series against the Blue Ridge League champions from Chambersburg, Pennsylvania. He slammed a pair of two-run homers to win the first game, 6–4, then added another home run in Game 3 and two more in Game 5. Parksley won the series in six games.

"Paul Richards, the kid infielder," returned to the Browns' camp in the spring of 1928.[11] He had spent the winter playing in Puerto Rico and Venezuela and submitted an expense account listing his travel costs from Puerto Rico to Florida aboard a United Fruit Company freighter. The club's business manager was not amused—and he wasn't paying, either.[12] The Browns had finished seventh for two straight seasons and had sold George Sisler, the best player in their history. Manager Dan Howley was trying out many youngsters, but he showed little patience with the nineteen-year-old from D ball. Howley thought Richards was loafing during one workout and lectured him loudly on the value of hustle.[13] Richards was sent down to Muskogee, Oklahoma, in the Class C Western Association.

He dominated the league. At the end of the season's first half he was named Muskogee's most valuable player and honored with a "day" at the ballpark and a wristwatch. In the game following the ceremony he played all nine positions.[14] He was primarily a shortstop but also appeared at third base and pitched. On July 22, taking the mound in relief against the Cardinals' Topeka farm club, he pitched left-handed to left-handed batters and right-handed to right-handers. When outfielder Charlie Wilson came up, he saw Richards take his position to throw lefty and jumped across the plate to the right-handed batter's box. Richards switched arms and Wilson switched sides. And again. And again. Finally, Richards dropped his glove, raised both hands above his head, and waited for Wilson to settle into his stance. As Richards told it, the umpire gave Wilson a walk when he took "a perfect left-handed curve through the middle."[15] Later Richards said that if he had known the rules, Wilson would have been out: "As soon as he walked across that plate he was out. He had to go behind the catcher."[16] (Rule 6.06[b] states, "A batter is out for illegal action when he steps from one batter's box to the other while the pitcher is in position ready to pitch.")

In August the first of Richards's Waxahachie High teammates advanced to the majors. First baseman Art Shires made a splash by batting .341 in thirty-three games with the White Sox, but he soon earned a reputation as a trouble-maker. He became one of baseball's flamboyant figures, calling himself "The Great Shires" and moonlighting as a wrestler. His big league career lasted only four years.

When Muskogee's season was over, Richards boasted, "I led the league in everything."[17] It was only a slight exaggeration. He was a 30-30 man with thirty-nine stolen bases and thirty-six home runs. He batted .314/.391/.578 and led in runs and total bases as well as homers and steals. Not surprisingly, a sportswriter called him "the best prospect in the league."[18] In eight games as a pitcher he walked more batters than he struck out and posted a 7.20 ERA with a 2-0 record. His defense was shaky; he committed thirty-two errors in seventy-eight games at shortstop and eleven more in fifty-seven games at third.

Wilbert Robinson had been tracking Richards's progress and wanted him back. Robinson had his Macon, Georgia, farm club in the Class B Sally League buy Richards's contract, then Brooklyn bought him from Macon for $5,000. When he arrived at the Dodgers' spring camp, "the kid infielder" was now "the $5,000 Western Association beauty."[19]

He opened the 1929 season as the Macon Peaches' third baseman. The *Macon Telegraph's* Jimmy Jones called him "a great hustler and scrapper."[20] The club moved into a new ballpark, named Luther Williams Field after the mayor, with distant outfield fences. On May 6 "the tall Texan with the poker face" hit the first home run out of the park to win a game in the ninth inning. Commissioner Landis came to dedicate the new field a week later. Richards hit an inside-the-park homer to win the 3–2 game for pitcher Buck Newsom, later known as "Bobo," who struck out eleven of the league-leading Tourists from Asheville, North Carolina. Richards was rewarded with a new suit; players, fans, and the commissioner shared a postgame barbecue.[21]

The Asheville club soon acquired Richards and put him in the lineup at third base. He remembered spending the most comfortable summer of his life in the Blue Ridge Mountains resort, enjoying what native son Thomas Wolfe called "the cool sweet magic of starred mountain night."[22] Richards's stint as a ballplaying Asheville Tourist was less than comfortable. He batted just .234/.270/.362 for the season and committed twenty-eight errors. His .895 fielding percentage was near the bottom among the league's infielders.

Asheville returned Richards to Macon after the season, since he still belonged to Brooklyn. In four years he had advanced only to Class B and would now repeat that level after his first year of poor performance. His quiet demeanor was also holding him back. Because he seldom showed emotion on or off the field, some in the Brooklyn organization questioned his desire and aggressiveness. Reflecting the views of management, syndicated columnist Grantland Rice said Richards was "a moody one. . . . He was not exactly listless, but lacked the fire normally expected of a young player and especially a promising rookie."[23]

In the spring of 1930 Richards saw that the Peaches were overstocked with infielders. Someone would have to go. He wanted to stay because he was dating "a beautiful blonde" in Macon. When the team's two backup catchers got hurt during spring training, he confidently assured manager Charlie Moore that he could catch. He soon had to prove it when Moore, the regular catcher, was disabled by a foul tip.[24]

That foul ball changed Richards's life. His skill as a catcher would be his only distinction as a major league player and helped establish him as a candidate to manage. The catcher's central role as a field leader and handler of the pitching staff has been an article of faith in baseball for more than a century. As early as 1888 former pitcher John Montgomery Ward wrote, "There are some cases in which a steady, intelligent catcher is of more worth to a team than even the pitcher, because such a man will make pitchers of almost any kind of material."[25] Recent research finds no hard evidence to support this shibboleth, but it persists.[26]

With his strong arm and the knack for leadership he had shown as far back as elementary school, Richards fit the job description, even though his tall, rangy build did not fit the traditional profile of a catcher. Charlie Moore said, "The first time he ever went behind the plate he was a better catcher than I ever was."[27] Richards committed a league-leading seventeen errors in eighty-six games but rediscovered his batting stroke, slugging sixteen home runs with a line of .304/.354/.507. Macon sports editor Paul S. Jones, writing for the *Sporting News*, named him one of the league's two all-star catchers.[28]

Macon easily won the second-half pennant with a 45-25 record. In the last game of the regular season Richards and six other Peaches took turns on the mound against Columbia, South Carolina, and pitched a seven-inning no-hitter in the nightcap of a doubleheader. Richards delivered with both arms during his inning.[29] He caught every game of the playoff series against the first-half winner, Greenville, South Carolina, and contributed four singles and a triple as Macon lost to Greenville in six games.

Richards went to spring training with the Dodgers in 1931. The *Brooklyn Eagle*'s Tommy Holmes wrote: "Richards has been bobbing around the minors for quite some time now. In spite of great natural ability in some directions, he didn't seem to have what a great outfielder, infielder, or pitcher needs." Holmes added that the youngster "showed astonishing development" in his first year as a catcher but was too inexperienced at the position to compete for a big league job.[30] Still just twenty-two years old, Richards was promoted to Hartford, Connecticut, in the Class A Eastern League. Macon manager Charlie Moore, business manager Earl Mann, and several other players went with him after the Sally League collapsed under the weight of the Depression.

By midseason the Hartford Senators were running away with the pennant, and attendance was sagging in every market. The league decided to split the season, awarding Hartford the first-half championship with a 44-17 record and starting over with a new race to give hope to fans of other teams. The Senators turned it up in the second half, finishing 54-22, thirteen games ahead of second-place Bridgeport. Richards and seven other Hartford players, including Van Lingle Mungo, a wild, hard-throwing right-hander, were selected for the *Sporting News* all-star team. Richards batted .301/.343/.500 with fifteen home runs in 402 at-bats. In a hundred games behind the plate his eighty-five assists were second in the league but so were his fifteen errors.

He later claimed to have come up with his first innovation while he was in Hartford. Many minor leagues had adopted night baseball, but the dim lights made it hard for pitchers to see the catcher's signs. Richards bought three bicycle reflectors and glued them to the bottom flap of his chest protector. He covered up one for a fastball, two for a curve, and all three for a changeup.[31]

Brooklyn had used up all of Richards's major league options, so his career had reached a turning point. The club would have to keep him or trade him. The prospect of moving up may have led him to a personal turning point: he got married.

Richards's off-season hangout was the Waxahachie firehouse. He had spotted Margie Marie McDonald when she visited her father's office at the gas company across the street. Nineteen years old, the slim, brown-haired, hazel-eyed Margie was considered a beauty. She had studied for a year at North Texas State Teachers College (now the University of North Texas) in Denton.

She had asked one of the firefighters to bring her some taffy from the state fair in Dallas. Richards, who had gone along to the fair, delivered the taffy and asked her out. After only three or four dates he proposed. Margie was shocked but said yes. Wasting no time, Paul borrowed five dollars and arranged for a friend to drive them 122 miles across the state line the next day to Love County, Oklahoma, where no blood test or waiting period was required before marriage. But when he and his driver came to pick her up, Margie had changed her mind. It took Paul several hours to talk her around. They were married on Valentine's Day 1932.[32]

The young couple may have eloped because they were afraid to ask Margie's father for permission. George McDonald, a hulking six-foot-six-inch plumber, had once beaten up a man who made a pass at one of his three daughters. He left the Lothario crumpled on the sidewalk, then turned himself in to the sheriff. That perceptive lawman noted, "Nobody has filed a complaint," and sent George home. Margie was the McDonalds' pampered baby daughter. Her father didn't see how a ballplayer could support her.

Two weeks later the newlyweds left for the Dodgers' spring training camp. For the rest of her life Margie followed her husband wherever baseball took him.[33]

1. Hank Greenberg, *The Story of My Life*, ed. Ira Berkow (New York: Times Books, 1989), 45–46.
2. Davi̇d Quentin Voigt, *From the Commissioners to Continental Expansion*, vol. 2, *American Baseball* (University Park: Pennsylvania State University Press, 1983), 218; George F. Will, "Fielder of Dreams," *New York Times Book Review*, May 7, 2006, online edition.
3. Harold Seymour, *Baseball: The Golden Age* (New York: Oxford University Press, 1971), 353.
4. Associated Press, *Atlanta Constitution*, October 2, 1926, 11.
5. Robert F. Burk, *Much More Than a Game* (Chapel Hill: University of North Carolina Press, 2001), 28–29.
6. *Brooklyn Eagle*, October 13, 1950, clipping in the Paul Richards file, A. Bartlett Giamatti Research Center, National Baseball Hall of Fame, Cooperstown, N.Y.; *New York Times*, September 4, 1961, 19.
7. *Waxahachie (Texas) Daily Light*, undated clipping (ca. February 1927) in the Richards scrapbooks.
8. *St. Louis Post-Dispatch*, March 11, 1927, 28.
9. *St. Louis Star*, March 2, 1927, page unknown, in Richards scrapbooks.
10. Richards's minor league statistics come from the *Sporting News* (hereafter *TSN*). Some of the on-base percentages are approximate because hit-by-pitch totals are not available for all years.
11. *TSN*, March 1, 1928, 1.
12. Paul Richards, taped reminiscences (undated; 1983 or later, cited hereafter as Richards Waxahachie tape), in the author's files. The freighter ticket is in the Richards scrapbooks.
13. *TSN*, March 15, 1928, 1.
14. Ibid., July 5, 1928, 9.
15. AP, *Kansas City Star*, July 23, 1928, 10; *TSN*, August 2, 1928, 9; *Chicago Tribune*, December 28, 1975, B8.
16. Paul Richards, interview by Clark Nealon, February 5, 1981.
17. Richards Waxahachie tape.
18. *Springfield (Mo.) News and Leader*, September 2, 1928, page unknown, clipping in Richards scrapbooks.
19. AP, *Atlanta Constitution*, January 7, 1929, 11; *New York Times*, January 19, 1929, 16; *TSN*, March 14, 1929, 2.
20. *Macon (Ga.) Telegraph*, undated (1929) clipping in Richards scrapbooks.
21. *Macon Telegraph*, May 7, 1929, 10; *Macon (Ga.) News*, July 29, 1979, B1; Macon Community Sports Committee, "Luther Williams Field 50th Anniversary Celebration," September 28, 1979, all in Richards scrapbooks; *TSN*, June 20, 1929, 2; *Atlanta Journal-Constitution*, August 15, 1999, G2.
22. Richards Waxahachie tape; Thomas Wolfe, "Return," *Asheville Citizen-Times*, May 16, 1937, online archive.
23. *New York Sun*, March 8, 1932, 32.
24. Richards Waxahachie tape; Paul Richards interview.
25. John Montgomery Ward, *Baseball: How to Become a Player* (1888; repr., Cleveland, Ohio: Society for American Baseball Research, 1993), 65.
26. Keith Woolner, "Is Mike Matheny a Catching Genius?" in Jonah Keri, ed., *Baseball Between the Numbers* (New York: Basic, 2006), 105–10.
27. Ed Linn, "The Double Life of Paul Richards," *Sport*, August 1955, 52.
28. *TSN*, January 1, 1931, 6.
29. Ibid., September 11, 1930, 9; *Atlanta Journal*, October 3, 1937, 4-B.
30. *TSN*, November 13, 1930, 1.
31. *Baltimore News American*, May 4, 1976, 5C.
32. Richards Waxahachie tape; Paula Richards interviews, interviews by author, 2006–2008. "The County of Love" still advertises itself as a marriage magnet. Its Web site (www.lovecountyokla.org) boasts of a wedding chapel on Marietta's main street.
33. Richards Waxahachie tape; Paula Richards interviews.

CHAPTER 4

Up and Down

Brooklyn had turned a page in 1932. Wilbert Robinson had been fired after eighteen years as manager. The sixty-eight-year-old Robinson was caught in the crossfire between the team's ownership factions: the heirs of Charles Ebbets, who supported him, and the McKeever family, who did not like anybody the Ebbetses liked.

His successor was Max Carey, a former star center fielder who had led the National League in stolen bases ten times in a twenty-year career with Pittsburgh and Brooklyn. The owners saw Carey as a tough, serious-minded counterpoint to Uncle Robbie, but many players thought the new manager was just a grouch. Since Carey had never managed, the club hired an experienced minor league manager and former Brooklyn favorite, Casey Stengel, as a coach.

The twenty-three-year-old Richards's chances did not look good. The Dodgers had two catchers his age but with major league experience. The regular, Al Lopez, had batted .269/.324/.328 in his second season. He was challenged by the huge Ernie Lombardi, who hit .297/.340/.412 in his first year. Nap Rucker, the Brooklyn scout, was loyal to the Texan he had signed. Rucker told Grantland Rice, "Right now the brightest future on the team belongs to young Richards." Rice noted Richards's lack of fire in earlier years but said he had blossomed after his conversion to catcher because he found that position more challenging.[1]

The Dodgers soon picked up a more experienced catcher when they traded Lombardi along with their leading hitter, Babe Herman, and third baseman Wally Gilbert to Cincinnati for the Reds' regular catcher, Clyde Sukeforth, second baseman Tony Cuccinello, and third baseman Joe Stripp. Even without hindsight (Lombardi won two batting titles and was elected to the Hall of Fame), it was a lopsided deal, brought on because Herman was holding out for more money.

After six seasons in the minors Richards made his major league debut on April 17, 1932, when he caught his Hartford battery mate Van Mungo in the season's fourth game on a cold day at Ebbets Field. Mungo pitched shutout ball for ten innings against Philadelphia, but so did the Phillies' Ed Holley. In the eleventh Philadelphia's star right fielder, Chuck Klein, singled, and first baseman Don Hurst doubled. Klein slid home as Richards put on the tag. Umpire Bill Klem started to raise his arm to call Klein out, then spread his hands and cried, "Safe!" Richards protested, "I didn't drop the ball." Klem told him, "Klein beat the throw." Klem explained that he first thought Richards had blocked Klein, but when the dust cleared he saw the runner's foot on the plate and reversed his call. The *New York Evening Journal*'s Max Kase reminded his readers that Klem was the man who said, "I never missed one in my life," but he had missed that one at least for a few seconds. Manager Carey praised his rookies: "A great young combination lost a ball game with battery work that would have won 99 games in 100."[2] Richards, batting eighth, went 0-for-4 but threw out one would-be base stealer.

Mungo, who went on to win 120 major league games, credited Richards for his development.[3] But Richards played only three games for the Dodgers, going hitless in eight plate appearances before he was sold to Minneapolis of the American Association on June 14. After his conversion to catcher, this was the second of three moves that would shape his career. The Minneapolis manager was Donie Bush, a former teammate of Ty Cobb's who had trained in

Waxahachie with the Tigers when Richards was a boy. Bush was a little switch-hitting shortstop and lead-off man known for his keen batting eye. He led the American League in walks five times. At forty-four he had managed three major league teams and won the National League pennant with the 1927 Pittsburgh Pirates, who were swept in the World Series by the Murderers' Row Yankees. Richards always acknowledged Bush as his most important mentor.[4]

The 1932 Minneapolis Millers were a veteran club. Thirteen of the eighteen players were older than thirty, including several who were on their way down after long careers in the majors. The Millers were in first place when Richards joined them and stayed on top the rest of the season. They finished with a 100-68 record, counting the postseason playoffs, but lost the Junior World Series to the International League champion Newark Bears.

Richards excelled in his first exposure to AA ball, the highest level of the minors. (Class AAA was not created until 1946.) He belted two home runs on June 29, then another one the next day. On July 8 he hit a homer and two doubles. The next day he homered again. In seventy-eight games Richards knocked in sixty-nine runs with sixteen home runs and a .361 average. The *Sporting News* named him the league's all-star catcher.[5]

Richards got a chance to catch several former major leaguers. Thirty-four-year-old right-hander Rosy Ryan, who had pitched for McGraw's Giants, won twenty-three games. Lefty Jesse Petty, thirty-seven, posted a 16-10 mark. The grayest of the graybeards, forty-two-year-old left-hander Rube Benton, had broken into the majors in 1910, when Richards was in diapers. In 1920 Benton was the first player to testify before a Chicago grand jury that he knew in advance about the Black Sox's World Series fix. Both the American and National League presidents blacklisted him, but Judge Landis ordered him reinstated.[6] In 1932 Benton won eighteen games for Minneapolis.

Richards said a young catcher handling veterans must "try and figure out exactly how this pitcher likes to pitch. Observing and catching him—this isn't as difficult as it appears—by applying yourself, you will start calling the pitches that he wants to throw rather than the ones you think he should throw. If you can do this, you build up a certain amount of confidence in the pitcher."[7] He learned that Benton had only one effective pitch, a sharp down-breaking curve. Whenever batters began to hammer the curve, the old-timer would bark, "Gimme a chance. Gimme a chance. Call for a fast ball once in awhile!"[8]

Richards described Bush as a strict manager, even with the former big leaguers: "I liked the way he handled men. And he was a student of the game."[9] Bush had been a top base stealer, swiping thirty-five or more in seven consecutive seasons. "Donie was a genius on baserunning, how to do it and how to defense against it," Richards said. "Donie stressed that with no outs the runner is NEVER doubled off on a line drive. NEVER."[10] As Richards explained it, "Sometimes you'll see a man doubled off on a line drive and later on somebody will say, 'He couldn't help it.' Well, that's wrong. He could help it. He could have stayed on the bag, for one thing, although I'm not advocating that. But you can teach a fellow not to break until he *knows* that ball is in the outfield or on the ground."[11] Bush encouraged aggressive base running: "The runner was never to be thrown out by the catcher; he has to take a chance on the pitcher picking him off. But you never were picked off unless you were trying to steal."[12] It was the first time a manager had taught Richards the nuances of the game.

Another pivotal moment in his life came near the end of the season when the Millers staged an "Appreciation Day" for players and fans. One fan drew Richards's name in a raffle; his prize was a set of golf clubs. He knew little about the game, but it would soon become his passion.[13]

After the season Bush and his hard-hitting young catcher were bound for the majors. Bush was hired to manage the Cincinnati Reds; Richards was sold to the New York Giants, a team in upheaval.

John McGraw had quit the Giants in June 1932 after thirty years as manager, leaving the club in last place and the players fed up with his abuse.

McGraw, the most successful manager in history to that point, had grown more tyrannical with age. "He played that 'Little Napoleon' bit to the very hilt," pitcher Carl Hubbell said. "If we won, it was something he had done, and if we lost the ball game, it was something some damn ballplayer did."[14] McGraw's successor, first baseman Bill Terry, had not spoken to him for months. Terry's first act, seconds after taking the job, was to fire trainer Doc Knowles, McGraw's snitch in the clubhouse. Terry instantly won the players' loyalty.

The thirty-three-year-old Terry had batted .401 in 1930 (only Ted Williams has hit .400 since), but he was an unconventional star. He quit baseball in 1918 and started a career as a salesman for the Standard Oil Company in his hometown of Memphis, Tennessee, before McGraw lured him back to the game four years later. Terry invested in Memphis real estate, building houses and flipping them for a quick profit. During his frequent holdouts for higher pay, he reminded sportswriters that he didn't need his baseball job. He was not yet independently wealthy, but by the time he died in 1989 he was worth nearly $30 million.[15]

Terry could lift the Giants only to a tie for sixth place in 1932. After the season he reshaped the team. Among his first acquisitions were two Texas catchers, Richards and Gus Mancuso. The son of a Sicilian immigrant who settled in Houston, the twenty-seven-year-old Mancuso had been fighting for playing time with the St. Louis Cardinals behind Jimmy Wilson, one of the league's top-rated defensive catchers. Terry traded two pitchers, a backup catcher, and an outfielder for Mancuso and a pitcher who didn't stick with the Giants. Terry called Mancuso the best catcher in the National League.[16]

As Terry built up Mancuso, one writer took note of Richards: "The youngster has free action behind the plate and has developed into sort of a stylist. He uses a light glove, which he handles with unusual dexterity and effectiveness."[17] The Giants sent Richards a contract for a $4,000 salary, the same as he had earned in 1932. This was a substantial paycheck at the bottom of the Depression, when one-fourth of American workers were unemployed. Other rookies were making as little as $3,000, and the major league average was $6,000 (roughly the same buying power as $91,000 today).[18] Richards asked for a $500 raise. In a letter to the Giants' secretary, James J. Tierney, he added: "Please do not consider my returning this contract as expressing any intention of becoming a holdout. . . . If you don't agree [to the raise], Mr. Tierney, I assure you that I may be slightly disappointed but not dissatisfied and it will not affect my spirit and enthusiasm for having the oppertunity [sic] to play with the World's best baseball club, The New York Giants."[19]

His groveling worked. Tierney replied: "In my thirteen years with this ball club I have never received a letter from a ball player meriting more consideration than yours above mentioned. Because of your attitude, which is greatly appreciated, I am enclosing herewith a new contract in the amount of $4500."[20]

Twenty of the thirty-five men on the Giants' spring roster were newcomers, but the biggest change was in atmosphere. Terry consulted his players, who were also his teammates, and listened to their advice, whether he took it or not. He drilled them on the fundamentals of base running and defense, something McGraw had not done in his later years. Although newspapermen painted Terry as cold and arrogant, many players saw him differently. Outfielder Joe Moore summed it up: "McGraw was a driver; Terry was a leader."[21]

As the Giants arrived in Los Angeles for spring training in 1933, the Depression's grip had become a stranglehold. Major league attendance had shrunk by nearly one-third from 1930 to 1932. While Richards got a raise, other players' salaries had been cut drastically for two years in a row.[22] Rosters had been reduced from twenty-five men to twenty-three.

As if the financial shock was not enough, on Friday, March 10, an earthquake jolted Southern California at 5:54 P.M. "with a roar and a crash that sounded like an explosion."[23] The panicky ballplayers spilled out of the Biltmore Hotel. Richards was with Margie and his sister, Lillie Belle, when the quake struck. Lillie Belle calmly remarked, "Why, look at those buildings falling." As aftershocks rattled throughout the evening, most of the Giants spent the night in the clubhouse at the ballpark, playing cards or curling up on equipment trunks to sleep. Richards took his wife and sister to a friend's house. The quake, centered in Long Beach, killed 130 people and injured five thousand.[24]

On the field Richards watched a master catcher at work. The *Sporting News* later described Gus Mancuso as "the National League's most skilled receiver of his time."[25] He was a small, swarthy man with a perpetual smile who said, "The catcher's got to have the pitcher's confidence. The main thing that I found was, rather than studying the hitters so hard, was to study your pitchers, their strengths."[26]

The Giants' ace, Carl Hubbell, was recognized as one of the league's best, but the gaunt thirty-year-old left-hander had never led in ERA or won twenty games, the common benchmark of excellence. His strength was the screwball, which broke opposite from a curve, away from right-handed batters. Terry had traded two starting pitchers to get Mancuso and was relying on a pair of young arms to take their place. Right-hander Hal Schumacher was just twenty-two and had won only six big league games. The broad-shouldered twenty-six-year-old right-hander Roy Parmelee, called "Tarzan" for his sculpted physique, had been trying to make the team for four years while walking more batters than he struck out. Mancuso said, "Parmelee had as much stuff as any four or five pitchers put together, but he didn't know where it was going."[27] In 1933 he led the league in hit batters and wild pitches. Terry understood that his staff presented a challenge to even the most agile backstop: Hubbell with his screwball, Schumacher's sinker, Parmelee's wildness, and veteran Freddie Fitzsimmons's knuckleball, a catcher's worst enemy.[28]

It was soon obvious that twenty-nine-year-old Travis Jackson could not take his regular place at shortstop. He and Terry were the only Giants left from

McGraw's last pennant winner in 1924, and Jackson was one of the new manager's closest friends. Terry had brought him to Memphis during the off-season to have his own doctor operate on both of Jackson's knees.[29] The rookie Blondy Ryan covered more ground in the field but could not match Jackson's bat. Without Jackson, *New York Times* columnist John Kieran commented, "The Giants were facing the season with four players and a prayer." He meant Terry, Hubbell, Fitzsimmons, and right fielder Mel Ott.[30] At twenty-four Ott was one of the league's most feared sluggers. He had won the first of his six home-run championships in 1932 with thirty-eight. After Ott and Terry the rest of the Giants' lineup didn't scare anyone. An Associated Press poll of eighty-one sportswriters picked the Pittsburgh Pirates to win the 1933 National League pennant. No one placed New York higher than third.[31]

Richards got into action in the season's fifth game on April 22 at the Polo Grounds, pinch hitting for Blondy Ryan in the ninth. He delivered his first big league hit, a single off Boston Braves right-hander Huck Betts. But now that Mancuso finally had a regular job, he wouldn't come out of the lineup. He caught every inning of the first twelve games before stepping aside to let Richards work the last three frames in the second game of an April 30 double-header. Richards didn't catch again for two weeks, as Mancuso went all the way in two twin bills. Richards pinch-hit on May 8, striking out against the Cardinals' Dizzy Dean. Richards got his first start in the season's thirty-first game, the nightcap of a May 21 doubleheader in St. Louis, going 1-for-4 and catching Fitzsimmons's knuckleball in an 8–4 loss. The Cardinals had beaten Hubbell in the first game, leaving the Giants in second place, three games behind Pittsburgh.

Margie joined her husband in New York, and they found an apartment near the ballpark. For small-town Americans of their generation, "the city was the home of liquor and bootleggers, jazz and Sunday golf, wild parties and divorce," as the historian Richard Hofstadter put it.[32] Margie made friends among the players' wives and enjoyed her time there, but the couple quickly returned home to Waxahachie after every season.[33]

By July 13 the Giants had opened a three-game lead over St. Louis. Hubbell relieved that day and held the Cardinals scoreless for the final three innings. During the next twenty days Hubbell did not allow a run. His forty-five consecutive shutout innings were a National League record, second in major league history only to Walter Johnson's skein of fifty-six in 1912. Sportswriters began calling Hubbell "King Carl."

Richards became Hubbell's personal catcher during the streak and was behind the plate for thirty-four of the forty-five innings. It was his first extended playing time, four starts and a relief appearance, but he did not take advantage, going hitless in fifteen times at bat.

New York clinched its thirteenth National League pennant on September 19; only the Chicago Cubs had won as many. John Drebinger of the *New York Times* wrote that the Giants overcame an "inferior attack" with "brilliant pitching and a firm air-tight defense"[34] Hal Schumacher won nineteen games; Fred Fitzsimmons, sixteen; and Roy Parmelee, thirteen.

Eight days later Richards caught Hubbell's one-hundredth career victory, King Carl's twenty-third of that remarkable season. Hubbell's 1.66 ERA was the lowest in the majors since 1919, the year Babe Ruth started hitting home runs in large numbers. Hubbell was named the NL's Most Valuable Player. He taught Richards one lesson that stuck for life. Hubbell's screwball was such a devastating pitch because it was a change of pace. "I just came right up [overhand] and turned it over, and it came out of the back of my hand," Hubbell explained. "And that slowed it up tremendously. The real effectiveness of the screwball was not the break at all. It's the speed of the ball."[35] When Richards became a manager, he demanded that every pitcher try to master a change-up.

Richards finished his 1933 season with two hits in the final game against Brooklyn. He stroked a fifth-inning double off Hollis Thurston, who had driven him to California seven years earlier. It was Thurston's last major league inning, and Richards scored the final run he allowed.[36]

The Giants met the Washington Senators in the World Series, the same match-up as the last time they had won a pennant under McGraw nine years earlier. They took the championship in five games as their pitchers allowed only eight earned runs. Mancuso did all the catching; Richards did not play.

If Richards learned anything from Mancuso, he never said so. Nor was there any reported friction between them; by all accounts Mancuso was one of the most likable men in the game. But Bill Terry made a deep and lasting impression on Richards with what he did right and what he did wrong. Forty years later, in an interview with Donald Honig, Richards assessed Terry in terms that foreshadowed his own managerial style:

Terry was probably the finest defensive manager that I knew in baseball. He concentrated almost entirely on defense. His theory was not to let the other club score and they'd beat themselves. Naturally, most ball games are lost rather than won. Terry took it far beyond anybody I ever knew—his entire approach to every game was defense. He didn't hit-and-run. He didn't go for the stolen base or any fancy offensive plays at all. He just figured to score three or four runs. And he had the good pitching staff to win—Carl Hubbell, Hal Schumacher, Roy Parmelee, Fred Fitzsimmons—and a good bull pen. . . .

Terry was not a personality manager. He had no feelings for the ballplayers, no particular friends except those who courted him. He had a couple of players who made a point of doing that, and he wasn't aware of the fact that that was what they were doing. That sort of thing was to the detriment of the other players, and they criticized it severely. He was hard to talk to. I stayed as far away from him as I could, frankly."[37]

• • •

The players' share of World Series money, based on gate receipts from the first four games, was the smallest since 1922 as the Depression held down attendance. None of the games was a sellout. Richards got about $4,600, doubling his salary.[38]

Paul and Margie lived with her family in the off-season. When they returned to Waxahachie, her sister Lucille, guardian of the household finances, asked them for $40 a month to cover room and board. Richards shocked the McDonalds when he peeled off $200 from his bankroll and paid for the entire winter in advance. By then he had won over "Mr. and Mrs. Mac" from their prejudice against their ballplaying son-in-law.[39]

Richards spent some of his windfall on a gift to his parents. He paid to install indoor plumbing at the Water Street house. When he asked his mother how she liked it, she said she would rather have a new dress. Della's ingratitude stung. Her son avoided her for several years while staying in touch with his father.[40]

Richards had failed to prove himself in his rookie year. His batting line was .195/.222/.230 in ninety plate appearances; three doubles were his only extra-base hits. Terry expected more from a player who had hit better than .300 with power in six of his seven minor league seasons. Looking forward to next year, Terry commented, "I believe Harry Danning is about ready to give Paul Richards a run for the second-string job."[41]

But Mancuso came down with typhoid fever during the winter. The more experienced Richards beat out Danning for the opening day assignment in 1934 and caught the first nine games before Mancuso regained his strength and his job. Richards managed only four hits in twenty-seven at-bats. If that did not sour Terry on him, Danning's performance did. Danning and Richards each caught in thirty-seven games, with Danning batting .330/.337/.433 in ninety-nine plate appearances to Richards's pitiful .160/.284/.173 in eighty-nine tries.

The Giants held a seven-game lead on September 4 and seemed poised to claim their second straight pennant. In the furnace of a pennant race Terry's club melted. While the Giants lost their last five games, the St. Louis Cardinals charged to the finish line by winning thirteen of their last fifteen and clinched the pennant on the final day of the season. Disappointed and taking flak from the press, Terry said, "Almost anything anybody wants is for sale or trade," excepting only Hubbell and Ott.[42]

When the 1935 season opened, Richards played only seven times, three of them as a pinch hitter, before Terry sold him to the Philadelphia Athletics on May 25. The Giants had put him on waivers, but no National League team wanted him.

The principal owner and manager of the Athletics, seventy-two-year-old Connie Mack, was called "The Tall Tactician" and "The Lean Leader," the nickname he preferred.[43] Managing from the bench in a business suit, he had won nine American League pennants, more than any other team, but the A's had started a downhill slide that would continue with few interruptions until he retired in 1950 at age eighty-eight. Mack had built a dynasty that claimed three straight flags from 1929 through 1931 before the Depression brought him down. After a third-place finish in 1933 he gutted his team on a single day, selling pitchers Lefty Grove and George Earnshaw and catcher Mickey Cochrane, among others, to raise the reported $250,000 he needed to pay off loans. The stars Mack sold were all older than thirty; he kept twenty-six-year-old first baseman Jimmie Foxx.

In 1935 Mack decided Foxx would be his catcher. The fearsome right-handed slugger known as "The Beast" had started his career behind the plate but moved to third base and then to first because the Athletics had Cochrane. He had not caught in seven years. "I am going to do my best for Connie and the club," he said gamely but added that catching was "bound to" hurt his hitting because it would be more tiring than playing first base.[44] Foxx had hit fifty-eight home runs in 1932, the closest challenge to Ruth's record of sixty, and won consecutive Most Valuable Player awards in 1932 and 1933. He ranked third on the lifetime home run list behind Ruth and Lou Gehrig.

The experiment lasted twenty-eight games. On the day he bought Richards, Mack restored Foxx to first base. At age twenty-six Richards got his first chance to play regularly, catching seventy-nine of 120 games after he joined the team. Before the 1935 season Mack had predicted the Athletics had a chance to win the pennant: "Don't be surprised if we do."[45] By the time Richards arrived, reality had bitten and they were in seventh place.

After riding the Giants' bench for two years, Richards showed early signs of reviving his batting eye. He hit his first big league home run on July 6 off Boston's Wes Ferrell. Richards slammed two more before the end of the month but only one after that. His two-run clout on July 30 beat the Yankees and Red Ruffing. But when he returned to the bench, Mack informed him he had missed a "take" sign. Wagging a bony finger in Richards's face, the manager lectured, "Don't let it happen again."[46]

Mack, a former catcher, did not like the way Richards handled Philadelphia's largely inexperienced pitching staff. Mack thought he called for too many curveballs, and the young pitchers couldn't throw them for strikes. In his usual mild language the exasperated manager said: "For heaven's sake, Richards, call for some fastballs. Good gracious, these kids can't pitch curves."[47]

Richards blamed a temper tantrum for his final break with Mack. In a game against Detroit the batter tried to bunt with a runner on first. The umpire called the pitch a ball, but Richards insisted it had tipped the bat. While he threw down his mitt and raged at the ump, the forgotten runner sneaked all the way to third. "I hit .268," he misremembered, "and got traded to the minors."[48] He hit .245/.310/.339 for Philadelphia. His .649 on-base plus slugging percentage, or OPS, ranked seventeenth among nineteen catchers with at least 250 plate appearances.

Richards had bought stock in his hometown newspaper, the *Daily Light*, and began writing an off-season column called "Sport Patter." As a writer he displayed a folksy touch. He predicted the winners of each weekend's high school and college football games and made fun of himself when he was wrong.[49] He worked as a high school football official and reported on many of the top college match-ups in Texas. Houston sportswriter Clark Nealon described him as a "quiet, almost solemn figure around the pressboxes."[50]

In his column of December 5, 1935, Richards recounted how he had discovered a promising young pitcher two years earlier. Six-foot-three-inch Almon Williams had been a basketball star for nearby Bardwell High, and Richards recruited "Ichabod" Williams for his semipro basketball team. Williams agreed to play basketball on the condition that Richards help him hone his pitching skills and arrange a professional tryout. Richards recommended the right-hander to his former boss Earl Mann, who was running the Atlanta Crackers of the Southern Association. Richards wrote, "The climax of this real-life drama was written just the other day when a bulletin from the Philadelphia Athletics baseball club briefly announced the following: 'Paul Richards, A's catcher, has been traded to Atlanta for Almon Williams.'"[51]

At twenty-seven Richards had blown his shot at the majors. With only 368 big league jobs available (on twenty-three-man rosters), and at least six times as many players in the minors to choose from, no team would give another chance to a player with a .216 batting average to show for three seasons. His demotion to Atlanta was the third move that shaped his career and the rest of his life.

1. *New York Sun*, March 7, 1932, 32.
2. Richards clipped and saved three newspaper accounts—from the *Brooklyn Eagle*, *New York Evening Journal*, and *New York Herald-Tribune*—of his debut, all dated April 18, 1932, and all in the Richards scrapbooks in the personal collection of Paula Richards. See also *New York Times*, April 18, 1932, 20.
3. *Sporting News* (hereafter *TSN*), September 7, 1944, 3.
4. Donald Honig, *The Man in the Dugout* (Chicago: Follett, 1977), 122.
5. *TSN*, November 17, 1932, 7. Details of the 1932 season were provided by Stew Thornley, whose Web site, http://stewthornley.net, covers the history of Minneapolis baseball.
6. Gene Carney, *Burying the Black Sox* (Washington, D.C.: Potomac Books, 2006), 111–18; David Pietrusza, *Judge and Jury: The Life and Times of Judge Kenesaw Mountain Landis* (South Bend, Ind.: Diamond Communications, 1998), 254–57.
7. Paul Richards, untitled 1970s manuscript "for high school, college and amateur managers and coaches" (hereafter Richards manuscript), in the author's files.
8. Paul Richards, *Modern Baseball Strategy* (New York: Prentice-Hall, 1955), 33.
9. Honig, *Man in the Dugout*, 122.
10. *Chicago Tribune*, February 27, 1979, C1.
11. Honig, *Man in the Dugout*, 122.
12. *Chicago Tribune*, February 27, 1979, C1.
13. Paul Richards, taped reminiscences (undated; 1983 or later, cited hereafter as Richards Waxahachie tape), in the author's files.
14. Carl Hubbell, interview by Walter Langford, June 15, 1982.
15. Peter Williams, *When the Giants Were Giants* (Chapel Hill, N.C.: Algonquin, 1994), 14–302.
16. *New York Times*, February 3, 1933, 22.
17. *TSN*, November 3, 1932, 5.
18. Charles C. Alexander, *Our Game* (New York: Henry Holt, 1991), 159; Lee Lowenfish, *Branch Rickey: Baseball's Ferocious Gentleman* (Lincoln: University of Nebraska Press, 2007), 242; Robert F. Burk, *Much More Than a Game* (Chapel Hill: University of North Carolina Press, 2001), 42. See the Web site for the Bureau of Labor Statistics, U.S. Department of Labor (http://data.bls.gov/cgi-bin/cpicalc.pl) for a handy way to calculate equivalents in today's dollars.
19. Paul Richards to James J. Tierney, January 19, 1933, Paul Richards Papers, in the personal collection of Paula Richards.
20. Tierney to Richards, January 23, 1933, in Richards Papers.
21. Williams, *When the Giants Were Giants*, 135–36.
22. Burk, *Much More Than a Game*, 42.
23. *Los Angeles Times*, March 11, 1933, 1.
24. *Waxahachie (Texas) Daily Light*, undated clipping (1933) in Richards scrapbooks; Williams, *When the Giants Were Giants*, 140–42; *Los Angeles Times*, March 12, 1933, E1 and 14.
25. *TSN*, November 16, 1944, 8.
26. Gus Mancuso, interview by Clark Nealon, ca. 1980.
27. Hubbell interview; Mancuso interview.
28. Warren Corbett, "Gus Mancuso," *The Baseball Biography Project*, Society for American Baseball Research, http://bioproj.sabr.org.
29. *New York Times*, October 22, 1932, 21.
30. Ibid., March 29, 1933, 20.
31. AP, *New York Times*, April 4, 1933, 22.
32. Richard Hofstadter, *The Age of Reform* (New York: Vintage, 1955), 294.
33. Richards Waxahachie tape.
34. *New York Times*, September 29, 1933, 26.
35. Hubbell interview.
36. Richards Waxahachie tape, confirmed by the game story and box score in the *New York Times*, October 2, 1933, 24.

37. Honig, *Man in the Dugout*, 127–29.

38. *New York Times*, October 7, 1933, 9.

39. Richards Waxahachie tape; Paula Richards, interviews by author, 2006–2008.

40. Paula Richards interviews.

41. *TSN*, February 1, 1934, 1.

42. Williams, *When the Giants Were Giants*, 180.

43. *Waxahachie Daily Light*, October 13, 1936, page illegible.

44. *TSN*, February 7, 1935, 5.

45. AP, *New York Times*, April 12, 1935, 29.

46. *New York Times*, July 31, 1935, 11; *Chicago Daily News*, February 6, 1945, 11.

47. *Washington Post*, April 6, 1940, 17. This is Shirley Povich's account, no doubt a paraphrase.

48. *New York Times*, October 18, 1972, 31; David Gough and Jim Bard, *Little Nel: The Nellie Fox Story* (Alexandria, Va.: D. L. Megbeck Publishing, 2000), 71. Richards sometimes identified the bunter as Charlie Gehringer, sometimes as Hank Greenberg.

49. *Waxahachie Daily Light*, various issues, 1935–46.

50. *Houston Post*, September 4, 1961, clipping in the Paul Richards file, A. Bartlett Giamatti Research Center, National Baseball Hall of Fame and Museum, Cooperstown, N.Y.

51. Paul Richards, "Sport Patter," *Waxahachie Daily Light*, December 5, 1935, page illegible (copy in the author's files).

CHAPTER 5

The Toughest Manager

F ormer major leaguers of the day commonly played out their careers in the minors. Even a minor league paycheck was more than most of them could earn outside the game during the Depression. Richards did not own a home; he and Margie still lived with her parents. He held off-season jobs as a high school football official and sportswriter, but he had no established profession besides baseball. Most important, the familiar rhythm of the game was the life he had known since he was seventeen. He was not ready to leave it. He never would be.

Demoted to Atlanta in 1936, he dropped two steps below the majors. That winter the Class A Southern Association and Texas League were elevated to a new 1-A classification.[1] Atlanta, with a population of about 300,000, usually led the circuit in attendance. The city's leading business, the Coca-Cola Company, had stepped in to keep the franchise afloat during the Depression. The aged Wilbert Robinson was the president of the Atlanta Crackers, and he had brought in Georgia native Earl Mann from the Brooklyn farm system as his assistant. When Robinson died on August 8, 1934, lawyer Hughes Spalding, who watched over Coca-Cola's investment, put Mann in charge. Not yet thirty years old, Mann had sold peanuts at Crackers games as a boy.

Earl Mann was "a big guy with tremendous charisma and personality"— blond, six feet three inches tall, and weighing more than two hundred pounds. He had a disappearing hairline and a smile as broad as his waistline.[2] He quickly proved himself one of the minors' savviest operators. In 1935 the pennant-winning Crackers drew a league-record 330,000 fans, more than five major league clubs had attracted. Mann won his players' loyalty by giving them a share of the purchase price when he sold their contracts. More than a generous gesture, it was an important strategic advantage that helped attract top talent to a team without a major league affiliation. He also slipped players hundred-dollar bills to reward outstanding performances.[3]

The Crackers played in one of the minors' storied venues, Ponce de Leon Park. Built in 1924, "Poncey" featured a majestic magnolia tree in center field, more than 460 feet from home plate (only Babe Ruth and Eddie Mathews hit balls into the tree), on a slope covered with kudzu, the voracious southern vine that devours houses, barns, and, it is said, the occasional slow-moving cow. The Southern Railroad tracks ran parallel to the right-field line outside the park; play sometimes stopped when thick smoke from the locomotives drifted over the field. Poncey had about fifteen thousand seats but could hold more than twenty thousand with standing room.[4]

Southern Association writers made the Crackers favorites to repeat in 1936.[5] Manager Eddie Moore returned, leading an experienced squad. Atlanta opened with a 25–5 surge and never lost its lead. In the second game of the season at Chattanooga, Richards threw out a base stealer, pounced on a bunt to start a double play, and picked a runner off second. The *Atlanta Journal*'s Guy Butler commented, "He catches a very fancy ball game."[6] Richards did some fancy running, too. In the eighth he reached base on a bunt, stole second, took third on the catcher's wild throw, and scored the go-ahead run.

After an early-season slump Richards hit a pair of two-run homers, a double, and two singles to drive in six runs in a victory over Little Rock. A few days later he hit three home runs in two games to tie for the league lead with eight. Jack Troy of the *Atlanta Constitution* began calling him "Pound 'Em Paul Richards," but his teammates succinctly nicknamed him "Slug."[7] By July 2 Richards was leading the team with a .371 average and forty-seven RBI, usually batting cleanup. He also filled in at second base.

With Nashville and Birmingham close behind, Earl Mann tapped his Brooklyn connection to acquire pitcher Emil Leonard. The twenty-seven-year-old right-hander, "a large, flabby sort of individual with a hairline in full retreat," was called "Dutch" after an earlier pitcher named Leonard.[8] Leonard had been a league-average pitcher for the Dodgers, a below-average team, but he had one problem: his catchers. He complained that they wouldn't let him throw his best pitch, a knuckleball. When Brooklyn manager Casey Stengel berated the portly catcher Babe Phelps for calling for too many of Leonard's mediocre fastballs, Phelps protested that the knuckler was hard to catch. Stengel snapped, "Don't you think it might be a little hard to hit, too?"[9] Because he needed Phelps's bat, Stengel shipped Leonard to Atlanta.

In half a season Leonard went 13-3 and led the league with a 2.29 ERA. "Richards was the first catcher I ever worked with who wasn't too timid to call for my knuckleball," he said. Richards told him, "You keep throwing it, and it's my job to catch it."[10] Richards caught most of them; he was charged with just ten passed balls. Two years later Leonard was back in the majors. He stayed there until he was forty-four, winning 173 more games, and became one of Richards's earliest boosters. Leonard told reporters, "He put me back in the big leagues after Brooklyn let me go."[11] Leonard was the first in a long line of reclamation projects that made Richards's reputation as a pitching guru. His ability to resurrect the careers of failed pitchers would become his hallmark.

Richards was also doing himself a favor he would not know about for twenty-two years. A North Carolina teenager with a not-so-fast ball, Hoyt Wilhelm, learned to throw the knuckler after seeing a photograph of Dutch Leonard's grip.[12]

Atlanta won the pennant with a 94-59 record, and the home attendance, more than 300,000, was the highest in the minors. The *Sporting News* named

Mann Minor League Executive of the Year.[13] Richards was the only unanimous choice for the Southern Association all-star team selected by sportswriters. He had made the all-star team in every minor league where he had played. In 117 games he batted .327/.392/.545 with fourteen homers while throwing out 38 percent of base runners trying to steal, above average for the league's catchers.

The Southeastern Conference, a big-time college football league, hired Richards to officiate at games that fall. Then he and Margie took off for winter ball in Panama, where a large expatriate U.S. population worked on the canal. His three-run homer against a U.S. Navy team clinched the league pennant for the Colón club. He also wrote for the *Colón Times Star* newspaper and tried tennis for the first time. He joked that he was mistaken for a star player, Vincent Richards.[14]

The Crackers returned most of their lineup and manager Eddie Moore in 1937, but the defending champions started slowly and sank to sixth place in May. Richards launched a twenty-game hitting streak in midseason as the club moved up to third place. With his twenty-ninth birthday approaching, he was discouraged that no major league team had shown interest after his outstanding performance in 1936. He was incensed when he learned that a radio announcer had called him "Old Man Richards." In August he told Earl Mann he was quitting baseball, but Mann persuaded him to stay until the end of the season.[15]

Atlanta finished third with a disappointing 84-66 record, twelve games behind the pennant-winning Little Rock Travelers. In 126 games Richards drove in seventy-six runs with eight homers and a line of .304./.360 /.406. The Associated Press named him the all-star catcher.[16]

As soon as the Crackers were eliminated from the postseason playoffs, Mann named Richards the new manager. "I think it's a great break that we have such a chap as Paul on our club," he said. ". . . It is our opinion that he has the background, experience, temperament and personality to make Atlanta a successful leader." Jimmy Burns wrote in the *(Atlanta) Georgian*, "Richards' selection is expected to be popular with the fans and the players." Years afterward Mann declared, "Richards was a managerial natural if ever there was one."[17]

Later Richards said: "I'll tell you when I decided to become a manager. When I found I wasn't going to be a .300 hitter in the big leagues. Of course, I found that out pretty early."[18] At twenty-nine he was the youngest manager in the league, but he did not lack confidence. In a guest column for the *Constitution*, he promised a hustling, running club: "If the Crackers finish at any point below first place, personally the season will be a failure." After twelve seasons as a ballplayer, he believed he knew how to create a winning team. The column was his first public expression of his baseball philosophy, one that would never change: "One thing I have learned in baseball is that a ball club that doesn't beat itself is hard to beat. By that I mean that a club which runs the bases correctly and throws the ball to the right base and in general forces the enemy to win the game on its merits, other than by errors on your part, will be hard to handle. The Crackers will drill continuously along these lines."[19]

A few days after Richards's appointment, his father died at sixty-eight. The cause of death was listed as pneumonia, but Jesse Richards had suffered a stroke a year earlier. The bond between the father and his only son had always been strong, even when Paul was keeping his distance from his difficult mother.

When Richards opened the Crackers' spring camp in Savannah, Georgia, in 1938, most of the regular lineup returned. He had a cast of veteran pitchers, including one born in the nineteenth century. Left-hander Leo Moon was nearing his thirty-ninth birthday (he subtracted one or two years for his "baseball age") and had already won 137 games in the Southern Association. Right-hander Bob Durham had won at least sixteen games in each of the three previous seasons. The most promising newcomer was a twenty-five-year-old lefty from the Cardinals' organization, Tom Sunkel. Another rookie, right-hander Luman Harris, had taken time off from his job in a Buck Creek, Alabama, cotton mill to sign with the Crackers the year before.[20]

Drawing on the lesson he had learned from Carl Hubbell, Richards began teaching the pitchers the change-up he called the "slip pitch," although he sometimes referred to it as a "dry spitter" because of its sinking action. He said he learned it from minor league veteran Deacon Johnson, who struck him out with one: "I'll swear the ball stopped out in front of home plate about six feet and after I swung the bat it came on through." As he described it, the pitcher palms the ball at the base of the first and second fingers, then rotates his hand clockwise with the thumb and fingers parallel to the ground, so the ball slips out between the index finger and thumb.[21] The result is a sinker that acts like the modern change-up thrown by Greg Maddux and Pedro Martinez. The slip pitch would become Richards's first prescription for every pitcher.

A rookie catcher came to camp with Richards: his nephew, Stan Bolton. Just twenty-one, Stan was farmed out and played six seasons in the low minors. When Richards became a big league general manager, he hired Stan as a scout for Baltimore, Houston, and Atlanta.[22]

The Crackers quickly learned that their teammate "Slug" was a tough boss. "You may think you'll continue to be the same person after you start to manage, but it just doesn't work," Richards said later. "As a manager you can be just close enough to appreciate your players' idiosyncrasies and witticisms, no closer."[23] In his first weeks on the job he established the style that would be his trademark. The *Georgian*'s sports editor, Ed Danforth, said: "Paul Richards has gone about his spring training after the manner of a college football coach. He has spent hours drilling his squad in elementary stuff."[24] The *Constitution*'s Jack Troy wrote: "For the first time in at least three years the players are being given independent instruction. And how they like it!"[25]

Richards told his players that base stealing and aggressive running would be a key part of the offense. He put them through drills on the fundamentals he had learned from Donie Bush. Richards also stressed aggressive defensive play. When his infielders handled a sacrifice bunt, he instructed them to look to throw out the lead runner rather than the bunter, even if it meant taking a gamble. It was a tactic borrowed from Bill Terry.[26]

Atlanta opened the season with an 8–5 victory over Knoxville, as Richards belted two home runs. He was soon suspended for three games for arguing too strenuously with an umpire, setting the tone for the rest of his career. When Atlanta won fifteen of twenty games to take over first place in June, the *Constitution*'s Ralph McGill wrote, "Richards is the first inspirational leader the Crackers have had in years—a leader and a performer, and not a berater and a boaster."[27]

Atlanta held on to the lead for the rest of the season, but Richards drove his players hard. He kept them after games for practice on plays they had botched. After one defeat he made them sit in the clubhouse in their sweaty uniforms until he finished a leisurely shower, giving them time to reflect on their shortcomings.[28] Richards always maintained that he did not care about players' off-field activities as long as they showed up ready to perform, but he discouraged them from attending movies because he thought it was bad for their eyes. However, he was a fan of westerns.[29]

The Crackers clinched first place on September 6, the franchise's third pennant in four years. The *Constitution*'s Jack Troy wrote that they were "the most spirited baseball club Atlanta fans have seen in more than a decade. . . . Paul Richards did a great job as a first year manager."[30] The Crackers finished 91-62 as Richards contributed thirteen home runs and batted .316/.392/.513. He led the league's catchers with eighty-two assists in 105 games, but his fifteen errors were the second highest. Atlanta won both rounds of the postseason playoffs to move on to the Dixie Series against the Texas League champion Beaumont Exporters.

Beaumont was a Detroit farm club whose roster included several men Richards would meet again: the third baseman and manager Al Vincent, pitcher Dizzy Trout, and outfielders Pat Mullin and Barney McCosky. A former Tiger pitching star, Schoolboy Rowe, spent the season with the Exporters as he tried to come back from a sore arm.

Only about seven thousand fans turned out in Atlanta for the first game. The Crackers filleted Trout with a five-run third inning and won, 7–3. In Game 2 Richards knocked in two runs with a first-inning single off Rowe as Atlanta took a 3–0 lead. Tom Sunkel pitched eight shutout innings, but Beaumont scored twice in the ninth and had the tying run on base when rain ended the game.

The Crackers needed ten innings to win the third game at Beaumont, 5–4, as Rowe took the loss in relief. Game 4 was deadlocked in the thirteenth when McCosky threw out an Atlanta runner at the plate. The tie game was called because of darkness and because the rules prohibited turning on the lights in midgame.

Atlanta pitchers had been complaining about the Texas League ball that was used in the games at Beaumont. They said the seams were flat, making it hard to put a break on their curve balls. Nonetheless, in Game 5 Richards started the ancient junkballer Leo Moon, who had won just five times during the season. In the third inning a foul ball landed in the Crackers' bullpen, and backup catcher Dewey Williams, accidentally on purpose, threw a Southern Association ball to his pitcher. Moon's eyes lit up when he gripped it. The batter hit into a double play, and Moon spun a three-hit shutout as Atlanta beat Dizzy Trout, 7–0. Atlanta became the first Southern Association champion to sweep the Dixie Series since it began in 1921.[31]

The *Sporting News* named Richards Minor League Manager of the Year: "No other pilot in the minors compiled such a record of conquests and though he had a good team behind him, much credit is due Richards for his adept management, ability to get along with his men, sound strategy and inspiration, both as a player and manager."[32]

In an interview with Wirt Gammon of the *Chattanooga Times*, Richards first used a phrase that became his mantra: "You have to learn what NOT to do, rather than what to do. I saw, for example, that it would not do to keep players in an uproar by riding them." Crediting Bush and Terry as mentors, he mentioned that Terry stressed the value of teamwork, with every player backing up his mates in the field.[33]

Paul and Margie did not stay long in Waxahachie that fall. Margie was pregnant and had found a doctor she trusted in Atlanta. They returned there for the birth of their first child on January 12, 1939. After the delivery the doctor told the new father, "You've got a goddamn redheaded girl." She was named Paula Del, the middle name honoring her paternal grandmother, Della. The baby weighed only four pounds, two ounces. When she came home from the hospital, she slept in a primitive incubator with a lightbulb for heat and newspapers for insulation. Her father soon set the contraption on fire, without injury to Paula.[34]

The Crackers began 1939 with the youngest team in the league. Richards hit his second straight opening day homer as right-hander Luman Harris beat Chattanooga, 7–1. But the story of the season was a crushing series of injuries to six regular players and as many pitchers. In one game Richards had his right fielder at first base, himself at second, the left fielder at third, and a pitcher in right. He had been diagnosed with water on both knees, on top of a painfully skinned arm, but had to keep catching because his backup was hurting worse. Richards said his left knee was the more troublesome, but the right one would plague him for the rest of his career. He played ten games at first base to ease the strain on his legs.[35]

The defending champions fell to last place in the first month but climbed to the top of the standings by May 23. Their season was a roller coaster, winning streaks followed by losing streaks, the results depending on who was well enough to take the field. Perhaps confused by shuffling so many players, Richards once left his own name off the lineup card, and his first-inning single was nullified.

Atlanta won its last five games to clinch fourth place and a playoff spot. Chattanooga, managed by future Hall of Famer Kiki Cuyler, squeaked in to the pennant with an 85-65 record. Memphis and Nashville finished one and a half games back and Atlanta two behind at 83-67.

The first round of the playoffs produced a pair of upsets. Fourth-place Atlanta swept first-place Chattanooga, while third-place Nashville beat second-place Memphis. In the finals the Crackers held on until the tenth inning of the seventh game, when Nashville pushed across the winning run.

Earl Mann blamed injuries for the club's failure to repeat as champions. He announced that Richards would return as manager. Morgan Blake of the *Journal* paid a watery tribute: "All hail to manager Richards for his magnificent work as a pilot of the boat through the shoals."[36] It was profitable sailing for Mann. The Crackers had again led the league in attendance and sold three players to the majors.[37] Although Richards was named the all-star catcher, he went behind the plate in just eighty-five games. His fifty-six assists ranked third in the league. He batted .300/.376/.409 but hit only three home runs.

Baseball celebrated its official centennial in 1939, commemorating the myth of Abner Doubleday's invention of the game. The marquee event was the opening of the National Baseball Hall of Fame and Museum in Doubleday's tiny hometown, Cooperstown, New York. It was a year of recovery for the industry as the Depression receded. Minor league attendance reached a record 18.5 million. Forty-four leagues started the 1940 season, the most in nearly three decades. The majors had restored the twenty-five-man roster. Their attendance in 1940 would approach the peak of ten million set a decade earlier. Night baseball, a novelty in only two big league ballparks in 1938, spread to eleven of the sixteen teams.[38] But just as the cloud of Depression began to lift, the outbreak of war in Europe cast an ominous shadow across the Atlantic.

Richards again fielded the youngest team in the league in 1940. His prize

rookies were a pair of powerful left-handed hitters: six-foot first baseman Les-
ter Burge and nineteen-year-old outfielder Willard Marshall, signed by Nap
Rucker out of Wake Forest College in North Carolina. The Nashville Vols
won twenty of their first twenty-four games to take the lead as Atlanta struggled. An eight-game winning streak in May lifted the Crackers above .500.
By mid-June they had climbed to second place, five games behind Nashville.
Commenting on the weak pitching, sloppy defense, and numerous injuries, the
Georgian's Ed Danforth asked, "What's holding the Crackers up? . . . It must
be Richards."[39]

On June 20 Atlanta drew a standing-room crowd for the game against
Memphis. With fans corralled behind ropes in the outfield, a player from each
team was stationed along the foul lines to help the umpires determine whether
balls went into the crowd on the fly for a ground-rule double. In the ninth the
Crackers' Emil Mailho lifted a drive that the Chicks' right fielder Babe Barna
caught as he fell among the spectators. Atlanta pitcher Wayman Kerksieck was
guarding that foul line. He told umpire Paul Blackard that Barna had leaped
and snared the ball in the air, then fell beyond the rope on his way down. Blackard ruled it an out, igniting a thunderous protest from Richards and the Atlanta
fans. The league president, Major Trammell Scott, came out of the stands to
escort the umpire off the field.[40] Scott fined Richards $100 and suspended him
for ten days for his "uncalled-for and unreasonable abuse of Umpire Blackard,
delaying game and refusing to leave field when ordered to go, all of which
incited a near riot."[41]

Atlanta won twenty-four of thirty-two games and was just .005 behind
Nashville by the end of July. Hit by more injuries and illness, the Crackers
could not catch up. On August 23 Richards, trying to beat out an infield hit,
slammed into Vols first baseman Mickey Rocco. He flipped over Rocco's back
and crashed down on his right shoulder. He did not catch again for the rest
of the season.[42] Nashville won its last thirteen games to finish nine and a half

ahead of Atlanta and beat the Crackers in the final playoff series. Earl Mann announced that his manager would return for a fourth season in 1941.[43]

Overcoming early pitching problems, Atlanta allowed the fewest runs in the league despite committing the most errors, on the way to a 93-58 record. Richards failed to hit .300 for only the second time in his twelve seasons in the minors, finishing at .271/.324/.357 with two home runs. With the shoulder injury, a broken finger, and his chronically painful right knee, he caught only sixty-nine games but played twenty-eight times at first base.

Before heading home, Richards stayed in Atlanta long enough to register for the new military draft. Adopted over the bitter objections of isolationists in Congress, the Selective Service Act brought the European war home to Americans for the first time. The law required all men aged twenty-one to thirty-six to register, although those with dependents were deferred from service. Nazi Germany now occupied most of Europe, but President Roosevelt promised America's mothers and fathers, "Your boys are not going to be sent into any foreign wars."[44] A week later he defeated Republican Wendell Willkie to win an unprecedented third term in the White House.

The draft posed a particular threat to baseball, since most players were of draft age. Reflecting the game's stature in American life, a Gallup poll found 84 percent of respondents believed big leaguers should be exempted from the draft until after the season, but Washington was not listening.[45] The minors had the most to fear, because their players tended to be younger and therefore less likely to be married with children or to have disabling medical conditions.

When Atlanta shifted its 1941 spring training camp to St. Augustine, Florida, Babe Ruth visited to play a round of golf with Richards, Mann, and the owner of the St. Augustine team, Fred Francis.[46] On the ball field Richards had to sort out the latest crop of rookies. The Crackers again opened the season with the youngest roster in the Southern Association; only six of the seventeen men had played at a higher level. Atlanta sprinted out of the gate, winning ten of the first eleven games, and the rest of the league never caught up. In the first month the Crackers reeled off a thirteen-game winning streak to lift their record to 26-5. Richards said it was the strongest minor league club he had ever seen.[47]

Richards platooned left-handed-batting rookie Pete Thomassie with right-hander Buddy Bates in center field, although the word *platoon* was not yet part of baseball's vocabulary; the strategy was called *alternating*.[48] Thomassie described Richards as "the toughest manager I ever played for," then added, "but he was also the best." He said: "One Sunday afternoon we blew a double-header and Richards kept the whole team in the clubhouse until 9 o'clock that night. Another time after we'd been licked twice, he wouldn't let us go home for supper. Instead, he kept us in the park for batting and fielding practice. Imagine that! A stiff workout after a doubleheader."[49]

Even as his club was winning, Richards continued to rage at umpires. He drew his annual suspension, three days this time, after another confrontation with ump Paul Blackard. Richards snapped, "We will win the Southern League pennant in spite of the umpires, [President] Scott and the seven other clubs." But Knoxville manager Fred Lindstrom complained, "Richards jumps up and tears into the umpires game after game. He goes berserk and he goes that way too often. The umpires get so they don't know what to do." Richards was ejected a dozen times during the season, his career high—so far. He had few reported run-ins with umpires during his playing career—he had been criticized for being too timid as a young player—but the responsibilities of managing transformed him into a ferocious intimidator. AP writer Romney Wheeler called him "the nearest approach to rampaging John McGraw the minors have seen in many years."[50]

The Crackers inevitably cooled off, going 15-15 in June, but clinched the pennant on August 28. They had held first place all season and finished 99-55, sixteen games in front of Nashville. Atlanta won with Richards's formula: pitching and defense. The Crackers allowed the fewest runs in the league but were also second to Nashville in runs scored. Les Burge belted thirty-eight homers, knocked in 146, and was named the league's most valuable player by managers. The thirty-two-year-old Richards caught only seventy-six games; his average fell to .244 with five home runs.

Although Atlanta lost the final playoff series to Nashville, Earl Mann called the '41 Crackers his favorite team for years. Despite a drop in attendance, it was also one of his most lucrative teams. He sold Burge and pitcher Bob Chipman to Brooklyn for a reported $50,000. The Dodgers also bought pitcher Emil Lochbaum for an undisclosed amount. The Giants paid $30,000 for Willard Marshall and second baseman Connie Ryan.[51] In four years as manager Richards had sent seven pitchers to the majors, not including his role in the comeback of Dutch Leonard.

Major league baseball in 1941 saw Joe DiMaggio hit safely in fifty-six consecutive games and Ted Williams bat .406. It was a golden season, the last before war and dramatic postwar change profoundly altered the game and the nation. December 7—the "date which will live in infamy"—changed everything.

While ballplayers worried about their draft status, club owners wondered whether they would be forced to shut down. In World War I the government's "work or fight" order had ended the 1918 major league season on Labor Day, with a special dispensation to play the World Series afterward. So many players went into military service or war-industry jobs that only one minor league completed the 1918 season.

Commissioner Landis, an ardent Republican, "wasn't much more welcome at the White House than the Japanese ambassador," according to Washington owner Clark Griffith. At Griffith's urging, Landis wrote to President Roosevelt on January 14, 1942: "If you believe we ought to close down for the duration of the war, we are ready to do so immediately. If you feel we ought to continue, we are delighted to do so. We await your order."

The president replied with the famous "green light" letter: "I honestly feel it would be best for the country to keep baseball going. There will be fewer people unemployed and everybody will work longer and harder hours than ever before. And that means that they ought to have a chance for recreation and for taking their minds off their work even more than before."[52]

During the off-season Paul and Margie Richards bought their first home after nearly ten years of marriage. It was a seventy-acre farm planted in pecan and peach trees, on the Fort Worth highway two miles west of Waxahachie's courthouse square. Land was cheap; the Depression had wiped out many Ellis County farmers, shutting down the cotton gins and the mill and ending the reign of King Cotton. The Richardses and three-year-old Paula moved into a two-story, ten-room frame house with double-deck wraparound verandas. Paula remembered that the old house, which was nestled in a grove of trees, seemed to sway in the prairie wind, the trees scraping its walls. Coincidentally or not, the property sat next to the Waxahachie Country Club's golf course.

A few dairy cows came with the farm. Paula regularly went with her father to the barn to feed them, and she developed a taste for the cottonseed pellets the cows ate. When a cow named Blossom kicked Paula in the head, her daddy took her to get ice cream instead of calling a doctor and warned her not to tell her mother. Margie did not find out about it until years later, when Paula began suffering headaches. "That was the only fight I ever saw my parents have," Paula said. "She read the riot act to him."[53] Richards was a halfhearted farmer. He invited boys from his Sunday school class at the First Baptist Church to visit, put them to work doing chores, and rewarded them with a game of catch when they were done.[54]

On opening day 1942 the impact of the draft was clear. More than half of the Southern Association's players were rookies. Atlanta had lost eight men to military service. The Crackers won thirteen of their first nineteen games to take over first place but soon fell back. Richards's center fielder was drafted, and a pitcher left the team for a job in a war plant. By midseason the minors had lost an estimated one-fourth of their players to the military or war-related jobs. More than three million men were drafted in 1942, three times as many as the previous year.[55]

Sharing the catching duties with Larry Smith, Richards threw out twenty-six of the first twenty-eight runners who tried to steal. In May he kept alive his streak of being suspended every year he had managed, drawing three days and a $50 fine for abusing an umpire.[56] Birmingham beat the Crackers on the next-to-last day of the season, knocking Atlanta out of the playoffs in fifth place. Richards hit .241/.364 /.338 and finished second in assists, although he had caught just seventy-seven games. For the first time since he came to Atlanta, he did not make the all-star team.

Only seventy major leaguers had been lost to military service in 1942 as the armed forces ramped up to train the millions of troops they would need for a worldwide war, but the minors were devastated.[57] Two-thirds of the leagues shut down for the duration of the war; just ten were left in 1943. Richards feared the Southern Association might fold, too. Several big league clubs had approached him about a playing contract, but none offered anything close to his $8,000 salary with Atlanta. Now he asked Earl Mann to release him so he could sign with the Detroit Tigers, the first big league team he had seen as a boy in Waxahachie.[58]

Ed Miles of the *Journal* wrote: "He was the fair-haired boy of Atlanta fandom, was popular with his players, though keeping a firm hold on the managerial reins. He was especially good at working pitchers, and had the weakness of the league's batters well-indexed in his orderly mind." The *Journal* saluted Richards in an editorial as "Mr. Atlanta": "He typified in many respects the city as it seems to be regarded in the hinterland. He was a hustler, and was never satisfied. Even if he won, he thought it might have been done better—say, more artistically, or more summarily. He was a hard loser. He never could reconcile himself to the fact that defeat sometimes is inevitable and might even be good for the soul. He had the obsession that the basic purpose of playing was to win."[59]

At age thirty-four Richards knew that his future lay in managing, not playing. Naturally, he wanted to lead a big league team. He was betting that a return to the majors as a player would bring him closer to that goal.

---

1. *Sporting News* (hereafter *TSN*), November 28, 1935, 3.
2. Tim Darnell, *The Crackers: Early Years of Atlanta Baseball* (Athens, Ga.: Hill Street Press, 2003), 62.
3. *TSN*, December 20, 1934, 7; August 8, 1935, 7; October 24, 1935, 7; December 2, 1953, 6; Darnell, *Crackers*, 62; Earl Mann, "Great Teams," undated interview for Georgia Sports Hall of Fame, *The New Georgia Encyclopedia*, www.georgiaencyclopedia.com/nge/Multimedia.jsp?id=m-3850.
4. Darnell, *Crackers*, 45–48; *TSN*, July 14, 1938, 14. The ballpark was razed in 1965; at last report the magnolia was still standing.
5. *TSN*, February 20, 1936, 8.
6. *Atlanta Journal*, undated (1936) and unidentified clipping in Paul Richards's scrapbooks, in the personal collection of Paula Richards.
7. *Atlanta Constitution*, undated clipping (1936) in Richards scrapbooks; *TSN*, August 27, 1977, 6.
8. *TSN*, May 26, 1938, 3. The description comes from *Washington Star* writer Denman Thompson, writing in the *Sporting News*.
9. Robert W. Creamer, *Stengel: His Life and Times* (1984; repr., Lincoln: University of Nebraska Press, 1996), 187.
10. *TSN*, October 1, 1942, 2.
11. *Washington Post*, April 6, 1940, 17.
12. Mark Armour, "Hoyt Wilhelm," *The Baseball Biography Project*, Society for American Baseball Research, http://bioproj.sabr.org.
13. *TSN*, April 15, 1937, 4.
14. *Waxahachie (Texas) Daily Light*, November 10, 1936, page illegible; unidentified clipping (1937) in Richards scrapbooks; *TSN*, April 1, 1937, 6.
15. *Waxahachie Daily Light*, October 9, 1937, page number missing; *TSN*, December 2, 1953, 8.
16. Unidentified clipping (1937) in Richards scrapbooks.
17. *Atlanta Journal*, undated clipping in Richards scrapbooks; *Atlanta Georgian*, October 3, 1937, clipping in Richards scrapbooks; *TSN*, December 2, 1953, 8.
18. Roy Terrell, "Hawkeye and His Boy Scouts," *Sports Illustrated*, April 17, 1961, 73.
19. *Atlanta Constitution*, December 4, 1937, in Richards scrapbooks.
20. *TSN*, April 11, 1964, 12.
21. Ibid., July 26, 1950, 16, and August 4, 1954, 6.
22. Scouting record provided by Jim Sandoval, cochair, Scouts Committee, Society for American Baseball Research.
23. *Chicago Tribune*, February 27, 1979, C1.
24. *Atlanta Georgian*, undated (1938) clipping in Richards scrapbooks.
25. *Atlanta Constitution*, March 4, 1938, page unknown, in Richards scrapbooks.
26. *TSN*, March 10, 1938, 8, and October 27, 1938, 9.

27. *Atlanta Constitution*, undated clippings (1938) in Richards scrapbooks. Sportswriter McGill later became the *Constitution*'s Pulitzer Prize–winning editor and publisher and a leading voice for tolerance during the civil rights era.

28. Ed Linn, "The Double Life of Paul Richards," *Sport*, August 1955, 53.

29. Paula Richards, interviews by author, 2006–2008.

30. *Atlanta Constitution*, undated clipping (1938) in Richards scrapbooks.

31. *TSN*, October 13, 1938, 8; October 27, 1938, 9.

32. Ibid., December 29, 1938, 2.

33. Ibid., October 27, 1938, 9.

34. Paula Richards interviews.

35. *Atlanta Journal*, undated clippings (1939) in Richards scrapbooks.

36. Ibid., September 14, 1939, 3; *Atlanta Journal*, undated clipping in Richards scrapbooks.

37. *Atlanta Journal*, August 10, 1939, 13; September 7, 1939, 2, 11.

38. Robert F. Burk, *Much More Than a Game* (Chapel Hill: University of North Carolina Press, 2001), 67–68; Lee Lowenfish, *Branch Rickey: Baseball's Ferocious Gentleman* (Lincoln: University of Nebraska Press, 2007), 308.

39. *Atlanta Georgian*, June 25, 1940, in Richards scrapbooks.

40. Ibid., undated clipping (1940) in Richards scrapbooks; *TSN*, September 27, 1940, 12.

41. Trammell Scott to Paul Richards, June 21, 1940, in Richards scrapbooks.

42. AP, unidentified clipping (1940) in Richards scrapbooks; *TSN*, August 29, 1940, 13; September 26, 1940, 11.

43. *TSN*, September 26, 1940, 11.

44. Robert E. Sherwood, *Roosevelt and Hopkins: An Intimate History* (New York: Harper, 1948) 190–91.

45. *TSN*, May 29, 1941, 2.

46. A photograph of the foursome is in the Paul Richards Papers, in the personal collection of Paula Richards.

47. *TSN*, May 22, 1941, 3.

48. Ibid., April 24, 1941, 11.

49. William Barry Furlong and Fred Russell, "He Put the White Sox Back in the League," *Saturday Evening Post*, July 21, 1951, 91; *TSN*, December 18, 1946, 10.

50. *TSN*, July 10, 1941, 11; *Atlanta Constitution*, June 5, 1941; UP, undated (1941); AP, May 21, 1941, all clippings in Richards scrapbooks.

51. Mann interview; *TSN*, November 27, 1941, 13.

52. David Pietrusza, *Judge and Jury: The Life and Times of Judge Kenesaw Mountain Landis* (South Bend, Ind.: Diamond Communications, 1998), 432–34.

53. Paula Richards interviews; Kelly McMichael Stott, *Waxahachie: Where Cotton Reigned King* (Charleston, S.C.: Arcadia, 2002), 133.

54. Buck Jordan, interviews by author, August 16–17, 2006, Waxahachie, Texas.

55. "War and Baseball," *Time*, July 20, 1942, online archive; "Inductions (by year) from World War I through the End of the Draft (1973)," U.S. Selective Service System, www.sss.gov/induct.htm.

56. *TSN*, May 14, 1942, 13; June 4, 1942, 13.

57. David S. Neft, Richard M. Cohen, and Michael L. Neft, *The Sports Encyclopedia: Baseball* (New York: St. Martin's Griffin, 2001), 228–29.

58. Paul Richards, taped reminiscences (undated; 1983 or later), in the author's files.

59. *Atlanta Journal*, undated clippings (1942) in Richards scrapbooks.

CHAPTER 6

Texas Tiger

Detroit's signing of Richards sparked speculation that he would replace manager Del Baker. Baker had led the Tigers to the 1940 American League pennant, but after slugger Hank Greenberg was drafted in May 1941, the club posted losing records for the next two years. General manager Jack Zeller insisted he wanted Richards strictly as a player: "He is a family man and fairly safe from the draft. There has been no thought of making him manager of the Tigers."[1] Richards was deferred from military service because he was married with a child.

The speculation about Baker's future turned out to be correct, but he was left dangling for two months before Zeller replaced him with Steve O'Neill. A former catcher and one of four brothers who played in the majors, the amiable fifty-one-year-old O'Neill had succeeded Hall of Fame pitcher Walter Johnson as Cleveland manager in 1935 and led the Indians to winning records in two-plus seasons.

Why not Richards? He had certainly proved himself in Atlanta, but few managers had been hired for major league jobs with only minor league experience. One was the most successful in history, the Yankees' Joe McCarthy, who got his first big league chance with the Chicago Cubs in 1926. McCarthy's rise was even more unusual because he had never played in the majors.

Besides Detroit, only two other teams changed managers for 1943. Richards had been rumored as a candidate for the Washington Senators job, but owner Clark Griffith followed his usual custom and hired from within, choosing long-time player and coach Ossie Bluege. Philadelphia's National League club, known as the Blue Jays that year, signed Bucky Harris, who had already managed Washington in two separate terms, Detroit, and Boston and would be hired three more times after Philadelphia let him go. Detroit chose O'Neill because he had paid his dues. After leaving Cleveland he spent five seasons in the Tigers' organization, managing two of their farm teams and serving as a coach under Baker.

In February 1943 the government called on major league baseball to "do its part" for the war effort. President Roosevelt's transportation chief, Joseph B. Eastman, asked Judge Landis to cut back on travel. With gasoline rationing in force and troops packing trains, a ubiquitous poster asked, "Is This Trip Necessary?" Landis ordered teams to abandon their spring training bases in Florida and California and train close to home.[2] Instead of enjoying springtime in the sunshine, Major leaguers worked out in snow, rain, and college field houses. Six clubs went to Indiana, including the Tigers, who went to Evansville; they formed the Limestone League to replace Florida's Grapefruit League.[3]

As draft calls swelled in 1943, the number of major leaguers in the military tripled to 219. White Sox manager Jimmy Dykes said, "Any team that can keep nine men on the field will be dangerous."[4] The Yankees' Joe DiMaggio had been deferred from service because he was married and the Red Sox's Ted Williams because he was supporting his divorced mother, a Salvation Army worker. They got no special favors, but throughout 1942 some writers and fans attacked both men as draft dodgers. Someone sent Williams an envelope containing a sheet of yellow paper. If it bothered him, he didn't show it; he won the triple crown, leading in home runs, RBI, and batting average. Williams signed up for navy pilot training and reported for duty in November. DiMaggio, pressured by his estranged wife (one headline read, "Love Me and Leave Me"), enlisted in the army.[5] Spring training opened without the game's two biggest stars.

The draft claimed the Tigers' ERA leader, right-hander Al Benton, who had pitched the most innings on the staff; promising outfielder Pat Mullin, who had hit .345 in fifty-four games; and two regulars, center fielder Barney McCosky, a .316 hitter in his first four seasons, and catcher Birdie Tebbetts.

Steve O'Neill planned to hand the catching duties to Dixon Parsons, who had batted just .197 with two home runs in his rookie year as Tebbetts's backup. When Parsons reported to Evansville with a sore arm, Richards won a share of the job.[6] Coming off a fifth-place finish, Detroit retained three-fourths of its infield—slugging first baseman Rudy York, second baseman Jimmy Bloodworth, and veteran third baseman Pinky Higgins—and two-thirds of its outfield, Doc Cramer and Ned Harris. (Cramer had been Richards's teammate on the 1935 Athletics.) The Tigers bought shortstop Joe Hoover, who had hit .329 for the Pacific Coast League Hollywood Stars. He was married with two children. To complete the outfield Detroit promoted the most celebrated rookie in the game, Dick Wakefield. He called himself "the original bonus baby"; he had signed for an unheard-of $52,000 and hit .345 in the Texas League.[7]

Except for Benton, the pitching staff was intact. One-time ace Tommy Bridges returned, but at thirty-five he was a once-a-week starter. Fireballer Virgil Trucks had won fourteen games with a 2.74 ERA as a rookie. The other starting jobs belonged to a pair of live arms who had been labeled disappointments: right-hander Dizzy Trout, rejected by the military because of poor eyesight, and blond, wavy-haired left-hander Hal Newhouser, who had a heart murmur.

Paul Trout gave himself the nickname "Dizzy" when Dizzy Dean was in his prime because Trout envied all the publicity Dean was getting. He explained, "It ain't because I got as much stuff as Diz but because I talk as much as him." Like Dean, Trout later turned to broadcasting. The six-foot-two, two-hundred-pounder had been trying to establish himself for four years but had trouble controlling his temper and his fastball.[8]

Hal Newhouser's story has been often and simply told: he was a loser and a hothead who alienated his teammates and walked everybody in the ballpark until Richards, the wise old catcher, settled him down so he could dominate weak wartime competition. Much of that familiar biography is false. In fact, the twenty-one-year-old Newhouser was a dominating pitcher in 1942, before Richards arrived, but it went unnoticed because his record was 8-14. All those losses weren't his fault; the Tigers scored no more than two runs in ten of his starts and were shut out three times when he was on the mound. Opposing batters hit .207 against him, the lowest average in the league. His 2.45 ERA was 61 percent better than the league average, and he led the league with 5.05 strikeouts per nine innings. With decent run support his record could have been 15-7, and he would have been hailed as "the left-handed Bobby Feller." Newhouser was wild—as was Feller—and was such a spoiled brat that nobody recognized how good he was.

Just before opening day President Roosevelt's manpower commissioner, Paul McNutt, issued a list of thirty-six industries whose workers were deemed essential to the war effort and would be exempt from the military draft. Baseball was not among them. Most essential workers were involved in manufacturing or farming, but newspaper and magazine writers were exempt and, eventually, those in the movie industry, who were churning out patriotic films glorifying the war effort.[9] McNutt explained, "The usefulness of the sport is a separate question from the 'essentiality' of individuals who play it. Thus it may well be that it is desirable that Blankville have a ball team. But Blankville may lose certain members of that team to higher priority industries—even members that might be 'essential' to winning the pennant. The pennant is not 'essential.'"[10]

The defending American League champion Yankees, even without DiMaggio, shortstop Phil Rizzuto, outfielder Tommy Henrich, and pitcher Red Ruffing, held their usual spot atop the AL standings in 1943. Detroit hovered around the .500 mark all season. Richards was doing most of the catching, but he was not hitting and was frequently replaced by pinch hitters. Tiger pitchers liked his unorthodox setup behind the plate. He moved so close to the batter that umpire Bill McGowan often ordered Richards to back up, lest he tip the bat.[11] Because of his bad knee, he could not comfortably drop into a full squat, so he stuck his right leg out to the side. "Strangely enough, the pitchers became accustomed to it and liked it better than the other style of catching," he recalled. Several said the stance presented a better target.[12]

It may have helped Richards throw out base runners, since he was in a half-crouch and could spring up to get the ball away quickly. Washington's George Case was the leading base stealer during the war with a 77 percent success rate. His sixty-one thefts in 1943 were the most in a dozen years. He named Richards as the toughest catcher to run against: "He always seemed to be guessing right along with me." Richards was not guessing; Case was giving himself away. Case had a chronic sore left shoulder, and when he prepared to steal he would tuck his arm against his side to protect it. He said, "Paul Richards, being a very shrewd man, picked it up."[13] At one point Case had stolen twenty-four bases in twenty-nine tries; Richards threw him out four of the five times he was caught.[14]

When Richards first came up with the Dodgers, coaches tried to teach him the catcher's traditional snap throw, a short-armed delivery that brought the ball back only to the ear. But he watched the Yankee great Bill Dickey and copied Dickey's full arm motion. "I believe the main flaw of many young catchers is that they throw standing flat-footed," he said. "What success I have achieved has been with a frontward movement. That is, I move toward second at the time I catch the ball. It saves precious seconds."[15]

He practiced throwing to second by placing a barrel next to the bag and dispatching his little daughter to chase down his errant pegs. Paula got the job because the Tigers' batboys demanded to be paid for it, and her tight-fisted daddy preferred free labor. She would scamper onto the field wearing a dress, never a baseball uniform.[16]

O'Neill installed Richards as Hal Newhouser's personal catcher. The young left-hander won his first game on May 21, striking out ten in thirteen innings to beat Boston 2–1. Newhouser fanned fourteen Yankees in his next start, then shut out Philadelphia on two hits. Connie Mack remarked, "How can you beat a pitcher like that?"[17] Newhouser's ERA was 0.90. He was getting little help; the Tigers stood at 16-16 at the end of May, in fifth place but just three games behind the Yankees.

On Sunday, June 20, fistfights between black and white patrons at Detroit's popular playground, Belle Isle, turned into an all-out race riot, one of the worst in U.S. history. Federal troops moved in to restore order. When it was over, thirty-five people were dead, most of them black, and more than seven hundred had been injured. Police shot seventeen black people, claiming all were looters, but shot no whites.[18]

The Tigers had a scheduled day off on Monday; Tuesday's game was canceled because public gatherings were banned. When the team resumed play on Wednesday with a doubleheader against Cleveland, more than three hundred soldiers were patrolling in and around Briggs Stadium. Newhouser registered his fifth victory in the first game, and Charles Ward of the *Detroit Free Press* wrote that he was "now recognized as the best lefthander in the league."[19]

In addition to many doubleheaders, the result of travel restrictions, teams had to cope with overcrowded trains and unreliable hotel accommodations. Sometimes four players shared a room with only two beds. Richards had been troubled by sleepwalking since childhood; Margie kept a flashlight beside their bed at home because the light would wake him. On the road his roommates piled furniture against the door to keep him from wandering outside.[20] One night he bunked with Trout, third baseman Pinky Higgins, and pitcher Roy Henshaw. Higgins and Trout warned Henshaw about Richards's night prowling: "Switch on the light. He'll come out of it right away." Richards remembered: "Henshaw snapped on the light every time I rolled over. Pretty soon he was doing it every time anybody rolled over." After a largely sleepless night the teammates nicknamed Henshaw "Firefly."[21]

On the morning of July 4 the Tigers' record was 31-30, only two and a half games behind the first-place Yankees. Newhouser's ninety-two strikeouts topped the league, but poor fielding and weak run support held his record to 7-6. Dizzy Trout was the team leader with nine victories. The loudmouth had become a workhorse, starting and relieving.

Trout carried the team in the second half as Newhouser's season turned sour. He lost nine straight decisions in July and August. When Wakefield butchered a fly ball and let two Boston runners score on August 19, the pitcher griped, "Well, that $50,000 prize blew another one for me."[22] It was not the first time Newhouser had showed up a teammate, either verbally or with a venomous glare at a man who had misplayed a ball behind him. Virgil Trucks recalled, "He was probably disliked more than any other ballplayer on any club I was on." *Detroit News* sports editor H. G. Salsinger sarcastically nicknamed Newhouser "Junior."[23]

The Yankees put on a second-half sprint and ran away with the pennant. The Tigers' 78-76 record left them in fifth place, twenty games behind, despite several star performances. Trout's twenty victories tied New York's Spud Chandler for the league lead. It was the first time Trout had posted a winning record, and he gave much of the credit to Richards.[24]

In his return to the majors Paul Richards delivered as an outstanding defensive catcher and unofficial pitching coach. H. G. Salsinger wrote: "He is one of the best throwing catchers in the game and is probably without equal in fielding foul flies. . . . He has handled pitchers with fine judgment and few flaws can be found with his mechanical play. Detroit's season would have been dismal without him."[25] Richards's eighty-six assists in one hundred games were second best in the league, but his bat was as useless as ever, even against wartime big league pitching. He hit .220/.307/.297 with five home runs, three of them during a two-week period in July. His .604 on-base plus slugging percentage ranked eleventh among twelve major league catchers with at least three hundred plate appearances.

Richards took Margie and Paula home to Waxahachie and picked up his jobs officiating at football games and writing and selling advertising for the *Daily Light*. He scored his most memorable news story in January. Driving home on a Saturday night, he heard a bulletin on the radio that an escaped prisoner was at large in town. Minutes later he came upon a sheriff's car upside down in a ditch. Deputy Jess White lay dying from two bullet wounds. Richards spotted a man sprawled nearby, handcuffed, barely conscious, and bleeding from a leg wound, with a gun on the ground beside him. The man admitted he had killed the deputy. Richards offered to trade him a cigarette for his story, but before telling it the escapee instructed the reporter that his name was J. B. Stephens, not "Stevens," as the paper had been spelling it. After Richards got his interview, the police took Stephens away, and Richards rushed to the office to write "the biggest scoop of my life." As he sat down at the typewriter, the danger of the encounter dawned on him: "I actually choked up. My fingers froze. I couldn't type a word, but became more frightened by the minute." He was able to write the story only after calming down for an hour. Eleven months later he wrote a front-page account of Stephens's execution.[26]

Hal Newhouser worked for the Chrysler Corporation during the off-season and began taking drafting classes. "I didn't know how long I was going to stay in baseball," he said later. "Not with the record I had."[27] Newhouser's record was 8-17, but the Tigers scored no more than two runs in ten of his losses. His ERA was 16 percent better than average, and opponents batted just .224 against him. His miserable second half—only one victory after July 7—and his clashes with teammates left him dejected. General manager Zeller made a deal to trade Newhouser for Cleveland right-hander Jim Bagby Jr., but Detroit owner Walter Briggs vetoed it.[28]

Newhouser and his wife, Beryl, welcomed their first child, a daughter, just before spring training. He said becoming a father made him realize it was time to grow up. In Evansville Richards worked with him day after day, making mechanical adjustments to his motion and teaching him a slider and the catcher's cure-all, a change-up, to go with his crackling fastball and sharp-breaking curve. Richards advised him that he could improve his control by "taking a little off" the fastball and curve. The veteran bluntly told Newhouser what he needed to do to fulfill his exciting potential. "I would talk to him and explain that he would have to control himself better so he could control his pitches," Richards said. "I even went so far as to warn him that his teammates were getting no little annoyed with his tantrums. . . . I told him some pretty bald truths. He took his lecture like a true sportsman. Despite his moody moments, Newhouser would always listen. He wanted to improve himself."[29]

Dale Stafford of the *Detroit Free Press* wrote that Newhouser seemed to display a "changed attitude" and could be ready for a breakout season, then added, "We'll believe it when it happens." The sneering remark enraged Newhouser, but he decided Stafford might be right.[30] Richards also had doubts; writing a guest column for the Associated Press, he predicted Trout would be "the 'lead dog' pitcher" for the Tigers.[31]

Detroit lost Dick Wakefield; pitchers Virgil Trucks, Tommy Bridges, and Hal White; second baseman Jimmy Bloodworth; and catcher Dixon Parsons to the draft. The Selective Service System was now calling up men with children or other dependents. Richards's Atlanta draft board reclassified him 1-A—available for immediate induction—and summoned him for a physical exam. Doctors declared him 4-F (medically unfit) because of his bad knee. Rudy York got the same exemption.[32] While Richards's status was in limbo, Jack Zeller acquired another light-hitting 4-F catcher, Bob Swift.

The St. Louis Browns opened the 1944 season with nine straight victories, the first three over Detroit. The league's perennial losers were inoculated against the draft. Eighteen of their players were classified 4-F, including the hard-hitting, hard-drinking shortstop Vern Stephens with his creaky knee. Others were beyond prime draft age. By the end of May the Browns had moved into first place, playing with unaccustomed confidence. "We looked around after we went around the league one time," second baseman Don Gutteridge said. "The other clubs looked bad, and we said, 'Hey, we can play as good as they can.' There wasn't no Joe DiMaggios."[33]

Baseball canceled all games on June 6, D-Day. The Allied landing in France was a momentous advance that brought victory in Europe closer, but the war was far from over.

With most of the stars and other regular players missing, the American League was tightly bunched around mediocrity; on June 13 only four games separated first place from last. Then Dick Wakefield came marching home. Wakefield had completed navy flight training, but the navy decided it had more than enough pilots. He and half his classmates were offered honorable discharges if they were willing to take their chances with the draft. Wakefield was. He returned to the Tigers, not knowing how long he would be allowed to stay.[34] In his first game on July 13 he drove in two runs as Detroit scored eight times in one inning against the White Sox. The Tigers put on an astonishing finishing kick, recording a 41-16 record during the last two months of the season.

Newhouser had already won sixteen and Trout fifteen; they accounted for nearly two-thirds of Detroit's victories. Both wild men had discovered home plate, reducing their walks dramatically. In an interview that sounds like the writer was putting words in his mouth, Newhouser said: "I owe most of what success I have attained to Richards. He taught me control of my pitches and control of myself. The latter was the most important." Richards shared the credit: "Newhouser has been a sort of community project with us Tigers."[35]

As August wound down, St. Louis began to play like the Browns, dropping seventeen of twenty-five games. Newhouser beat them on August 27 for his twenty-first victory, with Richards's double driving home the two winning runs. In an off-season newspaper article Richards called it "my biggest baseball day."[36] On Labor Day the Yankees swept a doubleheader from Philadelphia to take a half-game lead over the Browns and two and a half over Detroit. St. Louis had been in first place for ninety-six days.

For the next ten days the three contenders were separated by one game or less as the lead changed hands several times. O'Neill was down to two reliable starters: Newhouser and Trout, and then look out. The pair of aces started seventeen of twenty-eight games in the final month. On September 17 Detroit climbed to the top of the standings for the first time. The Yankees faded, while the Tigers and Browns elbowed each other in a sprint to the finish.

The nail-biting race came down to the final day. Detroit and St. Louis were tied for the lead on Sunday, October 1. Steve O'Neill had run out of pitchers. Stubby Overmire's arm was sore; Rufe Gentry, Johnny Gorsica, and Trout had pitched on Friday, Newhouser on Saturday. Those five had started 148 of the club's 153 games. In Friday's loss Trout had failed with two days' rest. Now O'Neill called on him after one day off. The big right-hander had already worked 344 innings, the most in the majors. His 349th inning was one too many. The Senators rapped out five hits in the fourth to put up three runs. The Washington starter, Richards's Atlanta reclamation project, Dutch Leonard, had been offered $2,000 by an anonymous caller if he would have a bad day. He had one of the best days of his career, holding Detroit to four hits in a 4–1 victory. Many of the 45,565 fans and all the Tigers stayed at the ballpark to watch the scoreboard for the outcome of the Browns-Yankees game. Detroit and St. Louis would be tied if the Yankees won.

St. Louis manager Luke Sewell went with thirty-five-year-old right-hander Sigmund Jakucki, who had been out of organized ball for six years, playing on semipro teams in Texas. A nasty, fighting drunk, Jakucki kept his pledge to Sewell and did not take a drink the night before, but he had made no promises about the morning. Properly fortified (teammates said he downed only one shot), Jakucki held the Yankees to six hits to bring the Browns their first, and only, pennant.[37] Their 89-65 record was the worst in history for a first-place team.

Steve O'Neill's pitching decisions in that final month could have given Richards a lesson in what not to do. Richards later said, "A tired pitcher is a badly handicapped pitcher." When he became a major league manager, he would not send a man to the mound with only one or two days' rest. He never adopted the conventional four-man starting rotation because he was convinced that any pitcher would be stronger with an additional day off.[38]

Newhouser and Trout notched fifty-six of Detroit's eighty-eight victories, the most wins by two teammates since Washington's Walter Johnson won thirty-three and Bob Groom twenty-four in 1912. The Tiger duo was a matched set. Newhouser topped the league in wins with twenty-nine; Trout was second with twenty-seven. Trout led in ERA at 2.12; Newhouser was second at 2.22. Trout's 352⅓ innings were the most by any pitcher in twenty years; Newhouser was second with 312⅓. Newhouser led with 187 strikeouts, followed by Trout with 144. In the Most Valuable Player balloting, ten writers named Trout as their first choice to 7 votes for Newhouser, but Newhouser won the award with 236 points to Trout's 232. (The voting system gave 14 points for a first-place vote, 9 for second, 8 for third, down to 1 point for tenth.)

Steve O'Neill attributed Newhouser's dominance to "control, a happy married life, a baby, control, an amazing change of disposition, the tremendous influence of Paul Richards, and control."[39] Newhouser walked fewer than three batters per nine innings; he had never been below five before.

Richards's hitting improved slightly to .237/.318/.310 as he caught ninety games. His backup, Bob Swift, batted .255/.331/.320, the best of his career, in seventy-six games.

Throughout the war baseball wrapped itself in the flag. Teams sponsored sales of war bonds, donated equipment to soldiers, and urged fans to return foul balls so they could be sent to military posts. The *Sporting News* offered free subscriptions for servicemen and regularly printed letters from the front testifying to the game's vital role as a morale booster, but there were dissenting voices. When teams played in front of servicemen, they sometimes heard a heckler shout, "Get a gun!" New York sportswriters Stanley Frank and Stanley Woodward returned from assignments as war correspondents to report that the soldiers' enthusiasm for baseball was greatly exaggerated. They urged cancellation of the 1945 season.[40] It nearly happened.

1. AP, *Chicago Tribune*, October 12, 1942, 25.
2. David Pietrusza, *Judge and Jury: The Life and Times of Judge Kenesaw Mountain Landis* (South Bend, Ind.: Diamond Communications, 1998), 434–35.
3. William B. Mead, *Baseball Goes to War* (Washington, D.C.: Broadcast Interview Source, 1998), 74.
4. David S. Neft, Richard M. Cohen, and Michael L. Neft, *The Sports Encyclopedia: Baseball* (New York: St. Martin's Griffin, 2001), 228–29; "Brave New Season," *Time*, April 5, 1943, online archive.
5. Ted Williams, with John Underwood, *My Turn at Bat* (1969; repr., New York: Fireside/Simon and Schuster, 1988, 97–100; Richard Ben Cramer, *Joe DiMaggio: The Hero's Life* (New York: Simon and Schuster, 2000), 202, 206–7.
6. *TSN*, September 7, 1944, 3.
7. UP, *Nevada State Journal*, October 25, 1942, 12; Donald Honig, *A Donald Honig Reader* (New York: Fireside/Simon and Schuster, 1988), 301.
8. *Sporting News* (hereafter *TSN*), April 1, 1937, 10; August 17, 1944, 15; August 31, 1944, 3.
9. UP, *Nevada State Journal*, April 13, 1943, 1.
10. Bill Gilbert, *They Also Served: Baseball and the Home Front, 1941–1945* (New York: Crown, 1992), 84.
11. *Washington Post*, October 8, 1945, 12.
12. Paul Richards, interview by Clark Nealon, February 5, 1981; Leo MacDonnell, "That Texas Tiger, Paul Richards," *Baseball*, November 1944, 408.
13. Donald Honig, *A Donald Honig Reader* (New York: Fireside/Simon and Schuster, 1988), 289. The quote is from an interview of Case in Honig's book *Baseball When the Grass Was Real* (Lincoln: University of Nebraska Press, 1993).
14. Unidentified (1943) clipping in Paul Richards's scrapbooks, in the personal collection of Paula Richards.
15. Richards interview; MacDonnell, "That Texas Tiger," 407.
16. Paula Richards, interviews by author, 2006–2008.

17. David M. Jordan, *A Tiger in His Time: Hal Newhouser and the Burden of Wartime Baseball* (South Bend, Ind.: Diamond Communications, 1990), 74.
18. *Chicago Tribune,* June 22, 1943, 1–2; UP, *Los Angeles Times,* June 22, 1943, 1; AP, *Chicago Tribune,* June 23, 1943, 2; "Deep Trouble," *Time,* June 28, 1943, online archive; William L. O'Neill, *A Democracy at War* (New York: Free Press, 1993), 240.
19. AP, *Chicago Tribune,* June 23, 1943, 22; AP, *Washington Post,* June 24, 1943, 17; Jordan, *A Tiger in His Time,* 85.
20. Paula Richards interviews.
21. William Barry Furlong and Fred Russell, "He Put the White Sox Back in the League," *Saturday Evening Post,* July 21, 1951, 91.
22. *TSN,* December 30, 1943, 17.
23. Frederick Turner, *When the Boys Came Back* (New York: Henry Holt, 1996), 19; Jordan, *A Tiger in His Time,* 90.
24. *TSN,* September 7, 1944, 3.
25. *Detroit News,* undated (September 1943) clipping in Richards scrapbooks.
26. *Salisbury (Md.) Times,* February 4, 1959, 30; *Waxahachie (Texas) Daily Light,* January 9, 1944, 1, and December 19, 1944, 1.
27. Jordan, *A Tiger in His Time,* 90.
28. *TSN,* September 10, 1947, 7.
29. Jordan, *A Tiger in His Time,* 95; *TSN,* April 2, 1947, 4; MacDonnell, "That Texas Tiger," 407.
30. Jordan, *A Tiger in His Time,* 97.
31. AP, undated (1944), in Richards scrapbooks. The story was datelined Evansville, so it appeared during spring training.
32. *TSN,* March 30, 1944, 18; September 7, 1944, 3; Jordan, *A Tiger in His Time,* 98.
33. Mead, *Baseball Goes to War,* 140.
34. *TSN,* July 13, 1944, 2.
35. MacDonnell, "That Texas Tiger," 407.
36. *Chicago Daily News,* February 6, 1945, 11.
37. *TSN,* October 5, 1944, 2, 28–29, 35; AP, *New York Times,* October 2, 1944, 14; "Streetcar Series," *Time,* October 9, 1944, online archive; Gilbert, *They Also Served,* 145–48; Jordan, *A Tiger in His Time,* 118–120; Frederick G. Lieb, *The Detroit Tigers* (New York: G. P. Putnam, 1946), 258–59; Peter Golenbock, *The Spirit of St. Louis* (New York: Harper Entertainment, 2001), 302–3; Mead, *Baseball Goes to War,* 117.
38. *TSN,* June 20, 1951, 6
39. Ibid., September 28, 1944, 2.
40. Richard Goldstein, *Spartan Seasons* (New York: Macmillan, 1980), 56–58, 106.

CHAPTER 7

Victory

In 1945 the *Sporting News* calculated that 487 current or former major leagu-ers were serving in the armed forces, but public support for baseball's "green light" was dimming. A Gallup poll found 46 percent of Americans favored con-tinuing the game, 41 percent thought it should shut down, and 13 percent were undecided. As the war entered its fourth year and the military was strapped for men, Selective Service reexamined many 4-F ballplayers, found some to be suddenly healthy, and drafted them.[1] But when Senators owner Clark Griffith paid his annual visit to the White House to deliver FDR's ballpark pass, the president urged baseball to continue so long as it did not divert healthy men from war work.[2]

As Richards arrived in Evansville to begin his twentieth season in baseball, Detroit's roster included only four holdovers from 1942: Doc Cramer, Rudy York, Hal Newhouser, and Dizzy Trout. The draft had caught up with Dick Wakefield in November. Third baseman Pinky Higgins was also called, though he was nearly thirty-six years old. But the Tigers had reason to be optimistic as they endured another chilly spring. Pitchers Al Benton and Les Mueller had received medical discharges. Benton had been the team's top reliever before the war; Mueller had had a brief trial in 1941.

Five days after President Roosevelt died, Detroit opened the season in St. Louis. Only 4,167 fans turned out on April 17, 1945, to see the defending American League champions. The Browns' Sig Jakucki, who had killed the

Tigers' pennant hopes in the last game of 1944, beat them 7–1 as Richards's homer provided Detroit's only run. In the home opener four days later Newhouser pitched eleven innings and drove in the winning run himself to defeat Cleveland 3–2.

Richards sprained an ankle and could not play for two weeks, but he found temporary employment as the interim manager when O'Neill was laid up with an attack of gout. While talking to a sportswriter about his minor league managing experience, Richards said he liked fiery players. The writer pointed out that Richards himself was a quiet sort. "That's right," he replied, "and if I were the manager, I wouldn't have Richards on the club."[3]

When Germany surrendered in May, the celebrations were muted by the continued fighting in the Pacific. President Truman cautioned, "Our victory is only half won."[4] But the end of the war in Europe meant some soldiers would be coming home.

On June 10 Richards hit his only major league grand slam, batting in all his team's runs in a 9–4 loss to Chicago. It was the fifteenth—and last—homer of his big league career. The Tigers settled into first place two days later and jockeyed with the Yankees for the lead. For the second straight year the military handed Detroit a midseason gift. In 1944 it was Dick Wakefield's discharge. Now it was Hank Greenberg's turn. Greenberg was mustered out on June 14, 1945. He had served with a bomber squadron in China before being assigned to stateside duty supervising training sites and had played only one ball game in his four years in the army. He was thirty-four; no player at any age had ever returned to the majors after such a long layoff. Looking ahead to the end of the war, some baseball men were predicting that the ex-soldiers would never regain big league form, so Greenberg's comeback was closely watched. The Associated Press's Whitney Martin wrote, "There isn't a fan or a rival player who doesn't wish for Big Hank anything but the best of luck."[5]

Greenberg took the field on July 1, welcomed by a cheering crowd of

47,729, the largest at Briggs Stadium so far that year. In the first game of a doubleheader against the Philadelphia Athletics, he drew one walk and made three outs against pitchers Bobo Newsom and Steve Gerkin. Coming up in the eighth against left-hander Charlie Gassaway, he drove a liner into the left-field seats for his first home run in four years, one month, and twenty-four days. Greenberg played in seventy-two of the Tigers' last eighty-one games and kept his batting average above .300 while suffering constantly from sore legs.[6]

The Tigers got more good news in Greenberg's first game. Al Benton, who had missed seven weeks with a broken ankle, relieved Trout and worked two scoreless innings to preserve a 5–0 shutout. Benton was the club's most consistent pitcher behind Newhouser, who was proving that his 1944 break-through was no fluke. Trout struggled with back problems and other ailments, barely keeping his record above .500.[7] Otherwise, the staff was thin; those three were the only double-figure winners. O'Neill used a seventeen-year-old home-town boy, right-hander Art Houtteman, in fifteen games and tried out another local product, lefty Billy Pierce, who had just turned eighteen.

The war suddenly ended and a new age began after the United States dropped atomic bombs on the Japanese cities of Hiroshima and Nagasaki. On August 15, 1945, President Truman announced Japan's surrender. It was the happiest day in American history. A soldier rejoicing in the streets of Washington, D.C., whooped, "We're all civilians now."[8]

On Labor Day the Tigers were hanging on to first place by two games over Washington and three and a half over St. Louis. Richards enjoyed the best game of his big league career at the plate on September 9 in Boston, clouting three doubles to drive in five of Detroit's six runs and scoring the other one himself in a 6–3 victory over the Red Sox.[9] But when the Tigers reached Washington on September 15, their lead over the Senators had shrunk to half a game.

Newhouser, who had won twenty-one games, pulled a muscle in his back on September 1. After five days off he took a shot of Novocain before he started against the Yankees. He threw a curve to Charlie Keller in the first and felt a stabbing pain. No more curve balls, he told Richards. Relying on his fastball and change-up, he gritted his way to a four-hit shutout. But he missed his next two starts when he felt more pain while warming up.[10]

Newhouser started the first of five games in Washington. After rain interrupted play in the second inning for one hour and six minutes, Richards persuaded O'Neill not to send the left-hander back to the mound. "Some pitchers can't warm up twice in one day and keep their stuff," Richards explained, "and Newhouser is one of them. This series is too important. We could get Newhouser out of there and save him for tomorrow."[11] That O'Neill agreed to remove his ace was a measure of his trust in his veteran catcher.

Detroit swept the doubleheader with Richards catching both games for the first time all season. The *New York Journal-American*'s Garry Schumacher wrote of the second game, "It was the tall, splintery catcher, Paul Richards, who won it for them."[12] Richards slammed a two-run double, gobbled up an attempted sacrifice bunt to cut down the lead runner, and threw out Washington's George Myatt on two steal attempts. No other Senator tried to run on Richards for the rest of the series. Newhouser, bolstered by another Novocain injection, started the opener of the next day's doubleheader but lost 3–2. In the second game the Tigers took a 5–2 lead into the bottom of the ninth. After Washington put the tying and winning runs on base in the ninth, Trout, who had worked a complete game the day before, relieved and threw one pitch to get the last out in Detroit's 5–4 victory. Following a rainout, Trout started the final game of the series, just two days after he had pitched nine innings. Washington knocked him out with four runs in the first. The Senators won for the second time in the five-game set, leaving the Tigers one and a half games ahead.

Detroit wrapped up the eastern trip by dropping two in Cleveland and came home to face the third-place St. Louis Browns. Newhouser, with five days' rest, was back in winning form. He pitched a four-hit shutout and batted in three runs with a double and a triple. The next day Trout made his sixth start in twenty days, with four relief appearances piled on top of that. As in 1944, O'Neill asked for more than Trout could give. Diz lasted only two innings, surrendering three runs, while the Browns' Nelson Potter spun a two-hit shutout.

Washington split a doubleheader in Philadelphia to stay one game behind, but the Senators' season ended a week ahead of everybody else's. Clark Griffith had not expected to be in a pennant race after finishing last the year before. He had agreed to turn his ballpark over to his tenant, the National Football League Redskins, so additional seats could be installed for football.[13] Washington's final 87-67 record meant Detroit had to win two of its last four games to take the 1945 pennant. After a day off and a rainout, Newhouser struck out ten Indians for his eighth shutout of the season, clinching at least a tie for first place. But the Tigers could not finish it off in the second game of the doubleheader, losing 3–2.

Detroit's final two games were scheduled in St. Louis on Saturday and Sunday, the last days of September, but rain canceled the Saturday game to set up a season-ending doubleheader. The Tigers needed to win one for the pennant. It was still raining in St. Louis on Sunday when Virgil Trucks, just discharged from the navy, walked to the mound for his first start in two years. He gave up a run in the first, but the Tigers tied the score and Richards's RBI single put them ahead in the sixth. When Trucks loaded the bases in the bottom of the inning, O'Neill called on Newhouser to nail down the pennant. Newhouser ended that threat but could not hold the lead. He gave up a run in each of the next two innings, putting the Browns in front 3–2 when Detroit came to bat in the top of the ninth. Rain was falling and visibility was poor, but the umpires were determined to play to the finish.

The Tigers filled the bases in the ninth, bringing up Greenberg to face the Browns' ace, Nelson Potter. "I took the first pitch from Potter for a ball," Greenberg recalled. "As he wound up on the next pitch, I could read his grip on the ball and I could tell he was going to throw a screwball."[14] Greenberg hit it into the left-field seats, just a few feet fair, for a grand slam that won the pennant. The now-meaningless second game was called after one inning as the rain continued, sending the AL champion Tigers home for a celebration and a World Series. Their .575 winning percentage (88-65) was a new low for a pennant winner.

Detroit faced the Chicago Cubs, who had clinched the National League pennant on the next-to-last day of the season after a tight race with the St. Louis Cardinals. Sportswriters and oddsmakers were divided over which team should be the favorite. *Chicago Sun* writer Warren Brown surveyed the war-depleted rosters and quipped, "I don't think either one of them can win it."[15] He looked like a prophet as the two league champions stumbled, bumbled, and bobbled through the first six games. Base runners fell down, balls dropped between fielders, wild and boneheaded throws ran up the scores. Tallying the errors, official and unofficial, the *New York Journal-American*'s Bill Corum was reminded of "the tall men versus the fat men's game" at a company picnic.[16]

The two managers started their ace pitchers in the seventh, and deciding, game at Wrigley Field. The Cubs' right-hander Hank Borowy, with one day's rest, volunteered to make his third appearance in four days. Newhouser had only two days' rest, but Trout had just one, so Newhouser got the ball.

Borowy threw only nine pitches. After the first three Detroit hitters singled to score the first run, Cubs manager Charlie Grimm brought in veteran right-hander Paul Derringer. Derringer walked two batters to force in another run. Richards was next. He had only two hits in fifteen at-bats during the Series. With the bases full he swung so hard at Derringer's first offering that he fell down. On a 1-2 count he hooked a double down the left-field line to knock in all three runners and give Newhouser a 5–0 lead before he threw a pitch. A huge photograph of that hit hung in Richards's home for the rest of his life.

As Richards was warming up Newhouser before the game, he had seen that the left-hander's fastball had no life and his curve was not breaking. Richards called for change-ups, one after another, keeping the Cubs off stride. In the later innings they switched to fastballs.[17] The Tigers added four more runs against six Chicago pitchers; Richards's second double batted in one in the seventh. He left the game in the eighth when a foul tip split the little finger on his right hand. Newhouser labored, giving up ten hits but walking only one while striking out ten. It was a gutsy performance by a weary pitcher who obviously did not bring his best stuff to the Series. He finished the 9–3 victory to give the Tigers the championship.[18]

The headline story of the Series was not the courageous pitching of Newhouser and Borowy, nor Greenberg's two home runs, nor Richards's seventh-game clutch hitting. Writers highlighted the lowlights, the stumblebum moments of both teams. "Incredibly inept incidents," Warren Brown alliterated. The *New York Times*'s Arthur Daley, apparently channeling Ring Lardner, wrote, "Thank heavens no one was kilt. But pardner, they was a couple of mighty close calls."[19] All hands agreed it was a fitting end to the travesty that was wartime baseball.

Newhouser won twenty-five games and led the league in victories, strikeouts, and earned run average, the pitcher's triple crown. He took home the Most Valuable Player award for the second consecutive year. The *Sporting News* named Richards to its postseason all-star team representing both leagues. He was the poorest player ever chosen for the team. He batted.256/.315/.355 in eighty-three games, but his .670 OPS ranked eleventh among catchers with at least 250 plate appearances. The writers honored him for his World Series heroics, coupled with his reputation for handling pitchers.

The war years elevated Richards from a failed major leaguer to barely a replacement-level hitter. His wartime batting line was .236/.313/.318 in 942 plate appearances, compared with .212/.284/.277 in 627 appearances before and after. He was thirty-four to thirty-six years old during the war. In his only chance at consistent playing time before that, when he was twenty-six and playing for the Athletics after two seasons gathering splinters on the Giants' bench, he had done better but not good enough: .245/.310/.339.

Given his record as an elite hitter in the minors and his prowess as a defensive catcher, he might have succeeded in the majors if he had had an opportunity to play regularly while he was in his prime. But when the Giants brought him up, he was stuck behind one of the league's top catchers, Gus Mancuso. Like countless others in the decades before free agency, Richards's career was stunted because of bad timing.

1. *Sporting News* (hereafter *TSN*), February 1, 1945, 15; "Amber Light," *Time*, February 12, 1945, online archive; Richard Goldstein, *Spartan Seasons* (New York: Macmillan, 1980), 204–6.
2. William Marshall, *Baseball's Pivotal Era: 1946–1951* (Lexington: University Press of Kentucky, 1999), 17.
3. David M. Jordan, *A Tiger in His Time: Hal Newhouser and the Burden of Wartime Baseball* (South Bend, Ind.: Diamond Communications, 1990), 132; *TSN*, May 24, 1945, 15.
4. David Brinkley, *Washington Goes to War* (New York: Alfred A. Knopf, 1988), 275.
5. Hank Greenberg, *The Story of My Life*, ed. Ira Berkow (New York: Times Books, 1989), 152.
6. Ibid., 153.
7. Frederick G. Lieb, *The Detroit Tigers* (New York: G. P. Putnam, 1946), 263.
8. David McCullough, *Truman* (New York: Simon and Schuster, 1992), 463.
9. AP, *Los Angeles Times*, September 10, 1945, A6.
10. Jordan, *A Tiger in His Time*, 145–48.
11. *Washington Post*, September 16, 1945, 8.
12. *New York Journal-American*, September 16, 1945.
13. *Washington Post*, September 25, 1945, 12.
14. Greenberg, *Story of My Life*, 155.
15. Warren Brown, *The Chicago Cubs* (New York: G. P. Putnam, 1946), 229.
16. International News Service, *Detroit Times*, in Richards scrapbooks.
17. Jordan, *A Tiger in His Time*, 162–63.
18. World Series game accounts from *Chicago Tribune*; *New York Times*; *Los Angeles Times*; Associated Press; International News Service; *Detroit Times*; *Nashville Banner*; Bill Gilbert, *They Also Served: Baseball and the Home Front, 1941–1945* (New York: Crown, 1992); Goldstein, *Spartan Seasons*, Greenberg, *Story of My Life*; Jordan, *A Tiger in His Time*; Lieb, *Detroit Tigers*.
19. Brown, *Chicago Cubs*, 229; *New York Times*, October 12, 1945, 8.

CHAPTER 8

Manager-in-Waiting

R ichards came home after the World Series to meet his new daughter. Margie and Paula had returned to Waxahachie before the end of the season because Margie was experiencing a difficult pregnancy. The baby, born prematurely in a Dallas hospital on September 15, 1945, weighed just two pounds, four ounces. She was named Lou Redith, variations on the names of several of Margie's relatives.[1]

Each Tiger's Series share was $6,445, the largest in history. Owner Walter Briggs, who made his fortune in the auto industry, arranged for the players to buy some of the first new cars to roll off assembly lines after civilian production resumed. Richards chose a pickup and used it to transport a male pony named Ginger home to six-year-old Paula. True to form, Richards found a bargain; he bought the pony from a Michigan farm that was going out of business. When Paula took Ginger for a test drive, he galloped for the barn as she screamed for help. Her father shouted that she couldn't have the pony unless she could control him. She remembered, "When it became obvious no one was going to save me, I did what he said, and Ginger and I had a great ride." Ginger survived for more than thirty years despite eating the cigarettes and drinking the beer Richards and his pals offered.

Paula had been mad about horses since her daddy took her to a pony ride near their apartment in Atlanta on the mornings before home games. Richards, who enjoyed betting on the races, borrowed a leaf from his father's book.

He taught her to read by placing the *Daily Racing Form* in front of her at the breakfast table. When she started school, Paula said, "I knew all about past performance but couldn't read Dick, Jane, and Spot." Her daddy sneaked her into the Detroit Fairgrounds, the city's pari-mutuel track, where no children under twelve were allowed. He dressed her in grown-up clothes, had her mother slather her face with makeup, and conned the gate attendants into believing she was a midget.[2]

Several hundred friends, neighbors, and notables from baseball and politics honored Richards at a banquet in Waxahachie on October 23. But the town's baseball legacy was crumbling. Jungle Park, where Richards first watched major leaguers in spring training, was "abandoned and overgrown with weeds." Richards and six other men leased the land for $500 a year and organized a fundraising drive to restore the grounds and build a new grandstand. A Baseball Jamboree dinner in February raised $2,000. That night the little ball yard was renamed Paul Richards Park.[3]

Detroit general manager Jack Zeller retired after the World Series. In one of his last acts he signed Richards for 1946.[4] Richards would not be dumped like most wartime players, but he was slated for a backup role behind Birdie Tebbetts. Tebbetts had lost three years in military service and was now thirty-three.

The Tigers brought fifty-six players to their prewar springtime home in Lakeland, Florida, including thirty-one military veterans and four others who had spent 1945 working in war plants.[5] Spring training began a month early in 1946 to give teams more time to sort out the returning players. The workouts produced an epidemic of sore arms and legs as the ex-soldiers and sailors struggled to reawaken muscles long unused. All big leaguers had come back alive except two short-term players, Harry O'Neill and Elmer Gedeon, but not all were whole. The Cardinals' pitching prospect John Grodzicki, a thirty-one-game winner in AA before the war, had taken shrapnel in his buttock and was trying to pitch while wearing a leg brace. He couldn't. Athletics left-hander Lou Brissie, his left leg shredded by an artillery shell, needed a cane to walk. He would return to action only after two years of painful rehabilitation. Others' wounds were not so visible. Athletics pitcher Phil Marchildon, who had spent months in a German POW camp, was weak, nervous, and constantly fidgeting. Washington pitcher Walt Masterson, who survived submarine warfare in the Pacific, said later, "When you get to the position where you don't care whether you live or die, you're kind of strange to be around."[6]

Though not wounded, others had sacrificed their baseball careers in their country's service. The Senators' shortstop Cecil Travis, whose .359 batting average in 1941 was higher than Joe DiMaggio's despite DiMaggio's fifty-six-game hitting streak, and Cardinals left-hander Ernie White, a seventeen-game winner that year, fought in the frozen Battle of the Bulge.[7] Travis's best postwar average was 107 points lower; White never won another game. Detroit center fielder Barney McCosky, a speedy twenty-five-year-old when he went into the military, was now twenty-nine and no longer so fast, suffering from back trouble. Birdie Tebbetts went to a hospital with dizzy spells and was treated for a stomach ulcer.[8]

The wartime stars now had to prove they were "real" major leaguers. Hal Newhouser acknowledged: "Well, anybody with any common sense would say, 'Well, yeah, you've been winning, but now the big boys are back. What are you going to do?'"[9] On opening day in Detroit Newhouser allowed a first-inning run to the St. Louis Browns. That was all. He struck out eight and Greenberg slammed a homer to give the Tigers a 2–1 victory. Besides Newhouser the lineup included just two holdovers from the 1945 opener, Richards and second baseman Eddie Mayo.

The big boys were back. Cleveland's Bob Feller and the Yankees' Spud Chandler pitched opening day shutouts. Ted Williams and Joe DiMaggio joined Greenberg in clearing the fences. The Giants' player-manager, Mel Ott, hit his

511th—and last—home run. Left-hander Harry Truman's ceremonial pitch in Washington, D.C., marked the first presidential opener since 1941. The eight opening day games drew 236,000, more than twice as many as in '45.

The *Sporting News* picked the Yankees to win the AL pennant, followed by Boston and Detroit. But the Red Sox reeled off a fifteen-game winning streak in April and May to take command of the race. The Tigers were eleven and a half games back when they arrived in Boston on June 8. In the first game of the next day's doubleheader Ted Williams homered, singled, and "nailed the right fielder to the fence with [two] line drives," as Richards remembered it. Richards was lifted for a pinch hitter and went into the clubhouse, where the second-game starter, right-hander Fred Hutchinson, was getting rubbed down and psyched up. Hutch was as hot-tempered as Newhouser but even more dangerous, because he was one of the strongest men on the team. He loudly told the trainer that Williams would not hit *him* like that. He would put Williams flat on his back with the first pitch. In the first inning Hutchinson knocked him down with the first *two* pitches. Then Williams blasted the longest home run of his life into the thirty-third row of Fenway Park's center-field bleachers, punching a hole through fan Joseph Boucher's straw hat. The homer is still memorialized with Boucher's chair painted red, surrounded by blue seats. It was a favorite Richards story: "Hutch didn't last very long in that game. Just an inning or two. I had to go into the clubhouse and there he is, good and mad. He's throwing chairs and equipment and whatnot. I got over near the door and said, 'Hutch, boy, you really scared that Williams.' I closed that door just as a chair came crashing against it."[10]

Boston swept the doubleheader and went on to win twelve straight decisions, with a tie in the middle of the streak. Richards banged his knee in a collision with Greenberg and did not catch for more than three weeks. He returned on July 3 when Newhouser started against Chicago. Ten White Sox struck out as they managed only three hits, but the game was tied 1–1 when Richards came to bat in the tenth. He doubled and Newhouser did the same to claim his fifteenth victory. Newhouser had silenced the doubters, though the doubts would resurface to sully his reputation after he retired. "I think I caught them all by surprise, because my pitching techniques had changed [since before the war]," he said. "Instead of ball one, ball two, it was strike one, strike two."[11]

Detroit went to Cleveland on September 22, 1946, for what the Indians' new owner, Bill Veeck, ballyhooed as "the pitching duel of the century": Feller versus Newhouser. Feller was chasing Rube Waddell's forty-two-year-old record of 343 strikeouts in a season. (Waddell's total was later discovered to be 349.) The match-up drew 38,103 fans to see the second- and sixth-place teams. Feller, working on two days' rest, gave up eight hits and walked four while striking out seven. He complained that all the Tigers except Wakefield were taking half-swings, just trying to make contact. Newhouser was superb, allowing two singles, no walks, and fanning nine to win a 3–0 shutout. When Richards singled to center in the ninth, bringing Newhouser to the plate, Cleveland fans gave the opposing pitcher a standing ovation. Richards's hit came in his last major league at-bat.[12] Catching fifty-four games, he batted .201 with a .581 OPS.

Feller broke the strikeout record in a rematch against Newhouser a week later in Detroit; it drew nearly forty-eight thousand on the last day of the season. Nobody realized that Newhouser had surpassed an even older Waddell record. Newhouser had averaged 8.46 strikeouts per nine innings, beating Waddell's 8.39 in 1903, but that statistic was not tracked at the time.

While it was a bad year for the Rube, Newhouser had a better year than Feller. In 292⅔ innings Newhouser's 1.94 ERA was the lowest in the majors; Feller's was 2.18. Newhouser allowed the league's fewest base runners per nine innings, with Feller close behind. Each won twenty-six games, but Newhouser lost nine to Feller's fifteen with a weaker team. Newhouser's performance was virtually identical to that of 1945. Contrary to his reputation as a wartime phenom, he continued to be an outstanding pitcher for four more seasons until his arm gave out.

Richards's influence was undoubtedly a major factor in Newhouser's success. Newhouser always said so, and Richards never shied away from the credit. But Richards also said: "Ninety percent of the pitcher's development is strictly up to the pitcher himself. He can be helped, of course, if he will listen and take advice."[13] The relationship between the battery mates was as important to his career as to Newhouser's. Richards's role in Newhouser's rise to stardom became the top line on Richards's résumé as he sought a major league managing job.

Only four of those jobs were open for 1947. After Joe McCarthy quit the Yankees in midseason, worn down by his own heavy drinking and owner Larry MacPhail's criticism, MacPhail turned to the great catcher Bill Dickey, but he could not put up with MacPhail, either, and quit with two weeks to go. Longtime minor league manager Johnny Neun finished the season. The Browns, who had returned to their accustomed seventh place, and two National League tail-enders, Cincinnati and Pittsburgh, were also looking for new leaders. The Yankees job was the plum, of course; none of the others was very attractive. MacPhail hired Bucky Harris, who had already managed four teams, including two terms in Washington. Johnny Neun took over the Reds, while the Pirates chose another pillar of the Yankees farm system, Billy Meyer. There is no evidence that any team considered Richards.

Richards signed to play for the Tigers again in 1947, but a few weeks later he was named player-manager of the International League's Buffalo club, now classified AAA. Detroit had a working agreement with Buffalo, and the Tigers were said to be paying $3,000 toward his $13,000 salary.[14] In an unusual profile of a minor league manager, *Sporting News* publisher J. G. Taylor Spink saluted Richards as "one of baseball's greatest teachers." Richards expounded on some of his ideas about developing pitchers: "The common mistake of many coaches is that they try to teach rookies to do something the way someone else did it, instead of developing an individual style suited for their arms or their ability." He believed a manager should never say "never" or "you can't do this," such as never throw a change-up on an 0-2 count or never throw a change-up to a pitcher. Speaking like an old catcher, he said it was the pitcher's responsibility to stop base stealers by holding runners close to the bag. He made his pitchers warm up from the stretch position at least 35 percent of the time so they would not lose their stuff with runners on. "A catcher's job is to help the pitcher," he said, "but the pitcher should go on from there and be responsible for his own salvation and success."[15]

At thirty-eight Richards was the International League's youngest manager. The team assembled by general manager Roger Peckinpaugh, a former big league skipper, was a mix of Tiger prospects and veterans, including several wartime big leaguers. The Tigers had few decent young players to offer. During the war Jack Zeller had liquidated the farm system because he believed it was an unnecessary financial drain, and his successors were just beginning to rebuild it.[16] Detroit sent its three brightest pitching hopefuls: right-hander Art Houtteman and lefty Billy Pierce, who had pitched briefly for the wartime Tigers as teenagers, and twenty-two-year-old left-hander Ted Gray, another homegrown Detroit product. Houtteman had been the International League's "19-year-old hill sensation" in 1946, winning sixteen games and leading the league in strikeouts.[17] By July he would be back in the majors to stay.

When the Bisons opened their 1947 season in Jersey City, Richards delivered a two-run homer, but his starter, ex-Tiger Les Mueller, was knocked out in the first inning as Jersey City won 11–5. It was an omen of dismal things to come; the team dropped to last place by the end of April. In his return to managing, Richards showed he was as demanding as ever. After his club played poorly in a night game at Baltimore, he ordered the players back on the field for additional batting practice and told the Orioles to send the electricity bill to him. He called midday workouts after other night games. When his short-stop committed three errors in the first game of a doubleheader, he made the offender take fielding practice between games in front of the crowd, one of the rare times he publicly showed up a player.[18]

He also terrorized International League umpires—and at least one fan. Enraged by an obnoxious heckler, Richards walked to the railing in front of the box seats and challenged the 230-pound noise maker: "Come on down here and let's do some swinging. . . . You're big enough to fight." Police officers jumped between them as the umpires threw Richards out of the game.[19] By mid-July he had been ejected twelve times. He was suspended for five days and fined $50 for what league president Frank Shaughnessy called "improper language in protesting a decision." In the first inning of Richards's first game after the suspension, he was ejected again. He complained that the umpires wouldn't even listen to him before they gave him the thumb.[20] Shaughnessy, a noted umpire baiter in his managing days, counseled Richards, "If you'd only watch your language, watch out not to call the umpires names, you'll be all right." Sportswriters nicknamed him "Popoff Paul" and "Ol' Rant and Rave," but Margie insisted, "He's never even raised his voice to the children."[21]

The home fans booed Richards when he came to bat for the first time after the suspension. He responded with a grand-slam home run. That victory over Rochester lifted the team into fourth place. *Buffalo Evening News* writer Cy Kritzer said Richards had developed Billy Pierce and Ted Gray into "the best pair of lefties in the International League," recalling Richards's success in turning around Hal Newhouser's career. Gray, just five feet eight and 149 pounds, learned a forkball and control. His 3.42 ERA was the lowest of the team's starters and he won eleven games. Pierce said Richards would "catch me when I pitched and tried to slow me down by holding onto the ball." The Tigers wanted the twenty-year-old kept to a light workload because he had suffered back problems.[22] In twenty-three starts and five relief appearances Pierce was the team's leading winner with fourteen but walked as many batters as he struck out.

The Bisons' final 77-75 record put them in fourth place behind Jersey City, Montreal, and Syracuse. In the first round of the playoffs Buffalo swept the pennant-winning Jersey City Giants in four straight, taking the first three games with come-from-behind rallies in the ninth. Richards was ejected from Game 2 when umpire Jim Honochick ruled he did not hold a foul tip on a third strike. He threw down his mitt and kicked it toward the mound. Shaughnessy fined him $100, but Richards must have been heeding the league president's advice; after twelve ejections in the first half, this was only his fourteenth of the season.[23]

Buffalo faced Syracuse in the Governor's Cup series to determine the league's representative in the Junior World Series (sometimes called the Little World Series) against the American Association champion. The Bisons fell behind, three games to one, but battled back with two straight victories. Suffering from a cold and fever, Richards started for the first time in Game 6, catching Billy Pierce. When a Syracuse runner was called safe on a close play at third, Richards asked his third baseman, Anse Moore, whether the man was safe or out. Moore said he was out, and the manager put up a long, loud argument. After the inning was over Moore told him the runner had actually been safe. Richards berated Moore for lying, then apologized to umpire Bill Tattler. When Tattler told his colleagues what had happened, one of the umps said: "Him apologize? Never."[24]

The sixth game was tied in the tenth inning when a Syracuse runner tried to score. Richards snared the relay from the outfield and sprawled across the plate, blocking the runner with his body. Cy Kritzer called it "the greatest play of the year in the International League."[25] Richards led off the twelfth with a single. He retired for a pinch runner who came around to score the winning run.

In the decisive seventh game Richards's sixth-inning homer tied the score, but Syracuse answered with six runs to win. Richards went 5-for-12 in the series while leading his fourth-place team to within one game of the playoff championship. Kritzer called him "the most brilliant and daring strategist that Buffalo baseball has known since the days of George Stallings."[26] (Stallings, best known as manager of the 1914 "Miracle Braves," had also won a pennant with Buffalo.) Richards caught just twenty-nine games during the season, batting .248 with a .716 OPS.

Soon after the playoffs the club fired Roger Peckinpaugh and made Richards general manager as well as field manager. Richards announced that the Bisons would go to Waxahachie for spring training in 1948. He declared that little Richards Park was the equal of International League fields.[27]

He arranged a game between some of his teammates from the sixty-five-win high school team and the current Waxahachie High team to raise money for construction of a clubhouse. There is no record of how much the Buffalo club paid Richards and his fellow leaseholders for the use of the ballpark, but the presence of a professional team for the first time since 1921 boosted his hometown's economy. His neighbors treated the Bisons to southern hospitality, offering them free access to the golf course, fishing boats, and movie theaters. Waitresses and cab drivers refused to accept tips. One local told Cy Kritzer, "Down here we don't tip white persons."[28]

When Richards took his club north, Margie was left to drive nine-year-old Paula and two-year-old Lou Redith to Buffalo. Before interstate highways the fourteen-hundred-mile trip was an ordeal. In what became an annual detour they stopped in the Kentucky bluegrass country so Paula could see the thoroughbreds. At Faraway Farm near Lexington she was allowed to pet War Admiral, the 1937 Triple Crown winner who had lost to Seabiscuit in a legendary match race. Whenever her daddy asked her to name the greatest athlete she had ever seen, she answered, "War Admiral." Paula grew up to be a horse breeder.

Richards didn't hesitate to pull Paula out of school. He told her that traveling to new places was a good education: "Nobody will remember whether you got a ninety-eight or a sixty-eight on that test." She learned to forge his autograph, and he paid her twenty-five cents for each photo she signed, but she had to nag him to collect. "He just wanted me to be independent," she remembered. "He said girls were not going to stay home and be taken care of. They would have to fend for themselves. He was a little ahead of his time."[29]

The Bisons had led the league in scoring in 1947 with the help of their cozy home park, Offerman Stadium. They continued to rack up runs in large numbers in 1948. In one game the team slugged a league-record ten homers, but its record stayed below .500 for most of the season.[30] With Pierce, Houtteman, and Gray promoted to Detroit, Richards had to piece together a pitching staff. Right-hander Clem Hausmann, a twenty-eight-year-old Texan, was again his ace, winning fourteen games. Saul Rogovin, a converted infielder who had been cut loose by the Giants, was begging for a job when Richards took him on in 1947. Richards revamped Rogovin's pitching motion, switching him from a three-quarters delivery to overhand, and caught all six of his starts.[31] In 1948 the tall twenty-four-year-old right-hander from Brooklyn won thirteen games. Richards also acquired his former Atlanta pitcher Luman Harris, who had been released by Washington after six seasons in the majors. The thirty-three-year-old Alabaman was the first of a cadre of younger men who would follow Richards from team to team for decades and become his faithful disciples.

That summer United Press columnist Oscar Fraley bemoaned the shortage of big league managing candidates in the minors. An unidentified club owner told him the only up-and-comers were Richards, Kiki Cuyler of Atlanta, and Bruno Betzel of Jersey City. Neither Cuyler nor Betzel ever managed in the majors. Fraley dismissed Oakland's Casey Stengel as "a nice guy" but a loser when he managed the Brooklyn Dodgers and Boston Braves.[32]

Battling injuries as well as weak pitching, Buffalo finished sixth with a 71-80 record. The Bisons' manager soon had a new job, as the newspapers told it. Detroit's first-year general manager, Billy Evans, fired Steve O'Neill after a fifth-place finish. Richards's name immediately leaped to the top of the list of potential successors. Detroit writer Watson Spoelstra pointed out that owner Walter Briggs preferred to hire managers from within the organization. A United Press reporter asserted, "An announcement of Richards's appointment will be made shortly."[33]

The writers failed to reckon with baseball's old-boy network. Billy Evans had come to the majors as an umpire in 1906, then served as general manager of Cleveland, farm director for the Red Sox, and president of the Southern Association. In forty-two years he had crossed paths with practically everybody in the game. Six days after firing O'Neill, Evans gave the job to the Tigers' farm director, Red Rolfe. It was a surprise choice; the former Yankees third baseman had coached at Yale but had never managed professionally. His connection with Evans went back much further; Evans had tried to sign Rolfe for the Indians when he graduated from Dartmouth College.[34]

There is no indication that Evans interviewed Richards or anybody else for the job. The old umpire may have shied away from a man with "Popoff Paul's" reputation. It was a disappointing setback for Richards, because Detroit was his best connection to the majors' old-boy network.

---

1. Paula Richards, interviews by author, 2006–2008; Texas Department of Health, Bureau of Vital Statistics, Index of Birth Records. The child's first name is misspelled "Loy" in the department's online archive. Thanks to Clyde Ziegler for finding her.
2. Paula Richards interviews. Racing historian Bill Mooney identified the track (e-mail to author, December 6, 2006).
3. *Sporting News* (hereafter *TSN*), November 1, 1945, 13; Billy R. Hancock, *A Story of Paul Richards Park and Waxahachie High School Baseball* (Waxahachie, Texas: Waxahachie High School RBI Club, 2008), 12–13. David Hudgins provided a copy of the lease agreement dated February 1, 1946.
4. *TSN*, December 13, 1945, 8.
5. Ibid., March 28, 1946, 16.
6. Frederick Turner, *When the Boys Came Back* (New York: Henry Holt, 1996), 117–18, 87–88, and 24; *Washington Post*, April 9, 2008, B7.

7. Turner, *When the Boys Came Back*, 22–23, 118.

8. *TSN*, April 4, 1946, 11; April 18, 1946, 6.

9. David M. Jordan, *A Tiger in His Time: Hal Newhouser and the Burden of Wartime Baseball* (South Bend, Ind.: Diamond Communications, 1990), 167.

10. Donald Honig, *The Man in the Dugout* (Chicago: Follett, 1977), 135–36; Leigh Montville, *Ted Williams: The Biography of an American Hero* (New York: Doubleday, 2004), 123.

11. Jordan, *A Tiger in His Time*, 177.

12. Turner, *When the Boys Came Back*, 204; *TSN*, October 2, 1946, 5.

13. *TSN*, April 2, 1947, 4.

14. Ibid., November 13, 1946, 18, and December 11, 1946, 19; *Syracuse (N.Y.) Herald Journal*, September 30, 1947, 24.

15. *TSN*, April 2, 1947, 4.

16. Ibid., January 8, 1947, 9.

17. Warren Corbett, "Art Houtteman," *The Baseball Biography Project*, Society for American Baseball Research, http://bioproj.sabr.org.

18. William Barry Furlong and Fred Russell, "He Put the White Sox Back in the League," *Saturday Evening Post*, July 21, 1951, 90–91; *TSN*, July 2, 1947, 28.

19. *Buffalo Evening News*, June 23, 1947, in Paul Richards scrapbooks, in the personal collection of Paula Richards.

20. *TSN*, July 23, 1947, 24; July 30, 1947, 22.

21. *Syracuse (N.Y.) Post-Standard*, October 30, 1947, 14; *TSN*, August 3, 1949, 26; Furlong and Russell, "He Put the White Sox Back," 92.

22. Bill James and Rob Neyer, *The Neyer/James Guide to Pitchers* (New York: Fireside/Simon and Schuster, 2004), 103.

23. *TSN*, September 24, 1947, 25–26.

24. Ibid., October 1, 1947, 26.

25. *Buffalo Evening News*, September 24, 1947, in Richards scrapbooks.

26. Ibid., December 16, 1947, in Richards scrapbooks; *Syracuse Herald Journal*, September 24, 1947, 28.

27. *Olean (N.Y.) Times Herald*, November 24, 1947, 15.

28. *TSN*, April 14, 1948, 1.

29. Paula Richards interviews.

30. Joseph M. Overfield, *The Hundred Years of Buffalo Baseball* (Kenmore, N.Y.: Partners' Press, 1985), 90.

31. Ralph Berger, "Saul Rogovin," *Baseball Biography Project*.

32. UP, *Waukesha (Wisc.) Daily Freeman*, August 3, 1948, 7.

33. *TSN*, November 17, 1948, 3; UP, *Syracuse Herald Journal*, November 12, 1948, 45.

34. *New York Times*, November 16, 1948, 43.

Nine Old Men and Mr. Sick

Richards's $16,000 contract with Buffalo had another year to run, so he was shocked when the club hired a veteran International League executive, Leo Miller, as assistant to the president. Richards went before the board of directors to ask how Miller's job affected his position as general manager. After Richards offered to resign, the Bisons' majority owner, Marvin Jacobs, reassured him that he still had full authority over the team. But Cy Kritzer commented that Miller's presence clearly put Richards "on the spot."[1]

Before bringing the team back to Waxahachie for spring training in 1949, Richards went to Miami in February to participate in the first ballplayers' golf tournament. He shot 75 and 83 to finish tenth, one stroke behind Dizzy Dean and three ahead of his pitcher Lou Kretlow. The tournament would become an annual tune-up for the season. Richards justified his golf addiction by explaining to his family that it was for their own good; he would need to stay active after he stopped playing baseball so he would not die young like so many ex-players.[2]

Detroit had ended its working agreement with Buffalo, so the Bisons were scratching for players. Richards visited the Tigers' camp in Lakeland to ask for handouts. He assembled the oldest roster in the league; sportswriters dubbed the Bisons the "nine old men."[3]

While Buffalo took over first place in June, the International League sensation was center fielder Sam Jethroe of Montreal. The Dodgers signed

Jethroe in 1948 and moved him directly from the Negro Leagues to AAA ball. He was thirty-one, although contemporary accounts placed his age anywhere from twenty-six to thirty. In 1949 the switch-hitting lead-off man batted .326 with a league-record eighty-nine stolen bases, including nine steals of home, seventeen triples, and 151 runs scored. IL president Frank Shaughnessy said: "He doesn't run. He skates."[4]

The story of Richards's strategy for containing Jethroe became one of the marquee illustrations of Richards's original thinking. It first surfaced in the July 27, 1949, issue of the *Sporting News* under the headline "Bisons Walk Pitcher to Slow Up Royals' Rocket, Jethroe; Novel and Daring Strategy Used to Keep Him from Swiping Hassocks." Cy Kritzer wrote: "Grab your hats chums, and get ready for the shock—it calls for walking the pitcher. The strategy also calls for something almost as extreme, forgoing a sure double play in order to make sure that Jethroe is retired. In other words the strategy is this: If you can't keep the Ebony Comet off the basepaths, keep a slow-running pitcher on base ahead of him."

According to Kritzer's account, Richards had used the ploy seven times by midseason. Kritzer described Richards's reasoning at length but, curiously, did not quote him directly. He quoted Montreal's manager, Clay Hopper: "I would do the same thing myself, if I had to contend with Jethroe's speed." Kritzer said Richards told his infielders that if Jethroe hit a ground ball with a man on first, they should throw Jethroe out rather than the lead runner, because they had no chance of doubling up the speedster.[5]

Other writers picked up the story, and it became a feature of every Richards profile. After a while Richards began telling it himself. Here is the version he gave Donald Honig twenty-five years later:

> We had it figured out that anytime [Jethroe] led off an inning and got on first, his chances of scoring were ninety percent. We had statistics on it.

So if we walk the pitcher intentionally and let Jethroe hit with the pitcher on first and two out, the only way that Jethroe's going to hurt us in that particular situation is with a triple. If he gets a hit, the chances are the pitcher is only going to second, and even though Jethroe is on base, he can't hurt us with his speed because he's got the pitcher in front of him. So we tried it, and it worked.[6]

Years afterward the Buffalo baseball historian Joseph M. Overfield mused, "Many had written about it and talked about it, but . . . I never could find anyone who had actually seen it." Overfield wrote to Jethroe, who owned a bar in Erie, Pennsylvania. Jethroe replied: "I don't know if he used it or not. I read it, same as you." Overfield went through box scores and newspaper accounts of every Buffalo-Montreal game in 1948 and 1949 and found no evidence to support the story. Buffalo sportswriter Joe Alli, who covered the team in those years, found no such incidents in his scorebooks.[7] Overfield's coup de grace was Alli's 1965 interview of Richards:

"'Paul, you know that never happened.'

"'That's right,' Richards laughed, 'it never did, but if you write that now, nobody will believe you and you will get letters from fans who will swear they saw it happen.'"

Richards told Alli he did come up with the idea: "We never got an opportunity to use it, but it did work for me once in Seattle."[8] He managed Seattle in 1950, but I could find no report of such a tactic; Richards may have been feeding Alli another line.

Overfield's 1987 article was the last word—until now. Richards gave his final version in an unpublished manuscript he left behind:

The minor league manager must either be a consistent winner or allow his imagination to come up with something unusual that will attract major league attention. Anything new, however, must have value and a strategical purpose.

Example: While I was managing Buffalo of the International League, the Montreal Club had an outfielder named Sam Jethroe. Sam's base running could be the difference between winning or losing in a close game. In one game we had a one-run lead. Montreal sent up a slow-running pinch hitter for the pitcher with two outs in the eighth inning. Not allowing it to be too obvious, we walked the pinch hitter. This could prevent Jethroe from leading off the ninth inning. For Jethroe to hurt us in the eighth inning, he would have to get an extra base hit. The records indicate that Jethroe scored eighty five per cent of the time he led off an inning and reached first. Many times he would steal both second and third.

This strategy, as most all other moves, can be offset by the opposing club. The pinch hitter could be given a steal sign. If he were successful, a single by Jethroe could tie the score. If he is out at second, Jethroe leads off the ninth.

After that game, Mr. Branch Rickey asked me to come by the Montreal office. He suspected that we walked the hitter to keep Jethroe from leading off the ninth inning. He told me later that he was able to get $50,000.00 more than he expected [for Jethroe] because of this unusual move.[9]

A likely explanation for the spread of this legend is Branch Rickey's well-known fondness for selling players to the highest bidder. In 1949, with Roy Campanella and Don Newcombe joining Jackie Robinson on the Dodgers, Rickey wanted to spread some of his black prospects around to other teams to advance the cause of integration—for the right price, of course.[10] As Richards suggested, Rickey could have used the story, or an embellished version of it, in touting Jethroe to other teams' executives at the All-Star Game in Brooklyn. Cy Kritzer's account appeared soon after the All-Star Game. Richards did not deny it because he needed "something unusual [to] attract major league attention" and help him get the big league job he craved.

Rickey sold Jethroe to the Boston Braves for a sum variously reported as $100,000 to $150,000. Jethroe was named National League Rookie of the Year in 1950 and led the league in steals in his first two seasons but soon dropped back to the minors as his age caught up with him.

Richards introduced another stratagem that became one of his trademarks—and this one actually happened. On August 25 Buffalo held a 3–2 lead over Toronto in the eighth inning when a Toronto batter singled off righthander Bob Hooper. The next hitter was the left-handed Bill Glynn. Richards shifted Hooper to first base and brought in lefty Jim Paxton. After Paxton retired Glynn on one pitch to end the inning, Hooper returned to the mound in the ninth. Richards had gained the platoon advantage without removing his starting pitcher. The incident drew little attention at the time, but when Richards used the same ploy in the majors two years later, it burnished his reputation as an innovator.[11]

After the Bisons lost twelve of sixteen games in July, their lead shrank to one and a half over second-place Rochester, with Jersey City and Toronto close behind. In the pennant-race pressure Richards erupted at umpire John Gallin, kicking dirt and drawing his ninth ejection plus a $100 fine and an indefinite suspension. Richards was reinstated after four days.[12]

Richards never let up as the Bisons clung to their lead. With just fourteen games left in the season, he ordered pitchers and slumping players to report for afternoon workouts before night games. Buffalo finished with a 90-64 record, five and a half games ahead of the Rochester Red Wings, giving Richards his third pennant as a minor league manager. "It was the greatest personal triumph of Richards' career," Kritzer wrote, "for he had built and managed the team

with a skill and a show of strategy that should win him the minor league manager of the year award."[13] It didn't. The forty-year-old Richards appeared in
only two games. After twenty-four seasons he was no longer a ballplayer.

Buffalo made short work of fourth-place Jersey City in the first round
of the International League playoffs, winning four of five games, but lost the
championship round to third-place Montreal in five.

In addition to bringing Buffalo its first pennant since 1936, Richards's club
attracted a franchise-record 384,000 fans. But the owners did not treat him like
a savior. As Richards had feared, they promoted Leo Miller to general manager
because they wanted a man who would work in Buffalo year-round. Richards
was offered only a one-year contract as field manager. He turned it down.[14]

He immediately became the most sought-after free agent in baseball,
according to the sports pages. He was mentioned as a candidate to manage the
Cincinnati Reds, Washington Senators, and St. Louis Browns. Richards had
reason to believe a major league job was waiting for him in Chicago. Although
the White Sox had risen from last place in 1948 to sixth in '49, general manager Frank Lane was feuding with the manager he had inherited, Jack Onslow.
After Richards and Lane met in New York during the World Series, the *Chicago Sun-Times* reported that Richards would be the Sox's new manager. But
the team's owner overruled Lane, and the White Sox announced that Onslow
would stay.[15]

Richards signed to manage the Seattle Rainiers of the Pacific Coast League.
The Rainiers were named after the nearby mountain and the beer brewed by
club owner Emil Sick. (He couldn't very well call it "Sick Beer.") Sick had never
met Richards but received strong recommendations from Boston Braves general manager John Quinn and *Sporting News* publisher Taylor Spink.[16] Seattle's
general manager was Earl Sheely, Richards's old-boy connection going back to
1926, when Sheely and his White Sox teammate Hollis Thurston drove teenagers Paul Richards and Jimmy Adair from Texas to California.

The *Seattle Times* introduced the new manager to fans in a seven-part series, describing him as "Buffalo's Miracle Man."[17] *Seattle Post-Intelligencer* sports editor Royal Brougham wrote: "Nobody out here knows the new manager of the Rainiers, few have ever seen him, but the rank and file of the clients are pleased and happy over the man from Waxahachie, Tex., who is taking over the Seattle helm. In the language of the barber shop, 'If the man has been on nine pennant winners, that's good enough for me.' We'll take him, sight unseen."[18]

Seattle did not have a working agreement with a major league club, so Richards and Sheely spent the winter piecing together a roster made up almost entirely of veteran players. United Press writer Hal Wood called the Rainiers "a flock of athletes who have seen better days."[19]

After Richards spoke to a civic luncheon in Palm Springs, California, during spring training, *Los Angeles Times* columnist Braven Dyer observed: "I doubt that there is a more erudite manager in baseball than the soft-spoken maestro of the Rainiers. His speech is so perfect that Paul would pass for a college professor in almost any type of forensic competition, and he's easy on the eyes, too."[20]

Richards was proud to be a self-educated man. In addition to his off-season job as a newspaper writer, he worked crossword puzzles, played Scrabble, carried a Bible in his suitcase, and read widely, especially in history. He studied military figures, including Field Marshal Erwin Rommel, the Nazi "Desert Fox," for insights into leadership. Remarkably, for the grandson of a Confederate veteran who named one of his dogs "Rebel," the leader Richards most admired was Abraham Lincoln.[21]

The Pacific Coast League opened its two-hundred-game season on March 28, 1950, two weeks ahead of the majors. Teams spent six days in each city, often playing seven games, including a Sunday doubleheader, and traveled on Mondays. Seattle won four of seven at Oakland, then came home for the opener at Sick's Stadium. Organizers of the opening day festivities wanted the

Texan manager to ride onto the field on horseback, but Richards vetoed the stunt. During the game he introduced himself to the league's umpires when he stalked out of the dugout to argue a balk call.[22] The Rainiers lost 4–0 to the Hollywood Stars.

After a month Seattle's record stood at 6-25, and the club was in the midst of an eight-game losing streak. AP writer Jack Hewins rendered Richards's drawl: "When Ah first arrived, people seemed to think Ah could take a crowd of men and make baseball players. Ah think Ah know a player when Ah see one, but Ah can't make one."[23] Richards was showing the strain. He kept the players for two hours of batting practice after they lost one night game. During a clubhouse tirade he kicked a door and broke his toe. He declined an invitation to speak at a sportswriters' luncheon: "I got nothing to say."[24] When the Rainiers returned from a road trip, they staged a "Welcome Home" night, setting off fireworks and pulling pranks to break the jinx.

Richards's club got off to an abysmal start and he was two thousand miles west of the nearest major league team, but his name was still bubbling in the rumor mill. White Sox manager Jack Onslow lasted only thirty-one games, losing twenty-two of them. When he was fired on May 26, Richards was again reported to be the choice to replace him. Instead, the Sox appointed coach Red Corriden as interim manager.[25] It cannot be proved, but it seems likely that Richards had promised to stay in Seattle for the entire season.

Even more intriguing, when the New York Giants lost seven consecutive games and fell to last place at the end of May, the grapevine said manager Leo Durocher would soon be out and Richards would take over. Durocher's wife, the actress Laraine Day, hosted a pregame television program; a New York wit quipped, "Laraine's running a better show from the Polo Grounds than her husband."[26] Although Richards had left the Giants fifteen years earlier, his friend Carl Hubbell was part of the front-office hierarchy as farm director. Nothing came of the speculation, but it is a fascinating exercise in what might have been. Durocher hauled the Giants out of the ditch to finish in third place, then led them to the pennant the next year, when Bobby Thomson hit "the Shot Heard 'Round the World."

During Richards's season in Seattle he left evidence of his most important strategic innovation. Every morning he clipped the newspaper box score of the previous day's game and taped it into a book. Thrifty as always, he used an appointment book left over from 1949. He recorded how his pitchers had fared against both left-handed and right-handed batters—at bats, hits, bases on balls, home runs. He tallied the same data for each of his hitters, keeping track of platoon splits. Some days he was in a hurry, spoiling his normally neat, classic penmanship.

After every weeklong series he turned to a blank page in the back of the book and totaled each player's results for the season to date. He calculated batters' averages against both types of pitching and pitchers' batting average allowed against both types of hitter. Then he added one more column, headed "B.A. with bases on balls."[27] Today the statistic is called on-base percentage, but that term was unknown when Richards became the first manager to track it. Present-day analysts consider OBP the best single shorthand measure of a hitter's value. Richards knew that in 1950, if not before.

Sportswriters and fans have been fascinated by the game's numbers since baseball's earliest days. The first primitive box score was published in 1845.[28] For most fans and professional baseball men, a hitter's worth was measured by his batting average and runs batted in. A few people inside and outside the game tried to develop a more accurate statistical picture. In 1913 Branch Rickey of the St. Louis Browns hired a young man named Travis Hoke, who counted bases—the number touched by a batter and by any runners he advanced—and the bases allowed by pitchers. Hoke reasoned, "The unit of achievement in baseball isn't a hit, it is a base."[29] As early as 1917 F. C. Lane, the editor of *Baseball* magazine, argued that walks were undervalued. Chicago writer Edgar

Munzel referred to a player's superior "getting-on-base average" in a 1946 story in the *Sporting News*, but he did not cite a statistic to measure it.[30] That is the only use of the term I found in a search of baseball's bible before 1954.

Of course, managers and sportswriters recognized that batters such as Babe Ruth and Ted Williams drew many more bases on balls than others, but few subscribed to the sandlot adage "A walk's as good as a hit." Williams's critics charged that he was too finicky about taking pitches that weren't strikes when he should have been whaling away.[31] The official stats did not count a player's "B.A. with bases on balls." In baseball, as in many other pursuits, if you don't count it, it doesn't count.

In 1947 Rickey hired the first full-time statistician, Allan Roth, who charted every pitch in Dodger games and produced unprecedented, detailed breakdowns of batters' and pitchers' performance in different situations. After Rickey left Brooklyn in 1950, the new management had no use for Roth's numbers and banished him to the press box to peddle his "trivia" to the writers and broadcasters.[32] Roth reached his widest audience in a 1954 *Life* magazine article under Rickey's byline, titled "Goodby [*sic*] to Some Old Baseball Ideas." Roth devised a "magic bullet" to predict a club's wins and losses. The first element of the long equation was [H + BB + HP] ÷ [AB + BB + HP] (hits plus bases on balls plus hit-by-pitch divided by at-bats plus bases on balls plus hit-by-pitch). That is the formula for what Roth called on-base average.[33]

When Richards was recording "B.A. with bases on balls" in Seattle, he was far ahead of nearly everybody else. He had learned the value of a walk from Donie Bush, whose ability to get on base was his hallmark. Although Bush's career batting average was only .250, his on-base percentage was .356. Richards posted OBPs above .350 nine times in his minor league career.

Richards's 1950 diary is the only one known to survive, so there is no way to tell when he started keeping the statistic. His daughter Paula watched him tape the box scores into a book every morning: "He always did it, ever since I can remember."[34] She was eleven in 1950; her memory goes back further. As late as 1968, when Earl Weaver became manager of the Baltimore Orioles, his use of statistical breakdowns was seen as an innovation. Weaver had worked for Richards as a minor league manager. It was not until 1982 that Oakland general manager Sandy Alderson made on-base percentage the cornerstone of his player evaluations. Alderson indoctrinated his successor, Billy Beane, whose devotion to statistical analysis was chronicled in the best-seller *Moneyball*. Other teams did not catch on until the late 1990s.[35]

The Rainiers finished sixth in 1950 with a 96-104 record. As stories continued to circulate that their manager was headed for the White Sox, some of the veteran players "doubtless heaved a sigh of relief at the report of his departure." Several made no secret of their dislike for the "stern disciplinarian."[36] Oakland columnist Emmons Byrne commented: "He may not be a lovable figure to his players, but he commands their respect. . . . Richards is quiet and reserved. He makes no attempt to win friends and influence people with funny sayings, public speeches or a magnetic personality. He believes there's only one place for a ball player or a manager to prove his point. That's on the field of play."[37]

Richards could have written that column. It fit the image he wanted to project, and he later used some of the same words to describe himself. By 1950 his persona was fully formed. He had honed his managerial style during nine years in the high minors. As the long Pacific Coast League season wound down in October, he knew he was headed to the majors.

---

1. *Syracuse (N.Y.) Herald Journal*, October 12, 1949, 29; *Buffalo Evening News*, undated (1948) in Paul Richards scrapbooks, in the personal collection of Paula Richards.
2. *Sporting News* (hereafter *TSN*), March 9, 1949, 9; Paula Richards, interviews by author, 2006–2008.
3. *TSN*, September 14, 1949, 29.
4. Larry Moffi and Jonathan Kronstadt, *Crossing the Line: Black Major Leaguers, 1947–1959* (Iowa City: University of Iowa Press, 1994), 50.
5. *TSN*, July 27, 1949, 10.

6. Donald Honig, *The Man in the Dugout* (Chicago: Follett, 1977), 136–37.

7. Joseph M. Overfield, "The Richards-Jethroe Caper: Fact or Fiction?" *Baseball Research Journal* (1987): 33–35.

8. Notes taken by Overfield from story in *Buffalo Courier-Express*, July 13, 1965, Joseph M. Overfield Papers, Buffalo and Erie County Historical Society Research Library, Buffalo, N.Y. It was later reported that the Giants walked a Dodger pitcher to keep lead-off man Maury Wills from stealing (*Baseball Digest*, September 1966, in the Overfield papers).

9. Paul Richards, untitled 1970s manuscript "for high school, college and amateur managers and coaches" (hereafter Richards manuscript), in the author's files.

10. Murray Polner, *Branch Rickey* (New York: Atheneum, 1982), 204.

11. *TSN*, September 7, 1949, 31.

12. Ibid., August 17, 1949, 21, and August 24, 1949, 32.

13. Ibid., September 7, 1949, 32; *Buffalo Evening News*, September 7, 1949, clipping in Richards scrapbooks.

14. Joseph M. Overfield, *The One Hundred Years of Buffalo Baseball* (Kenmore, N.Y.: Partners' Press, 1985), 91; *TSN*, September 7, 1949, 31.

15. *Chicago Tribune*, October 20, 1949, B1; AP, *Los Angeles Times*, October 11, 1949, C3.

16. *Seattle Post-Intelligencer*, October 23, 1949.

17. *Seattle Times*, several December 1949 clippings in Richards scrapbooks.

18. *Seattle Post-Intelligencer*, November 2, 1949, 21.

19. UP, *Nevada State Journal*, March 29, 1950, 8.

20. *Los Angeles Times*, March 4, 1950, B1.

21. Paula Richards interviews; Buck Jordan, interviews by author, August 16–17, 2006, Waxahachie, Texas; and Eddie Robinson, interview by author, August 18, 2006, Fort Worth, Texas.

22. *Seattle Post-Intelligencer*, April 5, 1950, 19; *TSN*, April 12, 1950, 22.

23. AP, *Walla Walla (Wash.) Union-Bulletin*, June 8, 1950, 50.

24. Ibid.; *TSN*, May 3, 1950, 35–36.

25. *TSN*, June 28, 1950, 36.

26. William Barry Furlong and Fred Russell, "He Put the White Sox Back in the League," *Saturday Evening Post*, July 21, 1951, 91; Gerald Eskenazi, *The Lip* (New York: William Morrow, 1997), 242.

27. Richards's 1950 diary is in the collection of the Ellis County Museum, Waxahachie, Texas.

28. Alan Schwarz, *The Numbers Game: Baseball's Lifelong Fascination with Statistics* (New York: Thomas Dunne Books/St. Martin's Press, 2004), 4.

29. Travis Hoke, "The Base in Baseball," *Esquire*, October 1935, 67, 140, online archive at www.baseballthinkfactory.org/btf/pages/essays/rickey/hoke.htm.

30. Schwarz, *Numbers Game*, 218; *TSN*, November 13, 1946, 19.

31. Leigh Montville, *Ted Williams: The Biography of an American Hero* (New York: Doubleday, 2004), 35–36.

32. Schwarz, *Numbers Game*, 56–57; *New York Times*, March 22, 1992, online archive. The *Times* article was written by broadcaster Vin Scully, a long-time friend, shortly after Roth's death.

33. Branch Rickey, "Goodby [*sic*] to Some Old Baseball Ideas," *Life*, August 2, 1954, 78–89.

34 Paula Richards interviews.

35. Schwarz, *Numbers Game*, 217.

36. *Seattle Times*, undated (September 1950) clipping in Richards scrapbooks; *TSN*, October 11, 1950, 36.

37. *Oakland (Calif.) Tribune*, August 11, 1950, 30.

CHAPTER 10

"The City That Championships Forgot"

The Chicago White Sox had never gotten over the Black Sox. After seven of their best players and one benchwarmer were banished for complicity in fixing the 1919 World Series, the Sox recorded only seven winning seasons in the next thirty years. Every other American League team had won a pennant during those decades. Sportswriter Bill Corum called Chicago "the city that championships forgot."[1] When the city council considered naming 35th Street outside Comiskey Park after the franchise's founder, Charles A. Comiskey, a local wit suggested a more appropriate name would be "Seventh Place." The White Sox were the Second City's second team; the North Side Cubs drew bigger crowds, usually by a large margin.

After the deaths of Charles Comiskey in 1931 and his son Louis in 1939, Louis's widow, Grace Reidy Comiskey, went to court to wrest control of the team from her husband's bankers. She ran the White Sox as a family business. Veteran baseball executives operated the club—first Harry Grabiner, then Leslie O'Connor—but family members filled other slots in the front office. The farm director, former pitcher Johnny Rigney, was the husband of Grace Comiskey's daughter Dorothy, who was the team's treasurer. A younger daughter, Gracie Lu, was listed as assistant secretary. The traveling secretary, Frank McMahon, was married to Grace's sister Alice; another brother-in-law had held the job before him. When Grace's only son, Charles A. Comiskey II, reached his twenty-first birthday in 1946, he dropped out of college to become president of the White Sox's Waterloo, Iowa, farm club. The next year he moved into the big league front office.[2]

Keeping kinfolk on the payroll was not unique to Chicago. Connie Mack and two of his sons operated the Philadelphia Athletics. Washington owner Clark Griffith employed four of his wife's nephews and the husband of a niece.[3] A big league franchise was a relatively small business with just a few year-round employees. The White Sox reported gross revenue in 1950 of $1.5 million, fifth highest in the eight-team American League, with a player payroll of $262,500, sixth largest. (That payroll is equal to about $2.3 million today.)[4]

After Chicago lost 101 games in 1948, Chuck Comiskey replaced Leslie O'Connor as vice president. The ballpark was less than a mile from the Chicago stockyards. Comiskey confided that "we've been getting a lot of complaints from the stock yards that a strong odor is coming from Comiskey Park."[5] He fired manager Ted Lyons and brought in Frank Lane as general manager.

The fifty-two-year old Lane started as a newspaperman and came to baseball by way of football. He played professionally for a short time and officiated college football games in Ohio with Larry MacPhail. Lane worked for MacPhail in the Cincinnati Reds and Yankees organizations. Before coming to Chicago, Lane was president of the American Association. He was known for his expensive tailored suits and had hard features softened by a head full of dark, wavy hair.[6]

Despite an improvement to sixth place in 1949, the White Sox lost ninety-one games. Lane wanted to fire manager Jack Onslow and hire Paul Richards, but Grace Comiskey controlled the checkbook. She refused to eat the final year of Onslow's contract. When the 1950 club lost twenty-two of its first thirty-one games, Grace Comiskey relented, and coach Red Corriden took over as interim manager.[7] The Sox lost ninety-four games and finished sixth.

As soon as the season ended, Lane got the manager he wanted and the forty-two-year-old Richards got the job he had been preparing for since he organized schoolboy teams in Waxahachie. Richards signed a contract for one year at a reported $25,000, with an oral agreement for a second year, plus five cents for each ticket sold above 900,000.[8] (At the time the average big league player made $13,000.)[9] Attendance at Comiskey Park had exceeded 900,000 twice during the postwar boom but had fallen to 781,000 in 1950.

After twenty-five seasons in baseball Richards did not doubt his ability to lead a major league club. In his first meeting with Chicago writers in October, he summed up his philosophy: "The most important thing to me is to get the other fellow out. Almost every game is decided by the loser giving it away rather than the winner winning it. A good defense, inclusive of pitching, is the most vital part of a successful team."[10]

Lane had acquired an entire new infield and several pitchers in his first two years at the helm, but he handed Richards an unimpressive club. When the 1950 All-Star Game was played at Comiskey Park, not a single White Sox player appeared in the game. Just two young Sox showed promise. Chico Carrasquel, a twenty-four-year-old rookie shortstop from Venezuela, had batted .282/.368/.365 and impressed with his deft fielding. The slim, five-foot-ten left-hander Billy Pierce, who had grown up under Richards in Detroit and Buffalo, was traded to Chicago in 1948. He lost more games than he won with the weak teams, but his ERAs were excellent. In 1950 he held opposing batters to a .228 average, second lowest in the league. He was still wild, but he was not yet twenty-four.

The Sox's leading slugger was Gus Zernial, a 210-pound right-handed batter who set a club record with twenty-nine homers in 1950. A handsome man nicknamed "Ozark Ike" after a muscular comic-strip character, he also struck out 110 times, the only batter in the league to reach triple figures, and was ridiculed for his lackadaisical defense in left field.[11] The big left-handed-batting first baseman, Eddie Robinson, contributed twenty homers after he was acquired from the Senators during the 1950 season. Robinson had survived both a wartime leg injury that threatened to end his career and the death of his baby daughter, but he was thirty years old and not likely to improve.[12] The slightly built second baseman, Nelson Fox, celebrated his twenty-third birthday on Christmas Day, but he had batted just .247 with no home runs and looked amateurishly awkward on the double-play pivot. Richards considered second base "our weakest spot."[13]

Behind Pierce's team-leading twelve victories, only left-hander Bill Wight and right-hander Ray Scarborough had won as many as ten games, and Scarborough's ERA was an ugly 5.30. Lane sent Wight and Scarborough to the Red Sox for Al Zarilla, an outfielder who had batted .325 in 1950, veteran right-handed curveballer Joe Dobson, and young left-hander Dick Littlefield.[14]

Richards brought pitchers and catchers to Palm Springs, California, on February 20, 1951, where they worked out for eight days before position players arrived at the regular spring training site in Pasadena. He drove to the West Coast from Waxahachie with his childhood pal Jimmy Adair, whom he had hired as a coach. After a short major league trial Adair had played and managed in the minors.

Doc Cramer also joined the coaching staff. Cramer had batted .296 in a twenty-year major league career that began under Connie Mack in 1928, when his teammates included Ty Cobb and Tris Speaker. Pitching coach Ray Berres, a holdover from the previous regime, had been a light-hitting catcher like Richards. Luman Harris, released by Baltimore, was working as a carpenter in Alabama when Frank Lane called and told him Richards wanted him as batting-practice pitcher.[15] Harris would stay at Richards's side for two decades.

Eighteen pitchers arrived in Palm Springs to compete for jobs. Pierce described their spring regimen: "Run, run, run, run, run." Richards explained, "A pitcher has to be in twice as good condition as any other player."[16] After the trade of Wight and Scarborough, the only holdover starters behind Pierce were right-handers Ken Holcombe, coming off a 3-10 record, and Randy Gumpert, who had gone 5-12. Joe Dobson, acquired from the Red Sox, had posted victories in double figures every year since he returned from World War II, but he was thirty-three years old.

Richards and Lane wanted to send second baseman Fox to the minors, but Ray Berres insisted, "He can play. He'll play for you if he has to play on crutches."[17] Richards agreed to watch Fox throughout spring training before making a decision. The "half-pint" claimed to weigh 160 pounds but refused to step on a scale to prove it.[18] He was listed at five feet ten, but nobody measured that, either. With his slender build, boyish face, and crew cut, he could have blended in among the bat boys except for the wad of tobacco swelling his cheek.

Richards brought a box of bats into the clubhouse and told Fox, "That's your new bat." It was a Doc Cramer–model Louisville Slugger, a "bottle bat" with a thick handle to help the hitter make contact. Fox said, "I could never hit with a bat like that." Richards replied, "Well, I want to tell you something, young fella. You're either going to learn to hit with that bat and how to bunt with that bat or you're going to be playing second base in Memphis." Cramer made him carry the bat around the ballpark and clubhouse, gripping it with his thumb and forefinger. Fox said, "Cramer told me that if he came up to me and was able to knock it out of my hands, he'd kick my butt." Cramer overhauled the left-handed hitter's approach at the plate, working with him on bunting and breaking quickly out of the batter's box. Fox said, "Ray Berres almost pitched his arm off giving me special batting practice."

In the field, Richards complained that Fox was getting knocked down by base runners on double plays because he threw cross-legged. "How he survived the season without getting hurt, let alone complete a double play, is a miracle," the manager remarked. To school Fox, Richards brought in Joe Gordon, who had just retired as a flashy-fielding second baseman for the Yankees and Indians. When a bad-hop grounder hit Fox in the mouth and dislodged a tooth, he spat out the blood and declined to see a dentist, saying, "It's not bothering me. I'll wait till after the season."

The intensive instruction transformed young Jacob Nelson Fox into Nellie Fox, who would win the American League Most Valuable Player award in 1959 and go on to the Hall of Fame. Fox's development also cemented Paul Richards's reputation as a master teacher of young players. Fox always gave credit to Richards, Cramer, and Berres, but Richards said: "Fox is just one of those kids who's got what it takes. . . . We just gave him a chance, that's all. He took it."[19]

As Fox and his teammates learned, there was no question about who was in charge. Pitcher Skinny Brown, who came with Richards from Seattle, said of him, "It was his way and no other way."[20] Twenty-two-year-old Joe DeMaestri was an impressionable rookie, but many others seconded his impression of Richards: "Ask anybody who played for him; they'll probably tell you the same thing. No conversation. No words of encouragement. Seldom a smile. He never got close to his players. But in a game he was always two, three innings ahead, like he knew what was going to happen."[21]

Richards's emphasis on fundamentals made a quick and lasting impact on first baseman Eddie Robinson. A native of Paris, Texas, Robinson had played four full seasons under managers Lou Boudreau in Cleveland and Joe Kuhel and Bucky Harris in Washington. "None of them seemed to be interested in teaching," Robinson recalled. He was also struck by the new boss's demeanor: "He had the air, the presence, of convincing people that he knew what was going on, he knew what was right. . . . I wanted to please him."[22]

One of the highlights of the Pasadena camp, at least from the players' point of view, was a visit by starlet Marilyn Monroe. She wore tight white shorts and high heels as she posed arm in arm with Zernial and Dobson.[23] Joe DiMaggio saw the photograph and asked Zernial about Monroe. Zernial gave DiMaggio her press agent's phone number, enabling the storied romance.[24]

The White Sox posted a 23-10 spring record, the best in the majors, although Richards used every player in camp. Despite their success in the standings (that didn't count), Richards kept players after games for extra practice. In a preseason assessment of his new team, Richards said, "According to information I received, the basic weakness of the Sox last season was lack of speed, especially in the outfield."[25] While Zernial's heavy feet and iron glove remained in left because Richards needed his bat, Zarilla, the new right fielder, was supposed to add speed and defensive ability. Richards was counting on rookie Jim Busby for center field. Busby was yet another Texan, a former sprinter at Texas Christian University. While managing Seattle the previous year, Richards had admired Busby when he batted .310 for Sacramento. Busby was a rarity for the White Sox, a homegrown player. The opening day roster exposed the desolate state of the farm system: twenty-five of the twenty-eight men had come from other organizations.[26]

As opening day approached, Richards's biggest worry was the pitching staff. Pierce and Dobson were the only proven starters. Five-foot-eight left-hander Marv Rotblatt made a strong showing in spring training. Richards said he would gamble on right-handers Lou Kretlow and Howie Judson, who had won a combined total of thirteen major league games. Judson and Rotblatt were products of the White Sox farm system.[27]

Most baseball writers acknowledged that Chicago had improved since 1950, but few thought the progress was significant because of the suspect pitching. The *Sporting News* poll of 204 writers tabbed the White Sox for fifth place, one slot above their previous finish. No one predicted they would rise higher than fourth. The writers picked the Red Sox and Giants as the likely pennant winners.[28] Although the Yankees had won World Series championships in

Casey Stengel's first two years as manager, Boston had finished just four games behind in 1950, despite losing Ted Williams for the second half of the season after he broke his elbow in the All-Star Game.

On opening day, April 17, 1951, the White Sox made Richards a winner in his first game as a big league manager when they beat the Browns in St. Louis 17–3. Three days later, in the home opener against Detroit, Randy Gumpert pitched a three-hit shutout. The game introduced Chicago fans to Richards's aggressive style. In the fourth inning Busby singled, then stole second and third on consecutive pitches. Richards leaned over from the third-base coach's box and told him, "Well, regardless of what happens, Jim, you've got to go home on this next pitch." He flashed the suicide-squeeze sign to the batter, Gumpert, and Busby scored on the bunt. "That was the birth of the Go-Go Sox," Richards recalled. Soon the fans were chanting "Go! Go!" whenever the home team put a runner on base.[29] The nickname stuck for the rest of the 1950s.

After Chicago won six of its first ten games, Frank Lane pulled off the deal that made his reputation. He orchestrated a three-way trade with the Indians and Athletics that brought the White Sox one of their signature players. Lane checked into New York's Commodore Hotel on Saturday, April 29, donned his pajamas, and put together "the biggest swap of the year" in more than twenty hours of almost nonstop long-distance calls that cost $250. He woke up Cleveland general manager Hank Greenberg twice— once at 1 A.M. and again three hours later. When he hung up the phone for the last time shortly after noon on Sunday, seven players had changed hands. Lane traded Zernial and outfielder Dave Philley to Cleveland. Greenberg added catcher Ray Murray and pitcher Sam Zoldak and sent the lot, plus $50,000, to the Philadelphia A's for Lou Brissie, the left-handed pitcher he wanted, and outfielder Paul Lehner. The Indians then flipped Lehner to Chicago along with the man the Sox coveted, Orestes Minoso.[30]

Minoso had lit up the Pacific Coast League in 1950 with a .339 batting average, forty doubles, ten triples, twenty homers, 115 RBI, and thirty stolen bases for San Diego. Richards, watching from Seattle, said, "He was just devastating the league with his hitting ability and his speed."[31] A Cuban, Minoso was a stocky right-handed batter who played third base and the outfield with more enthusiasm than skill. When Richards first brought up his name before the winter meeting in December, Lane questioned Minoso's fielding ability, protesting, "But he can't play anything." Richards replied, "Don't you worry about him playing anything. I'll find a place for him. We'll just let him hit and run."[32] Explaining the decision to get rid of Zernial, Richards pointed to the generous dimensions of the team's home field, with outfield fences measuring 352 feet down each foul line: "We are abandoning the idea of building with power hitters. We're going after speed and good defense. That's the only way you can win at Comiskey Park."[33]

He described Minoso as "the kind of player you need to win pennants. He's the guy we wanted. He'll show them something."[34] Richards called a meeting to tell the players they were getting a black teammate. Chico Carrasquel remembered, "He asked if there were any objections, but there were none."[35] The White Sox were only the third American League team to integrate.

Minoso was reported to be twenty-seven, but later baseball encyclopedias listed him as twenty-eight. (In his 1994 autobiography he made the improbable claim that he was twenty-five.)[36] He played professionally in Cuba and in the North American Negro leagues until Bill Veeck signed him for Cleveland in 1948. He had batted only fourteen times for the Indians in April and said he was happy for the chance to play regularly. He was puzzled when teammates began calling him "Minnie" and when fans and some opponents called him vile names. "I would answer with my smile," he said.[37] He became one of the most popular players in White Sox history and served as a community ambassador for the team for decades.

In the first game after the trade, on May 1 at home against the Yankees, Minoso hit a two-run homer in the first inning. But his error at third base let in two runs as the Yankees won 8–3. (New York rookie Mickey Mantle hit the first home run of his career in that game.) The next day Minoso booted a grounder in the ninth, allowing the two winning runs to score. The day after that Richards sent him to left field, although Minoso played both positions for the rest of the season.

Lane picked up Richards's reclamation project from Buffalo, right-hander Saul Rogovin. Detroit had given up on Rogovin because he had a chronic sore arm and sometimes fell asleep on the bench. He was accused of being lazy but may have suffered from a sleep disorder. Perhaps "Sleepy" Richards sympathized. He put Rogovin in the starting rotation and coddled him as he had in Buffalo, giving him extra rest between appearances.

On May 15 the White Sox were in Boston to begin their first trip to eastern cities. The *Tribune's* Irving Vaughn called it a "daffy afternoon." It was a day that stamped Richards as an innovator. The two teams swapped leads throughout the game. Ted Williams hit his three-hundredth career home run, but Chicago led 7–6 after eight innings. With the left-handed-batting Williams leading off the bottom of the ninth, Richards reached back to his brainstorm with Bob Hooper in Buffalo. He moved his right-handed reliever Harry Dorish to third base (Richards said he had never seen the pull-hitting Williams hit a ball to third) and brought in left-hander Pierce.[38] It worked; Pierce got Williams to pop out to shortstop Carrasquel, who was shifted close to the second baseman's normal position. Dorish returned to the mound, but he gave up the tying run. Twenty-nine veterans of the American League's first season were in the stands to celebrate the league's fiftieth anniversary, including Connie Mack, Clark Griffith, and Cy Young. None of them could remember seeing such a pitcher switch. The historian Peter Morris discovered that the switch had been used in the nineteenth century, when rosters were small and pitchers often filled in at other positions, but he found no examples of its use in the majors after 1909. Other sportswriters and former players said it had been done many times in the minors.[39]

The daffiness was not done. In the eleventh inning Nellie Fox hit the first home run of his career, after 804 at-bats, to give Chicago a 9–7 win. It was Fox's mother's birthday, and for years he called it "the most thrilling game" of his career.[40]

Starting that day, the White Sox won fourteen in a row and improbably charged to the top of the standings. Chicago writer Edgar Munzel commented, "They are a collection of castoffs and they have a burning desire to show the world that they are better ballplayers than they are rated by their previous employers."[41] The surging Sox were the talk of Chicago. When the team came home after winning eleven straight games on the road, several thousand fans met them at the LaSalle Street railroad station. Richards and a dozen players rode in a motorcade to city hall, where Mayor Martin Kennelly greeted them.[42]

That night the Sox beat the Browns 4–2 while New York lost to Boston, lifting Richards's crew into first place by percentage points over the Yankees. Fox hit in his eighth straight game, and Rogovin pitched his first complete game, a two-hitter. Eddie Robinson, who had knocked in thirty-five runs in the first thirty-three games, led his teammates in a "Hip-Hip-Hooray," a postgame cheer that had become a superstition during the streak. An Associated Press writer said the White Sox had gone "from rags to Richards," but the manager did not let first place go to his head. He ordered the players to come out for practice the next day, when no game was scheduled. "We didn't get into first place in the American League by resting," he said.[43]

Nearly thirty-five thousand people turned out on May 30 for a Wednesday afternoon doubleheader against the Browns. The Sox rewarded them with a sweep to extend the winning streak to fourteen. Fox raised his batting average to .370. He had hit three home runs in sixteen days. (He hit only one more all season.) Richards said the key to the club's success was speed and teamwork: "We don't have a standout star. But we do have a lot of players who are eager to play ball, and they're doing a wonderful job of it."[44]

"We're probably the runningest team in the league," he said. ". . . And as of now we've been getting as much benefit from our *reputation* as a running team as from actual running. Sometimes it's better to have one of your speed men *not* run, but stay on first base and upset the pitcher rather than go to second."[45] The Sox had already stolen thirty bases, compared with nineteen in the entire previous season. When Minoso reached first in a game against the Yankees, catcher Yogi Berra was so fixated on keeping him from stealing that Berra leaned forward and tipped Eddie Robinson's bat, interference that put Minoso on second and Robinson on first.

Frank Lane gave the manager much of the credit for the team's rise. John P. Carmichael of the *Chicago Daily News* wrote that Lane and Richards "so often thought as one man." They lived in the same apartment building that spring and had breakfast and dinner together when the team was at home, but, typically, Lane said, they seldom talked about anything except baseball.[46] They were complementary in one way: Lane was a motor mouth, while exasperated sportswriters often struggled to extract a complete sentence from Richards.

Following a day off (for all the players except Rogovin, who was summoned for bunting and fielding drills) and a rainout, the Philadelphia Athletics stopped Chicago's streak in a 5–1 victory. Chicago lost again the next day, then won six in a row to open a four-and-a-half-game lead over the second-place Yankees. The victories included a doubleheader sweep of the Red Sox on June 4 before the largest crowd of the season so far, 42,718.[47]

New York came in for three games starting on June 8. Yankees manager Casey Stengel said: "Look, don't fool yourself about that ball club. They're a pretty fair team. And the real difference between Chicago last year and this is that balls now are hit for outs that used to go for doubles and triples. Busby and Zarilla are catching them."[48]

Despite threatening weather a standing-room crowd of 53,940, the largest in Chicago baseball history, crammed Comiskey Park for Friday night's opener to watch Vic Raschi pitch the Yankees to a 4–2 victory. New York won again Saturday, 10–5. More than fifty-two thousand turned out for the Sunday doubleheader, and it was a rowdy crowd. Fans threw trash onto the field, and someone tossed firecrackers at Yankees right fielder Mickey Mantle. (A local bartender was arrested and fined $50.)[49] The teams split the two games and the Yankees left town just two and a half back. The three-day series drew 130,720, a franchise record. WGN-TV estimated that an additional three million watched the Saturday and Sunday games on television.[50]

The surprising Sox were "the darlings of baseball." Leading mass-circulation magazines *Life*, *Time*, and the *Saturday Evening Post* profiled the team and its rookie manager. The *Post* headlined its story "He Put the White Sox Back in the League." *Life* gave the "White Hot" Sox a five-page photo spread featuring a full-page shot of Richards coaching at third base.[51]

In an interview with *Sporting News* publisher Taylor Spink (or one of his ghost writers), Richards distanced himself from old-school managers: "The old idea of sitting on the bench and pulling strings, founded on the notion that ball players were puppets, is not the winning technique of today." He had already established his reputation as a handler of pitchers, but he was cagey about his theories: "I have a definite important notion about pitching which I do not want to spread around to the other 15 clubs of the majors. It is based on the idea that a tired pitcher is a badly handicapped pitcher."[52] This hints that he had started paying attention to pitch counts, a revolutionary notion at a time when a starting pitcher's ability to finish games was seen as a test of his manhood as well as his physical stamina.

Richards also believed in giving pitchers four days off between starts, while three days was standard until the 1970s. "I don't care what pitcher it is, he's always going to have more stuff with four days' rest than he has with three," he declared.[53] A manager could not follow a strict five-man starting rotation, as present-day teams do, because there were many more doubleheaders and days off for travel. The White Sox played twenty-six doubleheaders in 1951, scheduled on most Sundays and holidays to give fans two games for the price of one.

Baseball gospel held that pitching was the cornerstone of winning teams, but Richards phrased it as defense and pitching. When a writer asked him to explain the success of his unheralded mound staff, he replied: "I have Chico Carrasquel. I have Nellie Fox. I have Jim Busby. What more do you want?"[54]

Margie joined him in Chicago, bringing Paula, twelve, and Lou Redith, five. Paula recalled that her mother "always was dressed up when he came home. His meat was cut on his plate just the way he liked it. In return, she got everything she wanted."[55] The *Tribune*'s Rita Fitzpatrick described the thirty-nine-year-old Margie as "a softened edition of a Vogue model, 5 foot 5 inches in her stocking feet, brown blonde, blue eyed, with dainty hands and feet. She wears gray almost exclusively, and casual dresses, not suits." She claimed to know nothing about baseball ("Don't let her kid you," her husband remarked) and said she kept busy taking care of their home in Waxahachie.[56] Richards had bought a second farm, 150 acres planted in cotton. What the story did not say: Lou Redith was suffering from a congenital heart ailment, and her parents had brought her to Chicago for treatment at Children's Memorial Hospital.[57]

The White Sox hung onto first place through June as their business office was turning away requests for World Series tickets. "We are leading the league because we can do a lot of things," Richards told an Associated Press writer. "We can beat you a lot of ways—bunting, running, hitting and fielding. And we have had the pitching. But the most important thing to me is that we have players who like to hustle, rather than those you have to make hustle."[58]

Chicago writers were touting "the Miracle on 35th Street," but Richards had run out of magic. The club went 17-15 in June. The Yankees, Boston, and Cleveland were charging hard to create a pennant race that the *New York Times*'s John Drebinger described as "a four-ring circus."[59] On July 1 Chicago split a doubleheader with the Browns while the Yankees beat Boston to take over first place by percentage points. Richards "stalked off the field grimly" and barred reporters from the clubhouse for the first time.[60] The White Sox had been on top for thirty-four days.

On July 4 the Sox climbed back into first by a half-game. Baseball superstition held that the leader on that date would win the pennant, a superstition that had been correct two-thirds of the time in American League history.[61] Fox had been leading the league in batting average. When he faltered, playing on a bruised foot, Minoso took over the top spot. Robinson's sixteen home runs and sixty-eight RBI were second in the league. The team had scored the most runs in the league. The pitching, supposedly the weak spot, was the AL's best, giving up an average of just over four runs per game.

Saul Rogovin had been hammered in his first outing, but the twenty-seven-year-old castoff turned into the White Sox's most effective pitcher. He said rejoining Richards "was like coming home. I knew Paul had confidence in me."[62] In his next five starts Rogovin's record was 3-2 with a 1.52 ERA, but both his losses had been by a single run. He was still fighting a sore elbow and getting an extra day off between starts.

Nellie Fox led the fan balloting for the all-star team with more than 1.4 million votes. Carrasquel beat out the 1950 Most Valuable Player, the Yankees' Phil Rizzuto, at shortstop and became the first Latino player to start an All-Star Game. (That summer he broke Rizzuto's American League record by fielding 289 consecutive chances without making an error.)[63]

Chicago held a one-game lead over Boston at the all-star break, with the Yankees two games back. After the break the Red Sox came into Chicago riding a six-game winning streak. The makers of Hawthorn-Mellody Farms Yogurt (endorsed by Fox, Carrasquel, and Minoso) took out a full-page newspaper ad trumpeting, "All Chicago's Cheering: Go, Go, Go Sox!" The Cisco Kid Rodeo was playing at Wrigley Field, the hit musical *South Pacific* was at the Schubert Theater, and Dagmar was performing in burlesque at Minsky's Rialto, but 52,592 Chicagoans chose baseball that day.[64]

Fans began gathering outside Comiskey Park before noon for the double-header that would start at 6 P.M. Boston took the first game 3–2 as left-hander Mel Parnell pitched shutout ball until the ninth. The second game lasted seventeen innings, and so did Richards's starting pitcher, Rogovin, before he yielded the winning run to put Boston in first place by one game. The longest night game in American League history took four hours and one minute and ended forty-seven minutes after midnight on Friday the thirteenth.

On Friday night the teams topped that, playing nineteen innings in four hours and forty-seven minutes. Each side scored two runs in the first eighteen frames as the Red Sox starter, Mickey McDermott, pitched seventeen of them. Two Chicago errors helped Boston take a two-run lead in the top of the nineteenth. In their last chance the White Sox rallied with four straight singles and a sacrifice fly to bring home the winning run at 1:17 A.M. Boston was three percentage points ahead in the standings.

The players were back on the field barely twelve hours later. The Red Sox staged a ninth-inning rally to take a 3–2 lead. Chicago loaded the bases in the bottom of the ninth, but Floyd Baker popped out to end it. Boston left town with a one-game lead. Umpire Joe Papparella recalled, "It was the toughest series I ever worked"—fifty-four innings in four games over three days, each decided by one run, with first place on the line.[65]

While that showdown was going on, the Indians won two out of three from the Yankees. On the evening of July 14, 1951, Boston was one game in front of the White Sox, two and a half up on the Yankees, and three and a half ahead of Cleveland.

Chicago never regained first place. The Sox had been mediocre in June; in July they were awful, winning eleven games and losing twenty-one. The pitching got slightly worse, while the offense fizzled. Eddie Robinson hit only four home runs in a month as his batting average dropped twenty-two points. Busby's fell twenty-six points. Fox, who had reached .370 at the end of May, was down to .313.[66] Lane convinced Richards that the little second baseman was worn out and needed a day off, whether he wanted one or not. Richards told the story for years afterward:

> [Fox] sits down next to me and starts yelling at the pitcher, giving him hell, calling him everything. He goes on for nine innings like that, loud as he could. Doing it on purpose, you see, just to give me a headache. Finally I turned to him. "Foxie," I said, "Let me tell you something right now. This is the last time you're ever going to sit on this bench with me. I don't care if Lane or anybody else says you need a rest. You're not going to get it. Just remember that." Well, that satisfied him. He didn't want a rest.[67]

It is another good story ruined by the facts. Richards benched Fox for three games against Detroit on July 4 and 5.

Richards pointed to two defeats that killed his club's pennant chances. On July 20 Chicago trailed the Yankees by just three percentage points and was leading Washington 1–0 with two out in the ninth. When the count went to two-and-two on the Senators' Eddie Yost, the Sox were one strike away from first place. Lou Kretlow threw the third strike, as Richards saw it, but the umpire called it a ball. The Senators rallied to tie and won in the tenth.

A week later at Yankee Stadium the Sox came from behind to take a 4–3 lead in the top of the ninth and had the bases loaded when the game was called because of rain. The final score reverted to the previous inning, giving the Yankees a 3–1 victory. In the wet, wild ninth Richards accused Casey Stengel of stalling by changing pitchers four times while the rain pelted down. He complained that one Yankees reliever took nine minutes to walk in from the bullpen and warm up and that the groundskeepers were dawdling when they put the tarpaulin on the field. Raging, Richards stormed into the umpires' dressing room and said they "either are incompetent or should be investigated." In a postseason article for *Official Baseball Annual* he wrote, "That was the crusher."[68] The Yankees swept all three games of the series, dropping Chicago to fourth place, seven and a half games behind, on the last day of July.

And there they stayed. While the Yankees, Red Sox, and Indians swapped the lead in a tight pennant race, the White Sox went 16-13 in August and fell to 11-15 in September. As the team cooled off, Frank Lane said, "The most you can ask of any manager is that he get the most out of his material. No matter where we finish this year, Paul Richards has proved that he's strictly major-league in that respect."[69]

On August 3 the club was in Washington when Richards got word that his five-year-old daughter, Lou Redith, had died. The blonde child had been born with a heart defect, though the problem was not diagnosed until she was four. Doctors told the family that as Lou Redith grew bigger, her heart could not pump efficiently enough to keep her alive. Richards flew to Chicago to join Margie and Paula, and they went home to Waxahachie to bury their younger daughter. "Mother took it harder than Daddy," Paula said. "I don't think she ever got over it."[70]

He was away from the team for a week, leaving Doc Cramer in charge. But even after his personal loss Richards served notice that he had not given up on the season. After Cleveland swept the White Sox in three straight to regain possession of first place, he called a workout on an off day. This was a bedrock of his philosophy: "Preparing and teaching baseball is constant. Even major league managers must continue teaching during the championship season."[71] He put the players back on the field after games when they had botched a play and had them practice that play "not just eight or ten times, but fifty or a hundred times," Eddie Robinson said. "In those days players accepted it, and I think they accepted it from him without any problem because they would think it was going to help them get better."[72]

Although the Sox fell out of the race, the fans kept coming to Comiskey Park. On August 28 home attendance passed one million for the first time in the franchise's fifty-year history. Richards was absent that day. His mother had died August 23 at age eighty-one, three days after she fell and broke her hip. For the second time in three weeks he returned to Waxahachie for a funeral.[73]

The pennant race seesawed on without the White Sox. The Yankees clinched their third straight in a September 28 doubleheader against the Red Sox with a flourish befitting the two-time defending World Champions. Allie Reynolds pitched his second no-hitter of the season in the first game, an 8–0 victory, and Joe DiMaggio hit a three-run homer in the nightcap as New York cruised, 11–3. The White Sox's once-miraculous season ended with a whimper. They lost their final game to the last-place Browns as pitcher Ned Garver registered his twentieth victory out of only fifty-two won by his team.

Chicago's 81-73 record was twenty-one wins better than the previous year and the franchise's first winning season since 1943. The home attendance, 1,328,234, was 70 percent higher than 1950's and trailed only Cleveland's and New York's, with their huge ballparks. That earned Richards more than $21,000 on his nickel-a-head bonus for attendance greater than 900,000, a bonus almost equal to his salary.

Most important, in his first season as a major league manager Paul Richards created the "Go-Go-Sox," who ran and hustled and scratched and captivated the city. Saul Rogovin said, "He conned all of us into thinking we were better than we were."[74]

1. *New York Times*, June 19, 1951, 50; Bill Corum, *New York Journal-American*, reprinted in the *Sporting News* (hereafter *TSN*), December 1, 1954, 18.
2. *TSN*, March 31, 1948, 1.
3. One of the nephews, Calvin Robertson, and one niece, Thelma Robertson, changed their names to Griffith. Contrary to many published reports, neither was legally adopted by Clark Griffith, although they grew up in the Griffith household (Jon Kerr, *Calvin: Baseball's Last Dinosaur* [Dubuque, Iowa: Wm. C. Brown, 1990], 9–10).
4. *TSN*, October 31, 1951, 8, 13, 17, and June 14, 1952, 2. The figures cited in text come from a rare public accounting of baseball's finances, based on information supplied by the teams to the House Judiciary Committee's Subcommittee on the Study of Monopoly and reported in *TSN*. I used the Labor Department's inflation calcualtor at http://data.bls.gov/cgi-bin/cpicalc.pl to calculate the payroll in today's terms.
5. *Chicago Sun-Times*, August 28, 2007, online edition.
6. *Chicago Tribune*, April 6, 1951, B1; *TSN*, October 20, 1948, 22; Lee MacPhail, *My Nine Innings* (Westport, Conn.: Meckler Books, 1989), 7, 39.
7. *TSN*, October 18, 1950, 5.
8. Ibid.; *Chicago Tribune*, July 20, 1951, B2; David Gough and Jim Bard, *Little Nel: The Nellie Fox Story* (Alexandria, Va.: D. L. Megbeck Publishing, 2000), 69.
9. John Helyar, *Lords of the Realm* (New York: Villard, 1994), 12.
10. *TSN*, October 25, 1950, 1, 4.
11. *Chicago Tribune*, January 28, 1951, A3.
12. *TSN*, May 15, 1948, 5.
13. Neal R. Gazel, "Nellie Does Right by the White Sox," *Baseball Digest*, August 1951, 5.
14. *Chicago Tribune*, January 11, 1951, B2.
15. Jesse Outlar, "The Reunion of Richards and Harris," *Atlanta Journal-Constitution Magazine*, April 7, 1968, 27.
16. Billy Pierce, interview by Thomas Liley, February 24, 1992; William Barry Furlong and Fred Russell, "He Put the White Sox Back in the League," *Saturday Evening Post*, July 21, 1951, 91.
17. Ray Berres, interview by Norman Macht, March 8, 1996.
18. *TSN*, May 30, 1951, 3.
19. Gough and Bard, *Little Nel*, 73–76.
20. John Eisenberg, *From 33rd Street to Camden Yards: An Oral History of the Baltimore Orioles* (New York: Contemporary Books, 2001), 25.
21. Norman L. Macht, "Turn Back the Clock: Memories from Former Shortstop Joe DeMaestri," *Baseball Digest*, September 2003, 74–77.
22. Eddie Robinson, interview by author, August 18, 2006, Fort Worth, Texas.
23. *TSN*, March 21, 1951, 23.
24. Marc Aaron, "Gus Zernial," *The Baseball Biography Project*, Society for American Baseball Research, http://bioproj.sabr.org.
25. *Chicago Tribune*, March 22, 1951, B1; April 11, 1951, B1; December 18, 1975, C1.
26. Ibid., April 28, 1951, B3.
27. *TSN*, April 18, 1951, 16; April 25, 1951, 5; June 20, 1951, 5.
28. Ibid., April 18, 1951, 4.

29. Paul Richards, interview by Clark Nealon, February 5, 1981; *Chicago Tribune*, April 21, 1951, B1, and June 15, 1951, B1.
30. *TSN*, May 9, 1951, 7.
31. Richards interview.
32. Jerome Holtzman and George Vass, *Baseball Chicago Style* (Chicago: Bonus Books, 2001), 102.
33. *TSN*, May 9, 1951, 7.
34. AP, *New York Times*, May 1, 1951, 46.
35. Minnie Minoso, with Herb Fagen, *Just Call Me Minnie* (Champaign, Ill.: Sagamore, 1994), 50.
36. Ibid., 5. In the book Minoso says he claimed to be older so he would be eligible to join the Cuban army during World War II (which he never did) and so he could qualify for a visa to enter the United States. That claim produced a certain amount of head scratching. Why would he let the erroneous date stand for nearly fifty years, delaying his eligibility for his big league pension? Why would he allow managers and general managers to think he was older than he actually was? It also touched off a debate among baseball historians. Many had argued that his record qualified him for the Hall of Fame because segregation delayed the start of his career, but if he was only twenty-five when he became a regular player, he was not significantly held back by his color. Minoso married a much younger woman and fathered a child when he was in his sixties. Writer Steve Treder has suggested that Minoso may have lied to his wife about his age and stuck with the lie in the autobiography (Treder, "Minoso Made His Dream Come True," *Baseball Primer News Blog*, February 23, 2003, www.baseballthinkfactory.org/files/newsstand/discussion/minoso_made_his_dream_come_true/).
37. *Viva Baseball*, DVD, documentary directed by Dan Klores, Shoot the Moon Productions, 2005.
38. George Vass, "Juggling the Lineup," *Baseball Digest*, January 2001, online edition.
39. *Chicago Tribune*, May 16, 1951, B1; *TSN*, May 30, 1951, 14; Peter Morris, *The Game on the Field*, vol. 1, *Game of Inches*, (Chicago: Ivan R. Dee, 2006), 308.
40. *TSN*, May 30, 1951, 3; Gough and Bard, *Little Nel*, 79.
41. *TSN*, June 20, 1951, 5.
42. *Chicago Tribune*, May 29, 1951, B3; UP, *New York Times*, May 29, 1951, 40.
43. *Chicago Tribune*, May 29, 1951, B1; AP, *Charleston (W.Va.) Daily Mail*, June 19, 1951, 11.
44. *TSN*, June 6, 1951, 7.
45. *Chicago Tribune*, May 31, 1951, C5.
46. *TSN*, November 10, 1954, 11.
47. Ibid., June 20, 1951, 1.
48. *Chicago Tribune*, June 19, 1951, E1.
49. *TSN*, June 20, 1951, 2.
50. *Chicago Tribune*, June 11, 1951, E2; June 12, 1951, B2.
51. Furlong and Russell, "He Put the White Sox Back," 25; "Chicago's White Sox Are White Hot," *Life*, June 18, 1951, 27–31.
52. *TSN*, June 20, 1951, 6.
53. Donald Honig, *The Man in the Dugout* (New York: Fireside/Simon and Schuster, 1988), 141.
54. *TSN*, June 27, 1951, 10.
55. Paula Richards, interviews by author, 2006–2008.
56. *Chicago Tribune*, June 9, 1951, B3.
57. Ibid., August 4, 1951, A1.
58. AP, *Charleston (W. Va.) Daily Mail*, June 19, 1951, 11.
59. *TSN*, June 20, 1951, 3; *New York Times*, July 19, 1951, 31.
60. AP, *New York Times*, June 3, 1951, 154.
61. *TSN*, July 11, 1951, 24.
62. UP, *New York Times*, October 27, 1951, 28.
63. *TSN*, July 25, 1951, 6, and July 11, 1951, 2.
64. *Chicago Tribune*, July 12, 1951, W7 and A6.

65. Larry R. Gerlach, *The Men in Blue* (1980; repr., Lincoln: University of Nebraska Press, 1994), 140.
66. *TSN*, August 15, 1951, 18.
67. Honig, *Man in Dugout*, 138.
68. *New York Times*, August 22, 1951, 28; *TSN*, August 8, 1951, 9. The *Official Baseball Annual* article is quoted in Gough and Bard, *Little Nel*, 84.
69. Furlong and Russell, "He Put the White Sox Back," 92.
70. *Chicago Tribune*, August 4, 1951, A1; Paula Richards interviews.
71. *Chicago Tribune*, August 13, 1951, C1; Paul Richards, untitled 1970s manuscript "for high school, college and amateur managers and coaches" (hereafter Richards manuscript), in the author's files.
72. Eddie Robinson interview.
73. UP, *New York Times*, August 24, 1951, 9; *TSN*, September 19, 1951, 37.
74. *Scribner Encyclopedia of American Lives*, 2:731, undated photocopy in the Paul Richards file, A. Bartlett Giamatti Research Center, National Baseball Hall of Fame, Cooperstown, N.Y.

CHAPTER 11

The Wizard of Waxahachie

The 1951 White Sox displayed many of the hallmarks of what would become known as a Paul Richards team. They led the league in stolen bases and triples, emblems of speed and aggressive base running. The pitchers' 3.50 ERA was second to Cleveland's and not just because of spacious Comiskey Park: the White Sox allowed the fewest runs on the road of any American League team. The club hit eighty-six homers, the second-lowest total in the league, with only twenty-eight of them at home. Eddie Robinson tied Gus Zernial's franchise record of twenty-nine, but no one else had more than ten.

Richards and Lane patched together a fine pitching staff, although only Joe Dobson had previously won as many as fifteen games in a season, and a sore arm limited him to seven victories in 1951. Saul Rogovin, a washout in earlier big league trials, led the league in ERA at 2.78 and won eleven games. Rogovin said, "I still have quite a bit to learn about pitching, but everything I know about it was taught to me by Paul Richards."[1] Ken Holcombe, a thirty-two-year-old right-hander, lowered his ERA from 4.59 to 3.78 and won eleven games. His career victory total was eighteen.

Billy Pierce's record was just 15-14 because of weak run support, but his 3.03 ERA was fourth best in the league. The one-time wild young lefty cut his walks in half; his strikeout-to-walk ratio, 1.55, was third best. Pierce's wit was as quick as his fastball. One day, when the Yankees were hitting him hard and Jim Busby was chasing down their best shots in center field, Richards came to the mound to check on his pitcher. "Don't ask me how I feel," Pierce told him. "Ask Busby how he feels."[2]

Richards emphasized defense first. On offense he favored one-run tactics that hurt the team's run production. Chicago led the league in sacrifice bunts, giving up an out to move a runner ninety feet closer to home plate. The Sox stole ninety-nine bases, twenty-one more than any other club; their success rate was only 59 percent, about average for that time. Most analysts consider a rate of about 70 percent to be the break-even point where the bases gained are worth more than the outs lost.[3] The hitters were not patient, finishing fifth in walks. Lacking power and patience, the offense was inefficient. Despite a league-leading .270 batting average, Chicago finished fourth in runs scored.

Fielding, the third leg of Richards's winning triad, along with pitching and speed, is notoriously difficult to assess. One comprehensive measurement, the defensive efficiency rate, tracks how effectively a team's fielders convert batted balls into outs. The 1951 White Sox ranked second in the league at .720 compared with a league average of .707.[4] (Most of Richards's teams ranked high in this category.) Bill James's finely tuned system for awarding defensive win shares rates Busby, Fox, and Carrasquel among the best at their positions in the 1950s.[5]

Fox and Minoso blossomed into stars in their first season under Richards. Fox finished with a .313 batting average and .798 OPS while striking out just eleven times in 681 plate appearances. He was the type of player sportswriters and fans loved, a hustling, undersized overachiever who made the most of his meager talent and was a "holler guy" on the field. The playful poet Ogden Nash captured him in rhyme:

He uses a plug of tobacco a game,
And has never lost or swallowed same.
Nellie Fox so lives to play
That every day's a hollerday.[6]

Minoso, called "The Cuban Comet," led the league with thirty-one stolen bases (Busby finished second with twenty-six) and fourteen triples (Fox was second with twelve). Umpire Bill McGowan, a twenty-five-year veteran, said, "Orestes Minoso is the best base-runner—not base-stealer—I have seen since the days of Ty Cobb."[7] Minoso's .326 average was second in the league, and his .922 OPS was third best. He ranked in the top five in runs, hits, and doubles.

He also led the league in being hit by pitches—sixteen times. Black batters were far more likely to be targets than whites in the early days of integration.[8] In a rare display of anger Minoso once suggested he needed "a bucket of white paint" to stop pitchers from throwing at him.[9] But it is also true that he crowded the plate and his open stance had his body moving toward the ball as it was pitched, making it more difficult for him to duck. He topped the league in this category ten times, but his white teammate Fox was also annually among the leaders.

The stink of racism also tainted the baseball writers' choice for AL Rookie of the Year. In balloting by beat reporters, three from each AL city, the Yankees' Gil McDougald was named Rookie of the Year with 13 votes to Minoso's 11. Minoso was far superior in every offensive category except home runs; McDougald hit fourteen to Minoso's ten. Sportswriters at the time judged a player's worth primarily by his batting average, and Minoso hit .326, second in the league, to McDougald's .306. Frank Lane called the vote outrageous and speculated, "Could it be that some didn't know that Minoso was a first-year rookie or were some of them prejudiced in other ways?"[10] (McDougald was white.) Richards wrote, "I, for one, feel Minoso did more for our club than McDougald did for New York."[11] The *Sporting News*, in a broader poll of 227 writers, named Minoso the top rookie; he got 122 votes to 100 for McDougald.[12]

While the White Sox drew the biggest crowds in their history in 1951, total major league attendance fell for the third straight year, dropping 25 percent below the peak in 1948. Even after franchise shifts and expansion, per-game attendance did not recover until the mid-1970s. The Yankees played before more than two million home fans in 1950 but did not reach that level again for twenty-six years. Baseball's postwar "golden age" turned out to be only a golden moment. Two historic social changes rocked the industry in the 1950s: television and the shift of population to the suburbs and the Sun Belt.

Strife erupted in the White Sox front office during the winter. In January 1952 Chuck Comiskey resigned as vice president because he had been denied a pay raise and a long-term contract. Lane and Richards had gotten big raises, and young Comiskey thought it was his turn. But the club's board of directors—made up of his mother, sister Dorothy, and two lawyers, as well as himself—said no, and the Comiskey heir said goodbye. Although he returned to the White Sox in June, this was the beginning of a rift that eventually cost the Comiskey family control of the team.[13]

Richards and Lane stayed out of the office politics and set about building on the success of 1951. Lane acquired catcher Sherman Lollar from the Browns for a package of players; the key man was the Pacific Coast League MVP, outfielder Jim Rivera. Lollar had started his career in the Cleveland organization but could not dislodge the smooth-fielding Jim Hegan. Lollar was traded to the Yankees, where he sat behind Yogi Berra. Shipped to the bottom of the league, he took advantage of the chance to play more often in St. Louis and made the all-star team as a reserve in 1950.

Lane's moves did little to fill the biggest White Sox need. In a January article for the *Tribune*, Richards wrote, "We must find some batting power in order to win some of our well-pitched games this year." He said Lollar would add pop to the lineup, but the catcher had never hit more than thirteen home runs.[14]

In the *Sporting News*'s preseason poll, baseball writers picked Chicago to move up to third place behind Cleveland and New York in 1952.[15] The Indians' strong pitching staff made them the favorites, while the Yankees had lost Joe DiMaggio to retirement and second baseman Jerry Coleman to military service. Boston's Ted Williams, a U.S. Marine pilot like Coleman, was also recalled for his second wartime tour of duty.

Lane—no doubt with Richards's advice—sent a letter to White Sox players setting out plans for spring training. This edict vividly illustrates how teams exercised dictatorial control over their players before free agency. The first page and a half dealt with wives. They would be allowed to join their husbands at the Pasadena camp, at the player's expense, but the wives would be left behind when the team headed east on its cross-country barnstorming trip. Players were prohibited from bringing their cars to spring training for fear of accidents. Finally, players were not permitted to leave the team to pick up their families and bring them to Chicago. The wives had to get there on their own.[16] A player drew no salary during spring training. The club paid for his meals and lodging but not his family's, and he received $25 a week for expenses.

The largest opening day crowd at Comiskey Park since 1926, more than twenty-five thousand, watched the White Sox fall to Cleveland on April 15, 1952.[17] The Sox dropped their first four games and soon stumbled into a six-game losing streak. Still searching for a power bat, Lane swapped Jim Busby to Washington for outfielder Sam Mele (rhymes with "steely"), a right-handed hitter who had led the league in doubles the previous year and had hit all of his twelve home runs on the road. (Outfield fences at Washington's Griffith Stadium were even more distant than those in Comiskey Park.) That meant Minoso had to move to center field, where he was a downgrade from Busby, until the acrobatic "Jungle Jim" Rivera was reacquired in July.

On superstition day, July 4, Chicago was in second place, just two and a half games behind the Yankees. But the Sox dropped ten of fifteen during a swing through the eastern cities and fell to fifth. Richards fumed about his players' mental mistakes and finally exploded: "We've made enough rockhead plays of late to fill a stone quarry. We've been killing ourselves with stupid base-running, throwing to the wrong base, failure to take signs and that sort of thing. It isn't any one or two players. It seems to be a different one every day."[18]

After one of those rockhead plays, when his infielders convened under a pop fly and watched it drop among them, he hit on a novel solution: He told them Nellie Fox would be fined $100 if it happened again. In effect, he named Fox captain of the infield. He later put the same onus on shortstop Willy Miranda and third baseman Brooks Robinson in Baltimore.[19]

He also began to explode at umpires, bringing back memories of "Ol' Rant and Rave" in Buffalo. Richards had been on good behavior in his first year at Chicago and was ejected from only five games. In 1952 he was tossed nine times. In his first eleven seasons as a major league manager Richards rang up eighty ejections, ranking sixth among all managers in history. The men ahead of him—Bobby Cox, John McGraw, Leo Durocher, Earl Weaver, and Frankie Frisch—managed many more years.[20] "Umpires told me he knew words they had never heard before," broadcaster Ernie Harwell said. When television showed close-ups of his confrontations with the umps, horrified lip readers complained. The director began switching to a wide shot whenever Richards stalked out of the dugout.[21]

As the White Sox fell behind, Richards signed a contract extension for two more years.[22] Although attendance at Comiskey Park declined by ninety-six thousand from the 1951 record, it was still third highest in the majors as overall attendance dropped another 9 percent.

Chicago's 81-73 record was the same as in 1951, but the club climbed to third place behind New York and Cleveland. Lack of power was still the White Sox weakness. The team ranked next to last in home runs with eighty and fifth in runs scored. This time the Sox could not blame Comiskey Park; they scored the same number of runs at home and away. The trade of Busby and a sprained ankle that slowed Minoso for several weeks took some of the "go" out of the Go-Go Sox and cut their stolen bases from ninety-nine to sixty-one, still the most in the league. Their success rate barely improved to 62 percent, from 59 percent the year before.

Chico Carrasquel missed nearly two months with a broken finger, while several pitchers were sidelined with arm miseries, but the defense and pitching were effective enough to allow the second-fewest runs in the league. Joe Dobson rebounded to win fourteen games; his 2.51 ERA was the league's fifth best. Pierce followed at 2.57 and won fifteen. Both held opposing batters to an on-base percentage under .300, among the league leaders.

Chicago writer Edgar Munzel coined Richards's enduring nickname, "The Wizard of Waxahachie."[23] Frank Lane argued that Richards deserved to be Manager of the Year rather than Casey Stengel, who had won his fourth straight pennant and World Series, because Richards did more with less. "Our pitching staff was sneered at by the other clubs in the league," Lane said. While the Yankees had proven winners in Vic Raschi, Allie Reynolds, and Ed Lopat, and Cleveland countered with twenty-game winners Bob Lemon, Early Wynn, and Mike Garcia, Richards made do with castoffs and unknowns. Lane ticked them off: Pierce became a winner after Richards taught him the slider and got him to trust other pitches besides his fastball. Saul Rogovin went from the tenth man on the staff in Detroit to number two in Chicago, where he had won eleven games and then fourteen in two seasons. Right-hander Marv Grissom, rescued from the minors at age thirty-four, won twelve. Harry Dorish, another refugee from the minors, learned the slip pitch from Richards and became the team's top reliever. "Where else is there a manager who has molded a winning staff out of more erratic and aged material than we had?" Lane asked.[24]

In his 1955 book, *Modern Baseball Strategy*, Richards wrote, "Pitching is the backbone of any baseball team, and a good staff can keep a mediocre team in the pennant race almost indefinitely." He offered no magic bullet for developing and handling pitchers. He often said, "No two will ever be exactly alike."[25] He preached three principles: control, changing speeds, and proper rest. "Einstein couldn't be a smart pitcher unless he could throw strike one," he said.[26] When Richards arrived in Chicago, walks in the American League were at historic highs, because home runs were at historic highs and pitchers were nibbling at the corners to keep the ball away from the sluggers. The 1949 and 1950 seasons saw the highest walk rates ever.[27] White Sox pitchers issued 734 passes in 1950, second most in the majors. The next year, under Richards, the staff walked 549, fewest in the AL. He produced similar results when he moved to Baltimore.

Left-hander Bill Wight, later a respected scout of young pitchers, said Richards "emphasized changing speeds and varying pitches and concentrating on getting ahead of the hitter."[28] Richards wrote: "My best advice to every pitcher is to try to develop a change of pace as quickly as possible. Not only will you find it valuable in strategic pitching, but also less tiring on the arm. When you add the adverse psychological effect it has on the batter, it's easy to understand that the development of this pitch is worth whatever it may take to master the technique."[29]

In addition to his trademark change-up, the slip pitch, he also taught the slider, advising pitchers "to throw it like a football, with a spiral spin." He often said the slider was responsible for the falling batting averages that disturbed many old-time baseball men in the fifties and sixties. (Some observers called the slip pitch a slider, but Richards said it was not. The slider is delivered with a fastball grip and is thrown harder.)[30]

Because he usually gave his starters at least four days' rest, Richards never managed a twenty-game winner, but he scoffed at that measure of success. He reasoned that a pitcher working every fourth day might win twenty but lose fourteen or fifteen; a man making fewer starts with more rest might win eighteen while losing only seven or eight. The most successful manager in history, Joe McCarthy, also believed in four days' rest.[31]

Even on a five-day rotation Richards's best pitchers worked hard. Pierce's 240 innings were the seventh highest in the league in 1951; he reached a peak of 271 innings in 1953, third among AL pitchers. Virgil Trucks finished second in the league in 1954 with 264⅔ innings. Richards also used his top starters occasionally in relief, as did many contemporary managers.

He said a boy who wanted to be a pitcher should not play football or swim but should play golf (surprise) and box: "Now, I don't mean fighting, knocking one another silly. But boxing—throwing the arms forward in a straight blow or even hooking from either side, as long as the arm is extended to lengthen the muscles of the upper arm and shoulder. Boxing, golf and pitching are kindred arm sports."[32]

He believed in "the duster," his term for a knockdown pitch.[33] The young left-hander Bob Cain said Richards ordered his pitchers to dust off the next batter after a homer and knock down the home run–hitter the next time he came to bat. Cain didn't want to do it and was traded early in Richards's first season. In Baltimore six-foot-four reliever George Zuverink was the enforcer: "One time he brought me in and said, 'I want you to hit this guy right between the eyes.'"[34]

While Richards put his stamp on the rebuilt White Sox, Frank Lane also deserves credit because he made the deals that turned the franchise around. But many of the players Lane acquired were Richards's choices. In addition to those he had managed before, Richards had seen Minoso, Busby, Grissom, and Rivera on opposing teams in the Pacific Coast League. Because of the sorry state of the Chicago farm system, he and Lane had to gamble on young players and questionable veterans. Richards placed his bets on players he knew first hand, and Lane usually followed his lead. Later in his career Lane seemed driven to live up to his reputation as "Trader Lane" and "Frantic Frankie." He made nonsensical deals, such as swapping managers, traded away fan favorites Red Schoendienst in St. Louis and Rocky Colavito in Cleveland, and proposed trading the Cardinals' superstar Stan Musial until the owner overruled him.[35] Lane's hyperactivity in baseball's swap mart eventually became an end in itself, but Richards was able to channel the trader's energy in productive directions during their partnership in Chicago.

When Lane shipped pitcher Howie Judson to Cincinnati in December 1952, he disposed of the last holdover from the roster he had inherited four years earlier. The Sox publicity office said he had engineered seventy deals involving 180 players.[36]

Lane pulled off another big one in January 1953, acquiring first baseman Ferris Fain from the Athletics for first baseman Eddie Robinson and others. Fain had won two consecutive AL batting titles. Richards told Robinson that Lane made the trade without consulting him, but it bears Richards's finger-prints. While Fain was a left-handed line-drive hitter who could not match Robinson's power, he was usually among the leaders in on-base percentage (a term still unknown) and was ranked among the top glove men at first. He also came with a reputation as a drinker and a brawler. Although Robinson and Richards had developed a bond, Richards never hesitated to trade one of his favorites if he thought the deal would improve his team. Robinson's two seasons under Richards were the best of his career. He played five more years but said, "Playing ball was never fun for me after I left Paul."[37]

A few days later Lane sent three pitchers to the Red Sox for eight-time all-star Vern Stephens. Stephens was a rare commodity, a power-hitting shortstop. He had belted 231 home runs in eleven full seasons, but he was thirty-two, slowed by a bad knee, and may have been feeling the toll of his heavy drinking. Richards planned to move him to third base, giving the Sox an infield of four former all-stars.

The trades touched off an outbreak of pennant fever in Chicago. Richards told *Time* magazine, "Our goal is the top."[38] But in trying to climb higher than third place, Richards and Lane faced two insurmountable obstacles: the Yankees and the Indians.

The Yankees had been baseball's most successful team since they bought Babe Ruth in 1920. In the early fifties the juggernaut was at its peak, the strongest franchise in the history of the game. Surveying the talent in his dugout, Casey Stengel said, "I'm like a feller who ain't got nothing but caviar to eat."[39]

Cleveland, managed by Richards's former Brooklyn teammate Al Lopez, had assembled a sterling pitching staff that was perfectly suited for its cavernous ballpark. The best pitcher in the Indians' history, Bob Feller, was fading, but they had future Hall of Famers Lemon and Wynn as well as "The Big Bear," Mike Garcia, a barrel-chested Mexican American right-hander who was at least their equal for a few years. Center fielder Larry Doby, the American League's first black player, became a home run and RBI champion. The farm system contributed powerful third baseman Al Rosen, the 1953 AL Most Valuable Player. Second baseman Roberto Avila came from the Mexican League and won the 1954 batting title.

The Yankees and Indians captured every American League pennant from 1947 through 1958. They finished first and second every year from 1951 through 1956, with Cleveland winning only in 1954. Richards made his strongest bid to break up the duopoly in 1953, when the White Sox came home just three games behind second-place Cleveland.

By mid-June Hy Turkin of the *New York Daily News* had pronounced the pennant race "all-but-stone-cold-dead." On June 14 the "Frankensteinish conquering machine known as the New York Yankees" had won eighteen games in a row and opened a ten-and-a-half-game lead over Cleveland. The White Sox were in third place, thirteen and a half back. Richards conceded, "We don't figure to be any serious threat to the pennant romp of the Yankees, nor does anybody else."[40]

Not so fast: A week after their eighteen-win streak ended, the Yankees fell into a nine-game losing streak. Chicago made a run in June and July, winning fourteen of sixteen, and swept a three-game series at Yankee Stadium. In the third game Richards pulled his pitcher switch again. Pierce started but with two right-handed batters due to lead off the ninth, Richards moved him to first base and brought in right-hander Harry Dorish. Stengel countered with a left-handed pinch hitter, Don Bollweg. Richards was stuck because the rules require a new pitcher to face one batter. Bollweg tested first baseman Pierce with a bunt and beat it out, even though Pierce handled the ball cleanly. Richards argued the call and was ejected. Dorish then retired Gil McDougald, and Pierce went back to the mound to finish a 4–2 victory. After Richards used the switch in 1954, the rules were changed to allow a pitcher to move to another position and return to the mound only once during an inning, apparently for fear Richards would delay the game with multiple switches.[41]

The White Sox won eight straight and closed to within four games of New York on July 19 when the Yankees came to Chicago for a doubleheader. At least one hundred people spent the night outside Comiskey Park waiting for the ticket windows to open. A Chicago record crowd of 54,215 watched as the Yankees scored four runs in the ninth to take the first game, 6–2, then completed the sweep behind Vic Raschi's two-hitter. Richards claimed not to be discouraged: "It's a long way to October."[42]

That was the White Sox's high tide. They clung to second place until September 6, when Cleveland beat them in three of four games and passed them. New York ended the 1953 season eight and a half games ahead of the Indians for an unprecedented fifth consecutive pennant and went on to win an unprecedented fifth straight World Series.

The White Sox finished eleven and a half back, but their eighty-nine victories were the most for the franchise since 1920, the last year the Black Sox played. Chicago's offense improved to third best in the league. The pitching staff again was second in runs allowed.

Pierce staked his claim as an elite pitcher, posting eighteen wins and a 2.72 ERA while leading the league in strikeouts and opponents' batting average. Harry Dorish enjoyed the best year of his career with ten victories and eighteen saves, but Dobson and Rogovin declined. Minoso led the team with just fifteen home runs and an .876 OPS and placed fourth in the MVP voting. He and Rivera ranked 1-2 in the league in stolen bases. Rivera and Mele were the only other Sox to reach double figures in home runs.

Lane's big preseason deals did not pay off. Ferris Fain missed more than three weeks in August after he broke a finger in a fight at a nightclub outside Washington, D.C. Richards fined him $600 and commented, "And they wonder why managers go crazy."[43] Fain's batting average fell to .256, although his .750 OPS made him as productive as Eddie Robinson was for Philadelphia—when Fain was able to play. "They hit him third or fourth, and he was trying for the long ball," Pierce recalled, "and his batting average nosedived."[44] Vern Stephens failed to justify his $30,000 salary and was sold to the Browns on waivers in July.

Two midseason trades worked out better. In June the Browns' Bill Veeck was desperate to meet his payroll after fellow owners vetoed his bid to move the league's weakest franchise. He sent his top RBI man, former National League MVP Bob Elliott, and his pitching staff's leading winner, right-hander Virgil Trucks, to Chicago for three players and, more important, $75,000. In 1952 Trucks had pitched two no-hitters for last-place Detroit but won only three other games all season. He claimed to be thirty-four years old (he was thirty-six) but still had some fire left in his arm. He won fifteen games for Chicago, for a total of twenty with both teams, and placed fifth in the MVP voting. Elliott contributed little and was released in the fall.

Tiny Cuban right-hander Sandy Consuegra, acquired from the Senators in May, posted a 2.54 ERA with seven victories. He and Trucks would be the team's most effective pitchers in 1954.

After the season Richards organized a barnstorming team that played against Yankees pitcher Eddie Lopat's traveling band in western cities.[45] Richards had barnstormed every fall since coming to the White Sox, but this was the last time. Major league players had been showcasing their talents in fall visits to minor league towns for decades until television killed that form of baseball entertainment.

As the White Sox traveled north from spring training in 1954, they were scheduled to play a pair of exhibition games against the St. Louis Cardinals in Birmingham, Alabama, the epicenter of southern resistance to integration. The city commission had recently repealed an ordinance prohibiting blacks and whites from playing together in "any game of cards, dice, dominoes, checkers, baseball, softball, football, basketball or similar games," but a group called the Preserve Segregation Committee asked Richards and Cardinals manager Eddie Stanky to bench their black players when they came to Birmingham. Richards wired back, "I am very sorry, but that question of racial segregation was settled more than 2,000 years ago on Mount Calvary. . . . Christ Jesus died for us all." The games went on, with Chicago's Minnie Minoso and Bob Boyd and the Cardinals' Tom Alston in the lineups and black fans restricted to segregated bleachers at Birmingham's Rickwood Field. (The city's voters reinstated the segregation law in a June referendum.)[46]

Richards and Lane were again talking up their pennant hopes as the 1954 season began with a new city on the American League map. The St. Louis Browns moved to Baltimore, but only after AL owners forced their nemesis Bill Veeck to sell the team to a local group. Veeck had outraged fellow owners with his "undignified" but crowd-pleasing stunts—sending a three-foot-seven-inch pinch hitter up to bat was the most famous—and had enraged them when he advocated the "socialistic" notion that the visiting team should get a share of local television revenue. He argued that it took two teams to play a game, so both should be paid.[47]

Chicago started strong and took over first place on May 15, then won eight consecutive games. But the White Sox lost ground while they were winning, because Cleveland won eleven in a row. By the time Chicago's Pierce and Trucks stopped the Indians' streak on May 25, Cleveland had climbed to the top of the standings. Lane sent $100,000 and a utility infielder to Boston for former AL batting champion George Kell, who had been Richards's teammate in Detroit. The thirty-one-year-old Kell was a career .311 hitter and was considered the league's best defender at third.

On May 25 pitching ace Billy Pierce went down with a sore shoulder. He missed almost a month and sometimes needed extra rest between starts after he came back. He won only nine games. The injuries multiplied. Ferris Fain hurt his knee in June and was lost for the season. Six days later Kell tripped over first base and strained knee ligaments. When he returned to the lineup a month later, "playing on one leg," he was used primarily at first base to ease the stress on his knee.[48]

On July 4 Cleveland's Mike Garcia, Ray Narleski, and Early Wynn combined to hold the White Sox to one hit, Minoso's ninth-inning single. The defeat left Chicago in third place, seven games behind the league-leading Indians. Richards lamented, "And if we just had that big guy who would hit 40–50 home runs we'd win the pennant."[49]

They didn't, and they didn't. The White Sox hung around the fringes of the pennant race through July. Rookie left-hander Jack Harshman set a team record when he struck out sixteen Red Sox on July 25. He got many of them with the slip pitch he had learned from Richards. Catcher Matt Batts started calling it "The Thing" after Ted Williams asked him, "What's that thing he's throwing?"[50]

Harshman was a converted first baseman Richards acquired through the old-boy network. The New York Giants had given up on Harshman after a short trial, but Richards's old battery mate Carl Hubbell, head of the Giants' farm system, thought the pitcher showed promise. Hubbell recommended him to Richards because Hubbell wanted to make sure Harshman did not fulfill that promise with another National League team. Chicago bought him after he won twenty-three games for AA Nashville in 1953. Nineteen days after his strikeout performance he pitched a sixteen-inning 1–0 shutout against Detroit and finished the season with fourteen victories.

On July 29 the Yankees whipped the White Sox 10–0, pushing them seven games behind Cleveland and one and a half back of second-place New York. A photographer snapped Richards in the dugout, slumped over and hanging his head, an iconic picture of defeat. He insisted the camera "must have caught me when I was bending down to pick something up." He claimed Chicago was still in the race with fifty-three games to play.[51]

The Yankees reeled off a thirteen-game winning streak in July and a ten-game streak in August but could not catch the Indians. Cleveland took command by winning eleven straight in September on their way to an American League record 111 victories. The Yankees won 103 games, the most of any Stengel team, but their string of consecutive championships ended at five. The White Sox's ninety-four victories would have been enough to win the pennant in some seasons, but they finished third in 1954, seventeen games behind.

Virgil Trucks's 2.79 ERA was the league's fifth best, as he posted nineteen victories, the most by any pitcher under Richards, with a league-leading five shutouts. "Paul's the best manager I ever played for," Trucks said. "He saw me, and knew I had the goods, long before anybody else now in the big leagues."[52] Richards had caught "Fire" Trucks with the Tigers and had tried to sign him for Atlanta as far back as 1938, when he struck out 418 batters in 273 innings in Class D ball. Richards noted that Trucks was considered washed up after he lost nineteen games with Detroit in 1952: "All I can say is, I wish a few more like him would wash up around here."[53]

Two more of Richards's pitching projects, thirty-three-year-old right-handers Bob Keegan and Sandy Consuegra, contributed sixteen wins apiece and made the all-star team. Keegan, originally signed by the Yankees in 1943, had missed time because of military service and was held back by arm trouble.[54] He was thirty-two when he reached the majors in 1953 and had his career year in 1954. Consuegra recorded a 2.69 ERA, second best in the league.

Nellie Fox posted career highs with 201 hits and a .319 average. Twenty-eight of his hits were bunts, and he was thrown out only six times while bunting for a hit. Groundskeeper Gene Bossard helped him by sloping the foul lines inward so Fox's bunts would stay fair.[55] Minoso's .951 OPS was second to Ted Williams's 1.151. (Williams played only 117 games.) Minoso led the league in total bases, slugging percentage, and triples and was in the top five in several other batting categories. By most measures either he or Mickey Mantle was the AL's most productive hitter, though Yogi Berra won the MVP award.

Beginning in 1951, when Frank Lane brought Richards to Chicago, the White Sox posted winning records for the next seventeen years. After both architects were gone, the 1959 "Go-Go" Sox won the franchise's first pennant since the Black Sox with Nellie Fox, Sherman Lollar, and Billy Pierce as key contributors. In four seasons Lane and Richards had turned around a perennial loser.

Now Richards set out to prove he could do it again.

---

1. UP, *New York Times*, October 27, 1951, 28.
2. Donald Honig, *The Man in the Dugout* (Chicago: Follett, 1977), 138.
3. Jonah Keri, ed., *Baseball Between the Numbers* (New York: Basic Books, 2006), 122. The break-even point varies depending on the league's run environment. In a high-scoring league the loss of an out is more damaging.

4. The defensive efficiency rate measures the percentage of batted balls in play that are turned into outs by fielders. It tracks only batted balls that give a fielder a chance to make a play. Ignore strikeouts and home runs because the ball is not put in play, except for the rare inside-the-park homer. The formula is [[equation - hyphens are minus signs]](BFP - H - SO - BB - HBP - 0.6 x E) ÷ (BFP - HR - SO - BB - HBP). BFP stands for "batters faced by pitchers." Errors are multiplied by 0.6 based on the calculation that 60 percent of errors allow a batter to reach base. Other errors, such as wild throws that allow a runner to take an extra base, are ignored. DER is not a pure measure of fielding prowess. It is influenced by ballparks, ground ball/fly ball ratios, line drives allowed, and chance.

5. Bill James and Jim Henzler, *Win Shares* (Morton Grove, Ill.: STATS Publishing, 2002), 685, 694, 702.

6. Ogden Nash, "Behind Umpires' Backs Stars Relax," *Life*, September 19, 1955, 85.

7. *Sporting News* (hereafter *TSN*), July 4, 1951, 19.

8. Among the batters who were hit most often from 1947 to 1960, four of the top ten and nine of the top fifty were black, far more than the proportion of black players in the majors at the time. Minoso is number one on that list.

9. Jules Tygiel, *Baseball's Great Experiment: Jackie Robinson and His Legacy* (New York: Vintage, 1984), 309.

10. *TSN*, November 28, 1951, 2.

11. Paul Richards, "Orestes Minoso: Minnie by a Mile!" *Baseball Stars* (Dell, 1952): 60.

12. *TSN*, November 28, 1951, 2.

13. *Chicago Tribune*, June 11, 1951, B1. Chuck's sister Gracie Lu died in 1952. When his mother, Grace Comiskey, died in 1956, she left the majority ownership to her surviving daughter, Dorothy (*Chicago Tribune*, December 22, 1956, A1). The siblings squabbled for two years until Dorothy sold her controlling interest in the club to a syndicate headed by Bill Veeck in 1959, leaving Chuck with an office and a seat on the board but no duties (Hank Greenberg, *The Story of My Life*, ed. Ira Berkow [New York: Times Books, 1989], 225, 244).

14. *Chicago Tribune*, January 23, 1952, B3.

15. *TSN*, April 16, 1952, 4.

16. *Chicago Tribune*, February 15, 1952, C1; *TSN*, March 23, 1949, 11.

17. *Chicago Tribune*, April 16, 1952, C1.

18. David Gough and Jim Bard, *Little Nel: The Nellie Fox Story* (Alexandria, Va.: D. L. Megbeck Publishing, 2000), 95.

19. Paul Richards, untitled 1970s manuscript "for high school, college and amateur managers and coaches" (hereafter Richards manuscript), in the author's files.

20. Data compiled by Doug Pappas and provided by David Vincent.

21. Tom Keegan, *Ernie Harwell: My Sixty Years in Baseball* (Chicago: Triumph, 2002), 137; Paula Richards, interviews by author, 2006–2008.

22. *Chicago Tribune*, July 29, 1952, B1.

23. *TSN*, October 29, 1952, 19.

24. Ibid.

25. Paul Richards, *Modern Baseball Strategy* (Englewood Cliffs, N.J.: Prentice-Hall, 1955), 12, 205.

26. AP, *Lima (Ohio) News*, February 22, 1976, C8.

27. Steve Treder, "Eddie, Eddie, Eddie and the American League Walkathon," *Hardball Times*, September 1, 2004, www.hardballtimes.com.

28. John Eisenberg, *From 33rd Street to Camden Yards: An Oral History of the Baltimore Orioles* (New York: Contemporary Books, 2001), 28.

29. Richards, *Modern Baseball Strategy*, 43.

30. Larry Dierker, *This Ain't Brain Surgery* (New York: Simon and Schuster, 2003), 89; *New York Times*, September 22, 1968, 198; Richards manuscript.

31. Honig, *Man in the Dugout*, 141.

32. *Salisbury (Md.) Times*, March 21, 1961, 11.

33. Richards, *Modern Baseball Strategy*, 58.
34. Danny Peary, ed., *We Played the Game* (New York: Black Dog and Laventhol, 1994), 169; Eisenberg, *From 33rd Street to Camden Yards*, 27.
35. Stan Musial, as told to Bob Broeg, *The Man's Own Story* (New York: Doubleday, 1964), 177–78.
36. *Chicago Tribune*, January 28, 1953, B1.
37. Eddie Robinson, interview by author, August 18, 2006, Fort Worth, Texas.
38. "The Chicago Idea," *Time*, April 13, 1953, 58–59.
39. *New York World-Telegram*, March 12, 1958, reprinted in Peter Williams, ed., *The Joe Williams Baseball Reader* (Chapel Hill, N.C.: Algonquin, 1989), 169.
40. *TSN*, June 24, 1953, 6, 15.
41. David Nemec, *The Official Rules of Baseball* (New York: Barnes and Noble, 1999), 50.
42. *Chicago Tribune*, July 20, 1953, B2.
43. Ibid., August 4, 1953, B1.
44. Billy Pierce, interview by Thomas Liley, February 24, 1992.
45. *TSN*, October 14, 1953, 20.
46. Bruce Adelson, *Brushing Back Jim Crow: The Integration of Minor League Baseball in the American South* (Charlottesville: University Press of Virginia, 1999), 121–26; *TSN*, April 14, 1954, 20.
47. Gerald Eskanazi, *Bill Veeck: A Baseball Legend* (New York: McGraw-Hill, 1988), 103.
48. *Chicago Tribune*, July 4, 1954, A2; *TSN*, August 18, 1954, 9.
49. *TSN*, June 23, 1954, 11.
50. Ibid., August 4, 1954, 6.
51. Ibid., August 11, 1954, 11.
52. Larry Moffi, *This Side of Cooperstown* (Iowa City: University of Iowa Press, 1996), 18.
53. *Washington Post*, August 29, 1954, TA13.
54. *TSN*, March 2, 1955, 5.
55. Richards, *Modern Baseball Strategy*, 127; Joshua Prager, *The Echoing Green: The Untold Story of Bobby Thomson, Ralph Branca, and the Shot Heard Round the World* (New York: Pantheon, 2006), 67.

CHAPTER 12

"Daring Gamble"

On August 28, 1954, Baltimore newspapers reported that Orioles president Clarence Miles was courting Paul Richards to become the club's general manager. Frank Lane acknowledged that he had given Baltimore permission to contact his manager. "I don't blame anyone else for wanting Richards," Lane said. "We want to keep him. He has done a grand job."[1]

When the St. Louis Browns moved to Baltimore in 1954, the new owners had coveted Lane as their general manager, but Grace Comiskey refused to let him go. Richards's contract was due to expire at the end of the 1954 season. He wanted a three-year extension, but the thrifty Grace Comiskey offered only two. Reports surfaced in Chicago that Richards was tired of Lane's second-guessing (Lane was a notoriously emotional fan who anguished over every pitch) and that the Comiskeys, especially Chuck, resented the fawning publicity lavished on their manager. The *Tribune*'s influential sports columnist, Arch Ward, urged the Comiskeys to give Richards what he wanted: "Can't they remember the dreary years before they hit on a winning combination?"[2]

The Orioles gave Richards what he wanted. He resigned as White Sox manager on September 14, saying the chance to be both general manager and field manager was the deciding factor: "I'm running the show." As to the claims of discord, he insisted he was leaving with "nothing but the kindest feelings" for Lane and the Comiskeys.[3]

Lane grumped, "If he was second-guessed, he was second-guessed into a job that pays him $40,000 per year for four years." The contract was actually for three years with an attendance bonus of five cents for each ticket sold above 800,000. Lane had allowed Baltimore to approach Richards about the general manager's job and was not happy that Richards would also run the team on the field. Richards would have been free to go at the end of the season, so Lane had no recourse. It was widely reported that the Orioles had wanted Richards only as manager but gave in when he insisted on complete control.[4]

After a trip home to Waxahachie, Richards arrived in Baltimore ten days later to meet the local press, looking the part of a front-office executive in his double-breasted pin-striped suit. He told them, "The way I understand it, I am in charge of buying, selling and trading players."[5]

Except for Connie Mack, who had owned and managed the Philadelphia Athletics, no manager since John McGraw had been granted such broad authority. In most organizations the owner and/or general manager made most personnel decisions, while the manager's role was to run the team on the field. Although the manager was called "skipper" after the captain of a ship, sportswriter Ed Linn described the job as "a sort of glorified buck sergeant." Even the most successful pilot of the era, Casey Stengel, complained that Yankees general manager George Weiss sometimes made trades without consulting him.[6]

The Baltimore Orioles were sheep in birds' clothing, the sad-sack St. Louis Browns in black-and-orange plumage. Baltimore had welcomed its new team in 1954 with a parade, a chest-thumping display of civic pride, and an opening day crowd of more than forty-six thousand. Pitcher Duane Pillette thought: "How can they be so happy getting the St. Louis Browns? Don't they know we lost 100 games last year?"[7] The honeymoon ended just six weeks later when the Orioles lost their eighth straight game and the home fans booed them for the first time.[8] Attendance fell off in the second half of the season as the club again lost one hundred times and finished seventh under manager Jimmy Dykes. Baltimore drew slightly more than one million paying customers, nearly four times as many as the 1953 Browns, but far below expectations. The first franchise to change cities in fifty years, the Braves, had attracted a National League record 1.8 million in 1953, their first season in Milwaukee.

The 1954 Orioles stank. Third baseman Vern Stephens, whom Richards had dumped from the White Sox, led the team with just eight home runs and forty-six RBI as they scored the fewest runs in the league. Broadcaster Ernie Harwell quipped: "We called them the Kleenex team. They would pop up one at a time."[9]

Like Richards's home state, the Orioles had a lone star: Bullet Bob Turley, a twenty-four-year-old right-handed fireballer who was hailed as the new Bob Feller. In 1954 Turley led the AL in strikeouts, held opposing hitters to a league-low .203 batting average, and somehow managed a 14-15 record.

Richards traded him.

On November 17 the Orioles and Yankees announced the biggest deal in major league history. Seventeen players changed teams. The key pieces were Turley, smooth-fielding shortstop Billy Hunter, and twenty-five-year-old right-handed pitcher Don Larsen; they went to New York for outfielder Gene Woodling, a mainstay of Stengel's championship clubs; pitchers Harry Byrd and Jim McDonald; shortstop Willy Miranda; and two promising AAA catchers, Gus Triandos and Hal Smith, who were surplus because the Yankees had Yogi Berra and Elston Howard. The teams exchanged several minor leaguers to round out the trade.

The news hit Baltimore like bombs bursting in air. One fan told the Associated Press: "Richards must have lost his mind. When my son saw the papers he groaned so loud I thought his best friend had died." Another said, "It's like trading skilled mechanics for laborers."[10] Paul Menton of the *Baltimore Evening Sun* turned gray sky into purple prose: "Even the clouds were weeping as if to reflect the city's mood at the startling news that Bob Turley had become a Yankee."[11]

Richards had a ready answer: "If we hadn't been willing to trade Turley, we would have had to start next season with the same lineup which finished seventh in 1954. We had to take the initiative." As a result of the deal, he said, the Orioles had "gained a year, maybe two, in our rebuilding plans for a pennant club."[12]

The headlines around the American League said the Yankees had traded their way back into first place. *New York Times* columnist Arthur Daley summed up the conventional wisdom: "You are hereby invited to make early application for tickets to the opening game of the 1955 World Series, which will be played in Yankee Stadium on Sept. 28. The Bronx Bombers clinched next year's pennant yesterday by whisking away from the Baltimore Orioles two youthful strong-armed pitchers and a flashy shortstop in exchange for no one they'll miss."[13] Bill Corum of the *New York Journal-American* chimed in, "They were saying around baseball circles yesterday that George Weiss of the Yankees couldn't have done a more complete job on Paul Richards if he had used a gun."[14] The *Washington Post's* Shirley Povich reflected the despair of the league's also-rans: "The pattern hasn't changed, and it won't, as long as the Yankees can feed on the miseries of the second-division ball clubs and come up with the players they need."[15]

Richards replied, "What concern is it of mine who wins the pennant?. . . I want to get the Orioles out of seventh place."[16] He was applying Branch Rickey's guiding principle: Out of quantity comes quality. The Orioles' farm system had no quality players; the Yankees had more than anyone else. Richards was trading the present for the promise of the future.

A few writers gave him the benefit of the doubt. The *New York Herald-Tribune's* Red Smith said: "He is an exceptionally sound baseball man whose judgment must be respected. It is not inconceivable that this daring gamble may pay off. . . . The deal can't be bad for the Yankees. It may also be good for the Orioles."[17] Ed McAuley of the *Cleveland News* agreed: "With Bob Turley, the Orioles finished a bad seventh. Without him, they can hardly do much worse, and they may do a great deal better."[18]

Richards promised there were "more changes to come."[19] Within a month he completed a seven-player trade with his former Chicago partner Frank Lane, but the players involved were all journeymen. Richards sent two minor leaguers and $55,000 to Brooklyn for third baseman Billy Cox and left-handed pitcher Preacher Roe. Both had played important roles in winning pennants for the Dodgers, but they were past their thirty-fifth birthdays. Richards defended his deal for the senior citizens: "I know I have talked about building with young-sters. But I also want to put a presentable team out there by next April. This is one of those times we have to compromise while we develop the kids."[20] Roe chose to retire and acknowledged that he was thirty-nine years old, not thirty-seven as the record books said. The Dodgers sent right-hander Erv Palica to Baltimore in his place.

Richards plucked more veterans off the scrap heap. Pitcher Saul Rogovin had slipped back to the minors after enjoying his only success with Richards as his manager. Right-hander Jim Wilson, who had pitched for Richards in Buffalo and Seattle, came from the Braves for $40,000. Wilson had pitched a no-hitter in 1954 but was thirty-three years old.

Richards prescribed his favorite old-school remedies for a pitcher's sore arm: he ordered new acquisition Bill Miller and rookie Ray Moore to have their tonsils removed and told Moore to get some teeth pulled.[21]

He and other Orioles executives barnstormed around Maryland and Pennsylvania during the winter to drum up interest in the team. He returned to Crisfield for the first time since he played there in 1927. More than two hundred people welcomed him at a testimonial dinner, shouting, "We're with you, Paul." The guests included his old manager, Dan Pasquella, and Maryland state comptroller J. Millard Tawes, who, as treasurer of the Crabbers, had signed Richards's meager paychecks.[22]

Richards surrounded himself with a cadre of loyal assistants. He brought coach Luman Harris with him from Chicago. Harris had become a vital buffer between Richards and his players, an affable complement to the stern manager. Al Vincent, who coached for Detroit during World War II and managed against Richards in the Dixie Series in 1938, joined the staff. High school teammate Jimmy Adair was named manager of the Class D farm club in Paris, Texas. Sixty-three-year-old Dutch Dietrich signed on as a scout. As he had in Chicago, Richards kept the incumbent pitching coach, Harry Brecheen. A left-handed star who won three games in the 1946 World Series for the Cardinals, "Harry the Cat" finished his career with the Browns and came with the franchise to Baltimore. By all accounts the two worked well together, but Richards's confidence in his own knowledge of pitchers likely left his pitching coach with little authority.

Asserting his control over the organization, Richards summoned the Orioles' scouts and minor league managers to a "school" in San Antonio, home of their Texas League farm club. The first item on the agenda: a study of the rule book, "because 90 per cent of the people, including the players, don't know the rules." After repeating his mantra—"most games are lost, not won"—he said: "We hope that in this school we will bring out things that will help our managers and scouts teach our players basic fundamentals so that they will not make so many errors of omission. We will not discuss mechanical errors . . . you're going to have them as long as baseball is played."[23] After all, even Ty Cobb could drop an easy fly ball.

In the spring of 1955 Prentice-Hall published Richards's book, *Modern Baseball Strategy*. Instead of the anecdotes and reminiscences featured in most sports books, it was a serious, detailed guide for managers and coaches. That spring also saw the first publication (in the *Sporting News*) of Baltimore broadcaster Ernie Harwell's sentimental essay, "A Game for All America." He wrote: "Baseball is ballet without music. Drama without words. A carnival without kewpie dolls."[24]

The Orioles were more pratfall than ballet, more slapstick than drama, and a carnival with fun-house mirrors. The team Richards assembled was a collection of benchwarmers, has-beens, and never-would-be's. Only three of them had appeared in as many as 125 games the previous year: outfielders Chuck Diering and Cal Abrams and second baseman Bobby Young. None resembled an elite talent. Gene Woodling, the blocky thirty-two-year-old outfielder acquired in the Turley trade, was the best of the Orioles, but he had been a platoon player for New York, just one cog in Casey Stengel's machine. Richards was counting on him to play every day and bat cleanup. The *Sporting News* poll of writers picked Baltimore to repeat in seventh place.[25]

When the players arrived for spring training in Daytona Beach, Florida, Richards supervised two-a-day practices, moving around the field to give individual instruction to rookies and veterans alike. Dick Williams, a utility player for Baltimore and later a Hall of Fame manager, described how Richards and another manager he admired, Bobby Bragan, conducted spring training:

They began by taking the whole ball club to the on-deck circle. "This is what we do here. This is what we do going up to the plate as far as looking at the coaches and getting the sign is concerned." They talked about every play, offensively and defensively, around the home plate area. Same thing between home and first, how to run the bases. First base, breaks and leads. Offensive and defensive plays at first, second, short, third. Same thing in the outfield. All phases of the game. It used to take Richards about three days to get around the whole park, doing it for about two hours at a time. . . . It's like going back to kindergarten, so to speak.[26]

In Baltimore the anger over the Turley trade was replaced by excitement about the Orioles' new look. The team cut ticket prices and claimed season-ticket sales were running 90 percent ahead of the previous year.[27] (This is questionable, given the enthusiasm generated by the club's move to Baltimore in 1954.) As opening day approached, the new boss tried to tamp down extravagant expectations: "Don't look for any miracles. We're probably a year and a half away from being a serious pennant contender."[28] Even that forecast would prove to be extravagantly optimistic.

President Eisenhower threw out the first ball when Baltimore opened the 1955 season in Washington. The Orioles lost, 12–5. The next day they dropped their home opener to Boston, 7–1, as the Red Sox knocked out Richards's pitching ace, Joe Coleman, after two innings. Only about thirty-eight thousand fans turned out, eight thousand less than Memorial Stadium's capacity.

The Orioles lost their first six games. When Richards released the team's leading "slugger," Vern Stephens, barely a week into the season, only four players were left from the Browns who had come to Baltimore a year before. The roster included eight ex-Yankees.

Richards got his first victory on April 20 against New York. He also drew his first ejection as Orioles manager when umpire Red Flaherty tossed him for arguing balls and strikes. Four days later Saul Rogovin went ten innings to beat Washington, 2–1. "This was the best game I ever pitched," he exulted.[29] It was his only win for Baltimore; by July he had lost eight and was released. Richards used a different lineup in each of the first nineteen games. Baltimore lost fourteen of them. He tried nine starting pitchers in the first thirty games.

Orioles president Clarence Miles had promised to spend "whatever it takes" to build a winner, and Richards took him up on it.[30] Richards left the team several times to scout young players. In April he signed his first "bonus baby," Jim Pyburn, a twenty-one-year-old third baseman and outfielder who had been an All-Southeastern Conference end on Auburn's football team.

Pyburn said he was paid $48,000 in a combination of bonus and two years' guaranteed salary.[31] The signing revealed Richards's preference for tools over skills, in the language of scouts—youngsters with great athletic ability rather than baseball know-how. "Toolsy" players were Richards's weakness. He signed many, but few succeeded.

An eighteen-year-old third baseman from Monroe, Louisiana, Wayne Causey, received $32,000 plus a guarantee of three years at a $6,000 annual salary, big league money. High school pitcher Bruce Swango got at least $36,000. The right-hander signed with the Orioles even though fellow Oklahoman Mickey Mantle had called to recruit him for the Yankees.[32]

After the Swango signing, Baltimore papers reported that Richards had exhausted his $250,000 budget for player acquisitions and the owners had told him to holster his checkbook. President Miles denied it, and Richards continued to spend. In June he signed catcher Tommy Gastall, a quarterback at Boston University, and Bob Nelson, a high school first baseman from Dallas, for a reported $40,000 each.[33] (Published reports of the bonuses paid to young players varied widely.) The team's accountant, Joe Hamper, remembered: "Overnight, we went from a conservative organization to a very aggressive and, in some respects, reckless organization. It was a complete change in philosophy and a nightmare for those of us on the financial side, but the end result was the mentality that we were competitive and weren't going to back off."[34]

The bonus boys not only cost money, they displaced major league players. In a futile effort to hold down bonuses, baseball rules required any amateur player who was paid more than $4,000 to spend two years on the major league roster. They seldom played, but "Richards wanted us working out all the time," Causey recalled. "The bonus babies would have to come in and work out on the morning after night games, or when the team was coming off road trips. All the time."[35]

To compensate for the heavy outlays Richards unloaded most of his high-salaried veterans. Gene Woodling was batting only .221 and "was being booed out of town," in his words.[36] Woodling and Billy Cox, each of whom was making more than $20,000, went to Cleveland on June 15 for thirtysomething journeymen outfielders Wally Westlake, who was soon released, and Dave Pope. (Cox retired and the Orioles had to give the Indians some cash.) Pitcher Harry Byrd, who had come from the Yankees in the Turley deal, was sold to the White Sox for a reported $50,000. Backup catcher Les Moss brought another $25,000 from Chicago. Joe Coleman, a thirteen-game winner in 1954 but sore-armed in 1955, was released. None of the players Richards acquired was paid more than $15,000.[37]

Dave Pope was the first black player Richards brought to Baltimore. He was a thirty-four-year-old Negro League veteran who failed to produce as a left-handed-batting platoon outfielder. Two other African Americans, pitcher Jehosie Heard and young outfielder Joe Durham, had had brief trials with the 1954 Orioles.

No matter who wore the Orioles uniform, the results were the same. By July 4 the team had settled at the bottom of the standings with a 21–53 record. Fewer than seven thousand people attended the holiday game. A discontented fan complained, "Why should I pay big league prices to see a high school team play?" One local paper headlined: "Found: A Fan Who Likes Richards." Jimmy Breslin, a young reporter for the Newspaper Enterprise Association syndicate, called Richards "bewildered," a word nobody else ever applied to him. The manager told Breslin: "It's brutal. I didn't expect anything like this."[38]

Richards told another reporter, "Some spring, maybe three-four-five years from now, there'll be a fine young Oriole team out on our field to open the major league season and all I ask is that you observe ten seconds of silence in memory of Paul Richards—that's just in case, of course, that I'm not still here by then."[39]

Baltimore was shut out fifteen times in the first half of the season. Richards considered shortening the fences at Memorial Stadium to generate runs. The ballpark was a huge, oddly shaped layout, built for football. Center field was 450 feet deep and the left- and right-center power alleys were almost equally distant. Outfielder Gil Coan said, "You could use five outfielders out there."[40] White houses beyond center field reflected sunlight into batters' eyes. One day Richards had groundskeepers stretch a rope across the outfield during batting practice to see how a smaller field would play. Sportswriters suggested he concentrate on rebuilding the team rather than the park.[41]

He continued to shuffle personnel, trying out nearly anyone he could find. Bob Hale, a twenty-one-year-old first baseman for the Orioles' Class B farm team in York, Pennsylvania, impressed Richards during a midseason exhibition game and found himself instantly promoted to the majors. Hale hit .357 in 182 at-bats for Baltimore and stuck around for several years as a left-handed pinch hitter. The Orioles used fifty-five players during the season, including nineteen starting pitchers. Richards even begged his forty-year-old pitching coach to take the mound, but Brecheen refused.[42] When pitcher Duane Pillette was sent to the minors in July, none of the 1953 Browns remained.

In his most shocking move Richards released bonus pitcher Bruce Swango just two months after he was signed. The teenager had never appeared in a game. The Orioles put out the word that Swango had stage fright and could not pitch in front of crowds, but scout Jim Russo said that was a cover story: "The truth was he couldn't get the ball over the plate even in batting practice."[43]

"The Bruce Swango signing was when Paul decided he wasn't a very good scout," pitcher and future scout Bill Wight recalled. "Later on, when I was scouting for [Richards] he never went to a game by himself. He always went with three or four scouts and never gave an opinion until they gave their opinions. He was a brilliant baseball man, but he didn't have the knack for scouting."[44]

To alleviate the shortage of useful players, Richards placed Jim Pyburn on the disabled list with a bad back. A suspicious commissioner Ford Frick demanded an explanation. The commissioner ruled that teams would have to produce a doctor's statement before a bonus baby could go on the disabled list, and any time spent on the DL would not count against the player's two years on the roster.

Frick also refused to allow the veteran pitcher Don Johnson to go on the DL when Richards claimed he had a sore arm. Johnson said it was not so and accused Richards of damaging his reputation. Finally, the commissioner declared a Baltimore minor leaguer, Vincent Pignatello, a free agent because the pitcher claimed he had not received the salary he was promised.[45]

Symbolic of the Orioles' dismal season, their best-pitched game was a no-hitter that wasn't. On August 31 in Cleveland, Skinny Brown, in his third tour of duty under Richards, relieved Wight in the first inning after the Indians had scored five runs with nobody out. Brown finished the game with eight hitless innings (Cleveland, with the lead, did not bat in the bottom of the ninth), but it was not an official no-hitter.[46]

At least nobody could say the Orioles quit. They won fifteen of their last twenty games to vault over Washington into seventh place, thirty-nine games behind the pennant-winning Yankees. The Orioles' 57-97 record was three wins better than the year before.

The commissioner publicly chastised Richards again in September. This time Richards was caught hiding bonus pitcher Tom Borland by using him in an exhibition game under the name "Moreland." Baltimore had signed the Oklahoma A&M star for $40,000 but never filed his contract with the league office and sold him to Oakland of the Pacific Coast League in a flagrant violation of the bonus rule. Frick declared Borland a free agent, fined the club $2,000 and Richards $2,500, and put him on probation. Richards offered his resignation, but club president Miles refused to accept it and declared, "As long as I have anything to do with the club, Paul Richards will guide the destinies of the Orioles."[47]

Miles did not last long. The aristocratic lawyer owned just a small share of the team; he was the front man for several prominent business executives who had put up most of the money and sat on the board of directors. Resentment of Richards's spending and Miles's one-man rule had been building among them. "They were all powerful, successful men, and sometimes powerful, successful men don't make a great team," said Jack Dunn III, grandson of the owner of the minor league Orioles and now Richards's assistant.[48] Several directors were aghast at the money wasted on Bruce Swango and embarrassed by the underhanded dealings Commissioner Frick had revealed.

In November home builder James Keelty Jr. replaced Miles as president and operating head of the club, with investment banker Joseph Iglehart as board chairman. Both served without pay. Miles calculated that the franchise had spent $700,000 on player acquisitions during its first two years, most of it on Richards's watch. Jack Dunn later said, "Paul was the only man in baseball who had an unlimited budget and exceeded it."[49] After meeting with his new bosses, Richards said there would be no more big bonuses. Even then he hedged: he would gladly pay top dollar if he found the next Babe Ruth or Ted Williams.[50]

Keelty made a pilgrimage to the commissioner's office and promised that the club would sin no more. Frick agreed to lift Richards's probation, but it would not be the last time Richards was accused of flouting the rules. Stories continued to circulate that he paid young players under the table to get around the bonus limits, although many other clubs were accused of doing the same. Accountant Joe Hamper recalled a lockbox full of cash in the Orioles' offices: "I don't know that Richards had a key, but he always indicated where the money should go." Jim Russo said Richards used friends as bagmen to pass money to young players. "The only problem with the [bonus] rule was that it made liars out of people," Russo declared.[51]

Richards later scoffed at "the infamous bonus rule that nobody paid any attention to. I guess I was the only one that got caught." With a chuckle he added, "Of course, the clubs put the money under the table or something, or gave it to the old man [the player's father]."[52] One popular ploy was to give the father a job as a scout. Commissioner Frick attempted to ban that practice, without success.

Richards's first year running the show was a flop. He was found guilty of cheating and escaped a suspension only because Frick felt it would be too damaging to the team.[53] Attendance dropped by 20 percent. The Orioles' record barely improved. The wizard could not transform lead into gold, or even brass. He resorted to frantic wheeling and dealing that produced few quality players while loading the team with over-age journeymen and under-age bonus boys who took up roster spots but made no contribution.

His "daring gamble," the eye-popping trade with the Yankees, brought Gus Triandos, who played mostly at first base in 1955 but eventually became a power-hitting all-star catcher, and Willy Miranda, the regular shortstop for several years until his slick glove could no longer carry his slack bat. (Ernie Harwell remarked, "They said Willy hit left, right and seldom.")[54] Catcher Hal Smith showed no power and was traded the next year. No one else acquired in the trade contributed much. On the other end of the deal Bob Turley's seventeen victories in 1955 helped the Yankees reclaim the pennant. He later won a Cy Young Award. Don Larsen was a useful pitcher for Casey Stengel and made history with his perfect game in the 1956 World Series. The Yankees later traded him as part of the deal that brought them Roger Maris. Billy Hunter, who was supposed to replace the aging Phil Rizzuto at shortstop in New York, proved to be Miranda without the Cuban accent. On balance, the Yankees got the better of the trade. Later Richards said his only regret was trading *both* Turley and Larsen.[55]

Just one of Richards's first crop of expensive bonus babies went on to a significant career: Wayne Causey played eleven seasons, most of them as a utility infielder. Little noticed among the gaudy contracts, the Orioles' most important signing in 1955 cost them only $4,000.

---

1. *Chicago Tribune*, August 28, 1954, A1.
2. *Sporting News* (hereafter *TSN*), January 26, 1955, 15; *Chicago Tribune*, August 31, 1954, B1.
3. *Chicago Tribune*, September 15, 1954, C1; *TSN*, September 22, 1954, 5.
4. *TSN*, January 26, 1955, 15; Ed Linn, "The Double Life of Paul Richards," *Sport*, August 1955, 55.
5. AP, *Chicago Tribune*, September 25, 1954, B3.
6. Linn, "Double Life of Paul Richards," 49.
7. John Eisenberg, *From 33rd Street to Camden Yards: An Oral History of the Baltimore Orioles* (New York: Contemporary Books, 2001), 16.
8. *TSN*, June 9, 1954, 9.
9. Tom Keegan, *Ernie Harwell: My Sixty Years in Baseball* (Chicago: Triumph, 2002), 136.
10. AP, *New York Times*, November 19, 1954, 28.
11. *TSN*, December 1, 1954, 18.
12. Ibid., November 24, 1954, 3–4.
13. *New York Times*, November 19, 1954, 30.
14. *TSN*, December 1, 1954, 18.
15. *Washington Post*, November 19, 1954, 39.
16. James Edward Miller, *The Baseball Business: Pursuing Pennants and Profits in Baltimore* (Chapel Hill: University of North Carolina Press, 1990), 47.
17. *TSN*, November 24, 1954, 25.
18. Ibid., December 1, 1954, 18.
19. Ibid., December 8, 1954, 21.
20. Ibid., December 22, 1954, 7.
21. Ibid., January 19, 1955, 14, and December 29, 1954, 22.
22. *Salisbury (Md.) Times*, January 12, 1955, 10, and January 13, 1955, 12.
23. *TSN*, February 2, 1955, 17.
24. Ibid., April 13, 1955, 12.
25. Ibid., February 16, 1955, 15, and April 13, 1955, 5.
26. Donald Honig, *The Man in the Dugout* (Chicago: Follett, 1977), 201.
27. *TSN*, November 24, 1954, 21, and February 9, 1955, 25.
28. Ibid., March 30, 1955, 22.
29. Ibid., May 4, 1955, 11.
30. *Baltimore Sun*, October 29, 2003, online edition.
31. Jim Pyburn, interview by Brent Kelley, September 19, 1991.
32. Wayne Causey, undated interview by Brent Kelley; *TSN*, June 1, 1955, 8.
33. *TSN*, June 22, 1955, 9; July 6, 1955, 12; June 29, 1955, 10.
34. *Baltimore Sun*, October 25, 2003, online edition.
35. Ibid., September 16, 2006, online edition.
36. Larry Moffi, *This Side of Cooperstown* (Iowa City: University of Iowa Press, 1996), 56.
37. *TSN*, June 22, 1955, 9.
38. Newspaper Enterprise Association, *Joplin (Mo.) Globe*, July 2, 1955, 6.
39. *TSN*, July 27, 1955, 12.
40. Eisenberg, *From 33rd Street to Camden Yards*, 13.
41. *TSN*, July 13, 1955, 25.
42. Harry Brecheen, interview by Rick Bradley, October 26, 1992.

43. Eisenberg, *From 33rd Street to Camden Yards*, 42; Jim Russo, with Bob Hammel, *SuperScout* (Chicago: Bonus Books, 1992), 39.

44. Eisenberg, *From 33rd Street to Camden Yards*, 45.

45. *TSN*, August 10, 1955, 8; March 28, 1956, 28; August 10, 1955, 8.

46. Ibid., September 14, 1955, 17.

47. Ibid., September 28, 1955, 18; October 12, 1955, 16; October 19, 1955, 26.

48. J. Miller, *Baseball Business*, 48.

49. Ibid., 47–48.

50. *TSN*, December 7, 1955, 8.

51. J. Miller, *Baseball Business*, 48; Kevin Kerrane, *Dollar Sign on the Muscle* (New York: Fireside/ Simon and Schuster, 1989), 28; *Baltimore Sun*, October 25, 2003, online edition; Russo, *Super-Scout*, 43, 28–29.

52. Paul Richards, interview by Clark Nealon, February 5, 1981.

53. *TSN*, September 28, 1955, 18.

54. Eisenberg, *From 33rd Street to Camden Yards*, 33.

55. *TSN*, June 24, 1959, 1.

CHAPTER 13

The Oriole Way

T he letter from Lindsay Deal of Little Rock, Arkansas, who had played the outfield for Richards in Atlanta, introduced the Orioles to the young man who would become their first signature player:

February 13, 1955

Dear Paul,

I am writing you in regard to a kid named Brooks Robinson. I think he measures up to having a good chance in major league baseball. I think he is a natural third baseman, although he has been playing both second and third.[1]

Richards sent scout Dutch Dietrich to look at the boy. When Dietrich brought back a favorable report, the club's top scout, Fred Hofman, followed up and seconded Dietrich's recommendation. As soon as Robinson graduated from high school, the Orioles gave him a $4,000 bonus and flew him to Baltimore.[2]

When it came to Robinson, the competing factions in the Orioles' front office agreed. Dietrich was Richards's man. He had scouted Richards in high school and scouted for him with the Atlanta Crackers, Chicago, Baltimore, and later Houston and the Atlanta Braves.[3] "Bootnose" Hofman, a former catcher who was once Babe Ruth's roommate, was part of the scouting and player development team Richards inherited along with its chief, Jim McLaughlin.

McLaughlin had joined the Browns' front office in 1937 and was the only executive retained when the franchise moved to Baltimore. Soon after Richards took over as general manager, he summoned the forty-year-old McLaughlin to a breakfast meeting. "It was supposed to be my last meal," McLaughlin said.

When I got there, he must have expected me to defend the farm system, but I told him the truth: it was horseshit. We didn't have anything, because we hadn't been able to spend enough money. But I showed him how we might turn things around, and so he kept me on—and a few weeks later at a sports banquet I heard Richards give this speech about the farm system, and it was word-for-word what I'd told him. He just left out "horseshit." I knew I had him then: he didn't know any more than what I'd said.

McLaughlin was as arrogant, opinionated, and stubborn as Richards, so they were not destined to be friends. McLaughlin was determined to bring a scientific approach to appraising young players. He ridiculed the old-school scouts who believed "they could tell about a kid's makeup just by looking at him"—what they called "the good face." He pioneered physical and psycholog-ical testing of players. He devised a circular chart that he labeled "The Whole Ball Player." The top half covered the player's speed, arm strength, hitting, and other visible tools. McLaughlin instructed his scouts to learn about the bottom half of the circle, traits that "cannot be seen with the eye": intelligence, desire, teachability, family background, habits. He brought in FBI agents to teach scouts how to conduct a background investigation. He sent minor league managers to seminars designed by Dale Carnegie, the author of *How to Win Friends and Influence People*, to improve their communications skills.[4] "This may sound strange," one of the scouts, Hank Peters, said of McLaughlin, "but he didn't have a great love for baseball. He wasn't a guy who liked to go and sit at ball games."[5] McLaughlin was an administrator—a bureaucrat—who insisted on central control and was one of the first to use cross-checkers rather than betting on the opinion of a single scout: "We need a check and balance system with several scouts passing judgment, including the area supervisor." Another scout, Jim Russo, said, "He was years ahead of his time, a brilliant baseball guy."[6]

Most important, McLaughlin hired and trained the young men who would build the Orioles into the majors ' most successful team during a twenty-year period, from the sixties to the eighties. They included future Baltimore general managers Peters and Harry Dalton; future major league managers George Bamberger, Billy Hunter, Cal Ripken Sr., and the incendiary Earl Weaver, who led the Orioles to their greatest heights without taking the Dale Carnegie course.

Richards relied on his own coterie of trusted scouts, including Dietrich, Jimmy Adair, and later Hal Newhouser and Eddie Robinson, plus his contacts all over the country. When he got a tip like the one on Brooks Robinson, he would send his man to look at the player without informing McLaughlin. Harry Dalton said: "Paul would get a call from one of his cronies saying, 'This kid, boy, you've got to sign him.' And we would instantly give him $30,000, $50,000, $70,000, whatever it took."[7]

When the Browns moved to Baltimore, their farm system was the least productive in baseball, yet they had one of the largest organizations with thirteen teams. McLaughlin recommended dropping some of the farm clubs and putting the money into scouting, and Richards agreed.[8]

McLaughlin had established a minor league spring training base in the piney woods near Thomasville, Georgia, at an abandoned rest home for war veterans. It had eight military-style barracks with space for thirty cots in each, an administration building, a kitchen and dining hall, and four diamonds. Hundreds of hopefuls practiced together, wearing hand-me-down uniforms and numbers that rose into triple digits. The atmosphere was all baseball, all the time. Two ping-pong tables provided the only entertainment. There was nothing to do but play and talk baseball. This was not a new idea; Branch Rickey originated it with the St. Louis Cardinals and Brooklyn Dodgers.[9]

In 1956 the Thomasville camp opened with 236 players. Richards's top coach, the silver-haired Al Vincent, was in charge. Dozens of nonprospects had to be culled from the final rosters of the nine remaining farm clubs. The managers met with McLaughlin every evening at seven to make the cuts. Gathered in a conference room called the Bird's Nest, they graded each player on a scale of 1 (the best) to 4 in hitting, pitching, running, throwing, and power, but the grading was not exactly scientific. Earl Weaver observed, "Often one of us would rate a player one while two others would rate him a three or four in the same category." When the group decided to release a player, one of the managers had to give him the bad news. "Some of them cry, others get mad, a few go crazy," Weaver said. "One pulled a knife on me." The Bird's Nest sessions, over beer and cold cuts, lasted deep into the night, a time for the managers, scouts, and coaches to shoot the breeze and bond. "Some of those Thomasville days were the best days of my baseball life," Harry Dalton remembered.[10]

Cal Ripken Sr. said Richards prepared a "very small baseball manual" for the instructors. Dalton, Weaver, Ripken, and others later expanded it into a bigger book that guided the club's player development for decades. The bible came to be called "The Oriole Way," though those words did not appear in the original.[11] A later Baltimore catcher, Elrod Hendricks, said the Oriole Way meant "never beat yourself. And that's why we won so many close games. We let the other team make mistakes and beat themselves, and when the opportunity came we'd jump on it."[12] It was Richards's credo: Most games are lost rather than won.

Tension between the McLaughlin and Richards fiefdoms hung thick over the Orioles organization and spilled into Thomasville. Weaver recalled that Richards "would bring the minor league managers down to spring training and show us how he wanted things taught, so the instruction was all the same at every level." But scout Walter Youse said: "Every year Richards would send a representative down to the minor league camp in Thomasville, Georgia, and have him teach the players to do things Richards's way. But over on another field McLaughlin would be teaching them a different way."[13]

Despite continual conflict, McLaughlin stayed in the key player-development role for six years. He said, "Where Richards and I saw eye-to-eye was on pitching, the priority it ought to have in building the farm system."[14] McLaughlin's mission was to find promising young pitchers; Richards's passion was to develop them into winners.

More than eighty players had passed through the Orioles' roster during Richards's first year. He named Gus Triandos, Hal Smith, Willy Miranda, and Bob Hale as the team's foundation. He said the surprising Hale, who jumped from Class B to the majors and batted .357 in limited duty, was "too good to be true." (He was right.) Then he sent the youngster to have his tonsils removed. Bonus baby Wayne Causey got the same prescription. "We led the major leagues every year in, of all things, tonsillectomies," scout Jim Russo said. "Paul was from the old school that said, 'There's got to be poison in your system if you've got an injury'. . . and it was all silly and unnecessary."[15]

Catcher Hal Smith was named to the *Sporting News*'s 1955 rookie all-star team. He posted a respectable .271 batting average, but his "B.A. with bases on balls," or on-base percentage, was just .318, and he hit only four home runs. Triandos's twelve homers led the team. Baltimore writers and broadcasters chose Miranda as the Orioles' most valuable player. The switch-hitter enjoyed his career year at the plate with a line of .255/.313/.310 and hit his only home run inside the park, over the heads of outfielders who played him shallow. He never batted better than .217 again.

As Richards prepared for his second season in Baltimore in 1956, the farm system had nothing to offer. "Our youth movement will begin paying big dividends in a couple of years," he said.[16] In the meantime he scavenged scraps from other clubs as he scrambled to improve his ninety-seven-loss team. He acquired veteran utility infielder Bobby Adams and drafted Bob Boyd, who had fallen back to the minors after playing for Richards in Chicago. In Boyd and Hale, the Orioles had two left-handed first basemen with no power at what was traditionally a power position.

Richards and his family spent the Christmas season on the road. He drove to the West Coast for contract talks with some of the team's California players, then headed to Scottsdale, Arizona, to inspect his new spring training facilities. When he passed through Baltimore in January for the first time since the end of the season, some sportswriters griped that a general manager, unlike a manager, was supposed to work year-round. (If Richards was not in town, the writers had no stories.) Asked to predict how the Orioles would do in 1956, he blew off the question: "We'll finish in the league."[17]

When spring training opened, just seventeen of the forty-one players returned from Richards's first camp a year earlier. Outfielder Chuck Diering was the only holdover from the original Orioles of 1954. Baltimore's opening day lineup included only three men who had started the 1955 opener: Triandos, Smith, and Miranda. Besides them and twenty-two-year-old rookie center fielder Tito Francona, just back from the army, the rest of the starting position players were journeymen older than thirty.

After three straight losses in Boston, the club came home to find Memorial Stadium a bit cozier. Richards had moved in the fences, reducing the straightaway center field distance to 425 feet from 450, but the power alleys on each side were still a formidable 405. He said, "It's discouraging to hit a ball 430 feet to center field and have it caught."[18] Triandos celebrated with a homer to beat Washington 3–2 for the Orioles' first victory, but the attendance, 29,083 in chilly weather, was the smallest of the franchise's three openers.

Soon the Baltimore shuffle started again. Richards bought twenty-eight-year-old utility infielder Billy Gardner from the Giants and made him the regular second baseman. He took on another pitching project, twenty-six-year-old Billy Loes, sold on waivers by the Dodgers. The talented Loes had pitched for three Brooklyn pennant winners but was better known as an eccentric—a "flake," in baseball lingo. He said he didn't want to win twenty games because the team would expect him to do it again every year. He once explained that he had lost a ground ball in the sun. He complained of a chronic sore shoulder, but International News Service writer John Barrington said, "Dodger officials indicated a suspicion that the inflamed tendons might be located somewhat north of Billy's shoulder." Richards, suspecting that the problem was north of the shoulder but south of the brain, sent Loes to have three teeth pulled.[19]

The Orioles showed early signs of life. Their record climbed to 15-15 on May 16; it was the first time they had been at .500 after May 1 since coming to Baltimore. Richards shuffled the deck again. He traded his best hitter for average, thirty-six-year-old outfielder Dave Philley, and his top pitcher, thirty-four-year-old Jim Wilson, to the White Sox for his friend George Kell, pitchers Connie Johnson and Mike Fornieles, and outfielder Bob Nieman. Kell was thirty-three and slowed by a bad knee and back, but he had hit .312/.389/.429 for Chicago in 1955. Nieman was primarily a platoon player with some right-handed power. Johnson, a six-foot-four, thirty-three-year-old veteran of the Negro Leagues, had pitched for Richards in 1953. The deal looked like a steal for Baltimore. By this time Frank Lane had left Chicago, and Chuck Comiskey and his brother-in-law, John Rigney, were running the club in an uneasy partnership. It is likely that they wanted to shed Kell's $40,000 salary.

The trade touched off speculation that Richards intended to install the respected veteran Kell as the Orioles' manager and move into the front office full time. That speculation continued as long as Richards and Kell wore the same uniform, but Richards consistently denied it. Kell later said it was true.[20] He was one of the few players who had a personal relationship with Richards. They played golf together, and Kell even got away with needling him: "I teased him that he probably stood in front of the mirror every morning and said, 'I'm Paul Richards and I'm tough.'"[21]

The acquisition of Johnson came just a few days after Richards swapped outfielder Dave Pope back to Cleveland. Pope and first baseman Bob Boyd had been the only black players on the club. Baltimore's black newspaper, the *Afro-American*, questioned whether a racial quota was in force.[22] In fact, Pope had contributed next to nothing.

The Orioles' 15-12 record in May gave them their first winning month in Baltimore. They were just half a game behind fourth-place Boston on May 31. But when the June 15 trading deadline arrived, Richards contemplated desperate measures—or else concocted an elaborate joke. He offered to trade his entire roster for the roster of the Kansas City Athletics, who were trailing the Orioles in the standings. He may have been serious; although the A's finished last that year, they had more decent young talent than Baltimore. The infielders—flashy first baseman Vic Power, second baseman Jim Finigan, third baseman Hector Lopez, and shortstop Joe DeMaestri—were no older than twenty-eight, and Art Ditmar was a young, hard-throwing right-handed starter. The Athletics' general manager, Parke Carroll, apparently took the offer seriously but said he could not reach the team's owner to get approval in the few hours remaining before the midnight deadline.[23]

On June 15 the Orioles began an unusually long road trip that took them to every other city in the league. Playing seventeen of the next twenty-one games on the road, they lost fourteen of them to fall ten games under .500. That ended their hopes for a first-division finish. Richards later wrote:

Some of the games we lost were due to the kind of mistakes that are unpardonable. We'd let a rival runner work his way out of a run-down play, or throw the ball to the wrong base—or one of our hitters would forget to touch first on a double. After one comedy of errors that cost us a game against Washington, I locked the clubhouse door and made a brief speech to my players. "I wonder who named you fellows the Baltimore Orioles," I said. "You look more like the Baltimore Clowns to me."[24]

During a stop in Cleveland the club blew a 9–1 lead and lost. In an unusual lapse Richards ripped several players in the newspapers. When one unidentified Oriole was quoted making remarks that the manager deemed detrimental to the team, Richards locked the press out of the clubhouse and decreed that any interview with a player had to be conducted in his presence. After the writers raised the predictable furor, he reopened the doors a few days later.[25]

Although most sportswriters in Richards's day were far less aggressive and less critical than later, his relations with them were testy. He feuded with sports editors Jesse A. Linthicum of the *Sun* and Rodger H. Pippen of the *News-Post*, two old bulls who had covered the minor league Orioles as far back as 1914 and were the first to publish the name Babe Ruth. "Go ahead and get me fired," Richards challenged them. "I'd be the happiest man in the world if you'd get me fired. But I'll be damned if you'll make me quit."[26] Dan Parker of the *New York Daily Mirror* called him "one of most difficult of all subjects" for writers. Another New York reporter, Frank Slocum, wrote, "Richards had the warmth of an untipped waiter."[27] When asked whether sportswriters were qualified to second-guess a manager, Richards replied with typically precise words: "I would say they are *qualified* but not always *justified*. They would be justified only after they came to the manager to find out what he had in mind in doing whatever it was that didn't work. . . . I have observed that I have never been second-guessed on anything that *did* work."[28]

By the end of the 1956 season Richards had made the Orioles younger but had found only one player who could be called a prospect: the left-handed-batting outfielder Tito Francona. Signed by the Browns out of high school in

Pennsylvania, he had played only one full season in the low minors before serving two years in the army. He started the season as the regular center fielder but was batting just .146 on Memorial Day. For the next two months he hit close to .300 as Richards played him primarily against right-handed pitching. Francona had his first big day in a July 15 doubleheader against Detroit when he belted two home runs, one a grand slam. He hit safely in thirteen of fifteen games in July but tailed off to finish at .258/.334/.373.

On August 14 Bob Boyd returned to the lineup after missing nearly three months with a broken arm. He was batting .357 when he went down. Coach Luman Harris nicknamed him "The Rope" for his straight-as-a-string line drives.[29] To strengthen the offense Richards installed Boyd at first base and moved Triandos behind the plate. Richards traded his regular catcher, Hal Smith, to Kansas City for Joe Ginsberg. Ginsberg was nearly thirty, four years older than Smith, and a light-hitting backup, but Richards wanted the left-handed batter to play behind the right-handed Triandos.

Boyd batted .311/.395/.400 in seventy games. Triandos led the team with twenty-one homers, and the new left fielder, Bob Nieman, added punch. After raising his average as high as .362, Nieman finished at .322/.442/.497 with twelve home runs.

Richards had traded Harry Dorish and made six-foot-four right-hander George Zuverink the top reliever. The thirty-one-year-old sinkerballer was another pitcher of no distinction who prospered under Richards. Detroit had sent Zuverink to Baltimore on waivers in 1955. Richards liked his control and his calm demeanor in tight spots. After learning the slip pitch Zuverink saved sixteen games in 1956 and led the league with sixty-two appearances.

The Orioles' regular starting pitchers were all older than thirty: left-hander Bill Wight and right-handers Ray Moore and Connie Johnson. Johnson's 3.43 ERA was the best among the starters, but his record was 9-10. Richards said he had the best curve in the league and added a bit of hyperbole: "If that fellow had been pitching for the Yankees this season, he would have won 40 games."[30]

In September Mayor Thomas D'Alessandro proclaimed "Connie Johnson Day," and the Orioles honored the pitcher in a ballpark ceremony. It was an attempt to mend fences with black Baltimore. Those relations had been strained from the start, when the NAACP urged the American League not to put a team in the city because of its "rigid pattern of segregation" and "racist nature."[31] The *Afro-American* continually criticized the scarcity of black players. Sports editor Sam Lacy contrasted the Orioles with the National Football League's Baltimore Colts, "perhaps the most liberal organization in professional sports." The Colts fielded several African Americans, even including a quarterback, George Taliaferro.[32]

Although rural Maryland has roots in the South and Appalachia, Baltimore was an industrial port city with clearly defined white ethnic neighborhoods. By the mid-1950s the city's black population was growing fast. State law did not mandate segregation, but Baltimore's hotels were the last in the major leagues to open their doors to visiting black players.[33]

Naturally, suspicion about the Orioles' racial policies focused on the white Texan in charge. Richards bristled when a reporter insinuated he was a racist. "If you want to think that, okay," he snapped, "but go ask Connie Johnson and Bob Boyd if I'm prejudiced."[34] Long after Johnson retired, he said of Richards, "I don't think he liked blacks too much. He'd hide it in ways you wouldn't notice if you didn't come looking for it."[35] Boyd credited Richards for putting him in the lineup and helping him, then added: "He never broke his word . . . but he didn't like blacks. I was in enough team meetings where he would talk about the black players on the team . . . and he wouldn't say very nice things about them."[36] Black outfielder Joe Durham, who rejoined the Orioles in 1957 after two years in the army, was blunt: "The man was a hypocritical racial son of a bitch." Richards thought Durham was lunging at the ball, so he had coaches tie a rope around the young hitter's waist during batting practice to hold him back, oblivious to the symbolism of a white man, a black man, and a rope. Yet when Richards died, Boyd and Johnson called his home to offer condolences.[37]

Richards had brought the first African American players to the White Sox and the first significant ones to the Orioles. He had spoken out for integration in the 1954 controversy about exhibition games in Birmingham, Alabama. He believed his racial attitudes were enlightened. While managing Chicago he pointed to black and white players joking together in the shower and told Lester Rodney, a sportswriter for the Communist newspaper the *Daily Worker,* "You know, we white Southerners, when we get rid of the poison, we're more natural about white and black."[38] He put black players in the lineup if he thought they could help him win, but he was a product of his time and place. Every one of his closest colleagues in baseball was a white southerner.

The *Afro-American*'s Lacy perceptively wrote: "Richards wouldn't be human if he didn't have preference for personalities. . . nor would he be human if he didn't nurture prejudices. . . . There are some folk I don't like, and far be it from me to argue that I am free from prejudices . . . but I am convinced that [neither] Richards nor Stengel nor Lopez nor Dressen permits his dislike of a player to interfere with what he considers to be the most advantageous handling of the team." Lacy added, "I hope he stays, despite what he may think of me and I of him . . . personally."[39]

As the 1956 season wound down with the Orioles anchored in sixth place, their 69-85 record was twelve wins better than Richards's first season, the biggest step forward by any AL team. Baltimore's 571 runs and ninety-one homers were last in the league (they were the only big league team with fewer than one hundred homers), but the pitching and defense improved dramatically. The '55 team walked 625 batters, fifth highest in the league, committed the most errors, and gave up 104 unearned runs, more than any other club. In '56 the Orioles walked seventy-eight fewer, were charged with thirty fewer errors, and allowed thirty-four fewer unearned runs.

Still, sixth place was sixth place, and Richards was feeling pressure. His frustration boiled over to set a personal best: he was ejected from ten games, the most in any of his major league seasons. One anonymous player said, "What amazes me is that I know he has a real bad temper, but I never once saw him show it at one of his players."[40]

With one year remaining on Richards's contract, the owners gave him a two-year extension as both manager and general manager through 1959. At the same time President Keelty said the club planned to hire an executive vice president to oversee business affairs. This was an obvious, though unstated, attempt to rein in Richards's spending. Keelty insisted the owners had "the utmost confidence" in Richards and added, "As in the past, Mr. Richards will have full jurisdiction over all player personnel, both on the Baltimore club and throughout our farm organization."[41]

His bosses were fed up, but they would not challenge him directly. Orioles accountant Joe Hamper remembered: "The owners would talk to each other and say, 'We can't let him do this.' But they never talked to Richards about it. He intimidated them."[42] They had staked the future of the franchise on the prickly genius, had built him up as a savior, and were not about to admit they had been conned.

Besides the big bonuses for young players, Richards's personal spending provided fodder for office gossip. Hamper said Richards charged a limousine rental to the team when he attended an NFL championship game. Jim Russo remembered that Richards arrived at spring training and immediately sent all his clothes to the cleaners so he could put the bill on his expense account.[43]

The owners' choice to control the checkbook was forty-seven-year-old William Walsingham. A nephew of Sam Breadon, the former owner of the St.

Louis Cardinals, Walsingham had spent his entire working life in the Cardinals organization. He arrived in Baltimore bearing a carrot: "My position certainly does not curtail the authority and responsibility of Paul Richards as general manager." Then the stick: "I know of no successful baseball organization where a general manager is given carte blanche authority on player contract purchases or the disposal through sale or trade." Describing himself as the owners' representative (as if Richards didn't work for them), Walsingham said, "Paul and I will discuss any player transactions before they are consummated."[44] Maybe he believed it.

That fall Richards settled his family into a new home in Scottsdale, Arizona, near the Orioles' spring training site. It was his first and only move away from Waxahachie. He saw investment opportunities in the fast-growing resort area—and opportunities for more and better golf. Playing to a six handicap, he joined the Paradise Valley Country Club. Frequent partners included Dizzy Dean, Giants owner Horace Stoneham, and Chicago Cubs manager Bob Scheffing, who had homes in the area. The Richardses enrolled Paula in school and bought a pink ranch-style house with a cactus garden on Camelback Road between Scottsdale and Phoenix. He invested in the Northern-Aire Lodge and Country Club in Flagstaff.[45]

Richards brought sixty-five players to spring training in 1957, including the first products of his and McLaughlin's rebuilt farm system. He intended to keep twenty-year-old Brooks Robinson as a backup to George Kell, who had to be talked out of retirement. Robinson had batted .272 for Texas League San Antonio. Right-handed pitcher Charlie Beamon had beaten the Yankees in a September trial and was given a shot at the starting rotation but did not stick. A holdover from the Browns' system, twenty-nine-year-old outfielder Carl Powis, was a candidate to add power to the lineup; he had batted .330 with twenty-two home runs at San Antonio. Richards still called bonus baby Bob Nelson "the hitter with the most potential," although Nelson had batted .202

and had not hit a home run in ninety-nine at-bats during his mandatory two seasons on the roster.[46]

Robinson, who called his manager "Mr. Richards," described the youngsters' spring regimen: "We got to the ballpark at 10 o'clock in the morning, we'd work out, you'd do everything you had to do, then you'd play a game, and then you'd come back and work out in the afternoon. That's just the way [Richards] operated."[47]

Robinson and Powis were in the opening day lineup at Washington, with Kell playing first base. Powis drove in the winning run on an eleventh-inning sacrifice fly.[48] But by May 30 the Orioles had fallen to seventh place, ten games under .500. Powis, batting .195, went back to the minors. Richards had already been suspended for three games for bumping umpire Ed Hurley, and Robinson had undergone surgery for a knee injury. More injuries followed: a chipped vertebra for Gus Triandos, a broken hand for Tito Francona, and two beanings for Kell.

Richards added two more trick plays to the Orioles' bag. In an April game at Boston Kell, running from first base, intentionally allowed a ground ball to hit him. He was out, but he spoiled a sure double play. Kell said the team had worked on the play in spring training. The Red Sox howled, but umpire Joe Papparella said there was nothing in the rule book against it, and he wondered why base runners didn't do it more often. Within a few days the word spread. Cincinnati runners pulled it off in three different games. One of them, Don Hoak, brazenly picked up a ground ball before the fielder could reach it. The two leagues quickly adopted a rule interpretation permitting the umpire to call the double play in cases of obvious interference.[49]

Richards introduced catcher Joe Ginsberg to a bit of sleight-of-hand he claimed to have used in his Atlanta days. On a ball hit to the outfield with runners on base, the pitcher would move to back up home plate in case of a throw. As he ran past the catcher, they were to swap gloves. Richards reasoned that the catcher could snare the throw easier with the pitcher's glove than with his pillow-like mitt. The first time they tried it, Ginsberg and pitcher Bill Wight neatly pulled off the exchange—but Wight was a left-hander. "And here I am trying to get his glove on backwards, catch the ball and make a tag," Ginsberg said. "Now I'll tell you, that was the end of the glove-switch play."[50] (It wasn't; Richards later taught it to his catchers in Houston.)

In June 1957 bonus boys Bob Nelson, Wayne Causey, and Jim Pyburn completed their two-year sentences on the bench and were farmed out. Only Causey made it back to the majors. Nelson hung around the minors for four seasons, but Pyburn quit after one more year and became a football coach. He believed Richards "was highly overrated as a handler of people. . . . He really wasn't a motivator."[51]

Richards replaced them with three teenagers whose high school diplomas were barely dry: catcher Frank Zupo and right-handed pitchers Jerry Walker and Milt Pappas. Richards also imported more veterans. His Chicago center fielder Jim Busby came from Cleveland, and utility man Billy Goodman, a former AL batting champion, was acquired from Boston.

The club began to dig itself out of its hole behind strong pitching. Skinny Brown shut out Kansas City on two hits on May 19. Brown, a control pitcher who used a knuckleball as part of his junk collection, seldom completed a game but was a useful swing man, starting and relieving throughout Richards's time in Baltimore. Billy Loes won seven games by the end of June. Richards remarked, "I'd like to have more crazy pitchers like him."[52] On June 24 Brown shut out Detroit on five hits. The next day Loes won a three-hit shutout over Kansas City. The day after that Connie Johnson did the same. After a day off Ray Moore did the same to Cleveland, a fourth straight shutout. On July 11 the Orioles swept a doubleheader from the Indians to climb into fourth place and raise their record to 39-39, the first time they had been at .500 so late in the season since moving to Baltimore.

The home fans were taking notice; a Saturday doubleheader against the Indians and a Monday night game against the Yankees each drew more than forty thousand. Casey Stengel called Richards a "juggling genius" and added, "That man Richards has taken a bunch of hand-me-offs and made them into a respectable ball club."[53]

Baltimore stayed at .500 for only one day. Richards said, "We have been getting some amazing pitching, but the pitchers can't carry the load. We will have to get more punch at the plate in order to go places."[54] By the end of July his club had lost twenty-two of thirty-six one-run games. "When you lose 22 times by one run it means you were in the ball game," he said. "A hit here or there would have changed the picture."[55]

The eighteen-year-old bonus baby Milt Pappas had pitched only in batting practice during his first month with the Orioles when Richards put him on the disabled list in July. Doctor's orders, he said. The team physician had warned Richards that the youngster's arm was not mature enough to withstand professional pitching. Richards had personally signed Pappas, a Detroit native, although the hometown Tigers had been courting him for several years. "But I liked Paul Richards," Pappas said. His version of his disability: "Three or four days after I got there [Richards] asked me if my arm was sore and I said no. Then he repeatedly asked me the question, and finally he said, 'You know, isn't your arm sore?' I was eighteen; what the hell did I know? I finally said, 'Oh, yeah, my arm's sore.'" When Pappas continued to throw batting practice while on the DL, the Tigers, also sore, complained to the commissioner's office. Richards was ordered to put Pappas back on the roster, but there was no reported threat of suspension this time.[56]

The other eighteen-year-old pitcher, Jerry Walker, was a six-foot-one right-hander born in Harry Brecheen's tiny hometown of Ada, Oklahoma. Brecheen had scouted Walker while he went 52-1 for Byng High, and was impressed by his control. But in his major league debut, relieving in Boston's

Fenway Park before a crowd of 13,390, Walker walked the first two batters he faced and threw a wild pitch to the third one. Brecheen rushed to his side. "I said, 'Jerry, what's the matter?' He said, 'Listen, I never saw this many people in my life.' And so we had to take him out. He run [*sic*] off the mound."[57] Walker won his first game on September 4, shutting out Washington on four hits in ten innings. It was a milestone, the first victory by any of Richards's bonus babies, and an encouraging sign of things to come.

Brooks Robinson, who had been sent to San Antonio to rehabilitate his knee, was recalled on July 23. He spelled Kell at third, with Billy Goodman moving to second and second baseman Billy Gardner to shortstop, benching Miranda and his .194 batting average. By September Robinson was in the everyday lineup after Kell sprained his ankle.

The Orioles' record hovered just under .500. When they beat the Yankees and Whitey Ford on September 25, they stood at 73-76 with three games left against last-place Washington. They won the first two behind complete games by Skinny Brown and Bill Wight. On the final day Richards pulled out all the stops. He started his ace, Connie Johnson, on three days' rest and used nineteen players, including four pitchers. Baltimore won, 7–3, with a four-run uprising in the tenth inning. Robinson's double drove home the deciding run.

A 76-76 finish left the club in fifth place, twenty-one games behind the pennant-winning Yankees but only one game out of the first division. The Orioles allowed the third-fewest runs in the league and played eighty errorless games, a major league record, but they were next to last in runs scored. Attendance topped one million again, falling just short of the 1954 peak because of September rainouts. The team reported a profit of nearly $285,000, four times the previous year's earnings.[58]

The hope embodied in Brooks Robinson and Jerry Walker vindicated the strategy of building through the farm system. So did the blossoming of left-hander Billy O'Dell, a $12,000 bonus boy signed before Richards joined the franchise. O'Dell returned from military service to post a 2.69 ERA but a 4-10 record. The Orioles scored no more than two runs in eight of his losses. Triandos, still only twenty-six, led the team with nineteen home runs. But overall the Orioles were, as *Baseball Digest* described them, "Richards' Deluxe Retreads."[59] Six of the eight regular position players were twenty-nine or older, and four of the top six pitchers were past thirty.

George Kell retired at age thirty-five. He said later, "Paul told me when he went to Baltimore, 'I'm going to trade for you and make you the manager and I'm going to move into the front office as general manager.'" Richards now told Kell the owners had vetoed that plan. They wanted Richards in the dugout.[60]

Richards reunited with Eddie Robinson, who had been his slugging first baseman in Chicago. When Cleveland released the thirty-six-year-old in April, Robinson said, "I thought I'd like to be with Paul." Richards told him, "Well, Eddie, I can give you a job, but it ain't gonna pay much." Robinson signed on as a coach and was put on the roster for four pinch-hit appearances in September. He became a scout and troubleshooter, preparing for a career in the front office. The two Texans, a dozen years apart in age, forged a close friendship and professional partnership that lasted the rest of Richards's life. Robinson called Richards "my second father." The next year Eddie and his wife, Betty, named their first son Paul Richard Robinson.[61]

---

1. *Sporting News* (hereafter *TSN*), September 19, 1964, 3.
2. Ibid., September 19, 1964, 3, and June 15, 1963, 6.
3. Ibid., September 19, 1970, 42.
4. Kevin Kerrane, *Dollar Sign on the Muscle* (New York: Fireside/Simon and Schuster, 1989), 138–45; Earl Weaver, with Berry Stainback, *It's What You Learn after You Know It All That Counts* (New York: Doubleday, 1982), 121.
5. John Eisenberg, *From 33rd Street to Camden Yards: An Oral History of the Baltimore Orioles* (New York: Contemporary Books, 2001), 68.
6. *TSN*, February 24, 1960, 13; *Baltimore Sun*, February 9, 2004, online edition.
7. *Baltimore Sun*, October 29, 2003, online edition.

8. Steve Treder, "The Value Production Standings, 1951–1955," *Hardball Times*, September 19, 2006, www.hardballtimes.com; James Edward Miller, *The Baseball Business: Pursuing Pennants and Profits in Baltimore* (Chapel Hill: University of North Carolina Press, 1990), 50.

9. Eisenberg, *From 33rd Street to Camden Yards*, 72, 74.

10. Ibid., 74–75; Weaver, *It's What You Learn*, 101–3, 235–36; Terry Pluto, *The Earl of Baltimore* (New York: New Century, 1982), 30.

11. Cal Ripken Sr., with Larry Burke, *The Ripken Way* (New York: Pocket Books, 1999), xxv; Eisenberg, *From 33rd Street to Camden Yards*, 72.

12. Eisenberg, *From 33rd Street to Camden Yards*, 212.

13. Ibid., 69, 232.

14. Kerrane, *Dollar Sign on the Muscle*, 145.

15. *TSN*, October 5, 1955, 26 and March 28, 1956, 7; Jim Russo, with Bob Hammel, *SuperScout* (Chicago: Bonus Books, 1992), 41.

16. *TSN*, April 25, 1956, 11.

17. Ibid., January 18, 1956, 18.

18. Ibid., April 25, 1956, 11.

19. International News Service, *Mansfield (Ohio) News Journal*, May 15, 1956, 26; AP, *Ironwood (Mich.) Daily Globe*, June 14, 1956, 16.

20. *TSN*, May 30, 1956, 7; Eisenberg, *From 33rd Street to Camden Yards*, 38.

21. Danny Peary, ed., *We Played the Game* (New York: Black Dog and Laventhol, 1994), 279.

22. J. Miller, *Baseball Business*, 66.

23. *TSN*, September 27, 1961, 10. In the fall of 1964 Richards offered to trade his Houston roster for the Braves' roster. That was certainly a joke, since the Braves had Hank Aaron and Eddie Mathews, while the expansion Astros had castoffs and unproven kids (Dink Carroll, "When the Astros Tried to Trade Entire Team," *Baseball Digest*, March 1983, 51; *TSN*, December 19, 1964, 20).

24. Paul Richards, as told to Arthur and Milton Richman, "The Orioles Will Win the Pennant," *Saturday Evening Post*, April 15, 1961, 125.

25. *TSN*, July 11, 1956, 21.

26. Leigh Montville, *The Big Bam: The Life and Times of Babe Ruth* (New York: Doubleday, 2006), 36; Roy Terrell, "Hawkeye and his Boy Scouts," *Sports Illustrated*, April 17, 1961, 76.

27. *TSN*, April 17, 1957, 18, and March 27, 1979, 30.

28. Ed Linn, "The Double Life of Paul Richards," *Sport*, August 1955, 50. Emphasis in the original.

29. Bob Boyd, interview by Brent Kelley, February 15, 1991.

30. *TSN*, October 3, 1956, 29.

31. Jules Tygiel, *Baseball's Great Experiment: Jackie Robinson and His Legacy* (New York: Vintage, 1984), 313.

32. J. Miller, *Baseball Business*, 65–66.

33. Tygiel, *Baseball's Great Experiment*, 313.

34. Eisenberg, *From 33rd Street to Camden Yards*, 59.

35. Ibid., 60.

36. Larry Moffi and Jonathan Kronstadt, *Crossing the Line: Black Major Leaguers, 1947–1959* (Iowa City: University of Iowa Press, 1994), 54.

37. Eisenberg, *From 33rd Street to Camden Yards*, 62; Paula Richards, interviews by author, 2006–2008. In a conversation about her father's relations with black players, she volunteered the names of Boyd and Johnson, remembering their phone calls.

38. Irwin Silber, *Press Box Red: The Story of Lester Rodney, the Communist Who Helped Break the Color Line in American Sports* (Philadelphia: Temple University Press, 2003). Quoted in Lee Lowenfish's review of Silber's book, *Nine* 13 (2005), online edition.

39. *Baltimore Afro-American*, August 23, 1960, 10. The ellipses are in the original.

40. Ejections compiled by Doug Pappas and provided by David Vincent; Milton Richman, "The Ballplayers Give the Lowdown on A.L. Managers," *Sport*, October 1956, 82.

41. AP, *Chicago Tribune*, October 16, 1956, C5.

42. *Baltimore Sun*, October 29, 2003, online edition.

43. Ibid.; Russo, *SuperScout*, 41.

44. *TSN*, December 5, 1956, 24, and December 26, 1956, 6.

45. Ibid., January 9, 1957, 23; January 29, 1958, 11–12; May 20, 1959, 11.

46. Ibid., March 13, 1957, 32.

47. Louis Berney, *Tales from the Orioles Dugout* (Champaign, Ill.: Sports Publishing, 2004), 23.

48. Beginning here, except where otherwise credited, game accounts in this book come from *Retrosheet*. The information was obtained free of charge from and is copyrighted by *Retrosheet*. Interested parties may contact *Retrosheet* at www.retrosheet.org. At the time this book was written the *Retrosheet* play-by-play logs began in 1957.

49. Peter Morris, *The Game on the Field*, vol. 1, *Game of Inches* (Chicago: Ivan R. Dee, 2006), 296.

50. Bob Cairns, *Pen Men* (New York: St. Martin's, 1992), 99.

51. Jim Pyburn, interview by Brent Kelley, September 19, 1991.

52. Newspaper Enterprise Association, *Lima (Ohio) News*, June 30, 1957, 30.

53. UP, *Harrisburg (Pa.) Daily Register*, June 25, 1957, 7.

54. *TSN*, July 17, 1957, 13.

55. Ibid., August 7, 1957, 24.

56. Eisenberg, *From 33rd Street to Camden Yards*, 50–51; *TSN*, August 7, 1957, 24.

57. Harry Brecheen, interview by Rick Bradley. October 26, 1992; *TSN*, March 18, 1959, 9.

58. *TSN*, October 9, 1957, 24; September 25, 1957, 17; June 11, 1958, 11.

59. It was the headline on a September article, quoted by James Edward Miller in *Baseball Business*, 49.

60. Eisenberg, *From 33rd Street to Camden Yards*, 38.

61. Eddie Robinson and Betty Robinson, interviews by author, August 18, 2006, Fort Worth, Texas.

CHAPTER 14

Home Grown by 1960

D uring the winter of 1957–58 Jim McLaughlin hung a sign on his office wall: "Home Grown by 1960."[1] It reflected his confidence in the prospects he had found and was a challenge to his staff, but it may also have been a slap at Richards, who continued to load the Orioles' roster with shopworn veterans.

Richards needed to win—now. He said: "When I took over the club in September 1954, I was assured there was no particular urgency about building a winner. I later learned this meant that everyone was perfectly willing to wait as long as six months."[2]

At the winter meeting in Colorado Springs the majors scrapped the bonus rule that required high-priced youngsters to spend two years on the big league roster. Few of the 1950s bonus babies ever justified the investment—most notably, Sandy Koufax, Harmon Killebrew, and Al Kaline. Baseball men recognized that two years on the bench retarded the players' development, but Frank Lane gave the best explanation for the change: "I opposed the bonus rule because it required complete honesty and wasn't getting it from some clubs who were stooping to under-the-table payments."[3] The new rule allowed bonus players to be sent to the minors, but they could be drafted by other teams after four years (down from seven years) if they were not promoted to the major league roster.

The rule change backfired. Now that they could farm out their bonus babies, teams ratcheted up the bidding for young talent. The Milwaukee Braves paid seventeen-year-old shortstop Denis Menke a reported $125,000. In January 1958 the Orioles paid their first six-figure bonus to a high-school dropout from St. Louis, Dave Nicholson. He got a reported $105,000, plus new Pontiacs for him and his father. Nicholson was a six-foot-two, two-hundred-pound right-handed batter with fantastic power, another of the toolsy kids Richards loved. The eighteen-year-old said, "I like Paul Richards, and I honestly think the quickest road to the majors is through the Orioles' minor league system."[4] Team president James Keelty may have swallowed hard, but he promised, "There is more money where that came from."

"We're all a bunch of damn fools," Richards said, referring to all clubs, not just his own.

I'm going to retire in a couple of years and go back to Waxahachie, and the first thing I'm going to do is find me a tall old boy with long arms and big hands and I'm going to ask some friends of mine on the local newspaper to plant a few stories about how far he can hit a baseball. I don't care if he plays in the high school band. In a couple of weeks a few scouts will begin nosing around.

They'll ask the boy to work out for them, and he'll get a pained look on his face and say, "Oh, not again. I'm tired of working out for you guys." Then they'll go out in the town and begin to ask questions. You know how a small town is. I'll tip off a couple of friends, and they'll tell the scouts how this boy hit a baseball into Tarrant County one day and how another time he knocked all the bulbs out of a light tower 500 feet away.

"How much you want?" they'll ask the kid, and he'll say, "You make me an offer." Then the scouts will say, "How about $40,000?"

and the boy will laugh in their faces and say, "I've already been offered a lot more than that," and the scouts will go away to think about it.

Before it's all over they'll sign up that kid for $80,000, without ever seeing him swing a bat, and I'll take my cut as his agent and go find me another kid or two and pretty soon I'll be rich. And I won't feel bad a bit. Because this is just what's going on in the bonus business right now anyway.[5]

Reflecting his frustration with the failed bonus babies, Richards later advised a neophyte scout, "The best scouts are the ones who tell us who not to sign."[6]

The huge sums handed to untried teenagers stirred an angry, though futile, backlash from big league players. Only Ted Williams and Stan Musial were making $100,000 a year. Second baseman Billy Gardner was named the Orioles' most valuable player by writers and broadcasters after playing every game and tying for the league lead in doubles while being paid $17,000. Richards offered him a $2,000 raise. When Gardner protested, the general manager wrote him, "You can live very well on this in Triple A."

"I signed," Gardner said. "You didn't have a choice."[7]

Dave Nicholson arrived at spring training terrified by the burden of living up to his big contract, but he was an impressive sight. Fellow prospect Barry Shetrone said: "We used to just sit in amazement and watch him swing. I couldn't believe it. Everything was perfect—except he never made contact." Coaches immediately began tinkering with his swing, and that spooked him even more. Shetrone thought "they screwed him up," but Nicholson's minor league teammate Steve Barber believed, "He just couldn't hit the breaking ball."[8] Nicholson embarked on a long and frustrating odyssey to try to prove otherwise.

Entering his fourth season as boss of the Orioles in 1958, Richards had inched the club closer to the top of the standings every year. From fifty-seven games behind before he arrived, Baltimore moved up to thirty-nine behind, then twenty-eight, then twenty-one. Now he saw a chance to climb higher. The pennant-winning Yankees won ninety-eight games in 1957, and the White Sox, managed by Al Lopez, won ninety. Third-place Boston, with eighty-two victories, finished just five games ahead of Baltimore, well within reach.

Richards pulled in the fences at Memorial Stadium for the second time. Center field was shortened from 425 feet to 410, about an average distance, and the power alleys came in from 405 to 382, still pitcher-friendly. With characteristic attention to detail he erected new foul poles forty-five feet tall instead of thirty-four to give umpires a better chance of making the right call between a home run and a foul ball.

On opening day the Orioles looked a bit less like retreads. The starting lineup included Brooks Robinson at third, rookie Ron Hansen at shortstop, twenty-seven-year-old second-year man Al Pilarcik in right, and rookie first baseman Jim Marshall batting cleanup. But Richards had also reacquired thirty-five-year-old Gene Woodling, the outfielder who had been booed out of Baltimore three years earlier. "He had the guts of a burglar, to bring me back in that town," Woodling said later. "But that turned out to be the best thing that ever happened to me. I had three real good years for Baltimore."[9]

Another acquisition, left-hander Jack Harshman, who had broken in under Richards in Chicago, won his first five decisions, and Robinson was batting .370 in May, but by the end of the month Baltimore had sunk to last place. Hansen broke his hand in the season's sixth game, cutting short his rookie year. Marshall hit .215 and was put on waivers.

Nineteen-year-old Milt Pappas won a spot in the starting rotation, but Richards strictly limited his workload for part of the season. Pappas remembered, "No matter what count it was, what inning it was, what the score was, or what was going on, when I got to eighty pitches he pulled me."[10] Later accounts, including Pappas's, indicate that the pitch limit was in force all season, but it was not. Pappas came up with a sore arm in May and did not pitch for three weeks. He won a complete game against Kansas City on June 6, when he threw eighty-two pitches. That is the only contemporary record of his pitch counts, but broadcaster Ernie Harwell remembered: "Pappas pitched another month under the restriction. When the rookie's arm was OK again, Richards canceled the pitch count."[11] Pappas did not complete another game for seven weeks and finished only three of twenty-one starts, far below average. He said Richards's caution "probably saved my career."[12]

This became a permanent highlight on Richards's résumé: he was the first manager to impose a pitch count to protect a young starter. The historian Peter Morris, who specializes in finding "firsts," uncovered no evidence to dispute it.[13] But the story has been distorted over the years. Originally, it was that Richards put Pappas on a pitch count. Later it became that Richards enforced pitch counts to protect young arms. And that is the way sportswriters, old ballplayers, and Richards's cronies have handed it down. "He wouldn't let a young pitcher go more than seventy or eighty pitches," Eddie Robinson said in 2006. "He felt that their arms weren't developed. They might be big in stature, their bones had gotten big, but their muscles hadn't caught up with their growth. And he just didn't want to hurt a young pitcher."[14] That contention became the first line of defense when Richards was later accused of abusing the Orioles' "Kiddie Korps" in 1960 and 1961. The record shows that Richards did enforce pitch counts on an individual basis but not with all youngsters (see chapter 17).

By the time Pappas retired at age thirty-four, his lifetime record, 209-164, was virtually identical to his contemporary Don Drysdale's 209-166. Each started 465 games; Drysdale completed 167, Pappas 129. The Dodger right-hander was elected to the Hall of Fame. Pappas gained a reputation as a clubhouse lawyer and malcontent who looked to the dugout for relief as soon as he was assured of a victory.[15]

While Pappas was homegrown, if not yet fully grown, Richards picked up another castoff pitcher. The twenty-five-year-old right-hander Arnold Portocarrero had shown only occasional promise during four seasons with the Athletics. In his first appearance for the Orioles Portocarrero gave up two runs in two innings while walking four. Richards and Brecheen prescribed a total overhaul of his motion and his repertoire. They left his teeth and tonsils, if any, alone.

The new-model Portocarrero pitched six scoreless innings in his first start and reeled off six straight complete-game victories in June and July. "We've got him coming more overhand now," Brecheen explained. "He hides the ball better, and that now makes him more effective against left-handed batters." Brecheen and Richards also taught him a sinking two-seam fastball. "Porto" said, "You know, there isn't much that Richards and Brecheen don't know about pitching."[16] Porto posted a 15-11 record and a 3.25 ERA, tenth best in the league. It was the only time he won as many as ten games. As with many of Richards's projects, Porto's magic soon wore off. One writer dismissed him as a "puff-ball artist," and a player jeered that he could catch Porto's fastball "with a pair of pliers."[17] When Richards took on a failed pitcher, he changed the man's delivery and added pitches to his arsenal. The "new" pitcher could fool hitters for a year or two until they caught up with him. That is one explanation; another is that all but the best pitchers are inconsistent, unable to sustain success year after year.

The Orioles climbed into a tie for second place on July 26 but then lost eleven in a row and dropped to seventh two weeks later. With the Yankees leading second-place Boston by sixteen and a half games, Richards unleashed a broadside at the pin-striped dynasty: "The farce the Yankees are making of the 1958 American League pennant race is a catastrophe for the American League. . . . This domination by the Yankees, which has stifled interest and slowed down the turnstiles, isn't the result of a sudden development. It is caused by the relentless front-office drive of the Yankees while most of the other owners and their chief lieutenants were resting on their oars."[18]

After the season, in a *Look* magazine article titled "The American League Is Dying," Richards proposed breaking up the talent-rich Yankees farm system: "The *only* salvation for the American League is a *truly unrestricted draft*" that would allow teams to protect no more than the forty players on their major league rosters. A committee headed by Frank Lane had floated that idea in 1957, but New York and other clubs with strong farm systems ordered their minor league affiliates to vote it down.[19]

With the rest of the league tightly bunched behind the Yankees, Richards still had a shot at .500 and a spot in the first division. He pulled a new trick out of his bag on September 11 in Detroit. He posted a starting lineup that included pitchers Jack Harshman, listed as the center fielder and batting fifth, and Pappas batting seventh and playing second base. Richards explained that he was hoping for a first-inning rally so he could choose the pinch hitters to send up for the pitchers. It almost worked. Dick Williams led off the game with a single and, after two outs, the Tigers intentionally walked Bob Nieman to bring up Harshman's spot. Richards pinch-hit with Gene Woodling, but Woodling flied out to end the threat. In the bottom of the first Busby went to center field and Gardner to second base.[20]

Still looking for pitching help, Richards claimed thirty-six-year-old Hoyt Wilhelm on waivers. The Indians had dumped Wilhelm despite his 2.49 ERA; Cleveland general manager Frank Lane believed Wilhelm could not be trusted in tight spots because the catchers couldn't hold his knuckleball. After being wounded in World War II and languishing in the minors until he was nearly thirty because of the prejudice against knuckleballers, Wilhelm became a top reliever for Leo Durocher's New York Giants in the early fifties and was the first reliever elected to the Hall of Fame. Richards sent him out to start against

Boston. He pitched a strong complete game but lost 3–2. Richards gave him another start, then another.

The third one came on September 20, 1958, against the Yankees at Memorial Stadium. It rained all night and all morning, but Richards anticipated a big Saturday crowd, and CBS-TV cameras were on hand for the *Game of the Week*, so he begged umpire-in-chief Joe Papparella to let the teams play. Papparella agreed, on one condition: "I don't want to hear one word from you or your players about the rain or about me trying to drown you." Most of the Yankees regulars were in the lineup, although they had already clinched the pennant. Wilhelm and New York's Don Larsen matched shutouts for six innings. Papparella intended to call the game after seven, but when Gus Triandos homered to put Baltimore ahead 1–0, the umpire knew he had to give the Yankees a chance to come back.[21] Papparella may not have noticed what was unfolding: Wilhelm had not allowed a hit.

Richards had noticed and began putting his best defenders on the slippery field. Busby went to center in the seventh, pushing the swift rookie Willie Tasby to right in place of the slower Woodling. In the eighth Willy Miranda came in to play shortstop, and Brooks Robinson took over at third, sending Dick Williams to replace Bob Nieman in left field. The first Yankees batter in the inning, Norm Siebern, slashed a sharp grounder that second baseman Billy Gardner barely gloved. Elston Howard, up next, drove a hard liner to left that Williams caught—but he thought Nieman could not have reached it.[22] Richards, too nervous to watch, left the dugout and listened to Herb Carneal call the final inning on radio. With two out in the ninth, Casey Stengel ordered Hank Bauer to bunt for a base hit. Bauer fouled it into the mud, but he slipped and never got out of the batter's box, so he would have been out if the ball had stayed fair. Then Bauer popped out to Gardner to end the first no-hitter by a big league Oriole since 1898. Wilhelm had thrown ninety-nine pitches, eighty-seven of them knuckleballs.[23] He struck out eight and walked two; the only

Yankee to reach second base got there on a walk and a passed ball.

By making Wilhelm a starter, Richards added another boldface line to his résumé as a pitching master. "I'd always wondered why he'd been used in relief, coming in with men on base where one passed ball could hurt him," Richards said. "I thought that perhaps, if Hoyt started, the runners wouldn't get on base to begin with."[24] In fact, Cleveland managers Bobby Bragan and Joe Gordon had the idea first; they had given Wilhelm six starts, the first ones of his career.

Wilhelm's gem came in the middle of a three-game sweep of the Yankees but not even a seven-game September winning streak could boost the Orioles to .500. They finished 74-79, in sixth place, just three games out of the first division. They were seventeen and a half behind New York, again moving a bit closer to the top.

Baltimore's pitching and defense allowed the fewest runs in the league. Behind Portocarrero's franchise-record fifteen victories, Billy O'Dell established himself at age twenty-six with a 14-11 record and 2.97 ERA, fifth best in the league, though he was sent home early because of a tired arm. Jack Harshman was even better, ranking third in ERA at 2.89, but his record was 12-15. "In the overall picture, he was the top pitcher in the league," Richards said. "He'd have been a sure pop to win 20 games with a team like the Yankees. We didn't get him many runs."[25] The Orioles scored no more than two runs in ten of Harshman's losses. Young Pappas finished at 10-10 with a worse-than-average 4.09 ERA.

The team scored the fewest runs in the AL with the lowest OPS, .660. Gus Triandos's home run in the Wilhelm no-hitter was his thirtieth of the year, tying Yogi Berra's AL record for a catcher, but five of the eight Orioles with the most at-bats hit under .250.

One of them was twenty-one-year-old Brooks Robinson, who batted just .238/.292/.305 with three home runs in 145 games. "The pitchers didn't care whether he got a hit or not," Richards said. "They wanted him in there."[26] Robinson's Vancouver manager, Charlie Metro, said, "It seemed like the ball had eyes into his glove when he was fielding."[27] His arm was mediocre; his roommate, Ron Hansen, joked, "I used to yell 'Tag up' because it looked like a sacrifice fly when he threw to first base." Robinson compensated with a quick release; teammates said he always threw out the runner by a single step.[28] He eventually became a decent hitter and the club's most popular player. "In New York they named a candy bar after Reggie Jackson," sportswriter Gordon Beard said later. "Here in Baltimore, we name our children after Brooks Robinson."[29]

With the pressure of the bonus rule off, Richards signed a dozen more young players, including future major leaguers Jerry Adair and Pete Ward, bringing the Orioles' bonus payments to a reported $700,000 on his watch.[30] Harry T. Paxton wrote in the *Saturday Evening Post* that the owners had counted on Bill Walsingham to rein in Richards's spending: "It hasn't worked out that way. Walsingham handles various business and administrative affairs, but Richards continues to call the tune on player deals." President Keelty said, "We are not operating on a shoestring and we have 100 percent faith in Paul Richards."[31]

The latest rumor had Richards's Detroit teammate Fred Hutchinson taking over as the Orioles' manager (after he was fired by the Cardinals), with Richards moving to the front office full time. Richards denied it: "I'm perfectly satisfied with my setup in Baltimore as it now stands."[32] The owners were not. The Orioles had regressed after climbing to .500 in 1957, though, as Bill James has documented, it is common for a team to take a step forward and then fall back.[33] Home attendance plunged by nearly 20 percent to less than 830,000, the lowest in the club's five seasons. The franchise turned a tiny profit of $35,000 only because of revenue from network television's *Game of the Week*.

Richards and Keelty were lying about their mutual satisfaction. The delicate dance that ended Richards's reign over the Orioles had begun months earlier. Richards, typically, tried to spin the change as his own idea: "In July I decided the job was too big for one man, entirely too big for me. I reached my decision entirely on my own." He said he had considered George Kell and Fred Hutchinson as managers, "but after talking it over, it was obvious to me that the owners thought more of me as a manager than they did as a general manager."[34] That last part was true.

The Orioles' chairman, Joseph Iglehart, also served on the board of CBS and was impressed by the network's sports director, Bill MacPhail. The son of the mercurial Larry MacPhail had worked in baseball before going into television. When Iglehart broached his name, Richards said Bill was the wrong MacPhail. His older brother Lee headed the Yankees' farm system. Lee MacPhail said Richards was the first to approach him about coming to Baltimore when the Orioles visited New York late in the season: "I was taken completely by surprise."[35]

Iglehart soon invited the right MacPhail to lunch at the Racquet Club on Park Avenue in Manhattan and pitched the general manager's job to him. The forty-one-year-old MacPhail did not want to leave the Yankees, and his wife, Jane, did not want to leave their home in suburban Scarsdale, but Yankees co-owner Dan Topping told him GM George Weiss would be around for a long time, and advised him not to pass up the opportunity to run a team. (Weiss was forced to retire two years later.)

MacPhail was still wary: "I had heard rumors that there was disharmony in the Orioles organization, and if Paul and I were going to work together as a team I wanted to be sure that he was one hundred percent in favor of the move." He went to Memphis to meet Richards, who came up from Waxahachie, and got the reassurance he needed. He took the job for a $35,000 salary, less than Richards's, plus 5 percent of the net profits. MacPhail also gained a seat on the board, a distinction Richards never had.[36]

MacPhail's father had revived the failing Cincinnati and Brooklyn franchises, introduced night baseball to the majors, brought play-by-play broadcasts to New York, and had briefly run the Yankees. A belligerent drunk known as "The Roaring Redhead," he quickly wore out his welcome everywhere he went despite his success. His son and namesake, Leland Stanford MacPhail Jr., was, as John Helyar wrote, as different from his father "as a double was from a double play."[37] Short, pudgy, and bland of face and manner, Lee MacPhail spent fifty years in baseball while making no known enemies. His Baltimore assistant Jack Dunn III said, "If you can't get along with Lee MacPhail, you can't get along with anybody."[38] But MacPhail came to Baltimore with a cold-eyed understanding of the task before him: "Paul was not business-operation-minded. All of his energies were devoted to the field and they wanted someone to come in as general manager to supervise the organization off the field and to watch the exchequer. What they wanted in part was someone to say no to Richards when he chose to ignore the budget."[39]

When the Orioles announced the front-office shakeup on November 10, 1958, Keelty insisted that Richards had voluntarily given up the general manager's job. Introducing MacPhail, Keelty said, "He will have the authority to approve and conclude all major deals and will confer with Manager Richards on any contemplated transfer of player personnel." But Keelty went out of his way to soften the blow: "Richards is the best manager in baseball. With more time to devote to his players we think the Orioles will start moving upward." He noted that the team had advanced closer to first place every year since Richards arrived and had developed three frontline major leaguers—Billy O'Dell, Brooks Robinson, and Milt Pappas—more than any other AL team in the same period.

Given the disastrous Walsingham experiment, Baltimore writers were even more skeptical than MacPhail had been. When they asked who would have the final word on trades, MacPhail stepped in: "The setup between manager and general manager is traditional. I am a little surprised at the questions concerning authority. I talked with the owners and Paul and was told I would have the authority of general manager. But if there was any question of trouble arising, I wouldn't have taken the job."[40]

Months later Richards was still insisting that he had demoted himself: "The inception of the present pattern was all mine, and the final decision to get a general manager was mine. The recommendation to hire MacPhail was mine. What actually happened was that we screened managers and weighed general manager prospects available, one group against the other. After considering both groups, I took the job which I believe will give us the best balance between front office and field."

He reflected on his four years of "running the show":

When I came over [to Baltimore], the whole operation focused on a building job. I had to sign scouts, bird dogs [part-time scouts], players. [He seems to have forgotten Jim McLaughlin.] We had to go out and sign virtually everybody available simply to get into business. We were forced to sign many boys to major league contracts which complicated the front office operation, because waivers and options had to be watched closely. The job was in the front office for the first few years and there was little problem on the field. Then, finally, the number of major league players and prospects began to pile up and the time had come to assign one man to the front office and one to the field. . . .

I am completely satisfied as manager; I never will be a general manager and that's it.[41]

Those paragraphs contain some truths, some half-truths, and some lies. No matter what the spin, the Orioles' owners had clipped Richards's wings. The owners were businessmen, accustomed to employees who followed orders.

Paul Richards had one year left on his contract. As he reached his fiftieth birthday, he was clearly on the spot.

---

1. *Sporting News* (hereafter *TSN*), June 1, 1960, 4.
2. Paul Richards, as told to Arthur and Milton Richman, "The Orioles Will Win the Pennant," *Saturday Evening Post*, April 15, 1961, 125.
3. *TSN*, February 5, 1958, 8.
4. Dudley Doust, "Bonus Baby Blues," *Sports Illustrated*, July 14, 1958, online archive; *TSN*, February 5, 1958, 2.
5. "Events and Discoveries of the Week," *Sports Illustrated*, July 4, 1960, online archive.
6. *Everett (Wash.) Herald*, May 28, 2008, online edition.
7. John Eisenberg, *From 33rd Street to Camden Yards: An Oral History of the Baltimore Orioles* (New York: Contemporary Books, 2001), 45.
8. Ibid., 94.
9. Gene Woodling, interview by Jim Sargent, May 6, 1997.
10. Eisenberg, *From 33rd Street to Camden Yards*, 78.
11. *Detroit Free Press*, April 9, 2007, online edition.
12. Eisenberg, *From 33rd Street to Camden Yards*, 78.
13. *USA Today*, September 11, 2004, 4C.
14. Eddie Robinson, interview by author, August 18, 2006, Fort Worth, Texas.
15. Eisenberg, *From 33rd Street to Camden Yards*, 79.
16. *TSN*, August 27, 1958, 11, and February 25, 1959, 5.
17. Roger Williams, "Baseball's Week," *Sports Illustrated*, May 9, 1960, online archive.
18. *TSN*, July 30, 1958, 4.
19. Paul Richards, with Tim Cohane, "The American League Is Dying," *Look*, February 17, 1959, 44–47.
20. *TSN*, July 2, 1966, 4.
21. Larry R. Gerlach, *The Men in Blue* (1980; repr., Lincoln: University of Nebraska Press, 1994), 142–43.
22. Eisenberg, *From 33rd Street to Camden Yards*, 84.
23. Gerlach, *Men in Blue*, 143; *TSN*, October 1, 1958, 19.
24. Mark Armour, "Hoyt Wilhelm, Starting Pitcher," *Articles Related to Rob Neyer's Big Book of Baseball Lineups*, 2003, www.robneyer.com/book_03_BAL.html.
25. *TSN*, September 3, 1958, 16; June 18, 1958, 21.
26. Donald Honig, *The Man in the Dugout* (Chicago: Follett, 1977), 131.
27. Dave Brandon, "Then and Now: RC Q&A with Charlie Metro," May 28, 2007, www.royalscorner.com.
28. Eisenberg, *From 33rd Street to Camden Yards*, 104–5.
29. Tim Kurkjian, *Is This a Great Game, or What?* (New York: St. Martin's Griffin, 2007), 8.
30. *TSN*, November 19, 1958, 4.
31. Harry T. Paxton, "Baltimore's Bonus Baby Blues," *Saturday Evening Post*, August 9, 1958, reprinted in *TSN*, August 27, 1958, 11; *TSN*, September 3, 1958, 16.
32. *TSN*, September 24, 1958, 22.
33. Bill James, *This Time Let's Not Eat the Bones* (New York: Villard, 1989), 480.
34. *TSN*, November 19, 1958, 4.
35. Lee MacPhail, *My Nine Innings* (Westport, Conn.: Meckler Books, 1989), 59.
36. Ibid., 59–60.

Jesse and Della Richards, Paul's parents.
(Paula Richards collection)

Paul Richards at about age 8, ca. 1917.
(Paula Richards collection)

Captain of the undefeated Waxahachie High Indians, 1926.

(Courtesy of Buck Jordan)

With the Philadelphia Athletics, 1935.

(National Baseball Hall of Fame Library, Cooperstown, N.Y.)

Newspaper owner and sportswriter at the *Waxahachie Daily Light*, ca. 1940.
(Paula Richards collection)

With daughter Paula, at home in Waxahachie.
(Paula Richards collection)

With the Detroit Tigers during World War II. His unusual catching stance was the result of a knee injury.

(Photo by J.D. McCarthy)

BA with
B. on

AB	H	BB	HR		BA	Full
67	14	7	0	Berceaeus / Syomith	309	280
112	87	26	5	Lyon	330	450
94	30	5	6	Coleman	319	350
73	25	7	1	Vork	300	360
22	5	8	1	Gykild	230	430
78	26	12	6	Kinard	333	420
114	29	16	0	Albright	254	345
106	31	13	2	Selietta	244	370
16	5	2	0	Kithby	300	380
19	5	1	0	Fry	285	300
33	0	8	0	Sheely	000	250
48	15	8	9	Vire	191	270
40	12	2	2	Ihik	300	333
56	19	7	2	T. Orwin	340	384
29	9	1	0	Cheeten	310	340
91	25	8	0	Ramsey	275	330

AB	H	BB	HR	.13	BA	BH	
291	82	47	10	282	380	Daniel
297	82	47	10	253	320	Lyon
186	47	19	6	344	560	Coleman
284	92	16	9	183	234	Vork
82	15	6	1	204	380	Sykild
162	33	46	5	261	333	Theesen
46	12	5	2	284	395	Albright
250	71	41	7	231	300	Selietta
224	52	23	4	308	369	Kithby
185	57	18	8	276	395	Fry
237	63	43	2	210	420	Sheely
80	22	20	1	328	380	Vire
216	71	15	6	175	340	Ihik
40	7	10	0	240	295	T. Orwin
157	33	9	6	000	000	Cheeten
18	0	0	0	133	218	Ramsey
75	10	8	0			

Richards's journal of his season managing the Seattle Rainiers in 1950 includes his calculation of players' "B.A. with bases on balls," a statistic later known as on-base percentage.

Richards family, 1951. Left to right: Lou Redith, Paul, Margie, Paula.

Leaders of the White Sox, 1951. Seated, left to right: vice president
Charles A. Comiskey II, Richards, general manager Frank Lane. Standing:
Coaches Doc Cramer, Luman Harris, Ray Berres, Jimmy Adair.

(Paula Richards collection)

Richards with new White Sox acquisitions Minnie Minoso (center) and Paul Lehner, 1951.

(Paula Richards collection)

With White Sox pitchers Billy Pierce (left) and Randy Gumpert, 1951.

(National Baseball Hall of Fame Library, Cooperstown, N.Y.)

A familiar pose: Richards confronts an umpire.

(National Baseball Hall of Fame Library, Cooperstown, N.Y.)

At the Orioles spring training headquarters in Miami.

(Paula Richards collection)

Richards with White Sox manager Bob Lemon (left) and principal owner Bill Veeck, 1977.

(Paula Richards collection)

Richards's friends erected this monument at Richards Park in Waxahachie after his death.

(Photo by the author)

37. John Helyar, *Lords of the Realm* (New York: Villard, 1994), 282.
38. James Edward Miller, *The Baseball Business: Pursuing Pennants and Profits in Baltimore* (Chapel Hill: University of North Carolina Press, 1990), 62.
39. MacPhail, *My Nine Innings*, 60.
40. *TSN*, November 12, 1958, 6; November 19, 1958, 4; November 26, 1958, 13.
41. Ibid., May 6, 1959, 3, 8.

The Church of Johnny U

The bow-legged, round-shouldered quarterback handed off to a man called Horse. The play was "16 slant." When fullback Alan Ameche barreled one yard into the end zone at Yankee Stadium in the game's sixty-ninth minute, the Baltimore Colts won their first National Football League championship.

It was December 28, 1958. The Colts had come from behind to tie the New York Giants with seven seconds to play, sending the NFL title game into sudden-death overtime for the first time in history. Baltimore's quarterback, John Unitas, had told dancer Gene Kelly that football was a dance. Unitas choreographed the comeback victory.

The game "changed Sundays," as the later NFL commissioner Pete Rozelle put it. Forty-five million people watched on television right down to the thrilling end. "That's the game that changed professional football," said Don Shula, a former Colt defensive back and future coach. "The popularity of it started right there."

The NFL was still minor league. Unitas, the reigning MVP, was paid $17,500. In the 1950s big-time football meant Notre Dame, Ohio State, Oklahoma. Within a decade the professional game would surpass baseball as America's most popular sport.[1]

The Colts' stunning victory had its most immediate and dramatic impact in their hometown. Baltimoreans fell in love. Newcomer Lee MacPhail said,

"The Colts, at times during my stay in Baltimore, were almost like a religion to the sports fans of the city."[2] Orioles accountant Joe Hamper added: "And we were second-class citizens. The Colts sold out the stadium, and everybody, including myself, was a fanatic Colts fan."[3] The Colts were champions; they won again in 1959. The Orioles were still losers.

The club moved its spring training base to Miami in 1959 over Richards's objections. He preferred the dry Arizona heat to steamy Florida, but the owners wanted the spring camp to be more accessible to Baltimore fans. The team worked with travel agents to organize package tours. Richards sold his Arizona home and returned to Waxahachie every fall for the rest of his life.[4]

In Miami Richards was reunited with a teammate from New York and Atlanta, the former pitcher Frank Gabler. The Orioles' coaches paid Gabler's way to spring training purely for his entertainment value. Nicknamed "The Great Gabbo," he talked a better game than he pitched. He had posted a 16-23 record in four big league seasons. Richards called him "the funniest man in America" and loved to tell Gabler stories. One of the few printable examples: Gabler loaded the bases, bringing up a hitter who owned him. He threw the first two pitches wide, and manager Bill Terry visited the mound. Terry asked, "Gabe, are you afraid to pitch to this guy?"

"I'm not afraid to pitch to him," Gabler replied. "It's just a case of do you want them to get one run or four?"

In addition to providing comic relief, Gabler was one of the few men who could loosen up the starchy manager. As a contemporary, he could say things that Richards's coaches, even his closest associates, dared not.[5]

Before opening day Richards acknowledged, "We're desperate for hitting."[6] But the Orioles won three from New York on April 25 and 26, the first time they had swept a series in Yankee Stadium. Each game was decided by one run in the final inning. Baltimore left town tied for second place behind Cleveland, while the Yankees' record fell to 6-7. As New York continued to stumble, the timeless cry of "Break up the Yankees" was replaced by "The Yankees are broken." Richards was one of the first to see that the dynasty was ending: "It's bound to come, because other clubs, most notably our own, are working harder at digging up talent than they are."[7]

In May Richards optioned a disappointed and disappointing Brooks Robinson to the AAA Vancouver farm club. Robinson had missed most of spring training while fulfilling his six-month military reserve obligation, which kept him from being drafted for two years' service. He managed only five hits in twenty-five at-bats before Richards sent him down to play every day.

Baltimore's oldest pitcher and its youngest led the early-season charge. Thirty-six-year-old Hoyt Wilhelm won his first nine decisions, and twenty-year-old Jerry Walker took his first four. On May 22 Wilhelm held the Yankees hitless until Jerry Lumpe led off the eighth with a single. But Wilhelm's flutter-ball was torturing Gus Triandos. In Wilhelm's first 37⅓ innings Triandos committed eight passed balls. Wilhelm's catcher when he was with the Giants, Wes Westrum, offered some advice: "Whenever I caught Hoyt, I was so relaxed behind the plate, I was almost limp. If you tighten up, you're done."[8] No one could have been tighter than Triandos. "It was very tiring, very hot, and a long way back to the backstop to get passed balls," he said later. "You caught 98 percent of the knuckleballs, and then two or three would get by you in clutch situations, and they'd boo the piss out of you. . . . The more I caught [Wilhelm], the worse I got."[9]

On June 9, 1959, Baltimore beat Cleveland, 7–3, before the largest single-game crowd in franchise history, 46,601. Billy Loes, who had become Richards's relief ace, finished it with three no-hit innings. The victory lifted the Orioles into a first-place tie with the White Sox, the first time Baltimore had been on top of the standings as late as June. But the league was tightly bunched; only five and a half games separated first place from last. The Yankees stood at .500. The next day Cleveland's Rocky Colavito slammed four home runs to knock the Orioles out of the lead.

Baltimore hung in the race with Chicago and Cleveland on the strength of pitching and defense; the offense was the league's weakest. Richards recalled Brooks Robinson from Vancouver on July 8 and acquired the veteran first baseman Walt Dropo, a right-handed batter, to platoon with Bob Boyd. Richards was also platooning at shortstop, third base, and the two corner outfield positions. Casey Stengel remarked, "Richards is moving 'em in and out more'n I ever did."[10] It was true: In most seasons the Orioles used more different lineups than Stengel. In 1959 Richards put ninety-seven combinations on the field in 154 games, not counting pitchers. Stengel was "moving 'em in and out" because he had so many good players, Richards because he had so few.

Richards traded Jack Harshman, who had not won a game, and dropped Arnie Portocarrero from the starting rotation as his ERA climbed above 6.00. Right-hander "Fat Jack" Fisher was called up from Miami, giving the team three twenty-year-old pitchers along with Pappas and Walker. On July 9 Pappas and Walker pitched back-to-back shutouts in a doubleheader sweep of Washington. Pappas carried the team through July and August, winning eight of ten and saving two more. The pitch count was forgotten; he was leading the league in complete games. Wilhelm, after his 9-0 start, didn't win again for a month. A five-game losing streak dropped Baltimore to .500 on July 25.

Looking for punch in the outfield, Richards promoted twenty-one-year-old Barry Shetrone, a fast, rangy left-handed batter who had hit ten homers in half a season at Vancouver. Shetrone tripled and singled in his debut, then went 0-for-9. Richards and his coaches changed Shetrone's batting stance and thoroughly confused him. He had been an infielder in high school but was shifted to center field in the minors. When Richards put Shetrone in right for the first time, he let an easy fly ball drop. Richards told him, "Next time that happens, it's gonna cost you money." Shetrone recalled, "He expected you not to make any mistakes."[11] The rookie was consigned to pinch hitting and pinch running for most of the rest of the season, batting .203 in eighty-four plate appearances, and felt he never got a fair trial.

Richards made his debut as a congressional witness on July 30, 1959, before the Senate antitrust subcommittee. After the Giants and Dodgers abandoned New York in 1957, Mayor Robert Wagner had asked a Wall Street lawyer, William Shea, to find another big league team for the city. Unable to entice any existing franchise, Shea announced the formation of a third major league, the Continental League, and lined up investors in several markets, including New York. To free up some talent for the new circuit Senator Estes Kefauver of Tennessee introduced legislation limiting each major league club to no more than eighty players on its roster and in its farm system. Richards had proposed a similar idea in an article in *Look* magazine in February, so he was a logical witness.

In his testimony Richards backed away from some of what he (or his collaborator, *Look*'s Tim Cohane) had written.[12] Now he warned that the minors could not survive without subsidies from the majors. He advocated an NFL-style draft of amateur players to hold down bonuses and spread talent around. Hewing to the company line, he urged Congress to keep its hands off baseball. Commissioner Ford Frick, testifying the previous day, had promised that organized baseball would be helpful to the Continentals but dodged all specific questions about whether the majors would share players with the new league.[13]

The majors scheduled two All-Star Games in 1959 for the first time, to generate money for the players' pension plan. Richards was among many who didn't like the idea. He said sarcastically, "Why not have an All-Star Game every Monday?"[14] He liked it even less when the American League manager, Stengel, used three Orioles pitchers in the exhibition.

Baltimore reached the second all-star break on August 3 with a 53-53 record, tied for third place with Kansas City but eleven games behind the league-leading White Sox. During the break Richards and MacPhail made a decision. "We were going with the kids," MacPhail said. "It was time."[15] Richards's contract was extended through 1961. Chairman Joseph Iglehart said, "I think he's the greatest manager in baseball." The board promoted MacPhail to president after James Keelty resigned.[16]

The club had offered a longer contract extension, but Richards turned it down. He was protecting his options for the future. Although the Continental League existed only on paper, one of its franchises was promised to Houston, and a Dallas–Fort Worth syndicate was bidding for another. Both cities were also on the majors' unofficial list of potential expansion venues.[17] Richards would be the natural choice to run a new team in his home state.

The Orioles limped to the finish, dragged down by a succession of injuries. On September 11 two of Richards's twenty-year-olds started in a doubleheader against the White Sox at Memorial Stadium. Jack Fisher pitched a three-hit shutout in the opener for his first major league victory. In the second game Jerry Walker held the league leaders scoreless for nine innings, but Baltimore had not scored, either. "Richards asked how I was feeling and I said 'fine,'" Walker remembered. "So I stayed in the game, and in the twelfth inning I was still in the game. And it came to the fifteenth inning, and of course they had checked with me every inning to see how I was doing. So when it came to the fifteenth, they asked me how I was feeling and again I said, 'I'm fine.' So they let me go out in the sixteenth inning. When I came in, they said, 'That's it.' Fortunately Brooks got a base hit in the bottom of the sixteenth" to drive in the winning run.[18]

It was a shocking abuse of a prized young pitcher, a violation of Richards's tenet that young arms needed to be protected. He had been protecting Walker; the youngster had worked just 154 innings before that day and had completed only seven of twenty starts, with a 2.94 ERA. There is no record of Walker's pitch count. He recalled that he threw 178, but that is fewer than a dozen per inning—not likely.[19] He did not lose effectiveness in extra innings, retiring the Sox in order in the tenth, eleventh, twelfth, and thirteenth, giving up a walk in the fourteenth and a single in the sixteenth. But this was the second game of a twi-night doubleheader in September that lasted until after midnight, and Richards believed night games were harder on pitchers than daytime starts because the cool, damp air caused their muscles to stiffen.

Richards gave Walker six days off before his next appearance. He allowed four runs in six innings. After six more days' rest he gave up five runs in six innings against the Yankees. He was never the same pitcher. He struggled through five more seasons, none with a winning record, and was gone from the majors at age twenty-five. Walker said later: "People since have pointed back and said, 'Well, that's where you hurt your arm.' I can't say that I did and I can't say that I didn't. The next year I was not as effective. I had some physical problems, allergies and so forth. . . . I actually hurt my arm for the first time in Kansas City two years later, 1961."[20]

Why did Richards do it? This was the Orioles' third doubleheader in five days, but the bullpen was not overworked. Coming into September 11 the club was just two games out of the first division and a World Series share. Obviously, Richards badly wanted to win, but he always wanted to win every game. For a manager who drove scorekeepers dizzy with his lineup shuffles, perhaps the worst move he ever made was no move. It defies explanation.

The other kids were proving their worth. Brooks Robinson closed the season with a 20-for-50 splurge, raising his OPS to .708, almost equal to the league average. Pappas finished 15-9 with a 3.27 ERA. O'Dell and Walker each had ERAs below 3.00.

The Orioles' season peaked on July 19 when they stood at 48-43. In the last ten weeks they went 26-37. A final 74-80 record left them in sixth place, the same as the year before, but twenty games behind. After his 9-0 start Wilhelm ended the season at 15-11. His 2.19 ERA was the league's best. He had led the National League in his rookie year, 1952, and was the first to lead both leagues. The Orioles' 3.56 ERA was second best in the AL for the second straight year; they had four of the top ten on the leaderboard. But they again finished last in runs scored. Richards was moaning his familiar refrain: "What hurts us most is the lack of another dependable long ball hitter."[21] A different ballpark would have helped; even with its shorter fences Memorial Stadium was one of the worst in the majors for hitters.

The White Sox—still called the "Go-Go Sox"—won the pennant by five games over Cleveland. Nellie Fox was elected the AL's Most Valuable Player. Chicago's Al Lopez was the only manager to interrupt the Yankees' pennant run from 1949 through 1964; he had won in 1954 with Cleveland. New York's 79-75 record left the Yankees a distant third.

Lopez and Richards were contemporaries as players and managers and, briefly, teammates on the 1932 Dodgers. Ray Berres, who coached for both men, thought they were much alike and named them as the best managers he encountered in forty-four years in the game.[22] Analyst Bill James wrote: "Paul Richards's luck, in any area of his life, was never as good as Al Lopez's. He wasn't as handsome or as athletic. He didn't get to the majors as quickly. Lopez took over two good teams; Richards took on building projects." James described Richards as "a brilliant and talented manager [but] devious, a man who always had his own agenda."[23]

Many managers in Richards's situation would have been fired after the 1959 season. The team had gone backward for two consecutive years. He had never posted a winning record in five seasons. Lee MacPhail, the new president and general manager, was not one of Richards's confidants. When Richards recommended MacPhail for the job, he may have thought he could dominate the younger, mild-mannered executive. MacPhail wrote: "I tried to get close to Paul, and though everything was friendly, I could not seem to break through his shell. It was the manner of the man."[24] But MacPhail believed in Richards's approach to player development and was impressed by the prospects Richards and Jim McLaughlin had assembled.

On the last day of 1959 the Texas Sports Hall of Fame inducted Paul Richards, along with football coach Dana X. Bible and Southern Methodist star Doak Walker, whom Richards called the best football player he ever saw.[25] The honor reflected how far Richards had come from Waxahachie and recognized his status as a Texas icon.

1. Tom Callahan, *Johnny U: The Life and Times of John Unitas* (New York: Crown, 2006), 17–18, 151–75; the quotes are from p. 173.
2. Lee MacPhail, *My Nine Innings* (Westport, Conn.: Meckler Books, 1989), 62.
3. John Eisenberg, *From 33rd Street to Camden Yards: An Oral History of the Baltimore Orioles* (New York: Contemporary Books, 2001), 154.
4. *Sporting News* (hereafter *TSN*), March 18, 1959, 2; Paula Richards, interviews by author, 2006–2008.
5. *TSN*, May 17, 1961, 19; Eddie Robinson, interview by author, August 18, 2006, Fort Worth, Texas.
6. AP, *Warren (Pa.) Times-Mirror*, April 8, 1959, 10.
7. *New York Times*, April 15, 1960, 27. The writer was recalling a remark Richards made in April 1959.
8. *TSN*, May 13, 1959, 15.
9. Eisenberg, *From 33rd Street to Camden Yards*, 86.
10. UPI, *Morgantown, (W.Va.) Dominion-News*, July 23, 1959, 7.
11. Barry Shetrone, interview by Brent Kelley, August 10, 1992.
12. The *Look* article appears to have been written more by Cohane than Richards. The language does not match the many other published and unpublished examples of Richards's writing (Paul Richards, with Tim Cohane, "The American League Is Dying," *Look*, February 17, 1959, 41–47).
13. *TSN*, August 5, 1959, 17.
14. Ibid.
15. Eisenberg, *From 33rd Street to Camden Yards*, 97.
16. AP, *Frederick (Md.) News*, August 14, 1959, 2; James Edward Miller, *The Baseball Business: Pursuing Pennants and Profits in Baltimore* (Chapel Hill: University of North Carolina Press, 1990), 60.
17. *TSN*, August 5, 1959, 7; August 26, 1959, 22; October 28, 1959, 5.

18. Louis Berney, *Tales from the Orioles Dugout* (Champaign, Ill.: Sports Publishing, 2004), 32.

19. Eisenberg, *From 33rd Street to Camden Yards*, 83.

20. Berney, *Tales from the Orioles Dugout*, 32.

21. UPI, *Morgantown (W.Va.) Dominion-News*, July 23, 1959, 7.

22. Ray Berres, interview by Norman Macht, March 8, 1996.

23. Bill James, *The Bill James Guide to Baseball Managers* (New York: Scribner's, 1997), 195–98.

24. MacPhail, *My Nine Innings*, 63–64.

25. Texas Sports Hall of Fame induction program, December 31, 1959, in Richards scrapbooks, in the personal collection of Paula Richards; Paul Richards, taped reminiscences (undated; 1983 or later), in the author's files.

CHAPTER 16

Home Grown

S teve Barber was fed up. The twenty-one-year-old left-hander had been scuffling in Class D for three seasons, losing more games than he won and walking more batters than he struck out. "I was really wild," he said later. "One time a manager [Lou Fitzgerald] told me, 'I don't care if you walk five hundred guys, you're pitching nine innings tonight.' I walked the bases loaded in the first inning and he came out there and said, 'Well, you've got four hundred ninety-seven to go.'"

The Takoma Park, Maryland, boy had dropped out of the University of Maryland and signed with the Orioles for a $500 bonus. Barber bounced from Paris, Texas, to Dublin, Georgia, to Aberdeen, South Dakota, to Pensacola, Florida. Scouting supervisor Harry Dalton came to Pensacola and told him, "I hear you have an attitude problem." Barber answered, "I do. It seems to me that if I make it, it's all well and good for you, but if I don't it's no big deal because you don't have any money invested in me."

Barber moved up to AA Amarillo late in the 1959 season and pitched seven strong innings in his only start. Richards's roving instructor Eddie Robinson saw the game and brought Barber to Baltimore to work out in September. Richards watched him throw, then asked, "How come I've never heard of you?" The fresh rookie replied, "Probably because I'm not one of your fucking bonus babies."[1]

Richards liked fiery players. Even more, he liked pitchers who could fire the ball. Barber qualified on both counts. Richards sent him to the fall instructional league in Clearwater, Florida, where Harry Brecheen worked with Barber to improve his control, and he earned an invitation to the major league spring camp. He was no longer the neglected stepchild behind the high-profile prospects.

At the head of the line of those pitching prospects was Chuck Estrada, a Mexican American right-hander from Santa Margarita, California. He pitched a one-hitter in his first minor league season, led the Class A Sally League in strikeouts in his second, and (after a tonsillectomy) was named the outstanding AAA right-hander by sportswriters in his third. At Vancouver in 1959 Estrada struck out 177 in 182 innings. He turned twenty-two in February 1960, a week before Barber.

The Orioles brought up two other rookies from the Vancouver Mounties of the Pacific Coast League. Twenty-two-year-old shortstop Ron Hansen had missed one season because of back surgery, and his first trial with the parent club in 1958 was cut short by a broken hand. He batted only .256 for the Mounties but hit eighteen home runs. At six-foot-three he did not look like a shortstop; shortstops were little guys like Rabbit Maranville, Donie Bush, and Phil Rizzuto. The slick-fielding Hansen was drawing comparisons with the lanky one-time Cardinals star Marty Marion. Second baseman Marv Breeding was a graduate of Howard College in Florida (now Samford University), where he played baseball, basketball, and football with quarterback Bobby Bowden, later a prominent football coach.[2] After signing with Baltimore Breeding lost two years in military service and returned to hit .288 with twenty-seven stolen bases for Vancouver.

Along with the homegrown kids, MacPhail tapped the Dodgers' deep farm system in the never-ending search for a power hitter. Left-handed first baseman Jim Gentile had been in the Dodgers organization since 1952, hitting at least twenty-five home runs in all but one of his minor league stops while waiting for Gil Hodges to grow old. Roy Campanella nicknamed him "Diamond Jim" for his flashy wardrobe, but his temper attracted as much attention as his clothes and his slugging. He gained a reputation as a hothead and a whiner. In 1959 St. Paul fans voted him the most popular Saint; a few days later the team suspended him for insubordination. The Dodgers put him on waivers, but nobody claimed him, so they sent the twenty-five-year-old to Baltimore in a contingency sale. Baltimore would pay Los Angeles $25,000 if Gentile stuck more than thirty days into the season.[3]

Richards said, "We couldn't go with the same outfield as last year."[4] Gene Woodling was slow and aged, Bob Nieman was slow and aging, Willie Tasby and Al Pilarcik had not impressed. With many young pitchers in the pipeline, MacPhail traded Billy O'Dell and Billy Loes to the San Francisco Giants for outfielder Jackie Brandt, reliever Gordon Jones, and minor league catcher Roger McCardell, who never played for the Orioles. Brandt, a twenty-five-year-old right-handed batter, had hit .270 with twelve home runs and a .739 OPS, slightly below average. He was best suited for center field, but Willie Mays owned that real estate in San Francisco. Brandt won a Gold Glove for his play in left.

Swapping Brandt for Loes was a natural: one free spirit for another. Introducing himself to his new teammates, Brandt said, "My friends call me Flakey." He told reporters, "This year I'm going to play with harder nonchalance." The most famous Flakey story was the time he insisted on driving fifteen miles to a Howard Johnson's restaurant because it offered thirty-one flavors of ice cream. He ordered vanilla.[5]

Many familiar names were missing when the Orioles reported to Miami for spring training in 1960. Harshman, O'Dell, Loes, Nieman, Carrasquel, Miranda, and Zuverink were gone. On the first day Richards told his team that the White Sox had won the pennant with pitching and hustle, and "there isn't any reason in the world why you can't do it the same way."[6] *Chicago Tribune* writer Ed Prell labeled the Orioles "the team to watch in 1960 . . . the team of the future," and Arthur Richman of the *New York Mirror* even picked them to win the pennant.[7]

Steve Barber became the manager's pet project. Could Richards transform a Class D loser into a big league winner? Richards liked what he had seen in Barber's September workouts and believed in trusting his first impression of a young player. On a cold March day he drove to Bradenton, Florida, to watch Barber mow down the Milwaukee Braves. The manager sat in his car behind the dugout with the heater running and saw Barber "breaking bat after bat" with his sinking fastball. Minor league first baseman Boog Powell recalled, "The ball was just singing."[8]

Radar guns did not yet exist, but a photographer put six fireballers in front of high-speed cameras to find out who threw hardest: Sandy Koufax, Don Drysdale, Ryne Duren, Herb Score, Bob Turley, or the unknown Barber. Barber was clocked at 95.5 miles per hour, fastest of them all. Pointing to the rookie, Richards purred, "There's our surprise package."[9]

Jim Gentile struggled all spring. Shortly before the Orioles left Miami, Richards called him in. Gentile was braced for a demotion to the minors, but Richards told him, "Son, you can't be as bad as you look. . . . I'm going to give you 150 at-bats. If you hit, you're my first baseman. If not, on the thirtieth day, you'll be back with the Dodgers."[10]

Richards set out to turn the twenty-five-year-old Marv Breeding into an acceptable second baseman. He called Breeding an "ugly duckling" because of his awkwardness on the double-play pivot. Luman Harris said, "I bet Richards showed Breeding what he was doing wrong 500 times. It was the 501st time that Breeding caught on. He won't give up, that Richards." "Baseball is repetition," Richards told *Time* magazine. "Hundreds of moves all over again."[11]

Late in spring training the Orioles traded the veteran Billy Gardner to

Washington, leaving rookies Breeding and Jerry Adair as the only second basemen. Adair, twenty-three, had played basketball at Oklahoma State and batted .309 in the Texas League in his first professional season.

The Gardner deal brought catcher Clint Courtney back to Baltimore. He had played for the Browns and the '54 Orioles, but Richards had traded him. Courtney's eleven-year career launched a thousand stories. Nicknamed "Scrap Iron" for his toughness, he was one of the first catchers to wear glasses. The son of a tenant farmer originally signed with the Yankees but was sent to the Browns. He impressed his Texas League manager Rogers Hornsby (a hard man to impress) and was named the 1952 Rookie of the Year by the *Sporting News*. Courtney's on-field brawls, especially with New York's Billy Martin, were not the usual shoving matches; they drew blood. His Browns teammate Satchel Paige said, "There's the meanest man I ever met, but I'm glad he's on my side."

Courtney was country to the core. He owned a cattle ranch in Louisiana and sometimes loaded his hunting dogs and, allegedly, his smaller cows, into the backseat of his Cadillac, which was carpeted with empty beer cans. "I rode with Clint once," pitcher Dick Hall said. "It was like being in a barn."[12] A marginal left-handed hitter, the balding, bow-legged thirty-three-year-old "Scraps" quickly became a Richards favorite both for his hard-nosed play and his puppylike devotion to the manager. Courtney said, "If he told me to clean the floor, I'd put the broom up my ass and catch and sweep the floor at the same time."[13] When Richards went out to hit golf balls, Courtney shagged them. When Courtney took up the game himself, Richards gave him one free throw per hole; Courtney could pick up his ball and throw it whenever he wanted to.[14]

As opening day approached, Richards remarked, "I'm more eager to see what is going to happen this season than I ever have been in baseball."[15] He was going with the kids, but he was hardly a benevolent father figure. Brooks Robinson, who revered Richards, said, "You could get on an elevator [with him] in the morning and he wouldn't even acknowledge you."[16] The young Orioles referred to Richards as "Number Twelve," his uniform number. Some of them called Luman Harris "Twelve-and-a-Half" because he was the manager's alter ego. Harris, in his sixteenth season with Richards, played the good cop, "relaxed, laughing and cutting up." As third base coach, "Luman reads me like a book," Richards said. He sent Harris to the mound to change pitchers so there would be no argument from the man who was being relieved.[17]

In his usual pose, standing with one foot propped on the dugout step, Richards commanded the field. Jim Gentile said: "You know, he didn't say much. But you could tell when he was upset. He would grit his teeth, and this vein would just pop out on his neck." When a player left the dugout to use the bathroom, "Richards had like a clock in his head. If you were gone over, maybe, three minutes, he sent someone up after you."[18] *Time* called him "a lean, bronzed Texan right out of *High Noon*."[19] Richards's western heritage was an irresistible hook for big-city sportswriters, but he never wore a cowboy hat or boots. His black hair was salted with gray, his skinny neck corded.

Baltimore's opening day lineup against Washington in 1960 included rookies Gentile, Breeding, and Hansen, with Robinson at third, Jackie Brandt in center field, and Jerry Walker on the mound—six of the nine starters were younger than twenty-six. Gus Triandos, Gene Woodling, and left-handed hitting outfielder John Powers, a National League castoff, filled the other spots. Robinson, not yet twenty-three, was the veteran of the infield. "I guess it will be up to Woodling, Hoyt Wilhelm and me to keep the kids in line," he quipped.[20]

Richards was ejected from the opener for arguing balls and strikes, but the Orioles won 3–2, aided by Robinson's home run. After Pappas lost the next day, Barber was knocked around in his first start. Three days later Richards threw the young lefty into a game at Yankee Stadium in relief. The Yanks had battered Jack Fisher and Gordon Jones for twelve runs in the first two innings when Barber came on to mop up. He recorded four shutout innings, allowing only a hit and a walk. In his second start he pitched a complete game and held the Red Sox to one run for his first big league victory.

The Orioles put together a pair of five-game winning streaks and moved into first place on May 16, a half-game ahead of the White Sox and one game in front of the Yankees and Indians. They stayed there only one day but were back on top a week later.

Richards called up bonus baby Dave Nicholson in May. He was the tenth product of the farm system on the roster. Jim Gentile, a muscular six feet four himself, marveled, "He had a body like Superman."[21] Nicholson's performance was less than super; he struck out in more than 40 percent of his plate appearances.

On May 27 Baltimore was tied for first when Richards unveiled the innovation that became indelibly attached to his name. In 1959 Orioles catchers had allowed a record forty-nine passed balls, thirty more than any other team. Thirty-eight had come with Hoyt Wilhelm pitching. The demoralized Gus Triandos had set a record by committing twenty-eight passed balls, twenty-four while flailing at Wilhelm's knuckler. Richards had caught and managed knuckleball pitchers before, but many observers testified that Wilhelm's was in a different league. "He had the best knuckler I ever saw," Harry Brecheen said. While most knuckleballers admitted they had no idea where the ball was going, Brecheen said Wilhelm had command: "When he threw it overhand, it broke straight down. When he threw it from the side, it broke to the side."[22]

Richards commissioned the Wilson Sporting Goods Company to fashion a mitt forty-two inches in circumference, about half again as big as a normal catcher's mitt, at a cost of $400. He later said he got the idea from the giant floppy glove baseball clown Al Schacht used in his act. When Courtney wore the mitt to home plate in the bottom of the first inning at Yankee Stadium, the New York club protested. The American League's supervisor of umpires,

Cal Hubbard, cited the rule book: "A catcher may wear a leather glove or mitt of any size, shape or weight." Wilhelm pitched his first complete game of the season to beat the Yankees, with no passed balls. His catchers had committed eleven before that game; in his next 51⅓ innings they were charged with just one. "The damn thing really worked," Joe Ginsberg said, "except for one thing." It was next to impossible to dig the ball out of the mitt to throw out a base stealer. The Wilson Model 1050CL, called "Big Bertha" and "the elephant ear," became standard equipment whenever Wilhelm pitched, and Richards later used it for his knuckleball pitchers in Houston. In 1965 rule makers limited the circumference of catchers' mitts to thirty-eight inches.[23]

Wilhelm soon went back to the bullpen as the young pitchers, called the "Kiddie Korps," began taking regular turns in the starting rotation. Twenty-one-year-olds Pappas, Fisher, and Walker and twenty-two-year-olds Estrada and Barber joined the dependable Skinny Brown, now thirty-five and relying more on his knuckler.

Brown's family had nicknamed him "Skinny" in a bit of reverse psychology, because he was a chubby child.[24] He grew up to be a robust six feet two and 180 pounds. Richards said, "Harold Brown helped those young pitchers by not only telling them, but showing them, the value of strike one."[25] Brown averaged just two walks per nine innings during his fourteen-year career, ten of them with Richards. He believed he was one of the manager's favorites because he had been little Lou Redith Richards's favorite. "I got to know her in Seattle when she was four or five years old," he told Bill Tanton of the *Evening Sun*. "She used to come and hug me after the games. I just loved that little kid." In the last summer of her life a writer asked her to name her favorite player. She answered, "Brownie." When Tanton tried to question Richards about Brown's theory, the manager brushed him off: "The reason Skinny Brown is on this ball club is that he can play."[26]

Richards told the youngsters not to be too fine—just throw strikes.

"Everyone wonders where the kids get all their confidence," he said. "You'd have confidence too if you knew you could throw hell out of the ball. It's like having a .30-.30 out there on the mound."[27] He gave them at least four days' rest between starts. Jackie Brandt said: "Barber threw a shot put [a heavy sinking fastball]. Estrada threw the hardest. Pappas was slider, slider, slider. Fisher's fastball wasn't too much, but he had a grinding curveball. Walker tricked you." Harry Brecheen also named Estrada as the fastest, with "a smooth, easy motion which makes his speed more deceptive."[28]

Walker was inconsistent and did not earn his first victory until the last day of May, when he beat the Yankees and Whitey Ford. The next day Brown surrendered a first-inning homer to Mickey Mantle but did not allow another hit in a 4–1 win. In the final game of the series Wilhelm and Fisher gave up five runs. The Orioles battled back to tie, and Woodling won it with an eighth-inning homer. With the sweep Baltimore had won eleven of thirteen to take a two-and-a-half-game lead. The Yankees fell to .500.

While the Orioles' young pitchers were getting the headlines, the club was winning with its bats, a startling turnaround from previous years. In mid-June Baltimore led the league in runs scored but was next to last in ERA. The rest of the "Baby Birds" were proving themselves. "Don't call them kids," Richards cautioned. "They look like men to me."[29] Ron Hansen's batting average rose as high as .361. Jim Gentile, playing against right-handed pitchers in a platoon with Walt Dropo, was leading the team in home runs and batting .331. On June 16, 1960, he drove in a record seven runs in two consecutive innings with a pair of homers against Kansas City. Since most of his hitters were producing, Richards was content to stay with a set lineup except for the first base platoon and his inability to find a right fielder. Willie Tasby, once a top prospect, was dealt to Boston for Gene Stephens, but Stephens had evidently lost his batting stroke after spending several years as Ted Williams's late-inning defensive caddy. The Orioles picked up thirty-three-year-old Jim

Busby after he was released by the Red Sox and installed him in center, moving Jackie Brandt to right.

Baltimore held a two-and-a-half-game lead when the Detroit Tigers came to town on June 7. Detroit won four straight to knock the Orioles out of first place. As his club began a fourteen-game road trip, Richards said, "If the Orioles were going to fold, I figured this would be the time." They fell behind 5–0 in the third inning at Kansas City but came back to score once in the fourth. Brandt began talking it up on the bench: "We'll win this one yet. All we gotta do is score a run an inning for the rest of the game."[30] That's what they did, putting six straight 1's on the scoreboard to pull out a 6–5 victory.

At long last in a pennant race, Richards was more intense than ever. On June 27 umpire Joe Papparella ejected him for "the most insulting language I have heard in 23 years in the game."[31] When Pappas surrendered ten hits and four runs to the weak Washington Senators, the manager unloaded on him in a rare public scolding. He complained that Pappas had spent spring training saying hi to other players rather than getting into shape. After the diatribe Pappas won his next four decisions.[32]

On July 6 against the Yankees Richards uncharacteristically ordered two intentional walks in the first inning. Brown started and put runners on second and third with one out. Roger Maris was passed to load the bases for a possible double play and get a platoon advantage with the right-handed Bill Skowron coming up. Skowron struck out. After a wild pitch scored one run and advanced runners to second and third, Richards ordered a walk to Yogi Berra to bring up the weak-hitting Clete Boyer, who struck out to end the inning. The Orioles issued only nineteen intentional bases on balls all season, the fewest in the majors. Richards called the intentional pass "a dangerous gamble" but added, "It is a gamble, however, that a manager must make at times."[33]

Baltimore lost two to New York and three to Washington, falling to fourth place at the first all-star break, four games behind the league-leading Yankees.

The Orioles struggled for much of June and July. Barber had a 5-1 record at the end of May when he lost sight of home plate and did not win again for two months. He regained his form with a one-hitter against Kansas City on July 28, striking out ten. Barber led the majors in walks and topped the AL in wild pitches. Later in the season he tore up the clubhouse after Richards relieved him with two outs and the bases loaded in the ninth. Instead of punishment, the manager offered praise for his star pupil: "I was really proud of that boy. I hated to take him out, but it was the only thing to do."[34]

Brooks Robinson was shedding his "good field, no hit" label. After a slow start he raised his batting average to .300 in July and showed some power, often batting third in the lineup. He delivered eight consecutive hits in two games (separated by the July all-star break), going 5-for-5 and hitting for the cycle against the White Sox. He finished the month with his first grand-slam home run.

The Orioles won eight straight and trailed the Yankees by just .004 points when they went to New York on August 15, 1960. Richards said, "Nothing has convinced me we can't win it."[35] Hansen's homer boosted them to a 2–0 lead. When Mickey Mantle came to bat in the fourth, boos echoed around the triple-decked grandstand, which was less than half full. Mantle had failed to run out a ground ball the day before. Now his two-run homer tied the game. Jackie Brandt's home run gave the Orioles a 3–2 lead in the eighth when Mantle's turn came again. With Wilhelm pitching, Mantle lifted a pop foul near home plate, but Courtney, wearing the big mitt, dropped it. Then Mantle lined a two-run, game-winning homer. The next day Whitey Ford shut out the Orioles on three hits, lifting the Yankees a half-game ahead of Chicago and one and a half in front of Baltimore.

Barely two weeks later the Yankees came to Baltimore with a one-game lead. Ford, who had shut out the Orioles three times, started the opener before 44,518. Baltimore chased him with four runs in five innings while Pappas pitched a three-hit shutout. The next day Jack Fisher, in the midst of a streak of twenty-nine scoreless innings, blanked the New Yorkers as Robinson batted in the only two runs with a homer and a single. In the series finale Estrada pitched no-hit ball for six and a third innings—the Orioles had held the Yankees scoreless for twenty-four innings—then Wilhelm came on to finish a 6–2 victory. The sweep moved Baltimore into first place by two games with twenty-two left to play. Richards crowed, "We just stared 'em in the face and beat 'em down."[36]

In the 154-game seasons before expansion, each team played each of the others twenty-two times. Baltimore and the Yankees were even at 9-9 when the Orioles went to New York on September 16 to wrap up the season series. They trailed in the standings by just .001, and the league had authorized them to print World Series tickets. "We may win the pennant," Richards said. "Nobody else has won it yet."[37] Lee MacPhail chartered a bus to take the entire front-office staff to see the four-game set.

Whitey Ford went to the mound in the first game. He had not allowed a run in three starts against Baltimore at Yankee Stadium. This time he held the Orioles scoreless for eight and two-thirds innings. When Baltimore loaded the bases in the ninth, Stengel lifted his ace. Richards had Jim Gentile ready to pinch-hit against a right-handed reliever, but Stengel called on veteran lefty Bobby Shantz, even though the next two Orioles hitters were right-handed. "Gentile had been sitting on the bench all during the game and Stengel knew I was just waiting for the right spot to use him," Richards said.[38] Shantz gave up two runs but preserved the victory. The Yankees swept four in a row, behind home runs by Mantle, Berra, Roger Maris, Hector Lopez, and Tony Kubek, to beat Barber, Estrada, Fisher, and Pappas. Years later Skinny Brown faulted Richards for using the kids in such crucial games, especially because Brown and Wilhelm had a history of success against the Yankees. Brown said, "From there on it was downhill."[39]

New York went on to win its last fifteen straight, the greatest finishing kick in history. The Orioles clung to second place, eight games behind, with an

89-65 record. It was the highest finish of Richards's career as a manager. "I'm proud of these boys," he said. "I think they're pretty good, and they're going to get better. We got to a certain point, and we couldn't get any farther."[40] The Orioles allowed the fewest runs in the league, committed the fewest errors, and finished a surprising third in runs scored. Again the manager lamented, "If I had one more power hitter."[41] Home attendance climbed to a franchise record 1,187,849, third in the league behind New York and Chicago. The ball club sent out the unused World Series tickets as Christmas cards.[42]

"I'd have to say it was my favorite year of my career," Ron Hansen recalled in retirement. "I was a kid and everything was exciting."[43] Hansen led the team with twenty-two home runs in an era when Ernie Banks was the game's only power-hitting shortstop. Hansen was named AL Rookie of the Year, receiving 22 of 24 votes from writers; Gentile and Estrada got the other 2. Gentile slugged twenty-one homers and drove in ninety-eight runs in 384 at-bats, with a .904 OPS. Estrada tied Cleveland's Jim Perry for the league lead with eighteen victories. Pappas won fifteen, Fisher and Brown twelve, Wilhelm eleven, and Barber ten, all with better-than-average ERAs. Brooks Robinson established himself as a star with a .294 average, fourteen homers, and eighty-eight RBI. He won the first of sixteen consecutive Gold Gloves and finished third in the Most Valuable Player voting behind Maris and Mantle. "We had a real good year, our first good year, and we felt there were more good things to come," he remembered. "And I mean, the Yankees were supposed to win. They were the kings at that time, and we didn't feel bad. We felt like, 'Well, you know, there's next year.'"[44]

---

1. John Eisenberg, *From 33rd Street to Camden Yards: An Oral History of the Baltimore Orioles* (New York: Contemporary Books, 2001), 49, 92–93.
2. *Decatur (Ala.) Daily,* January 2, 2007, online edition.
3. Jim Gentile, undated interview by Jim Sanders, ca. 2002; *Sporting News* (hereafter *TSN*), September 23, 1959, 38; May 4, 1960, 17; May 17, 1961, 6.
4. *TSN*, December 9, 1959, 18.

5. *Baltimore Sun*, August 31, 2004, online edition; Eisenberg, *From 33rd Street to Camden Yards*, 122; Danny Peary, ed., *We Played the Game* (New York: Black Dog and Laventhol, 1994), 483.

6. UPI, *Chicago Defender*, June 8, 1960, 23.

7. *Chicago Tribune*, February 4, 1960, D1; *TSN*, June 15, 1960, 11.

8. Eisenberg, *From 33rd Street to Camden Yards*, 93.

9. Bill James and Rob Neyer, *The Neyer/James Guide to Pitchers* (New York: Fireside/Simon and Schuster, 2004), 126; Eisenberg, *From 33rd Street to Camden Yards*, 98. James and Neyer say the experiment was conducted by *Time* magazine after the season, but I could find no such story in *Time*'s archives. Eisenberg says it was reported during spring training by a Sunday newspaper supplement. That is the likelier explanation, because it would have been easy to arrange the photo shoots when the teams were in Florida in the spring. *Washington Post*, March 17, 1961, B1. The story referred to a comment by Richards in 1960.

10. Louis Berney, *Tales from the Orioles Dugout* (Champaign, Ill.: Sports Publishing, 2004), 10.

11. *TSN*, July 6, 1960, 3; "Two for the Money?" *Time*, September 26, 1960, online archive.

12. *TSN*, March 30, 1960, 9; *New York Times*, June 17, 1975, 36; *Baltimore Sun*, August 31, 2004, online edition.

13. Eisenberg, *From 33rd Street to Camden Yards*, 103.

14. Eddie Robinson, interview by author, August 18, 2006, Fort Worth, Texas.

15. *TSN*, April 27, 1960, 19.

16. Eisenberg, *From 33rd Street to Camden Yards*, 24.

17. *TSN*, September 20, 1961, 6, and October 3, 1964, 7; Roy Terrell, "Hawkeye and His Boy Scouts," *Sports Illustrated*, April 17, 1961, 71.

18. Gentile interview.

19. "Two for the Money?"

20. *TSN*, June 1, 1960, 4.

21. Gentile interview.

22. Eisenberg, *From 33rd Street to Camden Yards*, 85.

23. Paul Richards, taped reminiscences (undated; 1983 or later), in the author's files; Mark Armour, "Hoyt Wilhelm, Starting Pitcher," *Articles Related to Rob Neyer's Big Book of Baseball Lineups*, 2003, www.robneyer.com/book_03_BAL.html (2003); *TSN*, June 8, 1960, 13, and July 6, 1960, 4; Bob Cairns, *Pen Men* (New York: St. Martin's, 1992), 100; *USA Today*, May 6, 1986, 2C.

24. Harold Brown, interview by Brent Kelley, July 29, 1991.

25. *Baltimore Sun*, September 30, 1979, C5.

26. *Baltimore Evening Sun*, reprinted in *Dallas Times-Herald*, May 7, 1986, 1C.

27. "Young Orioles," *Time*, June 6, 1960, online archive.

28. Eisenberg, *From 33rd Street to Camden Yards*, 98; *TSN*, July 13, 1960, 28.

29. AP, *Los Angeles Times*, June 21, 1960, C5.

30. Paul Richards, as told to Arthur and Milton Richman, "The Orioles Will Win the Pennant," *Saturday Evening Post*, April 15, 1961, 126.

31. *TSN*, July 6, 1960, 26.

32. Ibid., July 13, 1960, 20.

33. Paul Richards, *Modern Baseball Strategy* (Englewood Cliffs, N.J.: Prentice-Hall, 1955), 50.

34. *TSN*, September 21, 1960, 7.

35. Ibid., August 24, 1960, 14.

36. *New York Times*, September 3, 1960, 12; September 4, 1960, 129; *TSN*, September 14, 1960, 4.

37. *TSN*, February 1, 1961, 7; "Two for the Money?"

38. Richards, "Orioles Will Win the Pennant," 124.

39. Eisenberg, *From 33rd Street to Camden Yards*, 107–8; Brown interview.

40. *TSN*, September 21, 1960, 7.

41. Ibid., October 26, 1960, 4.

42. Ibid., January 25, 1961, 23.

43. Eisenberg, *From 33rd Street to Camden Yards*, 108.

44. Ibid.

CHAPTER 17

Bound for Texas

As the 1960 presidential race between Richard M. Nixon and John F. Kennedy moved toward a tight finish, thirteen days in October rocked baseball. The Yankees outscored the National League champion Pittsburgh Pirates 46–17 in the first six games of the World Series, but Pittsburgh managed to win three of them. In the seventh game on October 13 Bill Mazeroski's dramatic home run in the bottom of the ninth gave the Pirates the championship.

Five days later the Yankees announced Casey Stengel's retirement after ten pennants in twelve seasons as manager. Co-owner Dan Topping, with much hemming and hawing, said Stengel had agreed to step down, but Casey told reporters, "Quit, fired, whatever you please. I don't care." Later he said, "I'll never make the mistake of being seventy again."[1]

National League owners, meeting in Chicago on October 17, inaugurated a new era in baseball history. They voted to expand the circuit for the first time since 1892, adding teams in New York and Houston to begin play in 1962. Sportswriter Jerome Holtzman commented, "The Continental League went phffft—and disappeared into the hot air from whence it came."[2]

The National League expansion stung their American League rivals, especially the Yankees, who enjoyed having the New York market as their exclusive preserve after the Giants and Dodgers went west. Yankees co-owner Del Webb was chair of the AL expansion committee and the "king-maker," as writer Shirley Povich put it. Without mentioning his own self-interest, Webb said the Nationals had "pulled a fast one on us" by grabbing the booming Houston market.[3] On October 25 the AL voted to expand—not in 1962 but in 1961. New franchises would go to Los Angeles and Washington, with the struggling Senators transferring to Minneapolis–St. Paul. Given the repeated threats from Congress to end baseball's antitrust exemption, the owners felt they had to put a replacement team in the nation's capital. That shut out a group of investors from Dallas–Fort Worth who had been leading contenders for a club.

With opening day less than six months away, the AL had to provide players for its new teams. Each existing club submitted a list of fifteen draft-eligible players from its forty-man roster and could lose seven of them for $75,000 apiece. In addition, the expansion teams could take one minor leaguer from each club for $25,000.[4]

In deciding who would be exposed to the expansion draft, MacPhail and Richards protected all their young major league pitchers and position players. Richards saw that he had no room on the roster to protect Chuck Hinton, a fast and powerful twenty-six-year-old who had batted .358 and .369 with twenty homers in each of his first two full minor league seasons after military service. Richards sweet-talked Hinton during the fall instructional league in Arizona, assuring the young man that he had a bright future in Baltimore. Richards persuaded Hinton to run into the outfield wall and fake a shoulder injury, then sent him home with his arm in a sling. It soon dawned on Hinton that the expansion draft was his ticket to the majors, so he told reporters he was not hurt.[5] Washington claimed him, and he went on to an eleven-year big league career.

For their final protected spot the Orioles had to choose between Dean Chance and Arne Thorsland, a pair of right-handed pitchers with just two years of professional experience. Each had posted a 22-12 record in the minors. While Chance had the better ERA, Thorsland threw harder and appeared to be more advanced; he had pitched one game at AAA Vancouver. Jim McLaughlin and his scouts wanted to keep Chance, but Richards insisted Thorsland was the superior prospect. Fred Hofman warned that Thorsland threw across his body, making him a candidate for injury because the delivery put extra strain on his arm. Richards's opinion carried the day, but the decision became the back-breaking straw in the conflict between the Richards and McLaughlin fiefdoms.

"It got to the point where you were either a 'McLaughlin player' or a 'Richards player' in the organization, and there were decisions made on that basis," Lee MacPhail said. "Paul and Jim just never could get along. They were always after each other." Richards was considered the indispensable man, so MacPhail fired McLaughlin. "I hated to do it," he said years later.[6] (McLaughlin gave a different version of his dismissal. He said the cause was the $80,000 bonus he paid to teenage pitcher Dave McNally without authorization.[7] By the time he told the story, McNally had become a star, making McLaughlin look prescient.)

McLaughlin's thirty-two-year-old assistant, Harry Dalton, replaced him. Dalton said of his mentor: "His legacy was organizing the farm and scouting department, and helping establish a strong pride in the organization. The Orioles became well respected, not only because of their success on the field, but a lot of baseball people thought the organization was run very well."[8] In addition to signing key players for Baltimore's pennant winners of 1966, 1969, 1970, and 1971, McLaughlin created a farm system for future general managers, including Dalton, Hank Peters, Lou Gorman, John Hart, and John Schuerholz.

Three of McLaughlin's last judgments proved to be correct. Dave McNally won 181 games for the Orioles, recording at least twenty victories in four straight seasons. Dean Chance won the Cy Young Award for the expansion Los Angeles Angels three years later and went on to 128 victories. Arne Thorsland's arm gave out. He never threw a pitch in the majors.

MacPhail signed Richards to a three-year contract extension with a $5,000 raise to $50,000. "I have said before, and I will say again, I am happy to remain in Baltimore as long as my services are in demand," Richards told the writers.

"My relationship with Lee MacPhail has been excellent and the performance of some of our young players has given me a lot of hope."[9]

The Richards family moved from the old farmhouse to a new one-story brick ranch-style house alongside the second green of the Waxahachie Country Club golf course. It was just a few hundred yards from the old house, atop a low hill overlooking the family's seventy acres. Paula had left for college. This would be Paul and Margie's home for the rest of their lives.

In January 1961 Richards traveled to Houston for a banquet welcoming the city to the major leagues—or, as the locals preferred, welcoming the majors to Houston. National League president Warren Giles and all seven of the circuit's managers attended (the Cubs job was vacant), along with an overflow crowd of thirteen hundred at the Shamrock-Hilton Hotel. Richards was the only American League manager on hand. Rumors were circulating that he would become the expansion franchise's first manager when it began play the following year, but he said the club never talked to him about the job.[10]

After the Baby Birds' near-miss, Richards's star was shining brighter than ever. Both the Associated Press and United Press International named him the American League Manager of the Year. CBS-TV's *Sunday Sports Spectacular* aired a ninety-minute documentary, "Paul Richards—Big League Manager." Wired for sound, he mused on what he called the paradox of baseball: "Maybe this is the wrong word, but it's strange and an oddity that we're looking for pitchers who can get bad balls swung at. We're looking for hitters who won't swing at bad balls.

"We're looking for ways and we're working on things to get people out and yet we're working on ways up here to keep this [batter] from getting out."[11]

Sports Illustrated's Roy Terrell portrayed Richards as a figure out of a western novel by Zane Grey or Max Brand, "a cold man and a hard one. Yet when he chooses to relax the imperious reserve that cloaks him he can charm a ballplayer right out of his spikes, and the loyalty he elicits from the few who know him well is a rare and unusual thing." Chicago writer Jerome Holtzman labeled him "Baltimore's most quoted sage since H. L. Mencken."[12]

On opening day of the expanded 162-game season the Orioles distributed thousands of bumper stickers and posters with their new slogan, "It Can Be Done in '61," in six languages, including Russian.[13] The club lost five of its first six games before beginning a steady climb above .500. In the latest version of his favorite whine, Richards told *Sports Illustrated*: "All this team really needs is that one big man. A monster who can hit 40 home runs and bat in 130 runs for you."[14] He had that man, but he didn't know it yet.

Jim Gentile opened the season in the same platoon role with Walt Dropo at first base. When the Orioles paid their first visit to the new Minnesota Twins (the former Washington Senators), Gentile, who had played for the Dodgers' St. Paul farm club, partied all night with friends. He insisted he didn't drink much, but he did not feel like playing on May 9. In the first inning Whitey Herzog, Jackie Brandt, and Brooks Robinson reached base, and Gentile poled a grand-slam home run to center field off the Twins' Pedro Ramos. Baltimore loaded the bases again in the second, bringing up Gentile to face reliever Paul Giel. On the first pitch Gentile belted a hanging screwball over the right-field fence. In the dugout Richards slapped him on the backside and said, "You know, son, I don't think that's ever been done before."[15] It hadn't. Tony Lazzeri, Jim Tabor, and Rudy York had hit two grand slams in one game, but no one had connected in consecutive innings. (In 1999 St. Louis third baseman Fernando Tatis hit two in the same inning.)

The next day Minnesota started a left-handed pitcher, and Gentile went to the bench. Two days later in Cleveland he got his first start against a lefty, Johnny Antonelli, and slammed a home run. The day after that he homered off left-handed reliever Bob Allen. Richards began playing Gentile no matter who was pitching. By the end of May Gentile was leading the league in homers and RBI, and Dropo was released. A writer asked Richards, "How in the devil did you ever come to go with that boy with what you knew [about his reputation]?"

"Hell, the boy's a human being," he replied, "and he had been kicked around a lot."[16] Given his own long road through the minors, Richards could empathize.

Now Richards's future was calling. Houston's new National League franchise had hired Gabe Paul away from Cincinnati as general manager. Paul began building a scouting and front-office staff to prepare for the club's debut in 1962 but soon clashed with the strongman in the Houston ownership group, Judge Roy Hofheinz. On April 27 Paul resigned to become GM of the Cleveland Indians.

Richards made the first move with a phone call to George Kirksey, executive vice president of the Houston club.[17] Their conversation violated baseball's rule against tampering with another club's employee. Kirksey—secretive by nature—embarked on a cloak-and-dagger courtship. He enlisted Richards's boyhood friend, the Reverend Clyde Verheyden, as his cutout and assigned Richards the code name Blackie. When Richards sent word that he did not think Houston could afford him, Kirksey signaled Blackie that money would not be an issue. The clandestine messages continued to flow between Houston and Baltimore as Kirksey pursued the most prominent Texan in the game.

The negotiations moved quickly. Kirksey and another minority owner of the club, Craig Cullinan Jr., went to Baltimore in May for a face-to-face talk. The Houston group agreed to Richards's terms at a June meeting in Cleveland: "It was with the understanding that I would have complete control of baseball." The owners would handle the business end. But he did not sign a contract, and the agreement was kept secret.[18]

Baltimore hovered around .500 through May and June. The pitching was inconsistent; both Pappas and Estrada missed time with sore arms. Steve Barber stepped up with a 7-3 record and three shutouts by the end of May. Skinny

Brown won his first five decisions, but Estrada, Pappas, and Fisher had a combined 4-11 mark.

On June 20 the club stood at 32-33, in fifth place. A wisecrack circulated in Baltimore: "It must be done in '61 or Richards is through in '62."[19] Then the pitchers revived. They allowed only five runs in an eight-game stretch beginning July 3 as the Orioles moved up to third place, seven games behind, at the first all-star break.

Because 1960's pennant-winning manager, Casey Stengel, was no longer with the Yankees, second-place Richards managed the AL all-stars. The first game was played on July 11 at San Francisco's Candlestick Park, where the notorious wind blew the Giants' wispy reliever Stu Miller off the pitching rubber for a balk. The National Leaguers won, 5–4.

In San Francisco, Houston writer Clark Nealon confronted Richards with knowledge of his deal to join the expansion franchise. The two had known each other since they covered college football together when Richards was moonlighting as a sportswriter. Richards persuaded Nealon to hold the story because no contract had been signed and his Baltimore bosses had been told nothing.[20] The secret was out, but it was distorted as it traveled along baseball's grapevine. On July 18 the Associated Press's national baseball writer, Joe Reichler, reported that Richards was going to Houston as field manager. A week later Reichler caught up and said the job would be general manager. That same day the *Baltimore News-Post* had Richards working with a Dallas–Fort Worth group to capture a team in the next round of expansion. Richards denied everything: "It's embarrassing to turn down jobs that haven't been offered. But what else can I do?" He told the *Dallas Times-Herald*, "I'm not going anywhere."[21]

The Orioles were not going anywhere, either, despite a remarkable surge. They played .610 ball (47-30) after the first all-star break but were never in the pennant race, as New York and the surprising Detroit Tigers pulled away. The Tigers feasted on the weak expansion teams, posting a 27-9 record against

Washington and Los Angeles. The Yankees, under new manager Ralph Houk, were slugging their way to a major league record 240 home runs as Mickey Mantle and Roger Maris challenged Babe Ruth's storied mark of sixty.

In July Skinny Brown pitched thirty-six consecutive scoreless innings. One game was a four-hit shutout of New York, the first time the Bombers had been held scoreless all season. Two days later Steve Barber blanked them again. The Orioles took three out of four at Yankee Stadium, but remained in third place, eight and a half games behind.

By August MacPhail had given Houston permission to talk to Richards, but the mention of his name was still forbidden in the Houston Sports Association's offices—until George Kirksey slipped. "We'll need to draw up a $50,000 life insurance policy for Blackie," he said, "and Mrs. Richards will need one, too."[22]

MacPhail believed the continuing speculation—would the manager go or stay?—was a serious distraction: "One could not blame him for wanting to make the move, but the publicity about the possibilities of his going ran on and on and in my opinion had a negative effect on the team. I think it also may have distracted Paul, and the Orioles may not have received the intense concentration that he usually gave to them." MacPhail told him to make up his mind by September 1.

Richards managed his last game on August 30 at Los Angeles. The Orioles belted five home runs to beat the Angels, 11-4, but Jack Fisher walked twelve. Richards thought the umpires were plotting to give him a going-away present. Plate umpire Ed Hurley made obviously bad calls against Fisher, hoping to lure their nemesis out to argue and add to his eighty ejections as a big league manager. Richards did not stir from the dugout as his seven years with the Orioles ended quietly.[23]

While the team flew home the next day, Richards detoured to meet Kirksey in Scottsdale, Arizona, and formally accept the Houston job. Richards returned to Baltimore for a brief meeting with MacPhail and an even briefer announcement of his resignation.[24]

Richards left the club in third place with a 78-57 record, eleven games behind the Yankees. Luman Harris took over as interim manager, and the Orioles finished the season in third place, thirteen and a half games back, with ninety-five victories, the most by any of Richards's clubs. The Yankees won 109 games and the Tigers 100. Steve Barber won eighteen for the Orioles with a 3.33 ERA and tied for the league lead with eight shutouts. Estrada went 15-9, but he and Barber walked more batters than any other pitchers in the league.

Jim Gentile had turned into the big man Richards long lusted for, finishing third behind Maris and Mantle with forty-six home runs and second to Maris with 141 RBI. Or so the record books say; decades later a researcher for the *Retrosheet* project discovered that Maris had been mistakenly awarded an RBI he did not deserve. Subtracting that one would have left him tied with Gentile for the league lead. When the researcher tracked down Gentile in Oklahoma, the sixty-five-year-old roared, "God damn it, I had a $5,000 clause [in his contract] if I led the league in RBIs. You think I can get those bastards to give it to me?"[25]

In seven seasons in Baltimore Richards transformed a woeful franchise into a winner, as he had in Chicago. Just as Frank Lane deserves to share the credit for the White Sox's rise, Jim McLaughlin made vital contributions to the Orioles'. Despite their mutual loathing, Richards and McLaughlin complemented each other. Richards provided the high-profile leadership that persuaded the owners to commit to his plan and stick with it, while McLaughlin supplied most of the scouts and players.

In his usual dry fashion Lee MacPhail wrote of Richards, "He had his pluses and minuses, but he was an excellent manager on the field, great with pitchers, a good judge of talent, and did a fine job with the Orioles."[26] John F. Steadman of the *News-Post* offered a grudging valedictory: "A controversial figure in his seven years here, he was respected for his baseball knowledge but kept his distance with the players and public and maybe at times was misunderstood. Certainly he exerted more influence on the changing, revised baseball picture in Baltimore than any other man."[27] The *Sun's* Bob Maisel concluded, "Whether you liked him or not, Richards will not be an easy man to replace."[28]

Later critics accused Richards of abusing the Kiddie Korps and ruining the careers of several of the pitching prodigies. Rob Neyer wrote: "In fact, aside from a brief stretch when Pappas was nineteen, I don't believe that Richards babied his young pitchers at all. Further, I believe that the combination of bringing them to the majors at such tender ages and *not* babying them goes a long way toward explaining why only Pappas won as many as a hundred games in his career."[29]

The record proves otherwise. Steve Barber won 121 games and pitched until he was thirty-six years old, battling a sore elbow and finishing up as a reliever. Jack Fisher's lifetime record is 86-139; he would have reached one hundred victories if he had not been sentenced to four years with the hapless New York Mets. Pappas, of course, won 209 games in a seventeen-year career.

The evidence that Richards enforced pitch counts is incontrovertible and comes from men who knew first hand: Pappas, Eddie Robinson, Larry Dierker, and Tony La Russa. Jim McLaughlin said, "He laid down numbers as laws."[30]

The indictment of Richards boils down to the early flameouts of Jerry Walker and Chuck Estrada. After Walker was ineffective in 1960, the Orioles traded him to Kansas City, where, as he said, he came up with a sore arm. But his decline started when Richards let him pitch the sixteen-inning game at age twenty. He was essentially finished at twenty-two. Estrada, after two strong seasons under Richards, dropped to 9-17 in 1962, although his ERA was still near the league average. The next year elbow surgery destroyed his career at age twenty-five.

No record of the Kiddie Korps' pitch counts survives.[31] They rarely started with less than four days' rest and often had more. While Richards was manager, all of them pitched into the seventh inning in most of their starts, except for the nineteen-year-old Pappas for part of 1958 and the twenty-one-year-old Walker in 1960, when he was struggling. Pappas's fifteen complete games at age twenty were second in the American League and his career high. He was in the top ten the next two seasons, so he evidently suffered no short-term damage. Barber completed fourteen starts at age twenty-three, the league's third highest. Estrada's twelve complete games at age twenty-two ranked sixth.

In the 1980s Craig Wright, the first man to put "Sabermetrician" on his business card, documented that a large number of pitchers who endured heavy workloads before age twenty-five soon blew out their arms. Physicians specializing in sports medicine have since confirmed that fatigue can contribute to injury. Richards also believed that "a tired pitcher is a badly handicapped pitcher."[32]

Wright posited, based on estimated pitch counts, that a young pitcher should not face more than thirty-one batters in a game. That suggests at least 100 to 120 pitches. Again, with the exceptions of Pappas and Walker, all the Kiddie Korps routinely faced thirty-one batters or more. The available evidence from the Kiddie Korps' workloads indicates that the pitch limit was 100 or 110. Those were the restrictions Richards set later in Houston and in his second tour with the White Sox.[33]

However, it is not unusual for two of five promising young pitchers to break down. It is so common that researcher Gary Huckabay coined the cautionary acronym TINSTAAPP—there is no such thing as a pitching prospect. Richards knew that; he said, "It takes five possible pitchers to get one pitcher."[34] From the five members of his Kiddie Korps, Richards produced one outstanding pitcher (Pappas), one good one (Barber), one fair one (Fisher), and, in Walker and Estrada, two proofs of TINSTAAPP.

Richards and McLaughlin left the Orioles with five regulars and five estab-lished pitchers younger than twenty-eight, plus a farm system brimming with prospects. When Luman Harris declined to be considered for the manager's job because he was going with Richards to Houston, MacPhail hired Billy Hitch-cock, a friendly, easy-going gentleman who was the anti-Richards. The club fell to seventh place in the ten-team league in 1962, and Hitchcock was fired the following year. MacPhail described Hitchcock as "a wonderful man . . . but he was a better guy than manager."[35]

Baltimore won its first pennant in 1966 under the tough ex-Yankee Hank Bauer, with Brooks Robinson, Steve Barber, Dave McNally, and Boog Powell as key performers—all products of the Richards-McLaughlin era. Richards's greatest contribution to the 1966 World Series champions was the man who wasn't there, Milt Pappas. The Orioles traded Pappas to Cincinnati for Frank Robinson, who won the AL triple crown and became the indispensable team leader.

---

1. Robert W. Creamer, *Stengel: His Life and Times* (1984; repr., Lincoln: University of Nebraska Press, 1996), 290–91.
2. *Sporting News* (hereafter *TSN*), October 10, 1960, 4.
3. *TSN*, November 2, 1960, 3–4.
4. *New York Times*, December 15, 1960, 64.
5. Earl Weaver, with Berry Stainback, *It's What You Learn after You Know It All That Counts* (New York: Doubleday, 1982), 118–19.
6. John Eisenberg, *From 33rd Street to Camden Yards: An Oral History of the Baltimore Orioles* (New York: Contemporary Books, 2001), 70; Weaver, *It's What You Learn*, 115–16.
7. Kevin Kerrane, *Dollar Sign on the Muscle* (New York: Fireside/Simon and Schuster, 1989), 146.
8. Eisenberg, *From 33rd Street to Camden Yards*, 68.
9. *TSN*, November 23, 1960, 40.
10. Ibid., January 18, 1961, 24, and September 6, 1961, 6; *Houston Post*, September 3, 1961, in the Paul Richards file, A. Bartlett Giamatti Research Center, National Baseball Hall of Fame and Museum, Cooperstown, N.Y.; Paul Richards, interview by Clark Nealon, February 5, 1981.
11. AP, *Zanesville (Ohio) Times Recorder*, April 2, 1961, 27.
12. Roy Terrell, "Hawkeye and His Boy Scouts," *Sports Illustrated*, April 17, 1961, 68; Jerome Holtzman, "Why Do Few Champions Repeat?" *Baseball Digest*, April 1961, 29.
13. "The Longest Season," *Time*, April 21, 1961, online archive.

14. Terrell, "Hawkeye and His Boy Scouts," 84.

15. Eisenberg, *From 33rd Street to Camden Yards*, 119.

16. *Houston Post*, September 4, 1961, in Richards's Hall of Fame file.

17. Richards interview.

18. Ibid.; Robert Reed, *Colt .45s: A Six-Gun Salute* (Houston: Gulf Publishing, 1999), 18, 49–52.

19. *Washington Post*, June 16, 1961, B2.

20. Richards interview. Clark Nealon added his own recollections to the interview. Richards did not dispute him.

21. AP, *Galveston (Texas) Daily News*, July 19, 1961, 10; AP, *San Mateo, (Calif.) Times*, July 26, 1961, 2; AP photo caption, July 26, 1961, in Paul Richards scrapbooks, in the possession of Paula Richards; *TSN*, September 6, 1961, 6. Stories in these papers quoted the *Baltimore News-Post* and *Dallas Times-Herald*.

22. Campbell B. Titchener, *The George Kirksey Story: Bringing Major League Baseball to Houston* (Austin: Eakin Press, 1989), 93.

23. Lee MacPhail, *My Nine Innings* (Westport, Conn.: Meckler Books, 1989), 70; Richards interview; *TSN*, September 6, 1961, 6.

24. *Baltimore Sun*, September 1, 1961, 25, and September 2, 1961, 13.

25. Alan Schwarz, *The Numbers Game: Baseball's Lifelong Fascination with Statistics* (New York: Thomas Dunne Books/St. Martin's, 2004), 253. The official record had not been corrected in 2008.

26. MacPhail, *My Nine Innings*, 70.

27. *TSN*, September 6, 1961, 6.

28. *Baltimore Sun*, September 2, 1961, 16.

29. Rob Neyer, *Rob Neyer's Big Book of Baseball Lineups* (New York: Fireside/Simon and Schuster, 2003), 34.

30. Eisenberg, *From 33rd Street to Camden Yards*, 78; Eddie Robinson, interview by author, August 18, 2006, Fort Worth, Texas; Larry Dierker, *This Ain't Brain Surgery* (New York: Simon and Schuster, 2003), 55; Buzz Bissinger, *Three Nights in August* (Boston: Houghton Mifflin, 2005), 177; Kerrane, *Dollar Sign on the Muscle*, 145.

31. Several researchers have developed methods to estimate pitch counts, but they are highly speculative.

32. Craig Wright and Tom House, *The Diamond Appraised* (New York: Simon and Schuster, 1989), 192–210; Buzz Bissinger, "My Right Arm," *Play*, online magazine published by the *New York Times*, June 3, 2007, www.nytimes.com/2007/06/03/sports/playmagazine/0603play-wood.html; *TSN*, June 20, 1951, 6.

33. Wright and House, *Diamond Appraised*, 211; Dierker, *This Ain't Brain Surgery*, 55; Bissinger, *Three Nights in August*, 177.

34. Clay Davenport, e-mail to author, March 19, 2007; *TSN*, December 11, 1965, 25. Huckabay wrote for *Baseball Prospectus*.

35. Eisenberg, *From 33rd Street to Camden Yards*, 120.

CHAPTER 18

The Man in the Dugout

There was a look fathers used to give their kids, where you just backed off when you saw it. Richards had that.
—**Fred Marsh**

When Paul Richards left Baltimore, he essentially closed his career as a field manager, although he returned to the dugout fifteen years later for one miserable season. In his first eleven seasons with the White Sox and Orioles, his teams won 859 games and lost 804, a winning percentage of .513, barely above average. He finished as high as second place only once. Still, sportswriters called him a wizard, even a genius, and he commanded wide respect in the game.

Any assessment of a manager's performance must begin with a threshold question: Does a manager matter? Many analysts have parsed won-lost records searching for evidence of a manager's impact. None of them has found it. "Managerial stats," Bill James said in 2006, "are closer to where batting stats were in 1878."[1]

Naturally, Richards answered the question with an emphatic yes: "If anybody tells you a manager has no effect on a ball club, he's telling you he doesn't know baseball."[2] He backed up his opinion this way: "There are an awful lot of small details that add up to the winning of a ball game, and it's up to the man in charge to see that his players are always drilled in and constantly alert to those things."[3] Dogged attention to those details was his hallmark. Orioles scout Jim Russo said Richards's approach was "teaching, teaching, teaching, 24 hours a day."[4] Richards believed there was no such thing as too much practice on the game's fundamentals, especially the fundamentals of defensive play and base running. He told Donald Honig:

> There's an old story about hitting a mule over the head with a two-by-four to get its attention. Well, you can't hit your ballplayer over the head, but you've got to get his attention and stamp the lessons into him. How many times have you heard a third base coach say he told that guy to tag up on line drives to the outfield? "I told him twenty times." Okay. But maybe he should have told that guy fifty times because twenty wasn't enough—because the guy still broke when the ball was hit and then wasn't able to get back and tag up and score when it was caught.[5]

Richards devoted one-fifth of his book, *Modern Baseball Strategy*, to defense: alignments, cutoffs, pick-offs, how to make a tag (straddle the bag), how to block home plate.[6] "You cannot assume a player has been taught a particular fundamental and then when he messes up in a ball game, blame him for it," he said. "You have to know that he's been instructed along those particular lines. Game conditions, the score, the inning, everything is a factor." He fined any of his coaches who could not tell him which way the wind was blowing. He said John McGraw did the same.[7]

Putting Brooks Robinson in the lineup is one of many examples of his preference for tight defense. Richards brought Jim Busby to the Orioles and carried his weak bat because Busby could cover Memorial Stadium's vast center field.

Richards used Willy Miranda as his regular shortstop for most of four seasons, although Miranda's on-base percentage was below .300 in the last three.

Richards's book contains far less about offensive strategy than about pitching and defense. He declares that the hit and run is overused and lists six things that can go wrong with it, then adds that there is always the possibility that the runner will advance from first to third without a head start. He favored the run and hit, where the runner takes off on a straight steal and the batter is not required to swing. He warned that there are more minuses than pluses for the squeeze bunt.[8]

In all his interviews and writings he offered practically nothing about instructing hitters. Eddie Robinson said, "He thought he was a good hitting coach, but he wasn't." Richards believed in the platoon advantage, and in addition to platooning players he constructed his lineups to alternate left- and right-handed hitters as much as possible.[9]

He was a scorekeeper's nightmare, shuttling players in and out. He used the whole roster and then traded for some more. Richards carried only nine or ten pitchers, so he had more bench players than present-day managers do. But he was no slave to "The Book," baseball's unwritten gospel. "Some managers play the game the orthodox way, so they won't be criticized if they fail," Richards told Ernie Harwell. "That's not good managing if deep down they know that bolder methods might have won for them."[10] That explains Richards's penchant for trying something new: his reliance on pitch counts and on-base percentage, the pitcher switch, the knuckleball catcher's oversized mitt.

Yogi Berra famously said baseball "ain't like football. You can't make up no trick plays."[11] Richards could, and he delighted in them. George Kell recalled one Richards devised in Baltimore: With runners on first and second he told Kell not to bunt the ball softly toward third base (the conventional move, so the third baseman would have to field the ball and leave his base uncovered) but to push it hard toward the second baseman. Richards reasoned that the second baseman would be hurrying to cover first and would not be able to make a play, so all runners would be safe. When it happened as he had predicted, Kell said, "Richards was so excited. It was like winning the World Series to him because he had introduced a play to major league baseball and it had worked."[12]

Richards agreed with Connie Mack that pitching is 75 percent of baseball.[13] Whatever the percentage, the belief that pitching is the most important part of winning is baseball's first commandment, embraced by nearly all managers and students of the game for more than a century. "Your team's strength begins with the pitching staff," Richards wrote. But each pitcher had to be handled differently: "No two will ever be exactly alike."[14] Above all, he wanted pitchers who threw strikes. Most of his teams were among the stingiest in allowing walks. Several of his better staffs were near the top in strikeouts as well.

Richards rarely ordered an intentional base on balls. In his book he put this in italics: *"The intentional pass is a dangerous gamble."*[15] Intentional walks were first counted in 1955. All his Orioles teams were at or near the bottom of the league in that category. In 1960, when he had the AL's best pitching staff, he issued only nineteen intentional walks. Casey Stengel, whose Yankees staff was almost as good, ordered thirty-three. Richards used the intentional pass only with runners in scoring position and first base open, most often in the late innings of tie games. He would walk a batter to set up a force play, to dodge the opposing team's best hitter, to get a platoon advantage, or to bring the pitcher to the plate.

The home run explosion in the 1950s accelerated the long-term trend toward fewer complete games and elevated the importance of relief pitching. Pitchers completed 40 percent of all starts in 1950; by 1960 that had fallen to 27 percent. Richards's teams were usually among the leaders in complete games, but he wrote in 1955, "I am strong for relief pitchers."[16]

During the 1950s most teams developed a relief ace, but his role was nothing like the modern closer's. With Harry Dorish in Chicago and George Zuverink and Hoyt Wilhelm in Baltimore, Richards deployed his top relievers in the conventional fashion for that time: usually in the sixth inning or later but sometimes earlier, no matter whether his club was ahead or behind. If the score was anywhere near close and the starter faltered, he brought on his best reliever. Still, he clung to the traditional notion that the bullpen was a place for pitchers who were not good enough to be starters. He put Wilhelm in the starting rotation. With the Atlanta Braves Richards converted another knuckle-balling reliever, Phil Niekro, into a starter, and Niekro won 318 games. When Richards returned to managing with the White Sox in 1976, he again made the league's best reliever, Goose Gossage, into a starter. It didn't work that time.

The spike in homers in the 1950s was far more dramatic than that in the 1990s.[17] This changed managers' in-game tactics. The number of sacrifice bunts fell by 13.5 percent during the decade as nearly all managers began to play for the big inning. Richards was behind the curve. He bunted more than any other manager of the 1950s.[18] His teams led the league in sacrifices five times. He often called for a bunt in the early innings and did not hesitate to sacrifice with his best hitters, such as Bob Boyd and former batting champions George Kell and Billy Goodman. A few years later he changed his mind: "The sacrifice is the most overrated tactic in baseball," he said in 1964. "The defense against the bunt in obvious situations has become so proficient as to make the value of it negligible. When you sacrifice, you are giving away one third of your inning. Too often you end up with your hitters bunting and your bunters hitting."[19]

When he took over the White Sox, he and Frank Lane built the offense around speedy line-drive hitters. Richards soon saw how things were changing and pined for a forty-homer slugger. His Go-Go Sox led the league in stolen bases every year, but after he moved to Baltimore he took fewer chances. His Orioles were near the bottom in steals.

A manager's most important responsibility is not to decide when to bunt or call for the hit and run or even when to change pitchers. His job is to lead men. A former Richards player, Whitey Herzog, said, "Your good manager, by hook or by crook, takes the potential and the personalities and he translates the whole mess into W's in the standings."[20] There is no formula for that.

Although Herzog could be tough, he stroked his players and tried to keep them happy. John McGraw was a tyrant who wanted to control everything his players did on and off the field, to the point of inspecting their restaurant checks to see if they were eating properly. According to one story, a reporter asked one of McGraw's young players if he was married. He replied, "I-I-I don't know, sir. You'll have to ask Mr. McGraw."[21]

Richards's style fell between McGraw's and Herzog's. Skinny Brown, who pitched for Richards on four teams, described him as "a great teacher. A stern taskmaster. It was his way and no other way."[22] Richards was respected by many but loved by none. That's the way he wanted it: "No manager ever tries to win the love of his players. All he needs is their respect." On another occasion he explained, "Managers who try to get too close to their players are making a mistake because invariably you'll get too close to two or three and leave the others out in the cold, and they're not going to like that." He added, "If you can't get them to respect you, you're in trouble."[23]

Richards earned respect because of his mastery of in-game tactics. Many players said he was always thinking several innings ahead. They knew he was on top of every situation and would give them every chance to win. His liberal use of platooning, pinch hitters, and defensive replacements meant that few players were rusting away on the bench. He had no doghouse; if he decided a man wouldn't do, he got rid of him. By keeping his distance from the players, he avoided charges of favoritism. He said: "I wanted a player to feel free to come to me with what he felt were constructive suggestions. It's true that I wanted to keep them at arm's length, but no further. The door was always open, as far as baseball was concerned, but 'Please don't ask me to have dinner with you or a drink with you or go visit your family.'"[24]

"Everybody knows I was Richards's favorite player, right?" Nellie Fox said. "He never talked to me. About all he'd say to me in a week was, 'Fox, go hit.'"[25] Pitcher Jerry Walker remembered, "He'd be sitting on the bench right next to you, get up and walk over to a coach, and tell the coach to go tell you to go to the bullpen."[26] Richards said, "You've got 25 different players and each one calls for different handling, and you'd better give them that handling." He had few hard-and-fast rules: no card playing for money and no children in the club-house, because if a player's child acted up it could cause friction on the team.[27] Instead of general rules he tailored his approach to match each player's makeup: "I look upon ballplayers as individuals, and I can understand their problems since I've been down the road myself. I was all different kinds of ballplayers. I was a ballplayer who was scared. I was a ballplayer who didn't hustle. I was a ballplayer who played only for myself. Then I began to get a little sense. I lost my fear, I began to hustle. I began to play for the team. So now I know how a ballplayer feels."[28]

Besides his success in developing pitchers, Richards's defining trait was his willingness to take a chance on a young player. Many managers would give a rookie a small number of at-bats and send him down if he didn't produce right away. When Richards believed in a young player, he put him in the lineup and let him learn on the job even if it took several years, as it did with Brooks Robinson and several of the Houston players Richards and Luman Harris nurtured later. When Richards arrived in Chicago and again in Baltimore, the farm systems were bare, so he used veterans as placeholders until he could develop young talent. By 1960 the twenty-three-year-old "veteran" Robinson was sharing the infield with three rookies, and the Kiddie Korps led the pitching staff.

Richards also gave opportunities to long-time minor leaguers other teams had rejected, including pitchers Saul Rogovin, Jack Harshman, and Bob Keegan, first baseman Jim Gentile, and second baseman Billy Gardner. Richards, who had spent most of his career in the minors, recognized that some players simply needed an opportunity.

He told George Kell, "I wouldn't be a good manager of the Yankees, because guys like Mantle and Berra wouldn't listen to me."[29] One veteran of the Yankees dynasty, junk-ball pitcher Eddie Lopat, was traded to Baltimore in the final year of his career. In his first encounter with his new manager, Lopat said, Richards showed him a certain grip and motion and told him, "If you do this I'm sure it can help you." Lopat mimicked the motion, then rotated his hand and arm to different angles. "I have that one here, here, here and here. What do you think I've been getting you out with all these years?" Lopat added: "Paul Richards was a strange man. He never said much, and I never quite knew what it was about."[30]

Richards never spoke of "clubhouse chemistry." There were few reports of dissension on his teams. The players who didn't like him—and many were in that category—usually kept their mouths shut in public. Although he would put up with characters like Billy Loes and Jackie Brandt, he surrounded them with solid citizens. Sixteen of his players were future managers, and many were elected player representatives by their peers.

Despite his protestations, some players did like him. Richards displayed considerable loyalty to his favorites, and they returned it. Kell, Fox, Saul Rogovin, Jim Busby, Harry Dorish, Skinny Brown, Jack Harshman, Gene Woodling, Dick Williams, Clint Courtney, and Dave Philley were among many who played for him more than once. Only the first two were stars. He traded several of them, then brought them back later. If he had to go after a veteran, he preferred someone he knew would respond to his leadership.

When Donald Honig interviewed Richards near the end of his career, he talked about Ty Cobb, whom he had watched as a boy during the Tigers' spring training in Waxahachie and cultivated when Cobb was an old man: "The drive he had to excel was incredible, and sometimes frightening." Honig asked whether Richards had seen anyone else with such drive. Richards mentioned Ted Williams—"as a hitter"—and four of his own players: Kell, Fox, Minoso, and Brooks Robinson.[31] That is as close as he ever came to naming his favorites.

What others called aloofness Richards called restraint. Unlike McGraw, there are few stories of Richards's chastising a player publicly or in front of his teammates. He told Honig: "It gets back to what I've always felt is absolutely essential to being a good manager. It's wrapped up in one word, one thing you must by all means be sure you're capable of understanding, and that is restraint. He must restrain himself when things are tough, when things are not going well. Restraint under duress is absolutely necessary."[32]

That restraint—whether the product of aloofness, shyness, or arrogance— meant he was not an inspirational leader. It is impossible to imagine Richards rallying his men to "win one for the Gipper." Except for his rages at umpires, his approach to the game was unemotional and analytical. Sportswriter Leonard Koppett said, "His baseball intelligence was certainly far above average among his peers, but he wielded it with a certain intellectual arrogance, conveying the idea that such and such a profound point was not just known by him, but only by him."[33]

Still, Richards formed warm and lasting relationships with many baseball men. His high-school teammate Jimmy Adair and Luman Harris, who pitched for Richards in Atlanta and Buffalo, followed him as coaches to Chicago, Baltimore, and Houston. Harris succeeded Richards briefly as manager of the Orioles and was his choice to manage Houston and Atlanta. Al Vincent, Richards's top coach in Baltimore, had coached for the wartime Detroit teams and had managed against him in the Dixie Series years earlier. Eddie Robinson played for him in Chicago and worked for him in front-office jobs in Baltimore, Houston, and Atlanta, then hired the elderly Richards as an assistant when Robinson was general manager of the Texas Rangers. Jim Busby began his major league career under Richards in Chicago and stayed with him as a coach in Baltimore, Houston, Atlanta, and Chicago again. Dave Philley played for him in Chicago and Baltimore and managed in Houston's farm system. Clint Courtney played for the Orioles and followed Richards to Houston and Atlanta as a minor league coach and manager. All were Texans except Vincent, Courtney, and Harris, who were southerners.

These were his cronies, his golf partners and dinner companions during many long seasons. Significantly, they were his employees as well. There is no evidence that Richards formed a close relationship with any contemporary manager or executive. He demanded followership as well as friendship.

Except for his cronies, Richards made no effort to win friends. He said, "I never want to hurt anybody's feelings—unintentionally."[34] His Orioles assistant, Jack Dunn III, was a respected executive whose family's roots in Baltimore baseball trace to the storied "old Orioles" of the 1890s. Ernie Harwell watched Richards ordering Dunn around like a lackey. Richards gave his golf clubs to Harwell on road trips so Harwell could check them with his own luggage, because the manager wanted to keep his golf addiction secret. Richards freeloaded at the top country clubs by persuading a member to give him access to the course. He would make bets with fellow golfers, then needle them to distract them.[35]

In Baltimore, and to a lesser extent in Chicago, Richards exercised more control over his roster than any other manager. As free agency and multimillion-dollar contracts transformed the baseball business, the present-day manager has ceded authority over the roster to the general managers and owners who write the checks. In the 1990s Whitey Herzog said, "Nowadays, it's hard to separate a [manager] from the payroll he's got. If your ballclub has money and you've got any brains at all, you're going to win."[36] Today the staggering amounts of money at stake, and the emphasis on individual statistics to determine who makes the money, have profoundly changed the manager's role. He must persuade fabulously wealthy players to put the team first. Tony La Russa explained, "So, in that sense, motivation has become more fundamental than the fundamentals."[37]

"Baseball's simplicity personifies its complexity," Richards wrote. "Translated, that means that every fan feels he knows more baseball than the manager."[38] Richards recognized that real power resided in the front office, not the dugout, and that is where he wanted to be. When he took off his Orioles uniform in 1961, he hoped to reclaim the power he had gained and lost in Baltimore and to make himself a Texas hero.

Marsh is quoted in John Eisenberg, *From 33rd Street to Camden Yards: An Oral History of the Baltimore Orioles* (New York: Contemporary Books, 2001), 29.

1. *Wall Street Journal*, October 21, 2006, P1.
2. Donald Honig, *The Man in the Dugout* (Chicago: Follett, 1977), 142.
3. Ibid.
4. Jim Russo, with Bob Hammel, *SuperScout* (Chicago: Bonus Books, 1992), 41.
5. Honig, *Man in the Dugout*, 123.
6. Paul Richards, *Modern Baseball Strategy* (Englewood Cliffs, N.J.: Prentice-Hall, 1955), 135–74.
7. Honig, *Man in the Dugout*, 142.
8. Richards, *Modern Baseball Strategy*, 93–95, 128–30.
9. Eddie Robinson, interview by author, August 18, 2006, Fort Worth, Texas; Richards, *Modern Baseball Strategy*, 180–81.
10. Ernie Harwell, "Baseball Wizard," *Parade*, March 16, 1958, 24.
11. Leonard Koppett, *A Thinking Man's Guide to Baseball* (New York: E. P. Dutton, 1967), 87.
12. Danny Peary, ed., *We Played the Game* (New York: Black Dog and Laventhol, 1994), 341.
13. *Chicago Tribune*, May 30, 1976, B1.
14. Richards, *Modern Baseball Strategy*, 12.
15. Ibid., 50.
16. Ibid., 72.
17. Research presentation on home runs by David Vincent, meeting, Bob Davids Chapter, Society for American Baseball Research, Arlington, Virginia, January 27, 2007.
18. Bill James, *The Bill James Guide to Baseball Managers* (New York: Scribner's, 1997), 284.
19. Frank Deford, "The Professional Opinion Is Mixed," *Sports Illustrated*, March 23, 1964, online archive.
20. Whitey Herzog and Jonathan Pitts, *You're Missin' a Great Game* (New York: Simon and Schuster, 1999), 139.
21. James, *Bill James Guide to Managers*, 97, 119.

22. Eisenberg, *From 33rd Street to Camden Yards*, 25.

23. *Sporting News* (hereafter *TSN*), April 27, 1955, 16; Honig, *Man in the Dugout*, 126–27.

24. Honig, *Man in the Dugout*, 129.

25. Randy Harvey, "From Waxahachie to the White Sox," *Dallas Times-Herald Sunday* magazine, August 29, 1976, 21.

26. Eisenberg, *From 33rd Street to Camden Yards*, 26.

27. *TSN*, June 13, 1951, 1; Honig, *Man in the Dugout*, 125, 130.

28. Roy Terrell, "Hawkeye and His Boy Scouts," *Sports Illustrated*, April 17, 1961, 74.

29. Peary, *We Played the Game*, 279.

30. Koppett, *A Thinking Man's Guide to Baseball*, 45; *TSN*, November 2, 1955, 13.

31. Honig, *Man in the Dugout*, 119–20.

32. Ibid., 126.

33. Leonard Koppett, *The Man in the Dugout* (New York: Crown, 1993), 196.

34. Tom Keegan, *Ernie Harwell: My Sixty Years in Baseball* (Chicago: Triumph, 2002), 137.

35. Eisenberg, *From 33rd Street to Camden Yards*, 29–30; Harwell, "Baseball Wizard," 25.

36. Herzog and Pitts, *You're Missin' a Great Game*, 141.

37. Buzz Bissinger, *Three Nights in August* (Boston: Houghton Mifflin, 2005), xxi.

38. Paul Richards, "Paul Richards Looks at Baseball," *Atlanta Braves Scorebook*, 1972, 41.

CHAPTER 19

Present at the Creation

W hen the Houston Colt .45s named Paul Richards general manager, sportswriter Clark Nealon applauded: "Who else?"[1] But Richards had not been the expansion club's first choice.

After the National League awarded new franchises to Houston and New York in October 1960, the teams had eighteen months to prepare to play in 1962. Houston's baseball decision makers were the men who brought Richards from Baltimore: executive vice president George Kirksey, a small-town Texas boy who became a leading sportswriter for United Press in New York and Chicago, and president Craig Cullinan Jr., a grandson of the founder of Texaco. The pair had spent nearly a decade trying to bring the majors to their hometown, relying on Kirksey's relentless energy and contacts from his sportswriting career and Cullinan's money and pedigree. But the principal owners of the franchise were R. E. "Bob" Smith and his partner, Roy M. Hofheinz.

Bob Smith was a barrel-chested, white-haired, sixty-five-year-old former oilfield roughneck who struck it rich—very rich. His wealth turned heads even among Houston's oil-soaked elite. As Harris County's largest landowner, he was a one-man planning commission; he would not sell land unless he approved of the buyer's plans for it.

Roy Hofheinz grew up skinny and poor and became fat and rich. He had been the boy wonder of Houston politics—a state legislator at twenty-two, Harris County judge (head of the county's governing body) at twenty-four, and mayor of Houston at forty. After he lost a bitter campaign for a third term as mayor, he joined Smith in real estate deals—marrying Smith's bankroll to Hofheinz's political connections. Hofheinz was forty-eight in 1960. Six feet tall, wearing heavy black-rimmed glasses, he looked like "he'd swallowed nine bowling balls." One associate said, "Roy Hofheinz could sell you a look at the moon. . . . He was the dumbest genius I ever met."[2]

Hofheinz envisioned the Colt .45s as the smallest part of the empire he would create: the first indoor stadium, air-conditioned to combat Houston's brutal heat and humidity, surrounded by hotels, convention centers, and amusement parks. He left the baseball decisions to Kirksey and Cullinan, and that suited them just fine. But as Kirksey, Cullinan, Smith, and Paul Richards would painfully learn, Roy Hofheinz ruled everything he touched.

The first general manager Kirksey hired, Gabe Paul, was a friend from his sportswriting days. When Paul quit barely six months after he arrived, Houston sportswriter Mickey Herskowitz said the veteran baseball executive "did not want Judge Roy Hofheinz breathing on his neck."[3]

When Richards agreed to terms as general manager at the end of August 1961, a relieved Kirksey declared, "We have the finest mind in baseball to direct the baseball affairs of the Colts." Bob Smith added, "This is a major accomplishment for the Colts and I personally feel that our baseball affairs are now in the best possible hands."[4] Richards signed for $60,000 a year for three years. The contract included language guaranteeing his authority over baseball operations. "My job is exclusively baseball," he said at a Houston news conference on September 7. "It goes without saying that the Texas angle was a factor in my decision." He endorsed Hofheinz's plan for a domed stadium: "It will be one of the greatest drawing cards for Houston that any town could have."[5]

Kirksey and Eddie Robinson were named assistant general managers, although Kirksey retained his title as executive vice president of the Houston Sports Association, the corporate owner of the team. Richards posed for photographers wearing a pair of six-guns on his belt. For a formal portrait of the team's leadership, Bob Smith stood in front—with Roy Hofheinz just over his left shoulder.[6]

Richards found that Gabe Paul had left him a functioning organization. Paul's scouts had signed eighty-two amateur players, and they were pursuing one of the most sought-after prospects in the country, Daniel Joseph Staub of New Orleans. Red-haired Rusty Staub was a powerful left-handed first baseman who had led his American Legion team, Crescent City Post 125, to the national championship. Every major league club was after him; the Red Sox even sent Ted Williams to visit his home. Houston scout Bobby Mattick reported, "I have never seen better coordination in a 17-year-old boy in my scouting experience."[7]

Richards wanted to close the deal personally as his first triumph for the Colts. One obstacle stood in his way: Hurricane Carla, the most powerful storm to hit Texas in more than forty years. As the category 5 hurricane screamed toward Corpus Christi, all planes were grounded. Richards took a train to Dallas, transferred to another train, and he and Kirksey reached New Orleans on September 11, 1961, just as Carla made landfall. They offered Staub $132,000. As Richards told it, "Rusty said, 'You know, you ought to sign my little brother.' And George said, 'Okay, we'll give him fifty thousand.'" They also hired Rusty's father as a scout. Richards acknowledged, "We did that quite often." He estimated the total package was worth at least $200,000 to the Staubs.[8]

Next on the agenda was naming a manager. Richards approved the choice before he formally joined the club, but it was not announced until he took over. Harry Craft, the last manager of the minor league Houston Buffs, became the first manager of the big league Colts. The forty-six-year-old Craft was born in Mississippi but grew up in Throckmorton, Texas, where he was a high school football star. He played center field for Cincinnati's 1939 and 1940 pennant winners, but his weak bat put him back in the minors. He was Mickey Mantle's manager for Mantle's first two seasons in the Yankees' farm system. In 1957 Craft became manager of the Kansas City A's but could not lift them out of seventh place in two-and-a-half seasons. He next joined the Chicago Cubs' "college of coaches," owner Philip Wrigley's disastrous experiment in rotating field leaders. In two short stints as head coach in 1961 Craft compiled a 7-9 record. He spent most of the season managing the Cubs' Texas League farm club in San Antonio and the AAA Houston team, which the Cubs shared with the Colts. In the last two months he moved the Buffs up from fifth place to fourth in the American Association with a 32-23 record.

Introducing Craft at a September 19 press conference, Richards said he had not interviewed any other candidate. He made the outlandish claim, "Of all the managers I worked against in my years in the American League, Craft, while he was at Kansas City, impressed me most with his moves."[9] Based on his work with Mantle and other Yankee prospects, Craft had a reputation as a teacher. He was a sensible choice for a team that planned to build with youth but a curious one because he and Richards had no history of close acquaintance. Craft's patron was George Kirksey. The two Texans had met in 1936 when the young outfielder was a rookie and Kirksey was a sportswriter, and they became friends.[10]

Craft was the manager, but the Colts were Richards's team. He hired his loyal cadre of coaches: Luman Harris, Jimmy Adair, and Jim Busby, along with Bobby Bragan, a Branch Rickey disciple who was a holdover from Gabe Paul's group. All but Harris were Texans by birth or residence. Craft was allowed to choose his pitching coach: the Oklahoman Cot Deal, who had played for him in winter ball, coached for Cincinnati, and managed Indianapolis to the 1961 American Association pennant.

The hiring of Harry Craft was not the biggest news in Houston that day. The National Aeronautics and Space Administration announced that Harris County would be the home of its control center for the historic effort to land a man on the moon and, as President Kennedy had pointedly added, "returning him safely to Earth." Houston was beside itself with pride. Alan Shepard and Gus Grissom had already flown in space, albeit briefly, and the astronauts were the newest American heroes. The Manned Spacecraft Center, later the Johnson Space Center, would raise Houston's name to the heavens and influence the baseball club's future. Its immediate impact was to delay construction of the domed stadium while unions battled contractors for higher wages on the $60 million "moon laboratory" job.[11]

When Richards arrived in Houston, he had less than five weeks to get ready for the expansion draft that would stock his new team's roster. He was outraged by the talent offered by the eight existing National League teams—or, rather, the lack of talent. Publicly he called it "the worst swindle since the Black Sox" and complained, "I figured the lists of players would be bad, but they are even worse than I thought they would be." Privately he told associates, "Gentlemen, we've just been fucked."[12] He and the new Mets' president, former Yankee general manager George Weiss, begged league president Warren Giles to rewrite the rules, but they got nowhere.

Unlike the hasty American League expansion, National League teams had a year to prepare for the draft, giving them an opportunity to game the system. They protected their top prospects by taking them off the forty-man roster before August 31, thwarting Richards's plan to snap up the best young talent. The draft eligibles included aging, high-salaried stars: pitchers Robin Roberts of the Phillies, Vinegar Bend Mizell of the Pirates, and Johnny Antonelli of the Braves; Cardinals second baseman Red Schoendienst and Cubs center fielder Richie Ashburn. Some clubs held on to marginal players throughout the season so they could dump them in the draft for a profit. Each expansion team could acquire as many as twenty-eight players at a cost of $2.1 million; each existing team would receive $525,000 if it lost the maximum seven men.[13]

Gabe Paul had hired Bill Giles, son of the National League president, as the Colts' traveling secretary and public relations man. The younger Giles said Richards asked him to go to his father's office and copy the league's secret waiver records to find out what other players might be available. Giles refused. He despised Richards, describing him as "a man of questionable character."[14] The night before the draft Richards proposed that Houston boycott—select no one. Roy Hofheinz and Bob Smith agreed, if the New York Mets would go along, but the Mets would not.[15]

Syndicated columnist Red Smith called the expansion draft "Warren Giles' square deal bargain basement."[16] It opened for business in the Julep Room of Cincinnati's Netherland-Hilton Hotel on October 10, 1961, the day after the Yankees defeated the hometown Reds in the World Series. Houston won a coin toss and picked first in the $75,000 round. Richards chose Eddie Bressoud, a backup shortstop for the Giants. The Mets took the Giants' third-string catcher, Hobie Landrith. Manager Casey Stengel explained, "You've got to have a catcher, or you'll have a lot of passed balls."[17]

Houston selected twenty-three players for $1.85 million. The only big names were thirty-six-year-old pitchers Sam Jones, a three-time NL strikeout leader, and Bobby Shantz, a former AL MVP who had been fighting a sore arm for years. (The five-foot-six-inch Shantz had the dubious distinction of being the only player chosen in both the American and National League expansion drafts.) The most promising youngster the Colts drafted was third baseman Bob Aspromonte, a Brooklyn boy from Sandy Koufax's high school. The Dodgers let him go although he was only twenty-four, but Richards called him "our best prospect."[18] One of Richards's $125,000 premium picks was infielder Joe Amalfitano of the Giants. Amalfitano quipped, "I'll have to go out and get another life insurance policy. I'm worth more than I thought."[19]

Few of them were worth much. Houston's nine pitchers had posted a combined 30-24 record in 1961, the Mets' 13-16. The Mets' hitters totaled fifty-three home runs, Houston's twenty-two. Richards put the best face on it to encourage the hometown fans: "We have a strong nucleus for a fine young club, which should help us build a contender in a hurry. . . . I was frightened a week ago when I did some talking, but had I known we would get the team we did I would never have opened my mouth." Later he vented his true feelings in a private memo: "The Houston and New York clubs were severely handicapped and were started under the most hopeless conditions that two teams could possibly encounter."[20]

By then the Colts had signed more than a hundred amateur players. Many joined the Arizona instructional league team, known as the Colt .22s, to work under Richards, Craft, and their coaches. The group included three $100,000 bonus babies: Rusty Staub, pitcher Wally Wolf from the University of Southern California, and shortstop Glenn Vaughan, a nephew of Hall of Fame shortstop Arky Vaughan.[21]

Construction finally began on the Harris County Domed Stadium on January 2, 1962. The Houston Sports Association staged a ground shooting rather than a groundbreaking. Richards joined Bob Smith, George Kirksey, Craig Cullinan, and local politicos to shoot into the ground with Colt .45 revolvers loaded with live ammo. Richards took time off to play in the Bing Crosby Pro-Am Golf Tournament at the Pebble Beach club in California before he accompanied Harry Craft and several players on a bus tour to pump up fan interest around Texas and across the border in Mexico.[22]

Richards picked up more major leaguers and ex-major leaguers during the winter. He traded his first draft choice, Eddie Bressoud, to Boston for another shortstop, Don Buddin. Buddin hit no better than Bressoud, but he had a higher "B.A. with bases on balls." Twenty-eight of the forty-one men on the Colts' spring roster were younger than thirty. (One player was in military service.) Richards brought more than a dozen other veterans to camp for tryouts. Several had slipped back to the minors after big league trials. His cronies Frank Gabler and Clint Courtney joined the spring coaching staff.

The Colts held spring training in Apache Junction, Arizona, a remote desert outpost thirty miles east of Phoenix at the foot of Superstition Mountain. Bob Smith and Roy Hofheinz owned land there and were trying to develop it into a resort. Houston writer Wells Twombly described the town as a "desolate home for aged scorpions." That was not the only wildlife; one morning pitcher Dick Farrell shot a rattlesnake in the dugout. During the next few weeks he polished off two more snakes, four jackrabbits, two lizards, and a quail. Courtney found a rattler enjoying the shade under his car. Lacking a six-gun, he used a bat to discourage it.

Life for the ballplayers was anything but wild. The *Houston Post*'s Mickey Herskowitz wrote, "Apache Junction has one drugstore, two gas stations, a laundromat, a supermarket, 33 real estate offices and one saloon, the Red Garter, where some of the Colt .45s do their serious training." Farrell said there were two saloons: "One's so bad that even *I* won't go in there, and the other one is full of coaches." The nearest movie theater was eighteen miles away, the nearest dog track thirty-five miles. The only diversion was a blonde named Betina, who showed up at the ballpark in a convertible and drove away each day with a different player riding shotgun.[23]

As the workouts began, Harry Craft said: "Every position on the Colt .45s will have to be won. There isn't a player who has made the team yet. . . . It is our plan to concentrate from the beginning on building a strong pitching staff backed by a tight infield and a fast outfield."[24] But none of the pitchers had worked as many as one hundred major league innings the year before. The biggest winner was Farrell, a hard-throwing right-hander known as "Turk," who had posted an 8-7 record as a reliever with the Phillies and Dodgers. The six-foot-four Boston Irishman had been a member of the Phils' infamous "Dalton Gang," a rowdy bunch of night crawlers and brawlers, and had worn out his welcome after one season with the Dodgers. Herskowitz wrote, "He threw a high fastball and liked a fast highball." Farrell was not the only one of the castoffs with issues. Bill Giles said, "We had drinkers, fighters, hot-check writers . . . just about everybody had some story that preceded them."[25]

There was no power in the lineup, either. The best hitter appeared to be thirty-one-year-old first baseman Norm Larker, who had finished second in the league with a .323 average for the Dodgers in 1960 but had never hit more than eight home runs in a season. Only four of the position players had appeared in as many as one hundred games the previous year.

George Kirksey hovered at Richards's elbow during spring training, trying to inhale the general manager's baseball knowledge. It was a role reversal; when the rookie Richards warmed the Giants' bench in the 1933 World Series, Kirksey was already a top sportswriter, covering the Series for a nationwide audience. Kirksey was sitting in the dugout when Colt pitcher Hal Woodeshick lost sight of home plate. Richards walked to the mound and spoke a few words to the left-hander. Woodeshick immediately began throwing strikes. Kirksey asked, "What did you tell him? What did you tell him?" Richards would not answer. After Woodeshick retired the side, Kirksey asked him what advice Richards had offered. "He told me to get the fucking ball over the plate," Woodeshick replied.[26]

The club posted the best record in the Cactus League, but Craft reminded the writers that the games didn't count. He developed a stock answer to the frequent questions about where his team would finish: "In San Francisco on the 28th of September."[27]

In Houston the first home of the Colts took shape under Richards's direction. Since the dome would not be ready for the 1962 season, Hofheinz built a $2 million temporary ballpark next to the construction site so fans could watch the new stadium rise. Colt Stadium was a makeshift structure of galvanized steel, with thirty-three thousand seats but no roof to shield fans from the blistering Texas sun. Richards designed the playing field as a pitcher's park, reasoning that his weak ball club would have a better chance of winning low-scoring games.

It was 360 feet down the foul lines, with center field 420 feet deep. "We'll have fewer home run areas than in other parks," he said. To further handicap hitters he planned to keep the grass high and the lights low.[28]

On April 10, 1962, master of ceremonies Morris Frank, a popular newspaper columnist, began the opening day festivities, "Friends, the National League has come of age and we have admitted it to the Lone Star State." After Frank introduced the requisite lineup of dignitaries, just as Bobby Shantz got ready to throw the first pitch, Paul Richards stood up in the press box and said, "Boys, someday when Houston is in the World Series and they are raising the pennant in center field, I hope you'll pause and give ten seconds of silence for ol' Richards."[29]

---

1. *Houston Post*, September 4, 1961, in the Paul Richards file, A. Bartlett Giamatti Research Center, National Baseball Hall of Fame and Museum, Cooperstown, N.Y.
2. Edgar W. Ray, *The Grand Huckster: Houston's Judge Roy Hofheinz, Genius of the Astrodome* (Memphis, Tenn.: Memphis State University Press, 1980), 30–283; John Helyar, *Lords of the Realm* (New York: Villard, 1994), 67–68.
3. *Houston Chronicle*, November 4, 2004, online edition.
4. UPI, *New York Times*, September 3, 1961, S4.
5. AP, *Los Angeles Times*, September 8, 1961, C5; *Sporting News* (hereafter *TSN*), September 13, 1961, 11.
6. Campbell B. Titchener, *The George Kirksey Story: Bringing Major League Baseball to Houston* (Austin: Eakin Press, 1989), 120.
7. Robert Reed, *Colt .45s: A Six-Gun Salute* (Houston: Gulf Publishing, 1999), 64.
8. Paul Richards, interview by Clark Nealon, February 5, 1981; Paul Richards, "Memorandum," February 9, 1966, 10, in Paul Richards Papers, in the personal collection of Paula Richards; *TSN*, March 21, 1962, 23; National Baseball Hall of Fame, www.baseballhalloffame.org/history/2005/050304.htm.
9. *Houston Post*, September 20, 1961, and Gabriel Paul, untitled Cincinnati Reds press release, January 1939, both in the Harry Craft file at the Baseball Hall of Fame; UPI, *Lowell (Mass.) Sun*, September 20, 1961, 39.
10. Titchener, *George Kirksey Story*, 43.
11. *TSN*, November 15, 1961, 2.
12. Ibid., October 11, 1961, 5; Helyar, *Lords of the Realm*, 465; Reed, *Colt .45s*, 57.
13. Reed, *Colt .45s*, 56; *New York Times*, October 10, 1961, 50; *TSN*, July 5, 1961, 5, and September 20, 1961, 2.
14. Bill Giles, with Doug Myers, *Pouring Six Beers at a Time and Other Stories from a Lifetime in Baseball* (Chicago: Triumph Books, 2007), 44–48. The quote is on p. 46.
15. Richards, "Memorandum," 2.

16. *Austin (Texas) Statesman*, October 14, 1961, 10.
17. Robert W. Creamer, *Stengel: His Life and Times* (1984; repr., Lincoln: University of Nebraska Press, 1996), 297.
18. *TSN*, April 18, 1962, 20.
19. AP, *New York Times*, October 11, 1961, 57.
20. *TSN*, October 18, 1961, 7; Richards, "Memorandum," 2.
21. *TSN*, November 8, 1961, 6.
22. Ibid., January 10, 1962, 25; Reed, *Colt .45s*, 68.
23. *TSN*, March 24, 1973, 8; Giles, *Pouring Six Beers*, 52–53; Reed, *Colt .45s*, 65–66; Mickey Herskowitz, "The Land of the Nonbreaking Curveball," *Sports Illustrated*, March 11, 1963, online archive. The *Houston Post* story from March 19, 1962, is reprinted in Mickey Herskowitz, *The Mickey Herskowitz Collection* (Dallas: Taylor Publishing, 1989), 243. Farrell is quoted in Reed, *Colt .45s*, 66.
24. *TSN*, February 21, 1962, 29.
25. Giles, *Pouring Six Beers*, 51.
26. Titchener, *George Kirksey Story*, 97.
27. Reed, *Colt .45s*, 81–82.
28. *TSN*, January 31, 1962, 13, and February 7, 1962, 28.
29. Reed, *Colt .45s*, 85–86, 88; Titchener, *George Kirksey Story*, 10.

CHAPTER 20

The Other Expansion Team

The visiting Chicago Cubs sent up rookie center fielder Lou Brock to lead off in the first major league game played in Texas. Bobby Shantz's first pitch was a strike. So were the next two, and Brock went back to the dugout. The tiny lefty allowed a single to Billy Williams but retired the side in the top of the first without giving up a run.

Third baseman Bob Aspromonte, leading off for the Colts, singled to left off Chicago starter Don Cardwell. Center fielder Al Spangler was next. The speedy left-handed batter had spent most of two seasons with Milwaukee but had never hit a home run in 245 plate appearances. This time his triple into the right-field corner was enough to drive in the first run in Houston's big league history. The Colts went on to win 11–2, as right fielder Roman Mejias contributed a pair of home runs. Morning rain held the opening day crowd to 25,271, well below capacity, but they were 25,271 happy Texans. Their new team was tied for first place with 161 games to go.[1]

Houston got off to a 5-3 start, while its expansion brethren, the Mets, lost their first nine in a row. After sixteen games the Colts had the best ERA in the majors, 2.00. Craft said, "If we keep getting this kind of pitching, this is going to be an interesting summer."[2] It could not last, of course. When they lost to the Milwaukee Braves on April 27, the Colts fell below .500 and never reached that level again. But they continued to draw big crowds; after eleven home games they were on pace for 1.5 million.

Opposing players soon came to dread their visits to Colt Stadium but not because they feared the home team. Cincinnati pitcher Johnny Klippstein said, "It was so hot that all you had to do was wiggle your finger to break into a sweat." Then there were the mosquitoes—mosquitoes the size of eagles, to hear the players tell it, mosquitoes that carried off small children. The little Pittsburgh shortstop Ducky Schofield, the son of Richards's Crisfield team-mate, said, "The mosquitoes were as big as me." Colt pitcher Ken Johnson remembered seeing dozens of them buzzing around his ankles on the mound: "I reached down and swatted at them and my white socks turned red."[3] Players carried cans of insect repellent in their back pockets and liberally sprayed the area around them, giving new meaning to the phrase "defending your position." Instead of standing for the seventh-inning stretch, fans ran for cover. The concession stands sold repellent, and groundskeepers fogged the grandstand before each game.[4]

In addition to the tall grass, dim lights, and distant fences, left-handed batters faced a stiff wind that constantly blew in from right field. The elements, natural and Richards-made, combined to make Colt Stadium the second-best pitcher's park in the league, after the new Dodger Stadium. Richards designed the park not only to help his club win but to make the players look better while they were losing: "We were actually being slaughtered pretty badly and had no chance to win a 2–1 or 3–1 or 3–2 game. We were completely outclassed, but it looked close because the elements—the fact of the lights and the high grass—kept anybody from scoring a lot of runs."[5]

Faced with such difficult conditions at home, the Colts should have welcomed road trips. Instead, they felt like sideshow freaks. To advertise to the world that Texas was in the big leagues, Hofheinz outfitted the team's traveling party in electric-blue western suits, blue cowboy hats, and orange, blue, and white boots. The costume designer, Evelyn Norton Anderson, said, "The team didn't like them at all—refused to wear them." The most contentious objector, first baseman Norm Larker, was fined several times for being underdressed. Other players "absent-mindedly" left their suits at the cleaners. By midseason the fancy outfits had disappeared. Anderson said Hofheinz was "furious about it, but he didn't win that one."[6]

As they traveled the National League circuit, the players faced the same predictable insults in each city, stories describing them as misfits, discards, and "discount merchandise." Turk Farrell fumed: "That stuff really tees you off. They don't give you any credit and it shows they haven't got any common sense. We're no picnic for anybody." Hal Smith asked, "If we're misfits, what about the teams we're beating?"[7]

By the end of May Houston pitchers had recorded six shutouts, and Roman Mejias had clubbed ten homers, more than in any of his previous full seasons. The Colts won four out of five during a visit to the league's powerhouses, the Dodgers and Giants. That lifted them into seventh place with a 30-35 record, but the rest of the season went downhill. As the losses mounted and the temperature climbed, more of Colt Stadium's brightly colored seats sat empty. A Sunday game against Cincinnati on July 1 drew only 6,666. On July 4, the traditional superstition day, the club was in eighth place, just one game behind seventh-place Philadelphia. Richards said, "I don't see how anybody can be disappointed in this team as long as we're ahead of anybody."[8]

The Colts' feeble offense hit bottom in August when they were shut out in three straight games and went thirty-eight innings without scoring. They fell into a nine-game losing streak, the longest of the year. After his fast start Roman Mejias collapsed, dragged down by nagging injuries. His OPS, .877 in the first half, fell to .634 in the second. He hit his twenty-first home run on July 15 but added only three more for the rest of the season. Mejias's wife and two children were trapped in Cuba when Fidel Castro's regime cut off emigration. Mejias spoke little English and was the only Latino player on the team, so his loneliness can only be imagined.[9]

Houston finished eighth with a 64-96 record, thirty-six and a half games out of first place but ahead of the Cubs and twenty-four games in front of the Mets, whose 120 losses were a twentieth-century record. The Mets were famously bad; the Colts were not bad enough to become famous. They also beat New York at the gate, drawing 924,456, sixth highest in the league, almost two thousand more than visited the Polo Grounds.

The Houston team was last in runs, homers, on-base percentage, and slugging percentage. By comparison, the pitching was a bright spot. The Colts finished seventh in runs allowed. Richards had chosen pitchers who could throw strikes; the staff posted the best strikeout-to-walk ratio in the majors. Turk Farrell, who had moved into the starting rotation, posted a 10-20 record, but his 3.02 ERA was the NL's seventh best, and he was fourth in strikeouts. He allowed more than three earned runs in only six of his twenty-nine starts. Ken Johnson finished 7-16, but his teammates scored no more than two runs in sixteen of his thirty-one starts. Johnson said: "If we gave up one run, we had a good chance of winning. Two runs, our chances were about 50-50. Give up three runs and we couldn't win at all."[10]

Craft kept his team fighting to the end. Beginning with a doubleheader sweep at Cincinnati on August 25, Houston went 19-12 for the rest of the season, giving reason for hope. George Kirksey said: "Most of our objectives were realized. We did not lose 100 games or finish last. . . . We have a foundation to build on, and by blending our upcoming players with the 1962 team, should begin the long, hard climb up the National League ladder."[11]

After the frustration of his first five years in Baltimore, Richards knew how hard the climb would be. The Colts could not get much better anytime soon. He needed to deflect the criticism that had dogged him during the dreary losing seasons with the Orioles, and he had to keep the fans coming out. Faced with the combination of a losing team, an uninviting ballpark, and punishing summer weather, attendance had fallen off badly in the second half of the season. Richards adopted a two-pronged strategy to improve the club on the field and at the gate.

The Colts had no recognizable star or fan favorite. Richards took another daring gamble to remedy that. He traded his only power hitter, Roman Mejias, to Boston for Pete Runnels, who had just won his second American League batting title. A native Texan who lived in the Houston suburb of Pasadena, Runnels was a ready-made hometown hero, but he was thirty-five years old, and his ten home runs in 1962 were a career high. Runnels's wife was overjoyed at the trade: "I won't have to pack another suitcase."[12] (It was an even better deal for Mejias. Boston owner Tom Yawkey and his staff succeeded in getting the player's family out of Cuba.)[13]

The second prong of Richards's strategy was to force-feed his best prospects to the majors, ready or not. Promoting a young player too soon could sap his confidence, perhaps permanently, but Richards had no better options. "If we have as many as three kids help us this season, we'll be three years ahead of our most optimistic planning," he said.[14]

At the end of Houston's first year in the majors, the franchise's minority owners were chafing under Hofheinz's dictatorial control. Craig Cullinan, the nominal president, found he had no authority, and other shareholders complained that Hofheinz would not let them see financial data. Bob Smith agreed to buy out the dissenters, returning their original investments and giving him and Hofheinz 96 percent of the stock.[15]

By this time Hofheinz's dome was in trouble. Architects had determined that it would cost far more than the $15 million budgeted for construction. Harris County Judge Bill Elliott said another bond issue was the only alternative. The site of the future stadium was a twenty-four-foot-deep hole in the ground that was derided as "Elliott's Lake." The city's political and business establishments swung their weight behind the third referendum in less than five years, and voters approved an additional $9.6 million worth of bonds in December 1962.[16]

The club bought an abandoned air force base near Moultrie, Georgia, for a Thomasville-style minor league training camp. It was not quite as primitive as the Orioles' Thomasville base; Moultrie boasted a swimming pool and a movie theater. Branch Rickey had established Dodgertown at a former naval air station in Vero Beach, Florida, to shield his black players from the South's Jim Crow laws, but the dormitories in Houston's Moultrie camp were segregated by race.[17]

Richards installed his own men in key roles throughout the farm system. Lou Fitzgerald would manage the AA San Antonio team with Clint Courtney as a coach. Former Orioles Billy Goodman and Dave Philley became the Class A managers. (A reorganization of the struggling minors abolished the B, C, and D classifications in 1963.) Grady Hatton, a holdover from Gabe Paul's tenure, led the AAA club at Oklahoma City.[18]

The farm director Gabe Paul had hired, Tal Smith, objected to the spring training regimen planned by Richards's managers and coaches. He asked them, "Who do you think runs this outfit?" Fitzgerald told him Richards was in charge of player development. "Smith said that he worked for Judge Hofheinz, not Richards, and he ran it his way," Fitzgerald remembered. He also heard Smith say, "All the bunch that Richards brought with him did not show [me] a thing. . . . They sat on their butts unless Richards was around, then they jumped like flies."[19] The confrontation, a replay of the Richards-McLaughlin turf battles in Baltimore, would grow into a fatal schism between Richards and Gabe Paul's men, who had transferred their allegiance to Hofheinz. When Richards named Eddie Robinson farm director, the judge kept Tal Smith to oversee stadium construction.

Richards had identified three prospects as the top candidates to make the team in 1963. Houston signed catcher John Bateman at a tryout camp for $76, reimbursement of his expenses for attending the camp. He hit twenty-one home runs in Class C ball in his first professional season. Bateman was a big, strong-armed kid from Killeen, Texas, who told the Colts he was nineteen when he signed; he was actually two years older. Richards called him "the next Gabby Hartnett."[20] The Colts' 1962 catchers had allowed twenty-five passed balls and seventy-four wild pitches, despite using the oversized mitt to catch knuckle-ballers Ken Johnson and Bob Tiefenauer. The job was wide open for Bateman.

The glossiest résumé among the rookies belonged to five-foot-seven-inch, twenty-one-year-old Ernie Fazio. A first-team All-America shortstop at Santa Clara University in California, he sparked the Broncos to a second-place finish in the College World Series. Scout Bobby Mattick, who had signed Frank Robinson and Vada Pinson for Cincinnati, said Fazio "has everything. He can run, throw, field, hit with power and has the instincts of a great player." He got a reported $75,000 bonus.[21]

Rusty Staub had lived up to his reputation in his first pro season, hitting .293 with twenty-three homers at Class D Durham, North Carolina. Midway through the Cactus League schedule, with the young left-hander batting over .400, Craft said, "Staub right now is the best hitter on our ball club." Staub had been ticketed for AA San Antonio, but Richards gave him a fielder's glove and told him to learn to play right field as well as his usual position, first base.[22] Staub celebrated his nineteenth birthday in April.

On opening day 1963 Fazio led off and played second base, and right fielder Staub batted cleanup. Bateman would have been in the lineup but for a broken thumb. But the schedule makers had dealt Houston a losing hand. The Colts played their first thirteen games against the Giants and Dodgers, first- and second-place finishers in 1962. The Colts won just four times, falling to last place behind even the Mets, and never raised their record to .500. The Mets got off to a stronger start in their second season; they lost only their first eight games, compared with nine the year before.

The rule makers also inaugurated a new deal. They expanded the strike zone vertically by several inches. The new definition: "The Strike Zone is that space over home plate which is between the top of the batter's shoulders and his knees when he assumes his natural stance." The previous rule, adopted in 1950, defined it as "between the batter's armpits and the top of his knees when he assumes his natural stance." Rules Committee members said they hoped to reduce the number of walks and speed up games. One catalyst for the change was the unseemly home-run outburst of 1961, the AL's first expansion season, when Roger Maris hit sixty-one, Mickey Mantle fifty-four, and six others clubbed forty or more. But homers had been increasing steadily since 1947. Batting averages and runs scored in the first two expansion years were about the same as in the 1950s. The balance between offense and defense was not broken, but the rule makers fixed it anyway. The taller strike zone severely depressed scoring. During the next five years, as pitchers and umpires adjusted, baseball entered its second dead-ball era.

With no baseball game to manage every day, Richards could devote more time to his golf game. Neither cold nor heat nor rain stopped him. He would say: "Well, the weather's bad, but it's the only weather we've got. Let's go play."[23] No round counted unless money was riding on it, sometimes big money. Bill Giles said Richards played for as much as $5,000 a round. He earned a reputation as a hustler. On occasion he would deliberately lose the first nine holes, then double the bet and win the back nine. A dentist, unable to cover his losses, paid off with free treatment for the Richards family. When Richards's nephew Stan Bolton brought his son Mike to visit, the boy asked how much money Uncle Paul made. Stan replied, "Paul Richards is paid very well, but he makes his real money on the golf course."[24]

Richards made his own rules. It was customary to concede an opponent's putt if the distance to the hole was shorter than the length of the putter's leather handle. Giles said Richards carried two putters in his bag, one with "short leather" to measure opponents' putts, the other with "long leather" to measure his own.[25] Others caught him improving his lie and teeing up his ball in the rough. A favorite course was the Champions Golf Club in Houston, owned by former PGA stars Jimmy Demaret and Jack Burke Jr. Burke chided, "Paul, damn it, you're the only guy out here that we've got any problem with riding his cart up on the green." Richards replied, "Well, if I'm the only one doing it, it's not gonna be a problem."[26]

Richards continued scouting young players and often came in to seal the deal personally on a coveted prospect. One was Jim Palmer, an all-around high school sports star in Scottsdale, Arizona. In addition to weighing bids from most major league teams, he was considering a basketball scholarship offer from coach John Wooden of UCLA, where Palmer would have been a team-mate of Lew Alcindor's (Alcindor later changed his name to become Kareem Abdul-Jabbar). Richards went to the Palmer home to make his pitch to the boy and his parents. "He was real casual," Jim Palmer recalled, "just grabbed my mother's putter, and he's putting and chewing peanuts [in the living room]. . . . He just had a certain arrogance." After Richards left without Jim's signature on a contract, the senior Palmers said, "You know, the Orioles seem like a bet-ter organization." Even though Houston was offering more money, Baltimore scout Jim Russo signed the pitcher for $40,000.[27]

Sportswriter Mickey Herskowitz called the Colts' 1963 season "a valley with very small peaks."[28] The club hit bottom in June when it lost ten straight, including four consecutive shutouts. Despite the sorry performance, Hofheinz extended Richards's contract for seven years, through 1970. "We told Paul to write his own ticket," the judge said. "I believe he has the best and longest con-tract in the major leagues. We are tying our baseball kite to the future and we believe Paul Richards is the best man in America to take us where we want to go."[29] Richards received the same $60,000 salary, with a portion deferred.

Staub, Bateman, and Fazio were not hitting, but neither was anybody else. Pete Runnels, a .300 hitter for five straight seasons, was struggling to raise his average above .240. Richards brought up twenty-one-year-old shortstop Jimmy Wynn, a five-foot-nine-inch speedster he had drafted out of the Cincinnati organization. After belting sixteen home runs in half a season at San Antonio, Wynn delivered nine hits in his first seven big league games. After Wynn appeared in thirteen games at short, Richards shifted him to center field, a position he had never played. The Colts were overstocked with utility infielders, but nobody they tried in center had produced much.

More rookies joined the expanded roster in September, and others were brought to Houston for workouts. Among them was Joe Morgan, a twenty-year-old second baseman in his first professional season. Morgan had led his Castlemont High team to the city championship in Oakland, California, and was a standout at Oakland City College, but every scout who saw him dismissed him as "a good little player." He was only five-seven. Houston's Bill Wight was the first to tell him, "You are really a good player."[30] Wight, Richards's former pitcher, was new to scouting and unsure of himself. He told Richards, "He's got a strong bat and he can run, but . . . he can't field a ground ball and he can't throw." Richards urged, "If you're going to make a mistake, make it signing him, don't make it not signing him."[31] Wight went to the Morgan home and accepted a beer from Joe's father. Then another one. He offered a $2,000 bonus. The elder Morgan sent his son out for more beer, and Wight eventually upped his offer to $3,000.[32]

In his second time at bat in the majors on September 22, 1963, Joe Morgan was due up against the Phillies with two out in the bottom of the ninth inning of a tie game, and the winning run on third. He looked around for a pinch hitter, but a voice from the dugout told him, "Go on up there and hit." He grounded a single to right to win the game. In the Phillies' clubhouse the enraged manager, Gene Mauch, demolished his team's postgame food spread. Some accounts say he told his players, "You got beat by a guy who looks like a Little Leaguer." Other versions say he compared his own players to Little Leaguers.[33]

Richards decided to showcase his prospects by fielding an all-rookie lineup in a late-season home game against the Mets. Larry Yellen, a twenty-year-old right-hander from Brooklyn, was tabbed as the starting pitcher, but Yellen was Jewish and the game was scheduled for Yom Kippur. Yellen's parents begged him not to disgrace the family by playing on the holy day. When the boy asked to skip the game, Richards apologized and moved his debut up a day.[34] Yellen pitched five innings against Pittsburgh, giving up just two earned runs, and left with no decision.

The Colts' lineup on September 27, 1963, averaged nineteen years, eight months old: Sonny Jackson at shortstop, Joe Morgan at second base, Jimmy Wynn in center field, Staub at first, Aaron Pointer in right, Brock Davis in left, Glenn Vaughan at third, and Jerry Grote behind the plate, with seventeen-year-old left-hander Jay Dahl pitching. The Mets battered Dahl for seven runs in the first three innings. Six other rookies also appeared in the game. The Mets won 10–3, but the lineup demonstrated the depth of the Houston farm system. The future Hall of Famer Morgan joined four more players who would be all-stars: Wynn, Staub, Grote, and pitcher Joe Hoerner.

Five of the rookie starters were African American. Jimmy Wynn said Richards took a "fatherly" interest in them, warning against the perils of nightlife. Wynn added, "I didn't see any difference in what he did with white players or black players." Wynn believed the franchise wanted to develop black stars because Houston's black residents had shown themselves to be potential customers when they provided crucial votes to pass the stadium bonds.[35]

Despite giving substantial playing time to the youngsters in September, the Colts again made the final month their best of the season with a 16-11 record. But they fell to ninth place at 66-96. Attendance plummeted by 22 percent to 719,502, lowest in the league; the novelty of major league ball had worn off. The Colts scored only 464 runs, fewest in the majors, and their 3.44 ERA was next to last in the National League. Richards cautioned that the club was "two or three years away from major progress."[36]

Houston's young players were still works in progress. Rusty Staub played regularly for all of 1963 while batting only .224 with a .617 OPS. Jimmy Wynn hit .244/.319/.372 in seventy games and struck out in nearly one-fourth of his at-bats. John Bateman led the team with a paltry ten home runs and fifty-nine RBI but struck out even more frequently and batted .210/.249/.334. Ernie Fazio posted a .184 average and had played his last game for the Colts. Third baseman Bob Aspromonte, not yet twenty-six, struggled, but Richards said, "Once I make up my mind that a player has the equipment to be great, it takes a long time for me to give up on him. The player has to convince me that I'm wrong."[37] As he had done with Brooks Robinson, Richards let them learn on the job.

Following the plunge in attendance and the drop to ninth place, Richards sought veteran help to lift the team toward respectability. He acquired Nellie Fox from the White Sox shortly before Fox's thirty-sixth birthday on Christmas Day. A twelve-time American League all-star, Fox was popular in Chicago, but he was no longer worth his $40,000 salary. He was a Richards favorite, but it was not a sentimental deal. Richards wanted the faded star to fill two roles: to inject some hustle and fire into his losing club and to mentor Joe Morgan.

With the additions of his high school teammate Archie Wise, nephew Stan Bolton, former Baltimore coach Al Vincent, and old standby Dutch Dietrich to the scouting staff, Richards had the full roster of his closest baseball friends and associates at his side. He enjoyed their company during long dinners at the best restaurants. Richards was not a heavy drinker; he drank occasional beers at the ballpark and at home but preferred a martini with dinner. "When he had two, he was tipsy," Eddie Robinson said.[38]

Judge Hofheinz had persuaded the town of Cocoa, Florida, to build an $800,000 spring training facility for the Colts. It had dormitories for 250 players, enabling the team to consolidate its major and minor league camps in 1964. Just nine miles from NASA's launch complex at Cape Canaveral, Cocoa Beach was the playground of the astronauts. Hofheinz wanted to associate the team with Houston's future as a space center.[39]

Only five players were left from the 1961 expansion draft: pitchers Turk Farrell and Ken Johnson, infielder Bob Lillis, third baseman Bob Aspromonte, and outfielder Al Spangler. The opening day roster mirrored some of Richards's early Orioles teams: ten men were older than thirty, and nine were twenty-one or younger. Richards said, "The Colt .45s will be a tougher team to beat in 1964 and I feel sure they will be more interesting to watch." But he would hazard only that they "might" move up in the standings.[40]

Right-hander Ken Johnson had compiled an 18-33 record over two seasons despite a 2.65 ERA in '63. Johnson begged the writers to stop calling him "a hard-luck pitcher." He protested, "If people call me that long enough, that's what I'll become." Johnson threw a knuckler and depended on excellent control plus "about 10 other pitches with about 18 different deliveries," including the slip pitch he had learned from Richards.[41] On April 23 the hard-luck pitcher spun a no-hitter against Cincinnati but lost the game 1-0 as the Reds scored in the ninth on two Houston errors.

Houston had settled into ninth place by the end of May. Pete Runnels, batting .196, was released. Staub's and Bateman's averages were hovering in the same neighborhood. Sportswriters predicted that Harry Craft would be replaced by Luman Harris, but Richards laughed it off: "If anything like that were true, I guess I'd know about it."[42]

Instead, Jimmy Wynn was the next to go. When he arrived at spring training, he had found uniform number 24 hanging in his locker—Willie Mays's number. "They said, 'We want you to be just like Willie Mays,'" he recalled.[43] The pressure was too much. Wynn was batting .234 while striking out nearly one-fourth of the time and was uncertain in center field when he was sent to

Oklahoma City on June 15. Staub, hitting .202, followed him on July 4. "It might as well have been the end of the world," Staub said later. "I bit my lip all the way to the airport to keep from crying. Then, on the plane, I broke down."[44] Bateman, at .200, soon joined them.

The Colts collapsed in the second half because they could not win on the road. Harry Craft's tenure as Houston's first major league manager ended on September 19, 1964. Craft said, "I've never felt that Paul and I were as close as a manager and general manager should be." To no one's surprise, third-base coach Harris succeeded him. The forty-nine-year-old Harris had spent twenty of his twenty-eight years in baseball playing or coaching under Richards. "I learned practically all I know about managing from Mr. Mack and Paul Richards," he said. "But there isn't anybody who can manage like somebody else. Sure, I'll make use of a lot of their ideas and methods, but I've got some thoughts of my own. So I'll manage like Lum Harris."[45]

The Colts finished the season with a 5-8 record under their new manager. After an ugly 7–0 loss to the Dodgers in the next-to-last game, Harris locked the clubhouse door and spoke to the players, asserting his authority for next year.[46] The club's 66-96 record and ninth-place finish were identical to the previous season's. So was their last-place standing in runs scored. The attendance, 725,000, was barely better than 1963's.

After right-hander Bob Bruce shut out the Dodgers in the final home game for his franchise-record fifteenth victory, Richards said: "We won our first and last here at ol' Colt Stadium. I just wish we'd won a few more in between."[47] His decision to build a pitcher's park had paid off; the Colts posted winning records at home in 1963 and 1964. But Colt Stadium was now history. The Colt .45s soon would be.

1. Colts game accounts are from *Retrosheet*; Robert Reed, *Colt .45s: A Six-Gun Salute* (Houston: Gulf Publishing, 1999); and Ron Briley, "The Houston Colt .45's: The Other Expansion Team of 1962," *East Texas Historical Journal* 32, no. 2 (1994): 59–74.

2. Reed, *Colt .45s*, 63.

3. Danny Peary, ed., *We Played the Game* (New York: Black Dog and Laventhol, 1994), 533, 547; Reed, *Colt .45s*, 77.

4. Bill Giles, with Doug Myers, *Pouring Six Beers at a Time and Other Stories from a Lifetime in Baseball* (Chicago: Triumph Books, 2007), 55; Jimmy Wynn, interview by author, February 28, 2007, Rosharon, Texas.

5. Paul Richards, interview by Clark Nealon, February 5, 1981.

6. Edgar W. Ray, *The Grand Huckster: Houston's Judge Roy Hofheinz, Genius of the Astrodome* (Memphis, Tenn.: Memphis State University Press, 1980), 396; Giles, *Pouring Six Beers*, 52; Reed, *Colt .45s*, 117; Peary, *We Played the Game*, 533.

7. Reed, *Colt .45s*, 109.

8. Briley, "Houston Colt .45s," 66–67; Giles, *Pouring Six Beers*, 53.

9. Ron Briley, "Roman Mejias: Houston's First Major League Latin Star and the Troubled Legacy of Race Relations in the Lone Star State," *Nine: A Journal of Baseball History and Culture*, 2001, online archive.

10. Reed, *Colt .45s*, 185.

11. Briley, "Houston Colt .45s," 71.

12. *Sporting News* (hereafter *TSN*), December 8, 1962, 21.

13. Briley, "Roman Mejias."

14. *TSN*, January 19, 1963, 4.

15. Reed, *Colt .45s*, 44.

16. Ray, *Grand Huckster*, 283–87, 333.

17. Joe Morgan and David Falkner, *Joe Morgan: A Life in Baseball* (New York: W. W. Norton, 1993), 48.

18. *TSN*, February 9, 1963, 11.

19. Lou Fitzgerald, letter to Paul Richards, February 10, 1966, in Paul Richards papers, personal collection of Paula Richards.

20. Reed, *Colt .45s*, 142; *TSN*, May 15, 1965, 5.

21. *TSN*, July 7, 1962, 24, 26.

22. Reed, *Colt .45s*, 147.

23. Eddie Robinson, interview by author, August 18, 2006, Fort Worth, Texas.

24. Giles, *Pouring Six Beers*, 46; Paula Richards, interviews by author, 2006–2008; Paul Bolton, e-mails to author, September 2006.

25. Giles, *Pouring Six Beers*, 45–46.

26. Mike Hastings, interviews by author, August–September 2006, Waxahachie, Texas; Eddie Robinson interview.

27. John Eisenberg, *From 33rd Street to Camden Yards: An Oral History of the Baltimore Orioles* (New York: Contemporary Books, 2001), 136–37; Jim Russo, with Bob Hammel, *SuperScout* (Chicago: Bonus Books, 1992), 71.

28. *TSN*, August 31, 1963, 11.

29. Ibid., July 20, 1963, 17.

30. Morgan and Falkner, *Joe Morgan*, 46.

31. Furman Bisher, "The Richards System," *Baseball Digest*, December–January 1966–67, 88. Wight later went with Richards to the Braves. Over three decades Wight signed Dale Murphy, Glenn Hubbard, Bob Horner, Dusty Baker, Jeff Blauser, David Justice, and Kent Mercker ("Braves Blog," *Atlanta Journal-Constitution*, May 23, 2007, online edition).

32. Morgan and Falkner, *Joe Morgan*, 46.

33. Ibid., 55–56; *TSN*, October 5, 1963, 39–40, and October 3, 1964, 10.

34. *Jewish Daily Forward*, August 30, 2002, online archive.
35. Wynn interview.
36. *TSN*, October 12, 1963, 37.
37. Ibid., June 27, 1964, 21.
38. Buck Jordan, interviews by author, August 16–17, 2006, Waxahachie, Texas; Eddie Robinson interview.
39. Ray, *Grand Huckster*, 287.
40. *TSN*, April 18, 1964, 42.
41. Ibid., May 9, 1965, 5; "Houston Colt .45s," *Sports Illustrated*, April 13, 1964, online archive.
42. *TSN*, May 23, 1964, 24; Reed, *Colt .45s*, 188.
43. Wynn interview.
44. Gary Ronberg, "Houston's Boy Is Now a Man," *Sports Illustrated*, August 14, 1967, online archive.
45. *TSN*, October 3, 1964, 7.
46. Ibid., October 17, 1964, 26.
47. Reed, *Colt .45s*, 201.

CHAPTER 21

Worst Enemy

The Harris County Domed Stadium would be ready for opening day 1965, giving the franchise a new start. Judge Hofheinz envisioned not just a ball club but a far grander empire with the dome as its centerpiece. According to Houston writer Clark Nealon, "Roy Hofheinz was in baseball to make money, not for the love of the game." The judge planned a Disneyland-style amusement park and a hotel-motel complex on adjacent land he and Bob Smith owned. The Houston Livestock Show and Rodeo was building a mammoth exhibition hall nearby to house its annual western extravaganza.[1]

The Colt Firearms Company had been happy to see a major league team named after its six-shooter, but the company had made no agreements about the sale of caps, shirts, and other souvenirs bearing the name and image of its product. When Colt demanded a share of the revenue, it played into Hofheinz's hands. He had never liked the nickname because it evoked Houston's past, not its future.

"From henceforth and evermore, Houston's baseball team will be known as the Astros," Hofheinz announced on December 1, 1964. The stadium would be the Astrodome. The amusement park would be Astroworld. The entire complex would be the Astrodomain. "The dome is so far ahead of its field that it is in the 21st century—just like the space program," the judge said. "The name and insignia will help dispel the image of Texas as a land of cowboys and Indians and it behooves every citizen in this area to call attention to the twentieth-century aspects of Texas and Houston."[2] Mickey Herskowitz pointed out that the team's new name "isn't one that can easily be shortened and still keep within the boundaries of good taste." Someone suggested the farm teams would be called the "Half Astros."[3]

No one knew what baseball would be like inside an air-conditioned building. On February 8 several Astros gave the dome a test drive in front of 250 writers and broadcasters from all over Texas. Rusty Staub hit two balls over the fence, coach Howard Pollet and front-office assistant Pat Gillick snapped off some curves, and Luman Harris tried a few knuckleballs. "It's even more remarkable than I thought it would be," Richards said. "We know now that the curve ball will break, the knuckler will dance, and the playing field is perfect."[4] No fly balls went anywhere near the 208-foot-high roof, but some fielders thought the flies were hard to see with daylight streaming through the 4,596 transparent Lucite roof panels. They could follow the ball easily after the lights were turned on, but it was an overcast day.

The full extent of the problem became embarrassingly clear when the Astros scrimmaged with their Oklahoma City farm club on the afternoon of April 8. It was sunny outside; inside, routine fly balls and pop-ups fell like hail, some as much as ten feet from the nearest fielder. The balls were invisible against the roof. Players wore batting helmets in the field. They put on sunglasses. The lights were turned on. Six runs scored on easy fly balls that were not caught. "It's impossible to play under these conditions," Richards fumed. "Sure, somebody will win and somebody will lose. But who's kidding whom? This isn't baseball."[5] Adding to the humiliation, sportswriters from around the nation had arrived to cover the first exhibition game against the Yankees the next night. The AP's Joe Reichler suggested, "A baseball game could be called on account of daylight." Hofheinz responded: "Never fear. I will not be the first man to call a game because of sunshine."[6]

The first exhibition game against the Yankees was played at night, so the crowd of 47,876 was treated to real baseball. Mickey Mantle hit the first home run in the dome. Hofheinz had planned a surprise to celebrate the Astros' homers, but by the eighth inning no Houston batter had cleared the fences. The judge could wait no longer. He ordered Bill Giles to press the "ecstasy" button on the control board for the 474-foot-long, four-story-high scoreboard. Roger Angell described the forty-five-second sound-and-light show: "Exploding ballpark, shooting cowboys, ricocheting bullets, a snorting steer with flags on his horns, mounted cowboy with lariat and a fusillade of skyrockets."[7] Nothing like it had ever been seen at a baseball game.

Nothing like the Astrodome had ever been seen anywhere. The dome spanned six hundred feet. All seats—even the $1.50 ones high above the outfield—were padded, another first in a sports stadium. The chairs were painted in a rainbow of colors. Some of the worst seats in the house were the most expensive: fifty-three luxury suites just below the roof rented for $14,000 to $35,000 a season, another innovation. Hofheinz took the idea from the Roman colosseum, which had private alcoves to separate nobility from commoner. Each suite in the Astrodome was decorated in a different theme—"Imperial Orient," "Roman Holiday," "Grecian Delight." Suite patrons enjoyed catered food, a refrigerator, a private bathroom, and a butler. The resourceful Bill Giles labeled the Astrodome "the Eighth Wonder of the World." Red Smith wrote warily, "This is the greatest change in baseball since Candy Cummings invented the curve."[8]

Hofheinz and his architects had thought of everything—except baseball. The exhibitions against New York and Baltimore passed uneventfully because of a welcome cloud cover during the day games. Richards said he would either paint the dome or cover it with a tarpaulin. He experimented with orange baseballs (the dye made them too slick to handle) and several shades of tinted glasses. Joe Morgan said, "The sunglasses turned everything into a sea-green mush where it was still impossible to pick out a fly ball against the roof."[9]

Hofheinz told Richards, "Well, look, our players will get used to that and the other players won't, and boy, we'll win fifteen or twenty more ball games than we should have." Richards replied: "That's not the way it's gonna work. It's gonna ruin our players, because they're gonna be embarrassed."[10]

The regular-season opener was played at night against Philadelphia. More than twenty astronauts threw out the first pitches before 42,652 pop-eyed fans. President and Mrs. Johnson joined Hofheinz in his luxury box overlooking right field. Phillies left-hander Chris Short shut out the home team, and the young third baseman Richie Allen won the game with a two-run homer.

Twenty-one-year-old Joe Morgan was the starting second baseman and second-place hitter. Although Nellie Fox had batted .265 in 133 games in 1964, he had retired to join the coaching staff. (He was later put back on the roster.) When Morgan came up in September 1964, Fox pulled him into a circle of veteran players, put his arm around the youngster, and told his teammates, "Listen, this guy is really special. I'm going to do the best I can to help him and I want you to do the same."[11] Morgan needed help in the field. He had hard hands, a weak arm, could not go to his right or pivot on a double play. Richards ordered coaches to hit him one hundred grounders every day during spring training. "It was [Morgan's] attitude that stood out more than anything," Pat Gillick said. "He knew what he had to do to succeed. He was very aggressive and had the kind of cockiness you like to see. He always thought positively."[12] Morgan delivered two hits and drew a walk on opening day, but his average soon settled into the .220s.

By the time the Astros played their first day game in the dome on April 25, the roof had been covered with seven hundred gallons of off-white paint, producing a bluish tint. Fielders handled a dozen fly balls without mishap, but the sky outside was cloudy.[13] Center fielders continued to lose sight of the ball when the sun was at a certain angle. On May 23 the Giants' Jim Ray Hart lifted a fly toward Jimmy Wynn. Roger Angell wrote, "Looking upward, Wynn pounded his glove confidently, then anxiously, and then froze in horror. The ball had vanished into a pure Monet cloud of overhead beams, newly-painted off-white skylights, and diffused Texas sunlight, and now it suddenly remateri-alized a good distance behind Wynn and plumped to earth like a thrombosed pigeon." Hart circled the bases with an inside-the-park "domer homer."[14] The next day painters put a darker coat above the outfield, making the Astrodome a cool island isolated from nature's vagaries. That seemed to solve the visibility problem, but it would soon create another one.

The Astros got off to a strong start. A ten-game winning streak boosted their record to 12-6 on May 1, just .021 points behind the first-place Dodgers. Most remarkably, Houston was leading the league in runs scored. The team had come from behind in the late innings to win six of its games. But in May the quirky schedule gave the Astros fifteen straight games against the Dodgers and Giants. The Astros lost twelve of them and fell to eighth place.

Opposing teams accused the Astros of manipulating the air-condition-ing so the "wind" would blow out when the home team was at bat. The club insisted it was not so. Visiting players complained about the scoreboard's loud, insulting messages, such as showing a cartoon of a man taking a shower when an opposing pitcher was relieved. *Sports Illustrated* remarked, "The visiting team has nine players, but the Astros have 10—nine men and a scoreboard." A blaring bugle and "C-H-A-R-G-E" spelled out in two-story-high letters fired up the fans, but the Mets' Casey Stengel griped, "I ought to be allowed to go out on the coaching lines and blow horns."[15] The board was a big hit with the paying customers, and they were coming out in unprecedented numbers.

The Astros fell to ninth place in June after an eight-game losing streak that included three consecutive shutouts. Jimmy Wynn was leading the club with an .877 OPS, but Joe Morgan was batting .232 and Rusty Staub .214. Richards and Harris kept them in the lineup, and they began to improve. By mid-July Morgan and Wynn, the smallest Astros, were tied with a team-best eleven home runs. Houston's attendance reached one million in the thirty-eighth home game on June 25. It was the highest in the league, more than the team had drawn in any previous full season.

The painted dome was effective in blocking out the sun—too effective; the grass died. Hofheinz said he would put down "undertaker's grass," the artificial greenery used around freshly dug graves. He ordered Tal Smith to find a substitute, and Smith discovered the plastic rug that became known as AstroTurf.[16] The turf could not be installed until after the season, so Hofheinz had the bare dirt painted green. "Ground balls inevitably picked up topspin and kicked up sheets of green dust," Morgan said. "Your life was literally in danger as these cannon shots came at you."[17] The players also discovered that batted balls did not carry well in the conditioned air. Only fifty-seven home runs were hit in the Astrodome all season, the fewest of any park in the majors.

Despite the pitcher-friendly surroundings, the Astros' ERA was second worst in the league. The pitching staff was a disaster area. Luman Harris used seventeen starters, including eighteen-year-old right-hander Larry Dierker. Richards limited Dierker to 110 pitches per start. One night he shut out the Mets for nine innings in a tie game, but Harris lifted him when he reached his limit, and Houston relievers lost it in the tenth.[18] Nothing helped stave off another ninth-place finish. The Astros lost ninety-seven games, one more than in each of their first three seasons. Asked to reflect on his club's performance, Harris replied, "I'd rather not."[19]

But the young players gave reason for hope. After his slow start Morgan finished with a .271 average and .795 OPS, setting team records for hits and walks. Wynn, in his first full season, slugged twenty-two homers and posted an .841 OPS. Staub, still just twenty-one, batted .256 with a .751 OPS, better than the league average. Despite the losing record, 2,151,470 fans turned out, second only to the Dodgers' attendance. The attraction was not the team but the dome. As Mickey Herskowitz wrote, "The game was quite incidental."

An additional one million people paid a dollar apiece for a tour of the empty Astrodome.[20]

Leaving aside its shortcomings as a baseball park, the Astrodome was Roy Hofheinz's crowning triumph. It would be inaccurate to say that the hosannas went to his head; his ego needed no boost. But his high-handed ways finally became too much for the gentlemanly Bob Smith. Some said the breach came when Hofheinz neglected to invite Smith and his wife to greet President Johnson on opening day, but Smith's associates believed the partnership had begun disintegrating long before that. One said the Smiths resented the judge's hogging all the credit for the Astrodome. In a later TV interview Bob Smith lauded Hofheinz's vision in building the dome, then added: "I'll give him credit. Of course, give him time and he'll take it anyway."[21] After her husband's death Vivian Smith said a combination of factors had soured him on his partner: Hofheinz didn't pay bills on time, insulted and humiliated people, and left Bob Smith to clean up his messes. "Bob didn't like the way Roy operated," she declared. ". . . Bob had to put up the money for everything. Roy didn't have any credit without Bob's signature."[22]

At a showdown meeting in May 1965, Hofheinz offered to buy most of Smith's stake in the Astrodomain for $7.5 million. Smith agreed, but he assured Richards and others that Hofheinz could never raise the money. Hofheinz did, by mortgaging most of what he owned. Although Smith did not want to sell, he stood by his word. In August Hofheinz became the owner of 86 percent of the stock.[23]

Richards said later: "When Bob Smith left, it became apparent to me that I would never get along with Roy Hofheinz. I mean, it was just impossible." On the day the sale closed, he went to Hofheinz: "I told him there's no way we can get along here, and if you will release me right now I can get another job. And he threw up his hands and said, 'Oh, no, don't leave me.'"[24]

The friction between them was well known. *Houston Chronicle* sports editor

Dick Peebles recalled: "When the judge first came into the baseball picture, a standing question was, 'How long will it be before the judge thinks he knows as much about baseball as Paul Richards?' The consensus was five years. As it turned out, it was only four."[25] Richards thought Hofheinz's "little clique" of Grady Hatton, Tal Smith, and business manager Spec Richardson had been undermining him. The judge believed Richards was talking about him behind his back—unforgivable disloyalty in his eyes.[26]

The lid blew off in December 1965. After Hatton led the Astros' Oklahoma City farm club to the American Association pennant, Richards gave the White Sox permission to interview Hatton for their managing job. It was a common courtesy in baseball to let an employee seek a better job, but Hatton had become a Hofheinz acolyte. Hofheinz thought Richards was trying to get rid of Hatton.

Richards and Luman Harris were scouting in Venezuela when the judge called a press conference to announce that Hatton would not be joining Chicago. As soon as Richards arrived home, Hofheinz summoned him to a Sunday meeting at the Astrodome. Richards demanded changes in the tangled lines of authority between his baseball responsibilities and Hofheinz's business affairs. Instead, the judge invited him to resign. Richards would not walk away from the five years remaining on his contract, so Hofheinz fired him. One of Hofheinz's men fired Harris by telephone.

Hofheinz immediately called in the press to introduce Hatton as the Astros' new manager and thirty-two-year-old Tal Smith as director of player personnel. The two would share the duties of general manager. Sitting beside the judge, Richards told the writers, "It's his team and he has the right to make a change."[27]

Bob Smith resigned from the board of directors and turned in his lifetime passes to the Astrodome. Columnist Red Smith described Hofheinz as "a stormy little man," clearly not referring to the judge's physique, and dismissed Tal Smith as "his stooge." The columnist added, "Paul Richards' exceptional ability is acknowledged everywhere in baseball."[28] C. C. Johnson Spink, who had succeeded his father as editor of the *Sporting News*, wrote, "It is a pity that in a sport not oversupplied with bold and modern thinkers, there wasn't room on one team for two original minds."[29]

After the Sunday press conference, writers Mickey Herskowitz and Dick Peebles commiserated with Richards in the Shamrock-Hilton Hotel bar. Herskowitz remarked, "Paul, the judge is his own worst enemy." Richards replied, "Not while I'm alive."[30]

The feeling was mutual. The two men were locked in a steel-cage grudge match over the $315,000 Richards was owed on his contract. It was the dirtiest fight of Richards's life. First Hofheinz cut off his paychecks and refused to reimburse him for outstanding expenses. Then the judge demanded immediate repayment of $19,500 that Richards had borrowed from the team. Richards tried to set up a meeting, but Hofheinz referred him to lawyers. When they met in January 1966, with attorneys present, Hofheinz declared that Richards had been fired for cause, so his contract was void. One of Hofheinz's lawyers said he would try to talk the judge into a $70,000 settlement if Richards would accept it. Richards would not. He turned the dispute over to the baseball commissioner.[31]

The new commissioner had been in office barely a month. After Ford Frick had announced his retirement, the owners conducted a six-month search before they chose the obscure retired air force lieutenant general William D. Eckert, known as "Spike," who had no previous connection with baseball and no public record of distinction. *New York World-Telegram* writer Larry Fox blurted the immortal description: "My God, they've elected the Unknown Soldier."[32] The truth may have been even more ludicrous. It was reported that baseball's search committee intended to hire the former secretary of the air force, Eugene Zuckert, but had mixed up the two men's names.[33] The owners persuaded Lee MacPhail to become Eckert's deputy and hand holder.

Richards took his grievance to his former Baltimore colleague, but MacPhail warned him that the commissioner might not be able to force Hofheinz to honor the contract. After their phone conversation Richards wrote MacPhail a confidential three-page letter outlining his grievances against the judge in rabid language:

This man is unprincipled and completely unreliable in anything that does not serve his own selfish interests. He would not hesitate to flush baseball down the drain if it served his purpose. His word is not worth five cents and neither is the word of anybody working for him worth that amount and if you don't know it now, you will before too long. You will also realize in time that this man is a danger and a menace to the best interest of baseball.

Richards's threat of a legal challenge was equally unsubtle: "For your sake as a friend and for the Commissioner's sake, and even for the best interests of baseball, I certainly hope and pray that court action is unnecessary."[34]

Hofheinz was building a case to prove that he had just cause to fire Richards and owed him nothing. The judge charged that Richards had neglected his job by spending too much time on the golf course, had won large bets from other golfers (causing ill will toward the ball club), had bounced checks, and had cheated on his expense account. As Hofheinz's lawyers moved around Houston looking for evidence to support the accusations, word quickly got back to Richards. Of course, he had spent many days playing golf. Of course, he had bet heavily—and won, more often than not. There are many examples of his chiseling on his expense reports. But he was not about to concede that these were firing offenses.

He prepared his defense by soliciting letters from associates and acquaintances to rebut the charges. More than a dozen testimonials, addressed "To whom it may concern," came from lawyers, businessmen, and doctors. H. J. Porter wrote: "It is my understanding that someone is attempting to spread the rumor that Paul Richards is a golf hustler and that he wins thousands of dollars per year playing golf. I consider the rumor erroneous and possibly malicious." The famed golf pro Jimmy Demaret said, "Paul Richards created an untold amount of baseball interest through his visits to Champions Golf Club." George Kirksey echoed, "He used his golf activities to help create interest in baseball." Craig Cullinan wrote that he had approved Richards's country-club dues as a legitimate business expense.

Hofheinz charged that Richards had given his nephew Stan Bolton a no-show job as a scout in California. Richards asked the Astros' area scout, his former pitcher Jim Wilson, to vouch for Bolton's work. He canvassed his baseball circle seeking evidence of interference by Hofheinz's men and examples of their personal and sexual transgressions.[35] Richards had warned MacPhail, "To take this thing to court would definitely be a blackeye [*sic*] to baseball, not only in Houston but over the entire country."[36]

The language of Richards's contract complicated matters. It specified that he would serve as general manager through 1970, drawing $45,000 a year, and that he would work four additional years as a consultant at $35,000 to $40,000 annually. Hofheinz's lawyers argued that he had not earned the money for those last four years, so they deducted that $145,000 from the contract. Richards contended the final four years' payments were deferred salary plus interest. Bob Smith backed him up with a sworn affidavit saying the deal called for an annual salary of $60,000, with a portion deferred.[37]

Richards prepared a sixteen-page memorandum for the commissioner, defending his work and detailing his role in the development of Joe Morgan, Rusty Staub, Jimmy Wynn, Sonny Jackson, and Larry Dierker, as well as two other prospects who never made it, pitcher Bruce Van Hoff and first baseman Chuck Harrison. Recalling how he worked out and signed Harrison, a Texas Tech football player, Richards remarked sarcastically, "I didn't play golf those two days." He wrote, "I feel that my accomplishments in Houston were superior to those of any other club in which I was employed."[38]

Eckert and MacPhail met with the feuding parties and their lawyers in February 1966. Richards offered to settle for $120,000 to be paid over three years, minus the $19,500 he had borrowed. He insisted that his future earnings not be deducted from the payments, as was customary when a man was fired and took another job in baseball. The meeting produced no agreement, but the commissioner instructed Hofheinz to pay Richards $10,000 while negotiations continued, covering his overdue salary and expenses.[39]

Out of baseball for the first time in forty years, the fifty-seven-year-old Richards toured spring training camps looking for work. He had never been fired before, but he had seen many other old baseball men making those same rounds like boys who were passed over when their fellows chose up sides on the playground. Fueling his anger, he claimed he had turned down four jobs after Hofheinz begged him to stay in Houston. Before he was fired he had been mentioned publicly as a candidate to manage the Mets after a broken hip forced Casey Stengel to retire, and Cincinnati general manager Bill DeWitt reportedly talked to Richards about managing the Reds. Now he told UPI's Milton Richman, "I'd be willing to do most anything, from handling a team in a rookie league on up."[40] He interviewed with his former subordinate Harry Dalton, the general manager in Baltimore. The Orioles didn't hire him, but that same week they hired a twenty-five-year-old schoolteacher, John Schuerholz, as a front-office assistant. By the end of March, Philadelphia general manager John Quinn had given Richards a scouting job.[41]

The period of unemployment allowed him to fulfill a long-standing wish. On March 12, 1966, he played a round of golf with the legendary, reclusive Ben Hogan. Former Masters and U.S. Open champion Cary Middlecoff joined them at Hogan's Colonial Country Club in Fort Worth. Hogan was fifty-three and retired from professional competition. He said, "I play with friends, but we don't play friendly games." Hogan shot a 68 on his home course, Richards 75, and Middlecoff 76. Richards framed the signed scorecard and kept it for the rest of his life.[42]

The Astros' new ruling triumvirate of Grady Hatton, Tal Smith, and Spec Richardson was purging the organization of Richards's influence. They fired Eddie Robinson and all the coaches except Nellie Fox. Dave Philley and Billy Goodman lost their jobs as minor league managers, and Richards's men were dropped from the scouting staff.[43]

Word leaked from the commissioner's office in May that Eckert had successfully mediated the dispute between Richards and Hofheinz. There was no public announcement, but UPI's Milton Richman wrote, "Richards settled for 25 cents on the dollar," $90,000.[44] The reports were premature. The two sides exchanged settlement offers into July. When he got no satisfaction from the commissioner, Richards appealed to baseball's behind-the-scenes power, Dodger owner Walter O'Malley. Richards said O'Malley told Hofheinz to pay him $40,000 annually for three years, with no deduction for any future baseball salary. That was nearly identical to Richards's original proposal in February.[45]

After finishing eighth in their inaugural season, the Colts/Astros were ninth for the final three years of Richards's tenure, losing at least ninety-six games each season. The club's record under Richards was 261-385. The Mets had lost at least 109 games in each of their first four years and stood at 194-452. Richards said, "It was very disappointing to have to leave a ball club with such great promise."[46] The young Astros, "as green as their infield rug," were pennant contenders in the first half of 1966, even landing on the cover of *Sports Illustrated*.[47] The tough New York writer Dick Young said, "When they hand out awards for this baseball season, let's not forget Paul Richards, who put together that amazin' team in Houston."[48] The Astros faded to eighth place and ninety losses, still the best performance in their short history.

Spec Richardson took over as general manager and, as Bill Giles put it, "spent much of his eight-year tenure being relieved by his fellow general managers of the burden of all that young talent Houston had been stockpiling."[49] Richardson traded Joe Morgan, Rusty Staub, Dave Giusti, Jimmy Wynn, Mike Cuellar, Mike Marshall, and John Mayberry—every one a future all-star. The Astros did not win a division championship until 1980 and did not reach the World Series until 2005. By then only Tal Smith was left from those who were present at the creation. He was not inclined to observe a moment of silence for ol' Richards.

---

1. Edgar W. Ray, *The Grand Huckster: Houston's Judge Roy Hofheinz, Genius of the Astrodome* (Memphis, Tenn.: Memphis State University Press, 1980), 290 and appendix A.
2. Robert Reed, *Colt .45s: A Six-Gun Salute* (Houston: Gulf Publishing, 1999), 208; *Sporting News* (hereafter *TSN*), December 12, 1964, 23.
3. Ray, *Grand Huckster*, 293, 382; *TSN*, October 31, 1964, 25.
4. *TSN*, February 20, 1965, 7, 10.
5. "Daymares in the Dome," *Time*, April 16, 1965; AP, *Victoria (Texas) Advocate*, April 9, 1965, 1.
6. Ray, *Grand Huckster*, 334.
7. Roger Angell, *The Summer Game* (Lincoln: University of Nebraska Press, 2004), 129.
8. *TSN*, April 24, 1965, 9–10; Bill Giles, with Doug Myers, *Pouring Six Beers at a Time and Other Stories from a Lifetime in Baseball* (Chicago: Triumph Books, 2007), 66–67; Angell, *Summer Game*, 128–31; John Helyar, *Lords of the Realm* (New York: Villard, 1994), 69–70; *New York Herald Tribune*, April 12, 1965, reprinted in *Red Smith on Baseball* (Chicago: Ivan R. Dee, 2000), 291.
9. *TSN*, April 24, 1965, 10; Joe Morgan and David Falkner, *Joe Morgan: A Life in Baseball* (New York: W. W. Norton, 1993), 66.
10. Paul Richards, interview by Clark Nealon, February 5, 1981.
11. Morgan and Falkner, *Joe Morgan*, 73.

12. Eddie Robinson, interview by author, August 18, 2006, Fort Worth, Texas; Giles, *Pouring Six Beers*, 255.
13. *TSN*, May 1, 1965, 24, and May 8, 1965, 13.
14. Angell, *Summer Game*, 125.
15. *TSN*, June 12, 1965, 9; Joe Jares, "The Big Screen Is Watching," *Sports Illustrated*, May 31, 1965, online archive.
16. Ray, *Grand Huckster*, 307; Helyar, *Lords of the Realm*, 71.
17. Morgan and Falkner, *Joe Morgan*, 67.
18. Larry Dierker, *This Ain't Brain Surgery* (New York: Simon and Schuster, 2003), 55.
19. *TSN*, November 20, 1965, 17.
20. Ray, *Grand Huckster*, 313; *Houston Post*, April 6, 1986, reprinted in Mickey Herskowitz, *The Mickey Herskowitz Collection* (Dallas: Taylor Publishing, 1989), 7.
21. Ray, *Grand Huckster*, 321.
22. Ibid., 326–28. Vivian Smith is quoted on p. 328.
23. Ibid., 318–29.
24. Richards interview.
25. Ray, *Grand Huckster*, 525.
26. Richards interview; Giles, *Pouring Six Beers*, 48.
27. Richards interview; Ray, *Grand Huckster*, 525.
28. *TSN*, January 1, 1966, 17; *Mansfield (Ohio) News Journal*, December 16, 1965, 33.
29. *TSN*, January 15, 1966, 14.
30. Richards interview; Ray, *Grand Huckster*, 525; Campbell B. Titchener, *The George Kirksey Story: Bringing Major League Baseball to Houston* (Austin: Eakin Press, 1989), 101.
31. Paul Richards, letter to William D. Eckert, February 3, 1966, Paul Richards Papers, in the personal collection of Paula Richards.
32. Leonard Koppett, *Koppett's Concise History of Major League Baseball* (New York: Carroll and Graf, 2004), 303.
33. Helyar, *Lords of the Realm*, 76; *New York Times*, June 11, 2000, online archive.
34. Paul Richards, letter to Leland S. MacPhail Jr., January 4, 1966, in Richards papers.
35. All these letters, dated December 1965 through February 1966, are in the Richards papers.
36. Richards to MacPhail.
37. Richards to Eckert; R. E. Smith, notarized affidavit, December 27, 1965, in Richards papers.
38. Paul Richards, "Memorandum," February 9, 1966, 1–16, Richards papers.
39. Richards to Eckert; Houston Sports Association check stub, dated February 25, 1966, in Richards papers.
40. Richards to MacPhail; UPI, *(Nampa) Idaho Free Press*, August 31, 1965, 7; *TSN*, December 11, 1965, 25; UPI, *Waxahachie (Texas) Daily Light*, March 1966 (day illegible), clipping in Paul Richards's scrapbooks, personal collection of Paula Richards.
41. *TSN*, March 12, 1966, 16, and March 26, 1966, 24.
42. Brent Kelley, "Ben Hogan," *About.com: Golf*, n.d., http://golf.about.com/od/golfersmen/p/ben_hogan.htm; Buck Jordan, interviews by author, August 16–17, 2006, Waxahachie, Texas. The scorecard is in the Richards papers. The signature of the fourth player is illegible.
43. *TSN*, January 8, 1966, 9.
44. Ibid., May 28, 1966, 27; UPI, *Connellsville (Pa.) Daily Courier*, May 10, 1966, 7.
45. Walter O'Malley, letter to Paul Richards, July 12, 1966; Paul R. Richards to William D. Eckert, July 13, 1966, in Richards papers; Richards interview.
46. Richards interview.
47. "Climbing into Orbit," *Time*, July 8, 1966, online archive; "Astros in Orbit," *Sports Illustrated*, June 6, 1966, front cover.
48. *TSN*, July 23, 1966, 16.
49. Giles, *Pouring Six Beers*, 48.

CHAPTER 22

Braves' New World

Richards's past now shaped his future. In June 1966 he returned to Atlanta, where he had started his managerial career twenty-eight years earlier, to become the Braves' director of instruction and development. President and general manager John McHale, who was briefly his teammate as a first baseman on the wartime Tigers, called Richards "one of the outstanding minds in baseball."

With the Braves in eighth place, sportswriters predicted Richards would soon replace manager Bobby Bragan. McHale's answer was ambiguous: "[Richards] has been a very good manager, but I would say this at this time, we did not hire him for that job."[1] Richards said bluntly, "No, I will not manage. . . . In my opinion, the fellow who develops the players and puts them up here in the big leagues is more important than the fellow who manages them after they get here. And that's what I've been hired to do—get them up here."[2]

Atlanta was the newest big league city. The Braves had moved south just thirteen years after they left Boston for Milwaukee. The club had set attendance records in Milwaukee, drawing more than two million each year from 1954 through 1957. After winning the World Series in '57, another pennant in '58, and losing a pennant playoff to the Dodgers in '59, the Braves fell out of contention and attendance slumped.

When the Braves opened the 1966 season in their new home, Atlanta Stadium "was rocking with 50,671 patrons intoxicated with pride."[3] The crowd whooped when the scoreboard flashed a message: "April 12 1861: First Shots Fired at Fort Sumter . . . April 12 1966: The South Rises Again."[4] But the next night only 12,721 showed up.

The Atlanta metropolitan area had a population of 1.1 million, and the club had the entire Southeast as its exclusive market. The Braves built a radio network covering most of the old Confederacy, but the gate was disappointing. While the team drew 1.5 million in 1966, triple the attendance in the lame-duck season in Milwaukee, it was only sixth highest in the National League. Still, the franchise posted a profit of nearly $1 million in its first Atlanta season, after losing money in Milwaukee.[5]

Richards made his first contribution to his new team when he counseled twenty-seven-year-old right-hander Phil Niekro. Niekro had been sent down to AAA Richmond after recording a 5.31 ERA and twelve bases on balls in twenty and one-third relief innings. He threw a knuckleball, but because he could not control it he had to mix in several other pitches, all hittable. Richards told him to throw the knuckler overhand instead of sidearm to improve his control. He said, "Tell you what, Phil, next game you pitch you just start off with the knuckleball and keep throwing it as much as you can, and don't throw anything else until you just can't get the knuckleball over."[6] After Niekro was recalled in August, he walked only eleven in thirty innings with a 3.30 ERA.

Atlanta was in seventh place with a 52-59 record on August 9, 1966, when Bobby Bragan was fired. His replacement, coach Billy Hitchcock, had failed when he succeeded Richards as manager of the Orioles, but he was another former teammate of John McHale's. Writers speculated that Hitchcock was keeping the chair warm for Richards.[7] Instead, McHale was on the hot seat. Three weeks later the Braves' chairman, Bill Bartholomay, promoted Richards to vice president with "full responsibility for the acquisition and development of players." McHale was kicked upstairs to handle business matters, although he retained the titles of president and general manager.[8]

Soon after Hitchcock took over, the Braves rallied to win seventeen of twenty-one games. They rose to finish in fifth place, so the manager kept his job. But Richards promised changes, saying no Brave was too valuable to trade.[9] Henry Aaron felt insulted. At age thirty-two, he led the league with forty-four home runs and 127 RBI in 1966, although his average fell to .279. The remark opened a rift between Richards and his biggest star that grew more bitter with the years.[10]

Richards did not trade Aaron; he did something even worse, from the fans' standpoint. He sent Eddie Mathews to Houston in December. The handsome, slugging third baseman was the team's other signature player. He had been an Atlanta favorite since he played for the Crackers and hit a home run into Ponce de Leon Park's magnolia tree, where only Babe Ruth had gone before. Mathews, who broke in with the Boston Braves, is the only man to play in all three of the franchise's hometowns. He was tied with Lou Gehrig for seventh place on the all-time home run list at 493 but had fallen off to sixteen homers with a .250 average at age thirty-four. After fifteen seasons with the Braves, Mathews learned of the trade from a sportswriter. Mathews was bitter, but Aaron was enraged by the slight. In his autobiography twenty-five years later Aaron said: "To me, that was vintage Richards. He was the kind of guy who would call you into his office and talk to you as he looked out the window, as if you weren't really there."[11]

John McHale also learned about the Mathews trade from a sportswriter. Reduced to irrelevance, McHale moved to the commissioner's office, where he succeeded Lee MacPhail as General Eckert's guide dog. Richards was named vice president of baseball operations. Bartholomay said no one would hold the title of general manager, while he would be more active in business affairs.[12]

In the Mathews trade Richards acquired two familiar faces from Houston, right-hander Bob Bruce and outfielder Dave Nicholson, the Orioles' bonus "Superman" who had been a super flop. In his only season as a near-regular,

Nicholson struck out a record 175 times with the White Sox. At age twenty-seven his career batting average was .204. *Sports Illustrated* labeled him "a chronic failure."[13] Richards was the only man who still believed in Nicholson; Richards had traded for him in his last deal before he left the Astros. Richards said Nicholson would spend the 1967 season in the minors to rebuild his confidence. "Then if he can't play in the big leagues, I'll go quietly."[14] It was Nicholson who went quietly; he played only ten games for the Braves, the last of his major League career. Eddie Robinson said: "The guy had all the ability in the world, but you never know. Sometimes the guys with the most ability don't have the desire. There's something missing in their makeup."[15]

Even without the fading Mathews, the Braves were by far the strongest team Richards had ever inherited. Although they finished fifth in 1966, their record was 85-77. Twenty-five-year-old catcher Joe Torre contributed thirty-six homers and 101 RBI with a .315 average. Lead-off batter Felipe Alou slammed thirty-one homers, batted .327, second in the league behind his younger brother Matty of Pittsburgh, and led the league in runs and hits. Rico Carty, the twenty-six-year-old left fielder, was third in average at .326.

The slugging Braves scored the most runs and hit the most homers in the NL. Phillies manager Gene Mauch remarked, "Pitching through that Braves' lineup is like going through a meat grinder."[16] Their power got a major boost from their ballpark. Frustrated pitchers nicknamed Atlanta–Fulton County Stadium "the launching pad."[17] Although its outfield dimensions were normal, it was one of the easiest home-run parks because it sat 1,050 feet above sea level, higher than any other big league venue. A batted ball travels farther in the thinner air at higher altitudes. Atlanta's hot summers also added distance. Aaron changed his batting style to take advantage of the ballpark, uppercutting the ball and becoming a dead pull hitter.[18]

While the stadium was a slugger's delight, it was a circular layout built for both baseball and football, so it had large foul territory that held down scoring except for home runs. Braves pitchers finished a respectable sixth in the league in ERA. Twenty-five-year-old Tony Cloninger and Richards's Houston draftee, Ken Johnson, led the staff with fourteen victories apiece.

A team with the magnificent Aaron in its lineup started with a solid foundation, but the NL was a league of superstars. Aaron was overshadowed by the incandescent Willie Mays and Roberto Clemente, the 1966 Most Valuable Player. San Francisco also had Willie McCovey and Juan Marichal; Philadelphia, young Richie Allen; St. Louis, Bob Gibson and Orlando Cepeda.

Richards did little to overhaul the Braves for 1967. To replace Mathews at third, he acquired Clete Boyer, a veteran of five Yankees pennant winners. The thirty-year-old Boyer was a stellar glove man and had become an average hitter with some power. He was the only new face in the lineup. Newcomer Bob Bruce joined the starting rotation with the veteran Ken Johnson and three young arms: Tony Cloninger, Denny Lemaster, and Dick Kelley. Right-handers Clay Caroll and Phil Niekro anchored the bullpen.

The defending champion Dodgers were reeling from the retirement of Sandy Koufax, finished by an arthritic elbow at age thirty. That left the Giants and Cardinals as pennant favorites, with Atlanta predicted to be in the middle of the pack again.

The Braves struggled to stay above .500 early in the season, as injuries devastated their pitching staff. Richards knew who he wanted to plug one hole in the rotation. On June 6 he traded backup catchers with the Phillies, giving up Gene Oliver for Bob Uecker. The thirty-three-year-old Uecker was a former Braves farmhand who could not hit major league pitching, but Richards had heard he could handle a knuckleball. Richards planned to convert Phil Niekro into a starter, and he needed a catcher who could hold "Knucksie's" specialty. When Uecker arrived in the Atlanta clubhouse, he was welcomed by a white carpet of towels leading to his locker and two notes. One, from the regular catcher, Torre, read, "Thank you very much. God bless you." The other said,

"Lots of luck, your buddy, Phil Niekro."[19] Uecker, a better comedian than ball-player, said his strategy for handling the knuckleball was to "wait till it stops rolling, then pick it up."[20]

Niekro started his first game of the season, and only the second of his career, a week after Uecker joined the club. He shut out Philadelphia on two hits. Uecker committed no passed balls, but Niekro was charged with two wild pitches. Niekro started twenty games and—shades of Hoyt Wilhelm—led the league with a 1.87 ERA.

Repeating his unhappy experience in Baltimore, the mild, pipe-smoking Billy Hitchcock proved unable to keep his players in line. Torre later said, "We led the league in drinking and hospitality" and acknowledged he was one of the most hospitable, along with Uecker and Boyer. Even the quiet Aaron, whose marriage was coming apart, joined the revels. A writer nicknamed the club "the playboys of Peachtree [Street]."[21] In June six Braves were fined $250 each for breaking curfew in Cincinnati.

A couple of weeks later Houston's Don Wilson no-hit Atlanta. On the flight to Los Angeles after the game Rico Carty called Aaron a "black slick," and Aaron went for him. As teammates leaped in to separate them, the aircraft began rocking with several large men jumping around. The pilot threatened to land and throw the Braves off.[22]

The ebullient Carty, a talented hitter who called himself "The Big Boy," was a lightning rod. Aaron thought he cared more about his batting average than about winning. Clete Boyer branded Carty a loafer. Carty carried his wallet in his back uniform pocket during games. Teammate Dusty Baker said, "That's why he never slid." He was a fan favorite who never tired of signing autographs but a liability in the outfield. When Richards chastised Carty and fellow Dominican Felipe Alou for fielding balls one-handed, Carty told him, "I catch [the] ball better." Richards said: "I guess he's right. With one hand he has half a chance less of making more errors."[23] Amid the turmoil Carty missed three weeks with a knee injury and his average dropped to .255.

As the Braves' injured pitchers returned, a modest five-game winning streak boosted them into second place on August 13, but they trailed St. Louis by eight and a half games. Atlanta's record was 61-51, the apex of the 1967 season. Then the wheels came off. The club went 16-34 the rest of the way and sank to seventh place. After the final game Aaron said, "Some of the guys gave up two months ago."[24]

Billy Hitchcock did not make it to the finish. When he was fired with three games to go, he said, "This comes as a relief."[25] It did not come as a surprise; rumors had been floating for weeks that he would be replaced by Luman Harris, whom Richards had installed as manager at AAA Richmond. That was Richards's plan, but Bill Bartholomay and others in the front office resisted reuniting the "old sidekicks." Before Bartholomay would go along, he made Richards promise to move into the dugout himself if Harris didn't work out. The club introduced its new manager at a press conference in St. Louis during the World Series. Harris said he had found out only that day that the job was his. A writer smirked, "Gee, it's a good thing you were in town."[26]

"I would say facetiously that Luman has had proper training for the job," Richards told the press. "He has been with me for 21 years." To the suggestion that Harris would be a puppet, Richards bristled, "That's simply not true." The fifty-two-year-old Harris said, "First, he made me a big league pitcher, then he made me a big league coach, and then he made me a big league manager, so why shouldn't I admire the man?"[27]

It was Houston and Baltimore all over again. Now that Richards had control of the ball club, he sprinkled his own men throughout the organization. Jim Busby, Billy Goodman, and former relief ace Harry Dorish joined the Braves' coaching staff. Bill Wight and Clint Courtney were hired as scouts. Richards would soon make Courtney a minor league manager. Completing the reunion, Eddie Robinson came aboard to run the farm system. After leaving Houston he had worked in the Kansas City Athletics' front office, but owner Charlie Finley was moving the team to Oakland, and Robinson did not want to go. Defending the hirings, Richards said: "They do a certain job for me, and that's all I care about. It is not a case of blind loyalty."[28]

The Braves' 77-85 record was their first losing season since they left Boston fifteen years before. Richards joked that he had considered taking over as manager "until I looked at shortstop and center field and the double plays we didn't make." He promised, "We are going to have some new faces in Atlanta next season."[29]

1. *Atlanta Journal*, June 26, 1966, 51.
2. *Sporting News* (hereafter *TSN*), July 16, 1966, 8.
3. *Atlanta Journal-Constitution*, April 12, 2006, online edition. The description is Furman Bisher's.
4. Henry Aaron, with Lonnie Wheeler, *I Had a Hammer: The Henry Aaron Story* (New York: HarperCollins, 1991), 181.
5. *TSN*, February 3, 1968, 29.
6. Paul Richards, interview by Clark Nealon, February 5, 1981; *TSN*, September 3, 1966, 19, and September 17, 1966, 7.
7. *TSN*, August 27, 1966, 14.
8. *Atlanta Journal*, August 31, 1966, 45.
9. Mark Stewart and Mike Kennedy, *Hammering Hank: How the Media Made Henry Aaron* (Guilford, Conn.: Lyons Press, 2007), 101.
10. Aaron, *I Had a Hammer*, 187.
11. Ibid.
12. *TSN*, January 21, 1967, 21–22.
13. Robert Creamer, "Boot a Few, Bat a Million," *Sports Illustrated*, July 15, 1963, online archive.
14. *Atlanta Journal*, March 19, 1967, in Paul Richards's scrapbooks, in the personal collection of Paula Richards.
15. Eddie Robinson, interview by author, August 18, 2006, Fort Worth, Texas.
16. *TSN*, April 15, 1967, 22.
17. Ibid., June 12, 1971, 36. Originally called Atlanta Stadium, the park was renamed when the Fulton County government agreed to contribute funding.
18. Aaron, *I Had a Hammer*, 199.
19. Phil Niekro and Tom Bird, *Knuckle Balls* (New York: Freundlich, 1986), 19.
20. *TSN*, August 9, 1969, 13.
21. Joe Torre, with Tom Verducci, *Chasing the Dream* (New York: Bantam, 1997), 100; Aaron, *I Had a Hammer*, 193.

22. Aaron, *I Had a Hammer*, 190–91; *TSN*, June 24, 1967, 10; UPI, *Lima (Ohio) News*, June 21, 1967, 38.

23. *TSN*, February 24, 1968, 28; Aaron, *I Had a Hammer*, 185, 195; Tim Kurkjian, *Is This a Great Game, or What?* (New York: St. Martin's Griffin, 2007), 64; Mark Mulvoy, "Things Are Different in Atlanta," *Sports Illustrated*, March 27, 1967, 53; *Atlanta Journal*, June 11, 1991, E6.

24. *TSN*, October 21, 1967, 15.

25. AP, *Cumberland (Md.) News*, September 30, 1967, 8.

26. AP, *Winona (Minn.) News*, October 8, 1967, 10; Jesse Outlar, "The Reunion of Richards and Harris," *Atlanta Journal-Constitution Magazine*, April 7, 1968, 24–27; *TSN*, October 21, 1967, 2.

27. Outlar, "Reunion of Richards and Harris," 27.

28. Mulvoy, "Things Are Different in Atlanta," 53.

29. *Atlanta Journal*, October 7, 1967, 1-B; *TSN*, October 28, 1967, 21.

CHAPTER 23

The End of Baseball as We Know It

Baseball was about to change. The face of change was Marvin Miller.

When the Major League Baseball Players Association hired Miller, a Steelworkers union economist, as its first full-time executive director in 1966, it unleashed the most powerful force the game had ever known—more powerful than Ruth or Landis or Rickey, more powerful than the nineteenth-century pioneers, Hulbert, Spalding, and Anson. That force was the players.

For baseball owners and executives Miller was the devil with a pencil moustache. They damned him through their pulpits in the press, and no voice was louder or more reactionary than that of Paul Richards. He called Miller "a little mustachioed four-flusher," among other choice names. The *Wall Street Journal*'s John Helyar wrote, "Paul Richards hated the union even more than he hated a ten-game losing streak."[1]

The players, on the other hand, were impressed by Miller's willingness to listen, his constant reminders that *he* worked for *them*, and his unshakeable calm. Joe Torre described him as a "small, soft-spoken man who mesmerized you because he kept making sense."[2]

The change began the first time Miller met with a committee of owners to set the terms for renewing the players' pension plan and health benefits. The owners had always decided how much they would contribute to the pension fund, and the players accepted it. Commissioner Eckert was walking toward a press conference to announce the new deal when Miller pulled him aside and told him there was no deal until the Players Association said there was.[3]

When the association's executive board met in October 1967, negotiations for the first labor agreement between players and management had been sputtering on and off—mostly off—for months. The twenty-two board members included five of Richards's current or former players: Torre, representing the Braves; Dave Giusti of Houston, Milt Pappas of Cincinnati, Dick Hall of Philadelphia, and Jack Fisher of the Mets.[4] It could be that Richards's men especially felt the need for an organization to protect their rights or that he had employed some especially intelligent players.

Miller believed the negotiations were making progress, so he and the player reps traveled to the majors' winter meeting in Mexico City at the end of November. According to Miller, the owners stood them up. He said the owners' negotiators had agreed to meet with the players in Mexico City, then reneged, claiming they did not have time. The player reps were furious. Their first response was to award Miller a three-year contract extension and a pay raise. National League rep Jim Bunning, later a conservative Republican senator from Kentucky, said the owners were pressuring the players to get rid of Miller: "Well, I have news for them. Marvin Miller will be around in his present job for a long time."[5]

American League president Joe Cronin told the writers that no bargaining session had ever been on the schedule. Richards followed him to the podium. "Somebody's lying, and I don't think it's the owners," he said. "If this guy [Miller] continues these tactics we'll just have to get in the gutter with him." Richards was just warming up. He said Miller's goal, obviously, was to abolish the reserve clause: "That'll be the end of baseball as we know it and that'll be a sad day in the lives of 90 percent of the ballplayers.

"The ballplayers don't know when they're well off. What kind of money are they going to make without the reserve clause? Peanuts: No owner is going to pay big money to a player he can't keep for the following year."[6]

In Miller's version of the scene Richards appeared, "highball in hand," and "sounded off with a drunken tirade directed at me. . . . The press was kind enough not to reveal that Richards had to be propped up to prevent his falling down."[7] (Richards was not known to drink a highball, whose definition does not encompass a martini.) Joe Torre confronted Richards in the back of the conference room and told him the owners had insulted the players. The catcher and the vice president argued loudly, but their words were not recorded. Torre believed his career with the Braves ended that night.[8]

The first encounter between Miller and Richards set the tone for years of mutual vituperation. When Miller returned home from Mexico City, he composed a blistering letter to the Braves' players, telling them their boss was "living in the past" and attacking Richards's character and the records of his teams. He decided not to mail it.[9]

Miller and Richards sniped at each other again during the 1968 season, when Miller protested to NL president Warren Giles about allegedly dangerous, wet field conditions in Atlanta for a Braves-Mets game. Richards responded that it was none of Miller's business. "I have never seen a player hurt on a wet infield," he wrote to Miller, telling him to "refrain from giving me advice regarding baseball players." Miller replied, "The health and safety of players is very much my business and the business of the Players Association."[10]

Richards was a company man to his bones. He had pursued the baseball life since he was a boy, and the game had rewarded him with forty years of steady employment at ever-increasing salaries in jobs with important responsibilities. It had made him famous. He relished the power he wielded over players: power to play them or bench them, trade them or release them, all for the good of the team—as he defined it. Though he was an anarchist with umpires and an experimenter with tactics and strategies, Richards was a conservative man. Any threat to baseball's status quo was a personal threat to him.

Richards was far from the only belligerent in baseball's front offices. When members of the White Sox filed a grievance about their seedy hotel accommodations in Baltimore, owner Arthur Allyn Jr. told the players that if they didn't want to stay in the hotel, the team would forfeit its games in the city. The commissioner ordered Allyn to find a better hotel.[11] The Cincinnati Reds complained that players were evicted from the first-class section on crowded planes (seats guaranteed by their contract) to make room for sportswriters. When Marvin Miller visited Cincinnati, general manager Bob Howsam invited the writers to sit in on the grievance meeting.[12]

Most writers were as hostile toward the union as Richards and the owners. The writers portrayed Miller as a Pied Piper leading gullible players off a cliff. One of the most rabid—and influential—was Dick Young of the *New York Daily News*, who said of "Comrade Miller": "He runs the players through a high-pressure spray the way an auto goes through a car wash, and that's how they come out, brainwashed." The *Atlanta Journal*'s Furman Bisher suggested that if stars like Jim Bunning were worried about the plight of players making the $7,000 minimum salary, they should donate part of their own paychecks to the less fortunate. "I cannot see the major league player demeaning himself to the status of a unionized laborer," Bisher wrote.[13]

Dick Kaegel of the *Sporting News* unwittingly explained the writers' hostility when he recounted conversations with player reps in Mexico City: "It was rather strange—guys who average $22,000 to $23,000 a season coming, baseball caps in hand, to newspaper reporters, who see such lofty figures only in their dreams."[14] Sportswriters were baseball's last romantics. They could imagine nothing more exalting than being paid to play the game. Even though they rubbed shoulders with the players daily, the writers—many of them union members, carrying a Newspaper Guild card—could not relate to a major leaguer as a fellow workingman. They were living not just in the past but in a gauzy vision of a golden past that never existed, when club owners were "sportsmen," and players, as so many of them naively said, "would have played for nothing."

Miller saw the players not only as workingmen but also as workers who were sorely oppressed. In his wildest exaggeration, he said they were "the most exploited people I have ever seen . . . worse than Cesar Chavez's grape pickers at the time."[15] No grape picker made $22,000 a year.

General managers had always advised players not to tell their teammates how much money they were making, so a man had no way of knowing where he stood on the payroll ladder. Miller asked each player to write his salary, anonymously, on a slip of paper. The survey revealed that the 1967 average was $19,000, the median $17,000 (half made more, half less). One-third of the players were paid $10,000 or less. (An average American worker made $8,000.)[16]

When the 1968 season opened, Richards had made good on his promise of new faces, beginning with eliminating the weaknesses up the middle. He acquired shortstop Sonny Jackson, whom he had signed for Houston, and handed second base to Felix Millan, a twenty-four-year-old Puerto Rican who was a favorite of Harris's from the Richmond club. "Millan is going to replace Bill Mazeroski as the best second baseman in this league," Harris predicted, "and I don't mean that as a knock against Maz."[17] Felipe Alou moved to center field. But Richards did not find the front-line starting pitcher he needed. He could not get rid of the controversial Rico Carty because Carty had contracted tuberculosis during the winter and would miss the entire 1968 season. He was the first of many casualties that sank Atlanta's pennant chances.

There is no evidence that Richards tried to trade Joe Torre after their Mexico City confrontation. No matter what their differences, a slugging young catcher was a prime asset. In May a beanball split Torre's palate and broke his cheekbone and nose. He did not help his standing with the front office when he was arrested for driving under the influence while on the disabled list.[18]

The Braves rallied from a slow start and closed to within one-half game of first place on the last day of May. Right-hander Ron Reed, a six-foot-six rookie who had played for the National Basketball Association's Detroit Pistons, won his first six decisions and made the all-star team. He credited Richards with teaching him the slider and slip pitch.[19] In June Richards dealt for his Baltimore bonus baby Milt Pappas, who had angered the Cincinnati management while serving as the team's player representative. Pappas had won 140 games in ten-plus seasons but was still only twenty-nine years old. He went on to win ten for the Braves with a team-best 2.37 ERA.

By July 4 Atlanta was tied for second place with San Francisco. Bill Bartholomay rewarded Richards with a three-year contract extension through 1971. "He's doing an excellent job for us," Bartholomay said, "and we're looking forward to the day we bring a pennant to the Southeast."[20] But the Braves were only three games above .500 at 41-38. The defending champion Cardinals had opened an eight-and-a-half-game lead.

The pileup of injuries continued, and the Braves sank steadily in the standings during August. Richards's refurbished team improved by four wins but was the definition of mediocrity: an 81-81 record, fifth place in the ten-team league. Aaron hit his five-hundredth home run on July 14 but finished with just twenty-nine and drove in only eighty-six runs, his lowest total since his rookie year. Launching pad or no, the Braves suffered a power outage: they managed only eighty homers.

They were not alone. The steady decline in run scoring that began when the strike zone was expanded in 1963 hit bottom in '68. Major league teams scored fewer than seven runs per game (by both teams), the lowest since 1908. One out of every five games was a shutout. Carl Yastrzemski won the American League batting title with an average of just .301. The acerbic Dick Young wrote:

"One of the favorites of the scoreboard quizzes flashed for fans in the new ball-parks is, 'Who was the last man to hit .400 in the majors?' The way things are going, the next question will be 'Who was the last man to hit .300?'"[21]

Baseball men offered various explanations for the leaguewide batting slump. Many thought the pitchers were better. "When I went to the big leagues the pitchers threw a fast ball and a curve," Richards said. "If they tried to throw anything else they were told to forget it." He believed experimentation started during World War II, when the inferior moundsmen were willing to try anything. "Now every pitcher has three pitches and probably four."[22] He had long blamed the slider for declining batting averages. He and others pointed to the growth of organized Little Leagues, where the biggest, strongest boy was usually put on the mound. White Sox manager Eddie Stanky maintained, "It's easier to teach a boy to be a pitcher than to be a hitter."[23]

Veterans also cited bigger gloves, manicured infields, and better position-ing of fielders. "Look at the difference in gloves," Richards said. "The gloves they used back in the '30s had short fingers and were small. With those gloves they have today they can catch anything they can get close to."[24]

Even the barnacle-encrusted baseball establishment agreed that something had to be done. Major league attendance had peaked at 25.2 million in 1965; in 1968 it was two million lower. That winter a Louis Harris poll found that football had surpassed baseball as America's favorite sport for the first time. The doomsayers were so loud that Roger Angell mused, "I almost looked for the obituary in the *Times* the next morning. (Pastime, National, 99; after a lin-gering illness. Remains on view at Cooperstown, N.Y.)"[25]

Against the backdrop of discouraging words and declining attendance, the game's establishment reluctantly embraced "that unthinkable concept, 'change.'"[26] Richards had suggested moving the pitcher five feet farther from home plate. That had worked in 1893, when establishment of the pitching dis-tance at sixty feet, six inches sparked a hitting explosion. During spring training in 1968 Richards experimented with a less radical change, placing the pitching rubber sixty-two feet, six inches from the plate.[27]

When baseball's rule makers met during the winter, they left the pitching distance alone but shrank the strike zone. The new zone reached from the batter's armpits rather than his shoulders to "the top of the knee." The committee also ordered the mounds lowered. The rule limited the mound to fifteen inches above the playing field; that was cut to ten.[28] In 1969 the major league batting average rose eleven points, to .248, and runs increased to more than eight per game, still below historical norms.

Marvin Miller and the owners squared off again in December 1968 over the pension plan. Owners refused to increase their contribution, despite signing the biggest network television contract in history. Miller announced that players would not sign their 1969 contracts until the issue was settled: "Signing without knowing what the new benefit plan will offer is like signing half a contract."[29] Nearly all players went along, including most of the stars. Mickey Mantle, who had decided to retire, held off announcing his plans and lent his support.[30] It was not a strike but a mass holdout.

Richards, the writers' reliable go-to guy for an inflammatory quote, came through again. He said Miller spoke for "a few rabble rousers and greedy players." Besides, the majors could use minor leaguers to fill in if there was a strike. Frank Lane implored, "Paul, for God's sake, stop talking. All you're doing is aiding the enemy." Richards was not the only loudmouth. Angels owner Gene Autry said the clubs might "close up shop" for a year or two, and he would get back in the saddle again. "I can still ride a horse and make $150,000 a year," the old movie cowboy said.[31]

The impasse dragged into February, with spring training drawing near. Only a few dozen players broke ranks and signed, including Atlanta pitchers Phil Niekro, Pat Jarvis, Ken Johnson, and Ron Reed. "The owners appear to be playing 'chicken' with us and I'm afraid they're going to miscalculate," Miller warned.[32]

"I don't think the players have enough guts to strike," Richards sneered. "They are bluffing." But he also criticized the owners. They had fired the feckless Commissioner Eckert, then deadlocked over choosing a successor. Richards said: "If the owners don't realize that this is an emergency and pick a commissioner, they might as well turn the game over to Miller. . . . It has been so long since baseball had proper leadership that the owners must absorb some of the blame."[33]

Unable to agree on a candidate, the owners named one of their lawyers, forty-two-year-old Bowie Kuhn, as interim commissioner. Kuhn had sat in on the negotiating sessions and had seen the players' determination first hand. He did not want to begin his commissionership by presiding over empty ball fields. More important, NBC sent word that it would not pay to televise games featuring minor leaguers. At Kuhn's urging, the owners' negotiators got down to business and settled the dispute just a few days after pitchers and catchers were due to report.[34]

After the settlement Richards fulminated, "Judge Landis would have ordered the owners to ignore Miller."[35] The comment reflected his ignorance of the law as well as his wrongheaded reading of the situation. Baseball would never be able to ignore Marvin Miller.

---

1. *Sporting News* (hereafter *TSN*), July 17, 1976, 17; John Helyar, *Lords of the Realm* (New York: Villard, 1994), 90.
2. Charles P. Korr, *The End of Baseball as We Knew It* (Urbana: University of Illinois Press, 2002), 42.
3. Marvin Miller, *A Whole Different Ball Game: The Sport and Business of Baseball* (New York: Carol, 1991), 86–89.
4. *TSN*, October 28, 1967, 30.
5. Miller, *Whole Different Ball Game*, 162–63; *TSN*, December 16, 1967, 31.
6. UPI, *Port Arthur (Texas) News*, December 2, 1967, 12.
7. Miller, *Whole Different Ball Game*, 162.
8. Ibid.; Korr, *End of Baseball*, 70.
9. Korr, *End of Baseball*, 69–70.
10. *TSN*, June 29, 1968, 4.
11. Ibid., September 28, 1968, 24.

12. Miller, *Whole Different Ball Game*, 156–57.
13. Korr, *End of Baseball*, 44–45.
14. *TSN*, December 16, 1967, 31.
15. Andrew Zimbalist, *Baseball and Billions* (New York: Basic, 1992), 75.
16. Robert F. Burk, *Much More Than a Game* (Chapel Hill: University of North Carolina Press, 2001), 155.
17. Gary Ronberg, "Felix Is One Sweet Ballplayer," *Sports Illustrated*, July 22, 1968, online archive.
18. Joe Torre, with Tom Verducci, *Chasing the Dream* (New York: Bantam, 1997), 103–4.
19. *TSN*, June 1, 1968, 12.
20. UPI, *Anniston (Ala.) Star*, July 9, 1968, 7.
21. *TSN*, June 8, 1968, 14.
22. Ibid., April 3, 1965, 29.
23. Ibid., June 8, 1968, 4.
24. Ibid., March 19, 1966, 16.
25. Roger Angell, *The Summer Game* (Lincoln: University of Nebraska Press, 2004), 197.
26. Leonard Koppett, *Koppett's Concise History of Major League Baseball* (New York: Carroll and Graf, 2004), 327.
27. *TSN*, June 22, 1968, 14.
28. UPI, *Bennington (Vt.) Banner*, December 4, 1968, 10.
29. *TSN*, September 21, 1968, 9.
30. UPI, *Los Angeles Times*, December 6, 1968, G1-2; Burk, *Much More Than a Game*, 161.
31. UPI, *Los Angeles Times*, December 6, 1968, G1-2; Helyar, *Lords of the Realm*, 91.
32. AP, *Manitowoc (Wisc.) Herald-Times*, February 25, 1969, 9; *TSN*, February 15, 1969, 33.
33. *TSN*, February 22, 1969, 43.
34. Ibid., March 8, 1969, 26; Burk, *Much More Than a Game*, 161.
35. *TSN*, May 24, 1969, 11.

CHAPTER 24

Half a Pennant

O n the field "the end of baseball as we knew it" came when the majors added four expansion franchises in 1969 and split each league into two six-team divisions, abolishing the traditional pennant races and creating postseason playoffs to decide the league championships. The World Series got colder.

Joe Torre was a holdout when spring training began. After hitting thirty-six home runs in 1966, he had fallen off badly. In 1968 he played only 115 games because of the beaning and a broken finger, and contributed just ten homers. Richards proposed cutting his $65,000 salary by 20 percent. Torre, predictably, did not sign. Richards sounded off: "I don't care if he holds out till Thanksgiving. . . . No more than he has contributed the last two years, it wouldn't hurt us if he did."[1] Torre was stung; he called Richards and asked whether he had really said that. Nothing personal, Richards told him. Torre told a reporter, "It was very personal with me. I respect the man's ability and his knowledge of the game. I just don't think he should have come out and said the things he did in public. He could have said what he wanted in the privacy of the clubhouse, but he never did."[2]

Bill Bartholomay persuaded Torre to report to West Palm Beach and meet with Richards. "The same deal stands—not one cent different," Richards told him. As Torre walked out, he handed Richards his business card from the Wall Street bond-trading firm where he worked in the off-season. As Torre described it, Richards disdainfully dropped the card into the wastebasket.

Within days Torre was traded to St. Louis for Orlando Cepeda. Torre and many writers believed his union activism, rather than his performance, was the reason.[3] Richards had been shopping him all winter—to the Mets for Nolan Ryan, not yet an established pitcher; to the Dodgers for pitcher Don Sutton and catcher Tom Haller; to Houston for Rusty Staub.[4] In each of those proposed deals Richards was seeking young players in exchange for his powerful twenty-eight-year-old catcher. Instead he got a thirty-one-year-old first baseman coming off the worst year of his career.

In 1967 Cepeda posted a .923 OPS and won the MVP award, but he slumped to .684 the next year. A boisterous, outgoing Puerto Rican, he was a clubhouse leader in St. Louis and would become the same in Atlanta—"a rah-rah guy," Aaron called him.[5] Cepeda could replace Torre as a power threat behind Aaron in the lineup.

Now Richards needed to replace Torre behind the plate. During spring training he assembled all the catchers and asked, "Can anybody here catch a knuckleball?"

The youngest of them stepped forward: "I can, sir."

"What's your name?"

"Bob Didier."

"Son, you're going to the majors."

Didier was twenty years old and had caught only 145 games in the low minors. "Well, I was young and dumb and I would say anything because I didn't know any better," he said later.[6] The youngster became Richards's latest project and won the everyday job.

Rico Carty, trying to come back from TB, did not make it out of spring training. He dislocated his throwing shoulder and underwent surgery.[7] The shoulder continued to pop out and sidelined him for most of the season, leaving Richards and Harris scrambling for a third outfielder. Otherwise, Richards stood pat with his .500 team. The "race for only half a pennant," as Red Smith put it, saw the Braves vying for the Western Division crown with San Francisco and Cincinnati, the second- and fourth-place clubs, in baseball's last true pennant race in 1968.[8] The favorite, Cincinnati, was beginning to build the "Big Red Machine" with 1968 Rookie of the Year Johnny Bench behind the plate, joining batting champion Pete Rose, first baseman Lee May, and third baseman Tony Perez.

The Braves started fast, and by the time they had been twice around the division they were tied for first place with the Dodgers and Giants on May 2. They would stay on top for fifty days. But San Francisco and Los Angeles were pitching better than Atlanta, and Cincinnati was scoring more runs. At the season's midpoint the Braves led the Dodgers by a half-game, the Giants by three and a half, and the Reds by four and a half. Held back by injuries, the Braves could not pull away. By September 1, 1969, the club had fallen two games behind San Francisco, with the Reds and Dodgers only a half-game back. Aaron said, "It's going to take about a 10-game winning streak by whoever wins it."[9]

Niekro had won eighteen games and was just out of the top ten in ERA. His rookie catcher, Bob Didier, said the secret to handling the knuckler was to keep your eyes wide open—"If you blink, you miss it." (He blinked at least twenty-seven times for passed balls.) Didier was batting over .250, better than he had done in Class A ball.[10]

It may have been a race for half a pennant, but it was some race. With three weeks to go, five teams separated by just two games were jostling for the Western Division lead: San Francisco, Cincinnati, Atlanta, Los Angeles, and Houston. The Astros lost their next six and fell back. For the stretch run Richards acquired forty-six-year-old Hoyt Wilhelm from the Angels. Wilhelm and a healthy Rico Carty carried the Braves to the finish line. Wilhelm saved four games and won two, while Carty batted .376 in September with a 1.031 OPS and twenty-five RBI in twenty-five games.

On Wednesday, September 17, the Giants woke up in first place. That afternoon they lost to Houston, putting Los Angeles on top. That night Atlanta beat the Dodgers and took over the lead. The next day the Braves lost for the third time in four games against the Dodgers and Giants, moving San Francisco back into the top spot by a half-game. Then the Braves took off on a ten-game winning streak that fulfilled Aaron's prediction. On September 28 Carty homered and drove in three runs as Atlanta beat San Diego 4–2 to clinch at least a tie for first place. Atlanta had two games left at home against Cincinnati.

Niekro started the first one on the night of Tuesday, September 30. He had already won four times in September, twenty-two for the season. Niekro singled and scored the game's first run in the third, but Cincinnati had taken a 2–1 lead when the Braves loaded the bases in the seventh, bringing up Rico Carty. The "Big Boy" capped his comeback season with a sacrifice fly that brought home the go-ahead run.

After Wilhelm retired the last six Reds to nail down the pennant, ecstatic Atlanta fans surged onto the field. Players lost their caps and fought to defend their gloves from souvenir hunters. Luman Harris emerged from the scrum minus his watch and glasses.[11] You'd have thought the South had risen again.

Eighteen years after they came to the majors together, Paul Richards and Luman Harris finished on top of the standings for the first time. Now they had to win the other half of the pennant. As a later Braves pitcher, John Smoltz, observed: "You grow up wanting to play in a World Series. No one says to you, 'Hey, someday you're going to pitch in the playoffs.'"[12]

Major league baseball's first postseason playoffs would be a best-of-five format. Except they weren't playoffs, according to the official doctrine; they were the League Championship Series, featuring the two division winners, rather than the multiple-round tournaments conducted in the minors and professional hockey and basketball.

Atlanta's opponent was the New York Mets, inevitably dubbed "the Miracle Mets" after they rose from ninth place to first. And they really did finish first;

their 100-62 record, seven games better than the Braves', would have won the pennant but for division play. Under the steadying leadership of manager Gil Hodges, the Mets had put together a young lineup with no regular older than twenty-six and three young pitching stars: Tom Seaver, Jerry Koosman, and reliever Tug McGraw. The Mets had overtaken Leo Durocher's Cubs down the stretch by winning thirty-eight of their last fifty games.

New York was favored in the championship series. The Mets looked to be the better team, and Atlanta had additional problems. Wilhelm was not eligible for postseason play because he had joined the Braves after September 1. Felipe Alou was hurt and available only to pinch-hit. While staggering home late after celebrating the division title, Aaron had lost his house key and gashed his hand when he broke a window to get in. He needed several stitches. (He told the team a cover story about climbing a fence.) Further, Aaron felt some of his teammates went into the series with a defeatist attitude. They had squabbled over how to divide up the smaller loser's share of playoff money. "I don't want to call names," Aaron said later, "but some were like, 'Oh, we're satisfied we made it this far.'"[13]

The two clubs' aces, Seaver and Niekro, were cuffed around in the first game. It was tied 4–4 in the seventh when Aaron homered to put the Braves ahead. Despite the sore hand, he batted .357 with three homers in the series. But Atlanta's defense fell apart in the eighth. A botched pick-off, a bungled double play, and a wild throw handed the Mets five runs and the victory. In the second game the Mets jumped out to an 8–0 lead and won, 11–6, as the Braves committed three more errors. Ron Reed, who was knocked out in the second inning, remembered: "When we lost two at home, there was absolutely no doubt we were going up [to New York] to lose. We knew we were going to lose up there. I don't think anybody thought we could win three in Shea [Stadium]."[14]

In New York Aaron's first-inning homer put the Braves ahead 2–0 in Game

3. When the first two Atlanta batters reached base in the third, the Mets' wild young flamethrower, Nolan Ryan, replaced starter Gary Gentry. Ryan finished the game with seven strikeouts in seven innings, allowing only a two-run homer to Cepeda, while the Mets came back to win 7–4 and sweep the series. Their miracle lasted through the World Series, where they beat Baltimore in five games.

On paper the Braves had no business winning even half a pennant. They finished fifth in the league in both runs scored and runs allowed. By scoring sixty more runs than they allowed, they could be expected to win eighty-eight games. Whether the five additional victories were a testament to Luman Harris's managing smarts or dumb luck is an enduring sabermetric debate.[15] Aaron's forty-four home runs and 1.004 OPS were second to the Giants' Willie McCovey's, but twenty-eight of Aaron's homers were solos. He totaled only ninety-seven RBI (batting himself in forty-four times) because there were few runners to drive in. The two hitters who most often batted in front of him, Felix Millan and Felipe Alou, had low on-base percentages. Hitting fourth behind Aaron, Cepeda was a disappointment with a .257 average and .753 OPS. As a result Aaron drew nineteen intentional walks, second in the league to McCovey's forty-five.

The *Journal*'s Furman Bisher later wrote that the '69 Braves "reflected hardly any of [Richards's] personality at all."[16] He was wrong. Richards's signature was all over the roster: tight defense and young players. Defense was the team's strength; Atlanta's defensive efficiency rate was the league's second best, and the Braves committed the fewest errors. Improving the defense had been Richards's primary goal in his trades for shortstop Sonny Jackson and third baseman Clete Boyer, the move of Alou to center field, and the promotion of Millan to play second. Cepeda, though coveted for his bat, wielded a better glove than the Braves' previous first basemen. Richards had acquired or promoted five of the eight everyday players: Jackson, Boyer, Millan, Cepeda, and Didier. More of his acquisitions stepped in when injuries struck. Tony Gonzalez replaced Carty and Alou; Gil Garrido subbed for Jackson.

The pitching staff also bore Richards's and Harris's stamp. They converted Niekro into a starter; he became the ace. They put a pair of youngsters into the rotation, eighteen-game winner Ron Reed and thirteen-game winner George Stone. They installed twenty-six-year-old side-armer Cecil Upshaw as the top reliever; he saved twenty-seven games. Richards's September deal for Wilhelm helped spark the championship drive.

Richards had inherited a strong nucleus of Aaron, Carty, and Alou. Aaron was the straw that stirred the drink, but Richards mixed the winning cocktail. Still, half a pennant tasted like near-beer.

1. AP, *Salisbury (Md.) Daily Times*, February 25, 1969, 11.
2. UPI, *Elyria (Ohio) Chronicle-Telegram*, March 23, 1969, D-5.
3. Joe Torre, with Tom Verducci, *Chasing the Dream* (New York: Bantam, 1997), 106–7.
4. *Sporting News* (hereafter *TSN*), March 29, 1969, 27.
5. Hank Aaron, with Lonnie Wheeler, *I Had a Hammer: The Hank Aaron Story* (New York: HarperCollins, 1991), 198.
6. *Atlanta Journal-Constitution*, September 30, 1989, E1.
7. Washington Post News Service, *San Antonio Express*, September 26, 1969, 57.
8. Red Smith, *Strawberries in the Wintertime* (New York: Quadrangle, 1974), 63.
9. Peter Carry, "Mad Scramble East and West," *Sports Illustrated*, September 8, 1969, online archive.
10. *TSN*, August 9, 1969, 13.
11. Ibid., October 18, 1969, 22.
12. John Feinstein, *Play Ball* (New York: Villard, 1993), 384.
13. Aaron, *I Had a Hammer*, 202; *Atlanta Journal-Constitution*, September 30, 1989, E1.
14. *Atlanta Journal-Constitution*, September 30, 1989, E1.
15. The win expectation developed by Bill James is called the Pythagorean winning percentage. The original formula was the square of the team's runs scored divided by the square of its runs scored plus the square of its runs allowed. Most sabermetricians believe any significant increase or decrease in victories is the result of luck or chance.
16. *TSN*, February 3, 1973, 35.

CHAPTER 25

"A Ghastly Mistake"

The *Sporting News* picked the Braves to repeat as Western Division champions in 1970, declaring they had "too much hitting power" to be denied.[1] Richards knew better. He set out to strengthen his pitching staff. He took a gamble on the Athletics' Jim Nash, who lived just outside Atlanta in Marietta, Georgia. Nash was a phenom when he broke in with the A's in 1966, posting a 12-1 record and 2.06 ERA. Two years later his ERA was 2.28, but in 1969 a sore arm limited him to 115 innings. The six-foot-four right-hander was only twenty-five. To get him Richards gave up thirty-five-year-old Felipe Alou, also coming off an injury-plagued season. Richards dealt young right-hander Jim Britton, a seven-game winner, to Montreal for lefty Larry Jaster. Like Nash, Jaster had been a rookie star in 1966, winning eleven games for the Cardinals, but he did not develop and the club let him go in the expansion draft. Britton was overjoyed to leave Atlanta. "I'd get a couple of starts and that was it," he said. "They [Richards and Harris] never told me where I stood . . . never talked to me. In fact, they never talked to anybody."[2]

A player in Britton's circumstances could only hope for a trade. Curt Flood, who was happy in St. Louis, was hoping not to be traded. When the Cardinals dealt their center fielder to Philadelphia, Flood refused to report to the Phillies and filed suit challenging baseball's reserve clause. Flood was making $90,000 a year, but he told broadcaster Howard Cosell, "A well-paid slave is nonetheless a slave."[3]

UPI's Milton Richman knew where to go for a comment on the lawsuit, and his old stand-by did not disappoint. If the reserve clause was struck down, Richards said, players would be here today, gone tomorrow. Owners would not care about keeping them happy and healthy: "We won't be having $15 a day meal money for the players, we'll have a training table instead. We won't be traveling in jet planes, we'll have a Greyhound bus pull up for the shorter trips. There won't be anybody taking care of a ballplayer's bags and carrying them to his hotel room. He'll have to carry them himself. Now we have surgeons and doctors taking care of their aches and pains. That'll be a thing of the past."[4] He warned that teams would be reduced to barnstorming like the Harlem Globetrotters, because hometown fans would not identify with the constantly changing cast of players.[5]

Soon after 1970's spring training opened, the ice in Richards's winning cocktail began to melt. Atlanta's number-two starter, Ron Reed, tripped over first base during a workout and broke his collarbone. Luman Harris believed Reed was poised to become one of the league's elite pitchers after winning eighteen games in his first season as a full-time starter.[6] Reed missed two months.

On the club's first West Coast trip in April, six-foot-six reliever Cecil Upshaw suffered a gruesome injury when he was showing some teammates how to dunk a basketball outside their San Diego hotel. As he jumped and slapped his pitching hand on top of an awning, his ring finger snagged on a sharp edge and was split open. Doctors considered amputation, but they were able to save the finger after several operations and nerve grafts.[7] Upshaw was lost for the season.

The pitching staff never recovered. Although Atlanta reeled off an eleven-game winning streak in April and May, moving up to second place behind Cincinnati, there was no race for the division title. The Reds, under new manager Sparky Anderson, won thirty-six of their first fifty. The Braves peaked in June, when they rose ten games over .500. For the rest of the season they went 47-67.

Atlanta fell to fifth in the six-team division with a 76-86 record. One of Richards's latest pitching reclamation projects, Jim Nash, was solid with a 13-9 record and better-than-average ERA, but Larry Jaster won just one game and spent most of the season at AAA Richmond. It was a sour, disappointing season after the semitriumph of 1969, "a lost season," the *Journal's* Wayne Minshew wrote.[8] Aaron said later: "Sixty-nine was just a freakish kind of year. . . . I didn't think it was a team that was going to build a dynasty."[9] Bill Bartholomay signed Luman Harris to manage for a fourth season. Asked what the team needed, Harris replied, "To win more games."[10]

Richards's only victory of 1970 came on the golf course. Shortly before his sixty-second birthday in November, he won Giants owner Horace Stoneham's annual tournament. More than sixty players and other baseball figures competed in Casa Grande, Arizona. Richards shot 73, 76, and 70 to win by four strokes over Cubs coach Peanuts Lowrey.[11]

Richards had founded his own golf tournament, the Waxahachie Classic. Beginning in 1967, he invited a few baseball friends to play after the season. Richards stage-managed the event, arranging for an Atlanta jeweler to provide prizes—free, of course. The tournament grew to a three-day gathering of dozens of players and former players. Eventually, he would take it on the road to resort areas, including Sea Island, Georgia; Las Vegas; and Guadalajara, Mexico. Waxahachie friends continued the classic for years after its founder's death.[12]

Mickey Mantle was the pigeon in one of Richards's golf hustles. The retired slugger, who lived in Dallas, accepted an invitation for a round at the Waxahachie Country Club. Richards recruited one of the club's top players, M. B. Few (who wouldn't want to play with the Mick?), and they demolished Mantle and his partner. Mantle demanded a rematch. When the appointed day came, Richards knew Few was out of town. Richards made a show of impatience, wondering why his partner was late. Finally he said, "Let's not wait any longer.

I'll take that old fellow on the practice green." He pointed to a skinny specimen wearing shabby work clothes and Hush Puppy shoes. "That old fellow" was a ringer: Richards's high school teammate Archie Wise, an excellent golfer with an uncanny knack for reading putts. Richards had arranged for Wise to take the day off from his job at the post office. They polished off the Mantle twosome and collected their money.[13]

The off-season news was not good. Rico Carty broke his knee playing winter ball in the Dominican Republic. After reconstructive surgery he would miss the entire season for the second time in four years. Richards signed him for a substantial raise anyway, a reward for his standout 1970 performance.[14]

The injury was the first of several that would open opportunities for young players. Twenty-five-year-old outfielder Ralph Garr had won two consecutive International League batting titles, hitting .386 in 1970. Clint Courtney had scouted him at Grambling State University in Louisiana. Other scouts said Garr could run but couldn't play. Courtney persuaded Richards to take him in the third round of the 1967 draft.[15] While leading his league in stolen bases for three straight years, Garr had picked up the nickname "Road Runner." The Braves licensed the name of Warner Brothers' "Beep! Beep!" cartoon character for use in promotions and souvenir merchandise, a first for a sports franchise.[16] Despite his speed, Garr was a poor outfielder. The club hoped to hide him in left field. Also in the outfield was twenty-one-year-old Dusty Baker, a high school football star in California who had signed with the Braves as a twenty-sixth-round draft choice in 1967. Third baseman Earl Williams was Atlanta's first pick in the inaugural amateur draft in 1965. He had turned down a college basketball scholarship.

Richards preferred to draft teenagers: "The young high school graduate is at a perfect age to learn baseball if he devotes his life to it. If he splits his time between baseball, football, sociology, basketball weaving [*sic*] and rock concerts, he can never be the ballplayer he might have been. Usually college is fatal to a career in baseball. . . . College is for football players, girls and others who can't play baseball."[17] He said multisport athletes faced pressure from family and friends to play football for State U but added, "The kids we really want out of high school, we seldom have too much trouble signing."[18]

Cepeda was the last Brave to arrive in West Palm Beach in 1971 after an extended holdout. He said there were no hard feelings between him and Richards: "I'm like Billy Graham. . . . I never hold a grudge."[19] Clete Boyer was feeling no Christian charity; he had also held out and had been forced to take a pay cut.[20]

The Braves' troubles started early in the season, as they struggled to stay above .500. Both Cepeda and Aaron had sore knees. Richards urged Cepeda to play through the injury, even if he could only pinch-hit much of the time.[21] When Cepeda was out of the lineup, Aaron moved to first base to rest *his* balky knee.

Boyer, seething over his contract dispute, popped off to a reporter when he returned to his old stomping grounds in New York. "There shouldn't be any place in baseball for a guy like Richards," he said. Boyer would "go anywhere just so I can get away from Paul Richards."[22] He said Harris was the manager only because he was Richards's crony. "You know why we lose on the road? There's no telephone direct to the dugout like there is in Atlanta, so Richards can tell (field manager) Luman Harris what to do. . . . Richards ain't never won a pennant in his life and he ain't never going to win one."[23]

When word of the interview reached Richards, he fired back: "I hate to admit that I pay that much to such a sorry player, one who is as scared as he is at home plate." He contended Boyer was plate-shy after a pitch broke his hand in 1968. While the Braves were in Montreal, Richards telephoned Boyer in the clubhouse and offered to release him if Boyer would forgo his sixty days' severance pay. After consulting Marvin Miller, Boyer refused to leave the team unless Richards put it in writing. The third baseman returned to Atlanta for a two-hour meeting with Richards. The club announced Boyer's release in a terse two-sentence statement. Boyer said, "I guess I talk too much sometimes."[24]

That was not the end of it. Richards had persuaded Boyer to return $10,000 of his severance check, in effect, buying his release. When the Players Association objected, the Braves had to give Boyer's money back. Many fans sided with Boyer, who owned a popular bar in Atlanta, and called for Richards's head, but Bill Bartholomay backed Richards. The Braves' clubhouse was in turmoil. "The tension is stifling," an unidentified player said. "We keep waiting for something to happen. You can feel that something is going to."[25]

That was not the end, either. Commissioner Kuhn revealed that Boyer had been under investigation for betting on football games. When no team showed interest in him, Boyer believed he had been blacklisted. He finished the season with AAA Hawaii, then moved farther across the Pacific to wind up his career in Japan.[26]

The abrupt dismissal of Boyer led other former Braves to unload on Richards. Shortstop Denis Menke, who had been traded to Houston in 1967, said: "I couldn't play for Richards. Who could? He'd never tell me what I was doing. It always came out in the papers. I'd rather a guy come up and tell me I'm lousy. Richards said more than anybody to hurt me."

Joe Torre, batting .355 for the Cardinals, said: "Call Richards a spur for me if you want to. . . . But it's enough to really hurt a guy when that guy (Richards) says he doesn't care whether you sign or not. Then you'd just as soon play somewhere else."[27] Even the *Sporting News*, no friend of outspoken ballplayers, editorialized that Richards's "views on labor-management relations would have delighted 19th century industrial tycoons."[28]

Boyer's departure opened third base for a young platoon of Darrell Evans, who batted left-handed, and the right-handed Earl Williams. Williams had been signed as a pitcher and outfielder but was converted into a full-time hitter when he displayed considerable power in his first minor league season. He also shared first base with the gimpy Cepeda and Aaron.

The Braves' catchers, Bob Didier and Hal King, were not hitting. On June 20, with the club in fourth place at 31-38, Richards and Harris put Williams behind the plate. Always willing to experiment, Richards had sent Williams to the instructional league after the 1970 season to learn to catch, but the twenty-two-year-old had caught exactly one professional inning before that day. Williams was a gifted athlete who attended college in the winter, but the midseason shift smacked of desperation.

Less than a month later Williams handled Niekro's knuckleball for the first time. The Dodgers' Maury Wills stole a base, but Williams cut him down when he tried it again. Williams caught seven innings with no passed balls. Niekro said, "I'm amazed at his ability to handle the knuckler." Soon Harris was calling him "the best young catcher in baseball." Williams was less enthusiastic: "I play where they put me. . . . I just want to play."[29] Williams caught seventy-two games and won Rookie of the Year honors after slugging thirty-three home runs.

When Cepeda underwent season-ending knee surgery in August, the Braves suddenly had a young lineup. Aaron was the only regular older than twenty-seven. He played most of the year at first base and hit a career-best forty-seven homers, including his six-hundredth. Only Ruth and Mays had gotten there before him. Aaron's .327 batting average was his highest in seven years. Bill Bartholomay signed him to the biggest contract in baseball history, three years at $200,000 annually, equivalent to about $1 million today.[30]

The club finished third in the division at 82-80, eight games behind San Francisco. Atlanta allowed more runs and homers than any other team in the league. Still, Bartholomay gave Luman Harris another one-year contract as manager.

Richards's contract had one more year to run. Looking ahead to the return of Cepeda and Carty, and buoyed by the emergence of his young players, he declared the Braves were "probably going to be the most explosive offense in baseball." He had a surplus of hitters, but he made no deals during the winter to improve the sorry pitching. "I'm willing to bank on what we've got, go with the players we consider competent, and if that's it, that's it," he told the writers. "I would take the consequences without regret."[31] In fact, he was hamstrung. He did not want to trade any of the youngsters. No other team would take Cepeda or Carty unless they proved they were healthy. Richards had his doubts, too: he did not sign them until they came to spring training and showed they were fit to play.[32]

During the winter baseball owners tried to break the Players Association. The ostensible issue was what the historian Charles P. Korr called "a relatively trivial pension-related matter."[33] The real issue was Marvin Miller. The owners' negotiator, John Gaherin, said, "Everybody wanted to shoot him but nobody wanted to pull the trigger."[34] Hard-line owners took the lead in forcing a confrontation. The Cardinals' Gussie Busch provided the players with bulletin-board material when he roared, "We're not going to give them another goddamn cent. And if they want to strike, let them strike."[35]

The players may not have understood the issues or the consequences, but they understood that the owners wanted to beat them. And they did not like to lose. The first players' strike in any professional sport delayed the 1972 season by ten days before the owners caved and put additional money into the pension plan. Eighty-six regular-season games were canceled.

Before the season opened, Luman Harris said, "I won't hedge on this statement one bit. This is the best personnel I have had at Atlanta. I have always wanted to be in a position where I had more good players than I had positions for them to play."[36] But the pitching was still weak. By the end of May Atlanta stood at 18-22, in fourth place, seven games behind division-leading Los Angeles. Rumors reached Bill Bartholomay that some of the Peachtree playboys were staying out late and showing up late at the ballpark, skipping fielding and batting practice. Speculation about Harris's job security was swirling, but Harris insisted he paid no attention to it: "The way I look at it, there's only one letter difference between hire and fire," he said. "I'll tell you this. I don't know what I or anyone else could do differently. When people who have proved they are good pitchers lose their stuff, when people make mistakes out on the field, or when fellows you know can hit don't, there isn't much anyone can do but sit on the bench and squirm."[37]

Richards scoffed at rumors of a managerial change: "Where do you get that kind of stuff? How can anybody knock his managing when he hasn't got anybody to manage? That's my job, getting the players. Fire me, not him."[38]

When Richards delivered the same message to Bartholomay, the owner took his advice. On June 1 Bartholomay announced a reorganization of the Braves' front office. Eddie Robinson became director of player personnel with responsibility for the major league team. Richards was reassigned as a "super, super scout," evaluating other teams' players for trades and instructing in the minors.[39] "I believe these new assignments should accelerate the Braves' player development program generally and specifically help the promising young pitchers in our organization," Bartholomay said. "This will be a better use of Paul's talents, and it will free him of office work here. He'll be like a senior consultant to me." The *Journal*'s Rod Hudspeth wrote, "The Paul Richards era is apparently over."[40] Richards told Robinson, "You're gonna get to fire Luman."[41]

Harris, trying to save his job, got tough. He said he would enforce a curfew on the road and fine any player who was late to the park. He yelled at catcher Earl Williams when he did not run out a ground ball.[42] But by August 7 the Braves had lost seven of their last eight games and dropped sixteen games out of first place. The team was in Cincinnati when Bartholomay flew into town, bringing the axe. Eddie Mathews was named manager. Harris left for his Alabama farm without speaking to reporters.[43]

Harris never spoke to Richards or Robinson again. Robinson said, "I wrote him one of the most sincere letters that I could ever write anybody, and he never answered."[44] Harris never managed or coached again, either. After two decades he was too closely linked to Richards.

The Braves' 70-84 record left them in fourth place, buried twenty-five games behind Cincinnati. When Richards's contract expired on December 31, 1972, it was not renewed. That was no surprise; his duties had essentially ended when Robinson was promoted. Richards's bitterness opened a rift between the two, because Richards thought Robinson cut him out of the decision-making loop. It took some time for the friendship to be repaired.[45]

The *Journal*'s Furman Bisher believed Richards had been a puppet, with Bartholomay pulling the strings on trades. Bisher later wrote that the owners wanted Richards to manage, but he refused: "He played golf with them, drank with them and was one of them, except in club memberships. It was to turn out to be a ghastly mistake for all concerned."[46]

For Henry Aaron, Richards's departure "called for a toast." Referring to Georgia's segregationist governor, Aaron said, "I think I would have welcomed Lester Maddox if he were replacing Paul Richards." In his autobiography Aaron added, "It might be my personal prejudice talking, but I've always believed that it took the Braves a long time to recover from Paul Richards."[47] Atlanta had only two winning seasons out of the next nine before winning a division title in 1982.

Richards was sixty-four and looking for a job. He did not find one. Much of the wizard's luster had worn off during the losing years in Houston and the in-and-out performance of the Braves. Although he had developed young stars for both clubs, he got little credit because the teams did not turn into consistent winners. He received scant praise for the 1969 division championship, since several top players, including Aaron, Niekro, and Carty, had been there before Richards arrived.

His union bashing did not necessarily work against him; many owners had expressed the same sentiments. But his well-publicized feuds with star players such as Aaron and Torre raised a red flag for any prospective employer. Those spats, combined with Richards's antiunion rants, stamped him as a dinosaur, unsuitable for a baseball industry that was increasingly dominated by wealthy outsiders who had made their fortunes in more conventional businesses. Who would an owner ask for references on Richards? Bill Bartholomay? Roy Hofheinz?

After he left Atlanta, Richards was never mentioned publicly as a candidate for a manager's or general manager's job. He would spend the next three years looking for a way back into the game that had been his life since he was a boy. When he finally found one, he would make another ghastly mistake.

---

1. *Sporting News* (hereafter *TSN*), April 11, 1970, 9.
2. Ibid., December 20, 1969, 6, 31.
3. Alex Belth, *Stepping Up: The Story of Curt Flood and His Fight for Baseball Players' Rights* (New York: Persea Books, 2006), 158–60. The quote is on p. 158.
4. UPI, *Monessen (Pa.) Valley Independent*, February 27, 1970, 6.
5. Belth, *Stepping Up*, 166.
6. *TSN*, March 28, 1970, 10.
7. Ibid., April 25, 1970, 9, and September 5, 1970, 30.
8. Ibid., October 3, 1970, 15.
9. *Atlanta Journal-Constitution*, September 30, 1989, E-1.
10. *TSN*, January 2, 1971, 46.
11. Ibid., November 21, 1970, 52.
12. Buck Jordan, interviews by author, August 16–17, 2006, Waxahachie, Texas.
13. Ibid.
14. *TSN*, December 26, 1970, 41; January 30, 1971, 36.
15. Ibid., March 25, 1972, 47.
16. Ibid., March 6, 1971, 35.
17. AP, *Fresno (Calif.) Bee Republican*, March 18, 1971, 31.
18. *TSN*, February 20, 1971, 42.
19. Ibid., March 27, 1971, 35.
20. Ibid., June 12, 1971, 15.
21. Ibid., August 7, 1971, 7.
22. UPI, *Bucks County (Pa.) Times*, May 29, 1971, 17.
23. AP, *Lawton (Okla.) Constitution*, May 28, 1971, 25.
24. *TSN*, June 12, 1971, 14–15.

25. Ibid., June 19, 1971, 16.

26. Ibid., June 26, 1971, 26; July 10, 1971, 35.

27. *Long Beach (Calif.) Independent,* June 16, 1971, 34. This is probably a wire-service story, but it was not identified as such.

28. *TSN,* June 12, 1971, 14.

29. Ibid., August 28, 1971, 34; September 18, 1971, 21; Jeffrey Katz, "Earl Williams," *The Baseball Biography Project,* Society for American Baseball Research, http://bioproj.sabr.org.

30. Hank Aaron, with Lonnie Wheeler, *I Had a Hammer: The Hank Aaron Story* (New York: HarperCollins, 1991), 216; for adjusting dollars for inflation, see U.S. Department of Labor, Bureau of Labor Statistics, http://data.bls.gov/cgi-bin/cpicalc.pl.

31. *TSN,* January 1, 1972, 43.

32. Ibid., March 18, 1972, 34.

33. Charles P. Korr, *The End of Baseball as We Knew It* (Urbana: University of Illinois Press, 2002), 105.

34. Robert F. Burk, *Much More Than a Game* (Chapel Hill: University of North Carolina Press, 2001), 176.

35. *TSN,* April 8, 1972, 24.

36. "Any One of Five Can Do," *Sports Illustrated,* April 10, 1972, online archive.

37. UPI, *Middlesboro (Ky.) Daily News,* May 31, 1972, 12.

38. *TSN,* June 10, 1972, 20.

39. AP, *Cumberland (Md.) Gazette,* June 2, 1972, 24.

40. *Atlanta Journal,* June 1, 1972, 1-D, 6-D.

41. Eddie Robinson, interview by author, August 18, 2006, Fort Worth, Texas.

42. *TSN,* June 10, 1972, 20.

43. *Atlanta Journal,* August 7, 1972, 1-D.

44. Eddie Robinson interview.

45. Ibid.

46. *TSN,* February 3, 1973, 35, and January 10, 1976, 2.

47. Aaron, *I Had a Hammer,* 220, 188.

CHAPTER 26

The Hustler

Afters twenty-two seasons as a major league manager and general manager, Richards set his sights higher. Even before he left the Braves in 1972, he began assembling a group of investors to bid for his hometown Texas Rangers.[1] Owner Bob Short had moved the Washington Senators to Arlington, a bedroom community between Dallas and Fort Worth. Short was hoping for riches but did not find them. Under manager Ted Williams, the Rangers lost one hundred games and drew fewer than 700,000 fans in the first season in Texas in 1972, barely more than in their farewell year in Washington. Short was heavily in debt from the moment he bought the Senators in 1969. His goal was "to sell the team at a substantial profit to some ego-crazed locals who were fair bursting at the seams with ready cash."[2]

Richards had no significant cash to put into the venture. He had little background in business; as a general manager his job had been strictly baseball. His assets were his reputation, experience, and connections. He put together a syndicate of wealthy acquaintances from Texas and Arizona that offered Short a reported $10 million, the same amount he had paid for the team, but Short rejected the deal in January 1973.[3]

On and off the field there were more signs of the end of baseball as Richards knew it. The Players Association won its most significant concessions so far in the 1973 contract. While defending the reserve clause from Curt Flood's challenge, the owners' attorneys had argued that employer-employee relations should be determined by collective bargaining. When the U.S. Supreme Court ruled against Flood in 1972, the justices invited Congress to decide the issue.[4] Since baseball had extolled the virtues of negotiation, the owners had to practice it. For the first time they agreed to loosen—ever so slightly—their dictatorial control over a player's career. The ten-and-five rule permitted a ten-year veteran who had spent five years with the same team to veto a trade. This was a direct response to Flood's central grievance, that he had been traded without his consent. Owners also accepted salary arbitration, relinquishing control of their payrolls. A player with at least three years' experience was entitled to have a neutral arbitrator choose between the club's offer and his counteroffer, based on the salaries paid to comparable players. That guaranteed virtually every eligible man an annual raise and eliminated some of the inequities between high-paying and low-paying teams. "The owners aren't bad," Richards observed. "They're dumb. Marvin Miller thinks about tomorrow. They think about yesterday."[5]

The American League adopted the designated hitter rule in 1973, a decision that could still start a brawl thirty-five years later. Despite the tighter strike zone and lower pitching mound established in 1969, offense had not recovered to 1950s levels, especially in the AL, and the circuit's attendance continued to decline. Richards endorsed the DH: "I give all the credit in the world to the American League for trying something different." Contrary to the conventional wisdom, he did not believe the rule would prolong sluggers' careers, because the legs go first. (He was wrong.) And he did not think it would keep starting pitchers in the game longer, because most managers would prefer to use a fresh reliever.[6] (Wrong again: The AL recorded more complete games than the National for decades.)

Richards was a sideline commentator on these events. For the first time since 1926, he had no reason to go to the ballpark. Later he might have found his niche as an outspoken talking head on ESPN, as some other managers filled their time between jobs, but TV sports networks did not yet exist. At home in Waxahachie Richards whiled away hours in his den, sitting in front of a portrait of himself in a Houston warmup jacket.[7] (The painting later hung in the men's locker room at the Waxahachie Country Club.) He began work on a new book about baseball strategy but never finished it. He spent most days on the golf course and many evenings hosting men-only cookouts. He liked to grill steaks under a shed next to his house, soaking the coals with lighter fluid and trying to make the flames leap to the ceiling. He never succeeded in setting it afire—Margie secretly had the building treated with fireproof material.

Some friction developed between the involuntarily retired husband and his wife of forty-one years. "Her hobby was going to the hospital," Paula Richards said facetiously about her mother. "That, and shopping." Richards eventually wearied of Margie's hypochondria and ordered her doctor to run every test imaginable. When her suspected "brain tumor" was diagnosed as a sinus headache, she seemed disappointed.[8]

Richards soon teamed with a fellow exile, the self-described hustler Bill Veeck. The former owner of the Indians, Browns, and White Sox had sold the Chicago club in 1961 because of his poor health. Veeck retreated to a Maryland farm he called "Tranquility" on the eastern shore of the Chesapeake Bay. Living there with his wife, six children, and four dogs, he entertained a parade of visiting sportswriters.[9] Like Richards, he was always good for a provocative quote. While Richards's bogeyman was the union, Veeck amused himself by tweaking baseball's commissioners and owners. He enraged them when he supported Curt Flood's lawsuit. Veeck, his friend Hank Greenberg, and Jackie Robinson were the only baseball figures to testify on Flood's behalf during the trial.[10]

Veeck's wife, Mary Frances, said, "Bill started out on the right side of the tracks and spent his whole life trying to get over to the other side."[11] His father, William Veeck Sr., was a Chicago sportswriter who became president of the Cubs. Young Bill helped plant the ivy on Wrigley Field's outfield wall. He made his name in baseball as a flamboyant promoter. His teams set attendance records—and won pennants—in Cleveland and Chicago. He introduced himself as "Veeck as in wreck," while he vexed his fellow owners until they ran him out of their lodge. Many of them were not eager to let him back in.

In October 1974 Veeck's friend Jerry Hoffberger put the Baltimore Orioles up for sale. Building on the foundation laid by Richards and Jim McLaughlin, the Orioles had reached postseason play six times in nine years, winning four pennants and two World Series, but their attendance had fallen below one million. Hoffberger and Veeck had tried to buy the Detroit Tigers together in the 1950s, and the two men remained close. Veeck had the inside track in negotiations for the Orioles, but the price of entry had soared. In 1959, when Veeck bought control of the White Sox, the franchise was valued at $5 million. Fifteen years later Hoffberger's asking price for a low-revenue team in a much smaller market was $12 million. Veeck didn't have it, so he began hustling up investors. He tapped Richards for his wealthy contacts.[12] Veeck was a long-time Richards admirer, but they were not close friends. The irony was thick. Richards was trying to return to the team he had built, while Veeck was seeking to reclaim the franchise he had lost when other owners refused to let him move the Browns to Baltimore.

Veeck believed he had a deal, but he was still scrambling to piece together financing when Hoffberger suddenly pulled the Orioles off the market without explanation. Veeck felt he had been double-crossed. At age sixty-one, he thought he might have lost his last chance to get back into the game. His friendship with Hoffberger ended in a lawsuit.[13]

Veeck and Richards were left outside with their noses pressed against the window, but not for long. An old Chicago friend, Andrew J. McKenna, told Veeck the White Sox were on the block. A former minor league owner and later chairman of McDonald's Corporation, McKenna may have been an emissary from the Sox's desperate owner, John Allyn. When McKenna explained the team's plight, Veeck said, "Let's go."[14]

John Allyn was broke. After seven losing seasons out of eight, White Sox attendance had dropped to 750,000 in 1975. The neighborhood around Comiskey Park had so deteriorated that many fans were afraid to go there at night. Allyn fell behind in payments to hotels, airlines, and to visiting clubs for their share of the meager gate receipts.[15] A Seattle group wanted to buy the team and move it. Here was Veeck's chance to return to his hometown as the savior of the White Sox. It was Richards's chance to return to the city where he won the nickname "The Wizard of Waxahachie." Old and creaky as they were, they jumped at it.

Needing to raise $8 million, Veeck cobbled together a rickety structure with more than forty investors. Veeck's prospectus listed Richards as director of player personnel and owner of 5 percent of the team. But most of the money was borrowed. One anonymous owner complained: "There is no equity in the Veeck deal at all. It's all loans—bank loans and subordinated debentures"[16] The debentures were IOUs with no collateral, a financial tool that gave Veeck and his partners a tax break.

American League owners seized on the financial house of cards as a convenient excuse to do what they wanted to do anyway: Keep Veeck out. The Angels' Gene Autry said, "I have to vote against a fellow who runs down baseball, then re-enters it."[17] Veeck needed a three-fourths majority, nine of the twelve owners, to approve the sale. At the December 3, 1975, league meeting in Cleveland, he did not get it. Rather than rejecting Veeck outright, the owners gave him one week to raise an additional $1.2 million and restructure the deal. AL president Lee MacPhail said disingenuously, "Everybody wants to see Bill have his chance." Veeck mused, "Maybe I am being hanged slowly."[18]

Veeck came up with the cash, but the owners, convening at baseball's winter meeting in Hollywood, Florida, again rejected his bid. Then Detroit owner John Fetzer spoke up: "We told them to go out and do it and they did it. We can't cry over spilt milk. Look, I don't like it any more than you do that we're allowing a guy in here who has called me a son-of-a-bitch over and over. But, gentlemen, we've got to take another vote." This time Veeck was approved, 10–2.[19]

When the decision was announced, Veeck kicked his prosthetic leg high like a Rockette. "I hope it's as much fun as I expect it to be," he told the writers at a joyous press conference. "It's not often a one-legged 61-year-old man gets started again in another go-round doing something he loves."[20]

The White Sox general manager, Roland Hemond, had expected to lose his job, because Veeck had always been his own GM. But Veeck had started cultivating Hemond months before, soliciting his ideas for improving the losing team. Veeck could appreciate how the club's poverty had shackled Hemond. Veeck told him, "I want you to let your imagination run rampant." The morning after Veeck won approval, Hemond noticed a circle of chairs and tables in the Diplomat Hotel's lobby. He suggested they put up a sign in the lobby saying, "Open for Business," and do their trading in public. Veeck was delighted: "What are you waiting for? Get it up."[21]

Veeck sat there for fourteen hours with Hemond and Richards, "operating in the open like honest men," making deals. The ink was barely dry on his ticket of admission to the owners' club, and already some of them were appalled. Bud Selig of Milwaukee sputtered, "This is a meat market." Veeck instructed the White Sox public relations director, Buck Peden, to call him every half hour. Picking up the phone, Veeck would say, "Hey, Buzzie," or mention the name of another general manager, and talk as if he were doing business. During his first twenty-four hours as White Sox owner, Veeck and his colleagues completed six trades.[22]

Veeck's carnival blared on. He named Richards the White Sox manager.

Richards had earlier been listed as director of player personnel, and that was the job he preferred, but he said, "Several years ago I made a half-promise that if Bill ever owned a ball club again I'd manage it for him." Veeck, out of baseball for fifteen years, called Richards "my security blanket." Veeck had often said he would want Richards as manager if he was stuck with a bad team, "because he gets the most out of 'nothing' players."[23]

"Paul wasn't at all keen about it," Hemond recalled. "He was fulfilling Bill Veeck's wishes." Richards urged Hemond to persuade the deposed manager, Chuck Tanner, to stay on as a coach: "He might be managing the club by July 4."[24] (Charlie Finley hired Tanner to manage the Oakland A's.)

Reaction ranged from skepticism to ridicule. Although Richards had been away from the game for just three seasons, he had not managed in fifteen. *Chicago Tribune* columnist Robert Markus wrote: "Richards was an excellent handler of pitchers and a consummate baseball strategist in his day. But this may not be his day." Phil Elderkin of the *Christian Science Monitor* gibed, "Bill Veeck got him his unconditional release from Madame Tussaud's Wax Museum." The White Sox relief ace, Goose Gossage, asked his wife, "Who the hell is Paul Richards?"[25]

That was the problem: Richards had skipped a generation of ballplayers. This sixty-seven-year-old relic of the Babe Ruth era would be leading men young enough to be his grandsons. Few of them had heard of The Wizard, much less of Waxahachie. Richards bristled at the repeated questions about his ability to handle "modern" players. "I've got the feeling you people think I've been in Siberia for the last few years," he grumbled.[26]

He recognized that the baseball business had changed and that a manager had to change, too: "What I mean is, you can't be a Simon Legree. You can't be a John McGraw and continually threaten your players with sending them to St. Louis or down the river, that sort of thing, because they know they have someone to intercede for them. The manager who is handling players today must be 100 percent right at all times, or he will be hearing from the players' commissioner." (He could not resist a jab at Marvin Miller.)

"I don't consider myself an old fogey. I'm sure I'll have a good relationship with the players. It's my job to manage and their job to play."[27] He was certain that one thing had not changed: how to win. "The teams which give away the fewest games usually win the pennants. That's what we're going to try to do—keep from giving away games."[28]

Veeck's exhilaration lasted just thirteen days. On December 23, 1975, arbitrator Peter Seitz decided a challenge to baseball's reserve clause by pitchers Andy Messersmith and Dave McNally. At issue was paragraph 10a of the uniform player contract. It gave the team the right to renew the contract for one year without the player's consent. The owners contended that, once renewed, the contract could be renewed again and again, forever. History was on their side; several courts had interpreted the clause that way. Even Curt Flood's lawyers had told the Supreme Court that teams had "a lifetime grip" on players.[29] Marvin Miller, not being a lawyer, took a more simplistic view: He thought "one year" meant one year.

Even though arbitrator Seitz was a lawyer, he agreed. To Seitz the case turned on the plain language of the contract. He said: "I am not an Abraham Lincoln signing an Emancipation Proclamation. Involuntary servitude has nothing to do with this case. I decided this case as a lawyer and an arbitrator."[30] A player could become a free agent by playing out his one-year option.

The wailing of baseball's panjandrums was drowned out only by the gnashing of their teeth. Commissioner Kuhn said free agency "would be a disaster for a great majority of the players, the clubs and, most of all, the fans." League presidents Lee MacPhail and Chub Feeney sang a mournful chorus: "It would do irreparable harm to baseball."[31]

Seitz's decision doomed Bill Veeck. Veeck came to Chicago short of cash, teetering on the edge of insolvency. He had no prayer of keeping up with the escalating salaries that would flow from free agency and arbitration. Veeck had been warning the owners for years that they should negotiate changes in the reserve clause while they could, because change was inevitable. They refused to listen, and now he would pay for it. It was, his biographer Ed Linn said, "a flagrant case of life being unfair."[32]

The owners were still in denial. Miller and the union were willing to negotiate a structure for free agency, but the owners dug in while they unsuccessfully appealed Seitz's decision in court. As desultory negotiations continued, the owners refused to open spring training. Despite what many newspapers persisted in reporting, it was a lockout, not a strike.[33]

That is, twenty-three owners locked their gates. Not Bill Veeck. He invited nonroster players (mostly minor leaguers) to begin training in Sarasota, Florida, on schedule, March 1. "Of course I'm doing it to attract attention," Veeck said. "Not to us, but to baseball and to the fact that it's a game played on the field with bats and balls, not in court with writs and pleas."[34] The Atlanta Braves followed suit a week later. Many major leaguers went to Florida and Arizona and organized workouts on their own, over Marvin Miller's objections. He thought it made them look too eager and encouraged the owners to stonewall. Players from several clubs practiced at Manatee Junior College in Bradenton, Florida—until the women's varsity softball team ran them off the field. "Even the girls won't let us play," lamented Pittsburgh's Dave Giusti.[35] After seventeen days Commissioner Kuhn ordered the camps opened while negotiations continued.

When Richards donned his White Sox uniform, the number on his back was the familiar *12*, but the fabric was unfamiliar; double-knit had replaced flannel. The lineup was also new; he had never managed with a designated hitter. Kicking off the first day's drills, Richards ordered: "Pitchers start running. And don't stop until the first guy throws up."[36] He had only twenty-two days to get ready for the season opener.

The club he inherited had finished 75-86 in 1975, fifth in the six-team Western Division. Veeck and Hemond had traded their best pitcher, twenty-game winner Jim Kaat, who was thirty-six. That left the paunchy knuckleballer Wilbur Wood to lead the pitching staff. The best of the position players were twenty-four-year-old all-star shortstop Bucky Dent and twenty-five-year-old catcher Brian Downing. Richards said all other jobs were open.[37] To add speed to the lineup Chicago acquired a Richards favorite, the Braves' "Road Runner," Ralph Garr. After batting .325 or better in three of his first four full seasons, Garr won a pay raise in arbitration from $55,000 to $114,500, then fell off to a .278 average in 1975.

The White Sox's strength appeared to be their bullpen, anchored by a pair of hard-throwing twenty-three-year-old hulks, right-hander Goose Gossage and lefty Terry Forster. The importance of the late-inning relief ace (not yet called a closer) was firmly established, but Richards clung to the notion that the best pitchers should be starters. He put Gossage and Forster into the rotation. Veeck endorsed the move with the logical explanation, "We're not going to have that many leads."[38]

The young Sox warily took the measure of their ancient manager. Gossage thought to himself, "Who is this old guy who never says anything?"[39] When Richards did speak, his words could scald. Sending Alan Bannister to the minors, he called the shortstop "a dead-ass ballplayer."[40] After first baseman Jim Spencer went 0-for-15 in exhibition games, Richards commented: "That boy came here and said it didn't matter whether there was a left-hander pitching against him or a right-hander because he hit them both the same. Well, he wasn't lying."[41] Bucky Dent diplomatically remarked, "Paul Richards is a straight shooter. He says what he thinks whether you like it or not."[42]

However reluctantly, The Wizard was back in the dugout. It was the only door open to him. He had to walk through it.

1. *Sporting News* (hereafter *TSN*), June 17, 1972, 14.
2. Leonard Koppett, *Koppett's Concise History of Major League Baseball* (New York: Carroll and Graf, 2004), 343; Mike Shropshire, *Seasons in Hell* (New York: Avon, 1996), 3.
3. *Dallas Morning News*, February 4, 1973, 2B; *Tucson (Ariz.) Daily Citizen*, January 12, 1973, 61.
4. See *Flood v. Kuhn*, 407 U.S. 258 (1972).
5. Koppett, *Koppett's Concise History*, 337–38, 341; Robert W. Creamer, ed., "They Said It," *Sports Illustrated*, March 5, 1973, online archive.
6. *Dallas Morning News*, February 4, 1973, 2B.
7. AP, *Lima (Ohio) News*, February 22, 1976, C8.
8. Paula Richards, interviews by author, 2006–2008.
9. Bob Addie, *Sportswriter* (Lanham, Md.: Accent, 1980), 246–47.
10. Marvin Miller, *A Whole Different Ball Game* (New York: Carol, 1991), 200.
11. John Helyar, *Lords of the Realm* (New York: Villard, 1994), 234.
12. James Edward Miller, *The Baseball Business: Pursuing Pennants and Profits in Baltimore* (Chapel Hill: University of North Carolina Press, 1990), 208; *TSN*, January 4, 1975, 38.
13. J. Miller, *Baseball Business*, 345.
14. *Chicago Tribune*, October 9, 2005, online edition. John Allyn was the brother of Arthur Allyn Jr., who had bought Veeck's interest in the White Sox in 1961.
15. *TSN*, August 16, 1975, 40.
16. *Chicago Tribune*, December 3, 1975, E1; Gerald Eskenazi, *Bill Veeck: A Baseball Legend* (New York: McGraw-Hill, 1988), 152.
17. Eskenazi, *Bill Veeck*, 152.
18. *Chicago Tribune*, December 4, 1975, C1.
19. Eskenazi, *Bill Veeck*, 153; Bill Veeck, with Ed Linn, *Veeck as in Wreck: The Autobiography of Bill Veeck* (Chicago: University of Chicago Press, 2001) 382. The narrative of Veeck's return to Chicago was written by his collaborator, Linn, after Veeck's death in 1986.
20. Veeck, *Veeck as in Wreck*, 382–83.
21. Eskenazi, *Bill Veeck*, 155–56.
22. Ibid.; Veeck, *Veeck as in Wreck*, 383; Bill Nowlin, "Roland Hemond," *The Baseball Biography Project*, Society for American Baseball Research, http://bioproj.sabr.org; *Chicago Tribune*, December 14, 1975, B1.
23. AP, *Annapolis (Md.) Capital*, December 18, 1975, 18; *TSN*, March 5, 1966, 13.
24. Roland Hemond, interview by author, October 18, 2006, Phoenix.
25. *Chicago Tribune*, December 18, 1975, C3, and May 30, 1976, B1; *Christian Science Monitor*, June 14, 1976, 27.
26. *Chicago Tribune*, January 10, 1976, F3.
27. *TSN*, January 24, 1976, 40.
28. *Chicago Tribune*, January 10, 1976, F3.
29. Henry D. Fetter, *Taking on the Yankees* (New York: W. W. Norton, 2003), 343–45.
30. AP, *Chicago Tribune*, December 24, 1975, A3.
31. Ibid.
32. Veeck, *Veeck as in Wreck*, 383.
33. M. Miller, *A Whole Different Ball Game*, 254–59.
34. *Chicago Tribune*, March 1, 1976, C1.
35. M. Miller, *A Whole Different Ball Game*, 260; *Chicago Tribune*, March 2, 1976, C1.
36. *Chicago Tribune*, March 19, 1976, C1.
37. *TSN*, March 6, 1976, 11.
38. Eskenazi, *Bill Veeck*, 161.
39. *Chicago Tribune*, May 30, 1976, B1.
40. Ibid., July 31, 1977, B4.
41. Ibid., April 7, 1976, E3.
42. Ibid., April 8, 1976, C1.

CHAPTER 27

"I've Been There, Wherever There Is"

*We direct your attention to second base, where three White Sox
veterans are coming back home to Chicago to honor America's Bicentennial
with an exact reenaction of* The Spirit of '76.

O pening day 1976 at Comiskey Park. Bill Veeck's first opener since 1961.
The showman made himself the show.

Who hatched the idea is not known, but when Veeck heard of it he crowed,
"If you've got the guy with the wooden leg, you've got the casting beat." To
reenact Archibald McNeal Willard's famous painting of three Revolutionary
War minutemen, Veeck wore a peg leg and played a fife; his faithful business
manager Rudie Schaffer beat a drum; and Paul Richards carried the thirteen-
star flag. Wearing wigs, bandages, and the tattered uniforms of General Washington's army, the trio marched to the flagpole in center field.

Paul Richards?

He was bribed. Richards often complained that baseball fans sang only the
first verse of *The Star-Spangled Banner*, with the lyrics asking plaintively, "Oh,
say, does that star-spangled banner yet wave?" He preferred the heroic conclu-
sion of the fourth verse: "And the star-spangled banner in triumph shall wave
/ O'er the land of the free and the home of the brave!" Richards always liked a

winner. He agreed to join in the stunt if he could recite the fourth verse to the crowd—he didn't try to sing it.[1]

The White Sox opener drew 40,318, the third-largest opening day turnout in franchise history. When the home team put a man on base, fans shouted, "Go! Go!" reenacting a chant first heard in Richards's first season in Chicago twenty-five years before. Wilbur Wood shut out Oakland, 4–0. With one out in the A's ninth, the crowd rose and cheered as Wood set down the final two batters.[2]

Gossage started the second game, striking out nine Minnesota Twins and holding them to three hits in a 4–1 victory. Richards remarked, "I don't want to criticize anybody, but how could you have a kid who can throw like that and not start him?" But Chicago soon fell below .500. Surveying the talent at his disposal, Richards said: "We're not going to overpower anyone. We'll have to bunt a lot, steal a lot and pray a lot."[3]

On their first visit to Yankee Stadium, the Sox showed off Veeck's new road uniforms: navy blue calf-length "clamdiggers" that were not tucked into the stockings, and navy jerseys with the shirttails hanging out. The Yankees protested that the flapping shirttails and white sweatshirts underneath were distracting. Umpires ordered Chicago pitchers to cut off the sweatshirt sleeves so they could not be seen. Richards griped that the Yankees' owner, George Steinbrenner, "should be worried about more important things, because he's in baseball on a parole and he's lucky to be out of jail." (Steinbrenner had been suspended from baseball after he admitted making illegal contributions to President Nixon's reelection campaign. He avoided prison by paying a fine.)[4]

As the losses mounted, opposing runners stole twenty-four consecutive bases off sore-armed catcher Brian Downing and his backup, Pete Varney.[5] Varney, wrestling with Wood's knuckler, dropped a third strike, then fumbled the ball again when he tried to tag the batter. If Varney didn't improve,

Richards warned, "he'll be gone from here." The manager also unloaded on twenty-six-year-old right-hander Bart Johnson, whose ERA had ballooned above 12.00: "I ain't giving up on him but that boy's got to change his entire approach to pitching."[6] After Richards worked with him, Johnson showed marked improvement for the rest of the season.

The Sox went an entire week in May without an extra-base hit, including a stretch when they scored once in thirty-three innings. Neither bunting nor stealing nor praying helped. Their fortunes turned dramatically worse on May 9 when Detroit's Ron LeFlore scorched a line drive that broke Wilbur Wood's kneecap. The left-handed knuckleballer was not only the ace, he was the greatest innings eater since the dead-ball era, averaging more than three hundred innings during the previous five years. He was lost for the season, and Chicago quickly sank to the bottom of the Western Division standings.

Instead of folding, Richards's club rallied with a ten-game winning streak, giving up only thirteen runs during that span. Newly acquired lefty Ken Brett pitched two shutouts and Bart Johnson added another. Chicago climbed to third place, three and a half games behind division-leading Kansas City, on May 26. The players were euphoric. To hear them tell it, the Wizard had not lost his touch. Bucky Dent compared Richards with his predecessor, Chuck Tanner: "With Chuck, if you did something good, he was always patting you on the back. He'd say 'Nice going' and stuff like that. But Paul doesn't say that. He assumes we're all professionals." Veteran outfielder Buddy Bradford added: "I don't really go for the rah-rah, the college type of manager. With Paul Richards you can go out and hit four dingers (home runs) and he won't say anything to you. But he won't go giving you a lot of jazz if you strike out four times, either."[7]

Richards took command of the pitching staff. "Well, one thing we've all noticed is how Paul teaches you basics, starts you from scratch," Terry Forster said. "Paul has us thinking about the whole picture—where you deliver the ball and how. He wants you to think. Think like hitters." Richards explained his hands-on approach:

I am the manager and I am also the pitching coach. Pitching is 75 percent of this game, and if a manager can't run his own staff without a middle man, then that doesn't make much sense to me. If you tell the boys something yourself then nothing's gonna get lost in translation.

And what I tell them is really pretty simple. Throw strikes. A pitcher in the major leagues has got to be able to throw a crucial strike at least 80 percent of the time he needs one. If he can't, he doesn't belong in the big leagues.[8]

Rookie right-hander Pete Vuckovich said, "This game is all confidence, and that's where he's helped all of us more than any place else." Gossage had been among the most skeptical: "No more, though. The man's unreal."[9]

As quickly as the White Sox had risen, they flopped back. Three weeks after the end of the winning streak, the *Tribune* called them the "Sagging Sox" and "Veeck's wrecks."[10] Then the front office made the move that turned the clubhouse sour. Pete Varney, who had been demoted to third-string catcher, was traded to the Braves and sent to the minors. Varney, the only Harvard graduate in the majors, was well liked and respected by his teammates; they had elected him their player representative. Many Sox thought that was the reason for the trade, rather than his .214 average and defensive shortcomings. Pitcher Dave Hamilton said, "I lost a hell of a lot of respect for this organization with that move."[11]

As Richards reached his fiftieth anniversary in baseball in June 1976, he remarked, "I've been there, wherever there is." But he poured fuel on the brushfire that was smoldering in his clubhouse. The Players Association and the owners were still negotiating the terms of free agency. Many players had refused to sign contracts so they could play out their options. "Marvin Miller with his silver tongue is ruining this game," Richards said. "I have my solution for all these boys who won't sign their contracts. Release them. It won't be chaos because none of them want to leave the security they've got. They're all like homing pigeons. They're making $70,000 a year or $80,000 a year to play baseball. They can't afford to stop."[12]

After thirteen months of negotiation the owners and the union agreed on a new structure for baseball. Players could become free agents after six years in the majors. It was not such a raw deal for the owners. A player they developed was bound to the team for six seasons, often until he was thirty or older. It was a significant sacrifice by the players, because the majority of them did not stay in the majors for six years.[13] But the agreement upended ninety-seven years of baseball history. It was, at last, the end of baseball as Paul Richards knew it.

Richards suddenly sounded like a Miller fan, if a grudging one. He said the union leader might be the single most important man in baseball history, even including Judge Landis: "You've got to admire Miller for what he's done for the players, but I hope he realizes we're going to need his help, or we'll all be going down the drain." Frank Lane could not believe what he had just heard: "Paul's finally got religion."[14]

The *Tribune*'s Robert Markus claimed the White Sox did have an official prayer: "Give us this day our daily run."[15] During one stretch the Sox scored just four times in five games. When they pushed across a run, Comiskey Park organist Nancy Faust struck up "Glory, Glory, Hallelujah." Gossage said, "You felt like you had to pitch a shutout to tie."[16]

At the all-star break Chicago was fifth in the six-team division with an almost-respectable 37-45 record. Veeck deployed a troupe of belly dancers to welcome fans back from the break. Richards thought the show "a little lewd."[17] Veeck had brainstormed promotional ideas during his years in exile, recording them on note cards. He unleashed new ones and some old favorites. On a single night he gave away a smoked trout, a typewriter to commemorate National Secretaries Week, and a four-foot-long submarine sandwich. He gave a woman a boyfriend and a man a girlfriend—both mannequins. He put a public address microphone in front of broadcaster Harry Caray, who led the crowd in singing "Take Me Out to the Ball Game" during the seventh-inning stretch.[18] Richards had exacted a promise that Veeck's stunts would not interfere with the games, but Veeck would eventually ignore it. One night Gossage warmed up amid a herd of cattle and horses that were sharing the bullpen, waiting to go on the field for another promotion.[19]

The sixty-two-year-old Veeck still rollicked through life at a breakneck pace. Roland Hemond quipped, "I tell people I worked for Bill Veeck five years, but it was really ten because I never slept." Veeck was said to drink a twenty-four-bottle case of beer every day, and he smoked at least three times that many cigarettes. Of course, his days were twenty hours long.[20] He held court far into the night in the Bards' Room, a dark, oak-paneled hideaway built by Charles Comiskey near the ballpark's press box.

Staying up late drinking was not Richards's style. "Paul used to find ways to disappear," Hemond recalled. While the owner and manager seemed to be polar opposites, Hemond said, "They were both great minds, creative, daring." Both read widely, and they shared a deep interest in American history. Hemond found Richards to be "very witty, with a great sense of humor."[21]

Veeck had already put the White Sox on the field wearing clam diggers. In August he dressed them in Bermuda shorts. In their first bare-legged appearance, on August 8 against Kansas City, the Sox stole five bases. Richards reported there were "no skinned knees," but he broke out long pants for the second game of the Sunday doubleheader, saying it was too chilly for shorts. The team wore the Bermudas in three other games. Margie came up from

Waxahachie for one of them because she had never seen her husband wearing shorts in public.[22]

As the Sox fell further behind and the clubhouse turned sullen, Richards seemed to lose interest. Hemond said, "His heart wasn't in it."[23] Richards often did not come out for batting practice and put on his uniform only a half-hour before game time. He had less and less to say to the players. Most tellingly, he seldom left the dugout to argue with umpires. For the only season in his twenty-one years as a manager he was not ejected from a single game.

Richards found the pace of travel draining. The rhythm of baseball had changed drastically since he was last in the dugout. When he managed in the 1950s, American League teams went no farther west than Kansas City and usually traveled by train. In 1976 virtually all travel was by jet, with trips to California and fewer days off. With most games played at night, the White Sox would board a plane after midnight and arrive at their destination in the small hours of the morning. The jetliners had no club cars where players, managers, coaches, and writers could gather to talk baseball. It was hard on a sixty-seven-year-old who hated to fly.

Richards's inattention cost his team at least one game. On July 25 Chicago led manager Gene Mauch's Minnesota Twins 5–4 in the sixth inning when left-hander Terry Forster loaded the bases. Richards brought in right-hander Francisco Barrios. "We couldn't believe it," Minnesota shortstop Roy Smalley exclaimed. "We were in the dugout, saying, 'Did he forget that Gene has Rod Carew, the best hitter in baseball, sitting over here?' [Mauch was resting the left-handed-batting Carew with a left-hander starting.] Richards signaled for the righthander, and Rodney was out of the dugout before Barrios got to the mound. Rodney hit the first pitch off the center field fence—a 410-foot rocket—for a bases-clearing triple. And we won the ballgame." Smalley called it the worst managerial blunder he saw during a thirteen-year career.[24]

Throughout the 1976 season Richards refused to discuss whether he would be back the next year. By August, with the Sox sinking toward last place, he pronounced judgment: "They plain can't play."[25] In earlier years he might have said that privately in a team meeting but never to a writer. The seething clubhouse burst open like a boil. Eight players spoke anonymously to Joe Goddard of the *Chicago Sun-Times*. Their complaints about the manager included "lack of instruction and communication . . . late arrival at the park and early departure . . . lack of encouragement . . . unpredictable lineups . . . failure to argue . . . no scouting reports." One player pronounced himself "completely depressed." Several criticized the coaches as well.[26]

The day after the story appeared, Richards called a team meeting. It lasted only ten minutes. He talked, they listened. "I told them a few things you can't print," he said afterward. "But I can say I let them know that I thought anybody making statements about the coaches and the way we do things ought to have the guts to stand up and be counted." He didn't ask who had sounded off: "I've got a pretty good idea about who did the talking, but they're guys who can't play a lick anyway." It was "a cheap shot" at the coaches. "The anonymous player who said we don't correct mistakes told a lie." He concluded, "As far as I'm concerned, it's all forgotten." Veeck dismissed the tempest as the inevitable tension on a losing team. But another anonymous player said: "Things are still horse bleep. Nothing's changed."[27]

Richards continued to insist there was no generation gap: "You know, I heard it said in 1926 that the players had changed. I heard it again in 1936, and '46, and '56, '66, and now again in '76. It's the same show, just a different cast. These ballplayers today are eager to learn, eager to win, and eager to do well."[28]

That was how September began. With the club in last place and attendance dwindling, Veeck put his promotional engine into overdrive in an effort to save the season financially. When the White Sox hosted the California

Angels on September 11, he ordered Richards to put coach Minnie Minoso into the lineup as the designated hitter. The Angels' Nolan Ryan had struck out eighteen Sox the day before; a fifty-three-year-old DH could hardly do worse. Minoso had not played in the majors since 1964, but he had been a player-manager in the Mexican League just three years earlier. He went 0-for-3, striking out only once against lefty Frank Tanana. The stunt may have achieved what Veeck wanted—twice as many people turned out the next day, but attendance was still less than twelve thousand for a Sunday doubleheader. Minoso started again and singled in his first time at bat, becoming the oldest man to hit safely in the majors. (That is, according to what was understood to be his age at the time; the mystery of Minoso's birth date is discussed in chapter 10, n.36.)

After sweeping back-to-back doubleheaders against the Angels and division-leading Kansas City Royals, the White Sox were only two games out of fifth place on September 13. Richards had never finished last, not even in the worst days in Baltimore, so he bridled when Veeck urged him to try out young players in the final two weeks of the season. The results were ugly; Chicago lost fifteen of the last sixteen games. Alan Bannister, recalled from the minors, said: "It was let's get the game over, let's hope it doesn't go into extra innings, when will October 2 ever come, and wait till next year. It was terrible."[29] Before it was over, Richards was in open revolt. Try out youngsters? Okay. He pinch-hit for Ralph Garr, his lone .300 hitter. He held first baseman Jim Spencer, one of his only power threats, out of two games against Kansas City.

On September 24 Veeck shattered whatever was left of his promise to keep the foolishness off the field. He sent the rubber-bodied clown Max Patkin to coach at first base.[30] Patkin had been a cornball favorite in the minors for decades, but his act—like Veeck's—was a bit tired. Veeck wanted Minoso in the lineup for the last home game. In what looks like a protest, Richards made out his batting order according to the players' numerical positions on the scorecard: catcher Brian Downing leading off, followed by the first baseman, second baseman, third baseman, shortstop, left fielder, center fielder, and right fielder, with DH Minoso batting ninth.

Chicago's 64-97 record was the worst in the American League. The Sox allowed the most runs and finished tenth in scoring. Richards said: "If there's a league in this nation that team could have won in, it has not been brought to my attention. And that includes Little League."[31] Given the last-place finish and the dissension, it was obvious that the manager could not return for 1977. Veeck named Bob Lemon the new manager. The former pitching star, who had just been inducted into the Hall of Fame, was a Veeck favorite from his 1948 World Series champion Indians. Lemon had managed the expansion Kansas City Royals to their first winning record in 1971.

Richards had no contract with Veeck—he said, "You didn't need one"—but he had been expecting to manage another year: "I wasn't exactly excited about it, but I would have done it. If I had wanted to manage badly enough, I suppose Bill would have let me. But I didn't want it that much." He played down the problems in the clubhouse: "Sure, there's a new breed of players and every club has a bad apple or two, but we didn't have much trouble with this team."[32] He stayed with the club as a roving minor league pitching instructor and scout, working from home in Waxahachie.

Although the Sox's attendance jumped by 20 percent to 915,000 in 1976, it was still tenth in the league. Veeck lost a reported $670,000. Now he faced baseball's new era—free agency—with no cash to bring to the table. "Don't bother drawing up a budget," he told Hemond. "We don't have any money. We'll think of something."[33]

Just twenty-two major leaguers were free agents. Most received multiyear contracts, including several totaling more than $1 million. Reggie Jackson set a new benchmark when he signed with the Yankees for $3 million for five seasons.[34] Veeck found two free agents in the bargain basement because they were damaged goods. Right-hander Steve Stone had a torn rotator cuff, an injury that was usually the final line on a pitcher's résumé. Third baseman Eric Soderholm missed the entire 1976 season with knee and rib injuries. Naturally, they came cheap.

Veeck also found an angle. He called it "rent-a-player." If a player had just one more year before he was eligible for free agency, his team could trade him and get something in return. Veeck sent his two young fireballers, Gossage and Forster, who were a year away from free agency, to Pittsburgh for outfielder Richie Zisk, a slow-footed slugger in the same category. He traded his twenty-five-year-old all-star shortstop, Bucky Dent, to the Yankees for another power hitter, Oscar Gamble, who had batted only .232 for New York, and minor league pitcher La Marr Hoyt. The Dent trade came just before opening day, when Veeck needed cash to meet his first payroll. The Yankees chipped in at least $200,000.[35]

By assembling a cast of sluggers, Veeck was playing against Comiskey Park's history; its spacious outfield was a graveyard for long fly balls. But his gamble with Gamble and his risk with Zisk paid off. "The South Side Hit Men" moved into first place in the second week of the 1977 season. Veeck boasted, "We're leading the league in standing ovations."[36] Gamble hit thirty-one homers, Zisk thirty, and Soderholm twenty-five. The Sox spent sixty-one days atop the standings, pulling as much as six and a half games ahead. At the all-star break they had a better record than the "Damn Yankees." Zisk remarked, "I think Bill Veeck has sold his soul to the devil."[37]

The club eventually sank to third but won ninety games, helped by its domination of the expansion Seattle and Toronto teams. Veeck broke his own franchise attendance record, set in 1960, by drawing more than 1.6 million. Major league general managers named him Executive of the Year. (Veeck remained bitter about his treatment by other owners and never attended league meetings.)[38]

Richards took on the duties of farm director after the 1977 season, but he still worked from home in Waxahachie. Of necessity, Veeck kept front-office expenses to a minimum. He, Hemond, Rudie Schaffer, and Richards were assisted by a few young gofers. To handle the farm system's paperwork for Richards, Hemond hired a recent Western Michigan University graduate who was living with his parents and was willing to work for $8,000.[39] Dave Dombrowski went on to serve as general manager of three teams.

The new manager of the AA Knoxville, Tennessee, farm club was a sore-armed thirty-three-year-old infielder, Tony La Russa. Hemond had recognized La Russa's sharp intelligence and hired him as a minor league player-coach. Hemond invited La Russa to the White Sox spring camp in 1976 and urged Veeck to get acquainted with him. Veeck, who never graduated from high school, was impressed that La Russa was attending law school in the off-seasons. The owner said, "This is an exceptional young man."[40] La Russa played sixteen years in the minors with five organizations and accumulated 132 major league games with a lifetime batting average of .199. He had appeared in nine games for Atlanta while Richards was general manager, but the two men did not meet.

"Tony had no preconceived notions about managing," Richards said, "so we didn't have to knock down any of his theories. We subjected Tony to a complete education on handling ballplayers."[41] The White Sox sent Knoxville their prize prospect: Harold Baines, the best thing to come out of the dreadful 1976 season. The Sox's last-place finish gave them the first pick in the amateur draft. Veeck had spotted Baines when the skinny left-handed batter was playing in Little League near Veeck's Maryland farm and drafted him over several higher-rated youngsters. Richards told La Russa, "You must make sure Harold Baines doesn't get abused." La Russa understood that if a pitcher threw at Baines, he should retaliate against the opposition's best hitter. Richards also ordered La Russa to hold the young pitchers to a hundred-pitch limit.[42]

"The South Side Hit Men" were Veeck's last triumph. After the 1977 season his rented players moved on, and he replaced them with other damaged goods. The combination of free agency and salary arbitration was driving payrolls skyward at a dizzying pace. The average salary rose from $51,501 in 1976 to $113,558 just three years later. Veeck lamented, "It isn't the high price of stars that is expensive, it's the high price of mediocrity."[43] Although fans complained about overpaid players, as they always had, the first eight years of free agency saw major league attendance climb by almost 50 percent.

The 1978 White Sox fell from ninety victories to ninety-one losses. In June Veeck fired Bob Lemon and installed coach Larry Doby as manager. Veeck had signed Doby as the majors' second black player in 1947; now Doby was second again, following Frank Robinson into the ranks of black managers. Some writers believed changing managers was a public relations move.[44] More likely, Veeck was burnishing his place in history.

The change accomplished nothing. The White Sox got worse under Doby and finished fifth in the seven-team division. "I was hoping for a reversal of form, but it just didn't happen," Veeck said.[45] He fired Doby after the season and went for another crowd-pleaser: thirty-six-year-old shortstop Don Kessinger, a popular player in Chicago during his eleven years with the Cubs. Kessinger had never managed and would continue as a part-time player.

The Sox hired two veteran managers, Bobby Winkles and Joe Sparks, to aid Kessinger. Richards helped run the 1979 spring training camp along with his minor league pitching coach, Ken Silvestri, and Tony La Russa.[46] La Russa had led Knoxville to the first-half championship in the Southern League, then joined the White Sox coaching staff when Doby became manager. La Russa would manage the AAA farm club at Des Moines in 1979.

"My satisfaction now comes from teaching fundamentals," Richards told a writer. "I miss managing, yes. I miss the paradise of day baseball, and the train rides where you had camaraderie with the writers and the players." As always, he preached the value of those fundamentals: "A common mistake is assuming all players know the basics we take for granted. A team that doesn't believe the A-B-Cs are worth emphasizing in a major league camp will be a very shoddy team."[47]

Comiskey Park attendance had fallen only slightly from the 1977 record, but rising salaries were sinking Veeck. He told Minnesota's Calvin Griffith, another owner who depended on his ball club for his living: "We are doomed. We are the last dinosaurs in a forest where there are no more trees to feed on." Veeck cut back to just four farm clubs; most teams had five or six. Many of his investors—he had more than forty partners—were clamoring to sell.[48]

To generate cash Veeck rented Comiskey Park for rock concerts. The 1979 season's lowlight came on July 12, Disco Demolition Night. As part of his effort to lure young people to Sox games, Veeck teamed with a radio station to promote an assault on the dance music that was assaulting the ears of radio listeners. Any patron who brought a disco record was admitted for 98 cents. Veeck planned to blow up the records between games of the doubleheader against Detroit. Nearly forty-eight thousand paid their way in, another five thousand stormed the gates, and fifteen thousand or so were left outside. Trouble started early, as fans Frisbeed their discs onto the field. At the end of the first game thousands of young people, high on beer and marijuana, surged out of the stands and trashed the field. Veeck would not allow mounted police and riot squads to enter the park. He let the kids tire themselves out. The second game was declared a forfeit because the umpires said the home team had failed to provide adequate security.[49]

The White Sox stayed near .500 until mid-June; by August 1 they had settled back to fifth place after seven straight losses. Don Kessinger had had enough. He resigned and never managed in the majors again, though he later coached at his alma mater, the University of Mississippi.

Tony La Russa became Veeck's fifth manager in less than four years. It was a bizarre choice, but Veeck was a bizarre man. La Russa was only thirty-four and had managed all of 180 games in parts of two minor league seasons. Veeck may have recognized a future star, or he may have been looking to leave a legacy, because he knew he would soon be gone from Chicago.

La Russa acknowledged, "I was paranoid about not doing the job right."[50] He had completed law school. Now his postgraduate baseball education began—on the field, in the clubhouse, and in Comiskey Park's dingy Bards' Room. La Russa joined Veeck's after-hours salon, mingling with Hemond, Richards, and visiting managers such as Sparky Anderson and Billy Martin. He had to listen to the older men's endless stories, but he also mined their brains. "They knew I had a lot to learn, but I had a willingness to learn," he said.[51] Hemond remembered, "Tony was very smart, asking many questions."[52]

Veeck loved a debate, and he loved an argument even more. He knew how to yank Richards's chain; the magic words were *hit and run*. Richards wanted to tear that page out of baseball's Book. La Russa disagreed and would not back down. "Paul said that Tony was special because he asked questions that would make Paul think deeply," Hemond said. "Nobody else had challenged him on some of those situations. . . . Paul was taken aback at times, but really seemed to enjoy it." Sometimes Richards wearied of Veeck's agitation and wanted a quiet dinner and an early exit. He would urge La Russa: "Let's defuse Bill tonight. [Whatever he says,] tell him, 'You may be right, Bill.'"[53]

Two eras rubbed shoulders in a postmidnight haze of smoke and alcohol. The baby manager was "consumed by the philosophy of Paul Richards," as La Russa's Boswell, Buzz Bissinger, recorded it: *"It's your ass. It's your team. It's your responsibility. There's a strategy for every situation. So start making some decisions."* Hemond said: "He learned at the feet of Bill Veeck and Paul Richards. It was beautiful to see."[54]

The White Sox, 46-60 when La Russa took over, played .500 ball in fifty-four games under the new manager but could not climb out of fifth place. Veeck said there was never any question that La Russa would return in 1980.

Veeck denied a report in a Caracas newspaper that the Sox's Venezuelan former shortstop, Luis Aparicio, had been offered the job.[55]

Richards was shuttling from Waxahachie to Chicago to the White Sox farm clubs. The seventy-year-old was spry enough to pitch the first inning of an old-timers' game at Richards Park in July 1979. He shot a first-round 73 in September's Waxahachie Classic, nearly equal to his age. He was playing in pain but refused to quit because he was leading the tournament. His appendix burst that night, and he survived emergency surgery.[56]

Richards's daughter Paula had been divorced from the actor she married and had moved back to Waxahachie. She began seeing the man who would become her second husband, Bill McQuatters. When the couple had dated as teenagers, her father had barely spoken to Bill. Richards's usual answer to any question was, "Umph." Twenty years later he was not so picky about Paula's suitors; Bill was her father's new best friend. "Daddy had found a live one," Paula said, "and he wasn't going to let him get away."[57]

When La Russa prepared for his first spring training as White Sox manager in 1980, he nominated coach Bobby Winkles to be camp coordinator. That is a crucial role: organizing the practice schedule so players don't waste time standing around; making sure each pitcher gets enough work, each hitter gets enough swings, and each man gets a full dose of the fundamentals. Winkles, a former coach at Arizona State University and manager of the Angels and A's, had the experience and skill to handle it. But Richards asked La Russa, "Do you have any credibility with that team?" No, La Russa answered. He recalled, "It was typical Paul." Richards warned that if Winkles ran a successful spring training, the players would look to him as their leader. La Russa had to earn their respect: "It's your ass on the line." La Russa ran the camp himself.

"Here's the P.S. to that story," he said years later, after he had won more games than any manager except Connie Mack and John McGraw. "I have coordinated my camp every year since, because Paul also told me, 'Every year your credibility and respect are zero. It starts with the spring training program.'" La Russa credits Richards for "one of the most valuable pieces of advice" he ever received. "It's tempting to protect your backside," the old wizard told him, by managing according to The Book so writers and other critics won't second-guess you. "Trust your gut, don't cover your butt." La Russa said, "I've lived with it ever since."[58]

Richards was shepherding several young pitchers through the farm system. The first of them arrived in the majors in 1979, a pair of twenty-one-year-old left-handers who provided some of the only bright spots on the losing team. Steve Trout had been Veeck's first-round choice in his first draft, 1976. Trout was rated a decent prospect, but Veeck made him a number-one pick for sentimental reasons: he was the son of Richards's teammate Dizzy Trout, who had been a Veeck hanger-on. As a rookie Steve Trout went 11-8 with a better-than-average 3.89 ERA. Ross Baumgarten was even better at 13-8 and 3.54. He was another sentimental choice—Chicago drafted him in the twentieth round as a favor to a friend of Hemond's who managed one of the Baumgarten family's furniture stores.[59]

Two more rookies were bidding to join the starting rotation in 1980. Right-hander Richard Dotson had been the Angels' top draft choice in 1977. Richards spotted him in rookie league and recommended that the Sox get him as part of a multiple-player trade. Britt Burns was discovered by an unlikely scout: the *Tribune*'s book reviewer, Robert Cromie, tipped Veeck about a large left-handed kid who had won eighteen straight games for Huffman High School in Birmingham, Alabama.[60]

Veeck said Chicago had the best collection of young arms since Richards's Baby Birds in Baltimore: "After four years of shadow-boxing, we're ready to play winning ball."[61] The baby Sox and their baby manager justified the owner's optimism as soon as the 1980 season opened, despite a killing schedule: nineteen April games against the Eastern Division powers New York, Baltimore, and Boston. The Sox beat the Yankees in four of six, the Orioles in five of seven, and split six with the Red Sox. On May 1 Chicago led the Western Division by one-half game over Billy Martin's Oakland A's.

Rich Dotson won three of the April games. Britt Burns allowed only one run in his first twenty-one innings. Thirty-year-old right-hander Ed Farmer, who had been passed around to six teams, turned into a relief ace on Richards's recommendation.[62] Peter Gammons of the *Boston Globe* said the Sox owed their early success to the pitchers Richards had developed. Although Dave Dombrowski had assumed the title of farm director, he told Gammons, "Every final pitching personnel decision is made by Richards." Gammons said there were two possible explanations for the Sox's wealth of pitchers: "One answer is 'luck.' The other answer is 'Paul Richards.'"[63]

Richards also led an overhaul of the White Sox's catching corps. The team had tried four catchers in 1979. Only twenty-six-year-old Marvis Foley survived the cut. The left-handed batter started the 1980 season in a platoon with Bruce Kimm, who was drafted from the Detroit farm system. Kimm's sole distinction was his service as the personal catcher for the short-lived phenomenon Mark Fidrych.[64] Richards said he evaluated the catching candidates using a method no one had ever heard of: "I've always kept the earned run average of catchers."[65] (The term refers to the ERA of a team's pitchers while a particular catcher was behind the plate.) Analyst Craig Wright first published a breakdown of catchers' ERA nine years later; he said the statistic was used in Japan. Recent research suggests the differences in catchers' ERA are largely random.[66] Richards's new backstops were no improvement over the ones he jettisoned.

The Sox's early spurt was an illusion. They dropped below .500 on June 18 and lost sixty of their last hundred games to repeat in fifth place. But Richards's young pitchers continued to shine. By July the rotation featured second-year men Trout and Baumgarten plus rookies Burns, Dotson, and La Marr Hoyt, a future Cy Young Award winner. At twenty-five Hoyt was the oldest. Burns led the league in ERA for half the season, finishing third at 2.84 with a 15-13 record. Ed Farmer saved thirty games. But Chicago scored the fewest runs and committed the most errors in the league.

Bill Veeck's carnival folded its tent. His money and his health were gone. He was suffering from emphysema, was partially deaf, and had undergone surgery on his remaining leg after a fall. When he sold the club before the 1981 season, he said, "Now Calvin [Griffith] is the last of the dinosaurs."[67] Richards resigned and returned to Waxahachie, but the seventy-two-year-old was not done.

1. Bill Veeck, with Ed Linn, *Veeck as in Wreck: The Autobiography of Bill Veeck* (Chicago: University of Chicago Press, 1962; reprint edition, 2001), 385; *Chicago Tribune*, April 10, 1976, I1.
2. *Chicago Tribune*, April 10, 1976, I1.
3. Ibid., January 10, 2008, online edition; April 4, 1976, B1.
4. Ibid., April 21, 1976, C1, and April 22, 1976, C1.
5. *Sporting News* (hereafter *TSN*), June 19, 1976, 10.
6. *Chicago Tribune*, April 25, 1976, B2, and May 2, 1976, B2.
7. Ibid., June 19, 1976, 10.
8. *Chicago Tribune*, May 30, 1976, B1.
9. Ibid., 3A.
10. Ibid., June 14, 1976, E1.
11. Ibid., June 17, 1976, C1.
12. Ibid., June 15, 1976, C1.
13. Charles P. Korr, *The End of Baseball as We Knew It* (Urbana: University of Illinois Press, 2002), 182–85.
14. *TSN*, July 17, 1976, 17.
15. *Chicago Tribune*, July 4, 1976, B2.
16. *TSN*, July 24, 1976, 31; *Chicago Tribune*, March 21, 1977, E3.
17. *Chicago Tribune*, July 17, 1976, SD1.
18. Ibid., April 25, 1976, B2; Veeck, *Veeck as in Wreck*, 387.
19. Phil Pepe, *Talkin' Baseball: An Oral History of Baseball in the 1970s* (New York: Ballantine, 1998), 220–21.
20. John Helyar, *Lords of the Realm* (New York: Villard, 1994), 239.
21. Roland Hemond, interview by author, October 18, 2006, Phoenix.
22. *Chicago Tribune*, August 9, 1976, E1, and August 21, 1976, 3; *New York Times*, October 20, 2005, online archive.
23. Hemond interview.
24. *Minneapolis Star-Tribune*, June 30, 2007, online edition.
25. *TSN*, August 21, 1976, 15.
26. *Chicago Sun-Times*, August 31, 1976, 84; September 1, 1976, 124.

27. *Chicago Tribune*, September 1, 1976, E1, and September 2, 1976, C1; *Chicago Sun-Times*, September 2, 1976, 152.

28. Randy Harvey, "From Waxahachie to the White Sox," *Dallas Times-Herald Sunday* magazine, August 29, 1976, 24.

29. *Chicago Tribune*, April 16, 1978, B1.

30. *TSN*, September 25, 1976, 1.

31. *Chicago Tribune*, March 12, 1980, E1.

32. Paul Richards, interview by Clark Nealon, February 5, 1981; *Chicago Tribune*, November 19, 1976, C3.

33. Helyar, *Lords of the Realm*, 237; Hemond interview.

34. Robert F. Burk, *Much More Than a Game* (Chapel Hill: University of North Carolina Press, 2001), 207.

35. Veeck, *Veeck as in Wreck*, 386. Some sources placed the Yankees' cash contribution as high as $500,000 (*TSN*, April 23, 1977, 19).

36. *Chicago Tribune, July* 5, 1977, C2.

37. Veeck, *Veeck as in Wreck*, 387.

38. *TSN*, November 12, 1977, 35–36.

39. John Feinstein, *Play Ball* (New York: Villard, 1993), 217–18.

40. Hemond interview.

41. *Chicago Tribune*, February 27, 1979, C1.

42. Buzz Bissinger, *Three Nights in August* (Boston: Houghton Mifflin, 2005), 112, 177.

43. Korr, *End of Baseball*, 189; *TSN*, November 15, 1980, 6.

44. *TSN*, July 22, 1978, 26.

45. Gerald Eskenazi, *Bill Veeck: A Baseball Legend* (New York: McGraw-Hill, 1988), 16.

46. Tony La Russa interview, telephone interview by author, November 16, 2007.

47. *Chicago Tribune*, February 27, 1979, C1.

48. Helyar, *Lords of the Realm*, 238; Eskenazi, *Bill Veeck*, 165.

49. Veeck, *Veeck as in Wreck*, 394–95; *TSN*, July 28, 1979, 20.

50. Bissinger, *Three Nights in August*, 97.

51. La Russa interview.

52. Hemond interview.

53. Ibid.; La Russa interview.

54. Bissinger, *Three Nights in August*, 97 (emphasis in the original); Hemond interview.

55. *TSN*, September 1, 1979, 54, 57.

56. *Waxahachie (Texas) Daily Light*, July 9, 1979, 1; *Baltimore Sun*, September 30, 1979, C1; Paula Richards, interviews by author, 2006–2008.

57. Paula Richards interviews; Bill McQuatters, interview by author, May 18, 2007, Fernley, Nev.

58. La Russa interview.

59. Veeck, *Veeck as in Wreck*, 391.

60. Ibid.; TSN, May 17, 1980, 7.

61. *TSN*, April 12, 1980, 18.

62. Ibid., January 5, 1980, 48.

63. *Boston Sunday Globe*, May 4, 1980, 51; *TSN*, May 17, 1980, 12.

64. *TSN*, May 10, 1980, 13.

65. *Boston Sunday Globe*, May 4, 1980, 51.

66. Craig Wright and Tom House, *The Diamond Appraised* (New York: Simon and Schuster, 1989), 22; Jonah Keri, ed., *Baseball Between the Numbers* (New York: Basic, 2006), 106.

67. Helyar, *Lords of the Realm*, 243.

CHAPTER 28

Fadeaway

I think that's a wonderful standard to earn: the baseball man.
—Tony La Russa

Baseball was bracing for another strike in 1981. After just five years of free agency, star players were commanding mind-boggling dollars. Dave Parker and Nolan Ryan topped the million-dollar salary mark. The Yankees signed Dave Winfield for ten years and at least $13 million. (His contract included a cost-of-living increase.)[1] To rein in the runaway market, owners proposed that a club signing a top-tier free agent be required to give up one of its players to the club that lost him. A free-agent signing would be much like a trade. The Players Association said no.[2]

"Now the only people making any money out of baseball are the players and the agents," Richards groused. He blamed big-spending owners who did not mind losing money because they were looking for fame and/or a tax shelter. He named the Angels' Gene Autry and the Yankees' George Steinbrenner, two of the most active bidders in the free-agent market. Richards derided general managers who cheerfully spent the owners' money because they cared more about protecting their jobs than about the long-term interests of the game.

Richards proposed signing amateur players to ten-year contracts, buying out their arbitration and early free-agent seasons.[3] Making long-term commitments to amateurs was too much of a gamble, but he was on the right track. Teams later embraced a lower-risk alternative by signing their young major leaguers to multiyear deals before they were eligible for arbitration.

The unemployed Richards's old-boy network provided him with a safety net. Eddie Robinson, now executive vice president and general manager of the Texas Rangers, brought Richards on board in February 1981 as a scout, instructor, and troubleshooter. Robinson said: "He is without question the most knowledgeable baseball man I have ever been associated with. He'll see all our minor league players and spend a lot of time watching the major league club. Pitching will be his No. 1 responsibility, but when he sees anything else out of line he'll report to me and something will be done about it." Although it was a role reversal—Robinson the boss and Richards his employee—Robinson later explained: "I don't like to say he worked for me. We worked together."[4]

Eddie Chiles, a self-made multimillionaire in the oilfield services industry, had bought the Rangers in 1980. Chiles was famous throughout the Southwest for his radio commentaries, which began, "I'm mad." He was mad about government regulation of business, and he spent $1 million a year buying commercial time on hundreds of stations to spout his conservative views. While railing against the federal government, he garnered tens of millions in federal loan guarantees to build offshore drilling rigs.[5]

Chiles was a friend and golf partner of Richards's and Robinson's. One day Chiles suggested that Richards buy the drinks at the nineteenth hole. "After all, Paul's got more money than the rest of us."

"I will have," Richards told him, "if you insist on staying in baseball."[6]

Working for Chiles was nothing like being his pal. He was an abusive boss who berated and humiliated employees. Robinson said, "Eddie came in and wanted to run it like the Western Company," his oil and real estate conglomerate.[7]

Robinson hired another old-school baseball man, Don Zimmer, as manager in 1981. Zimmer had seven years' experience leading the Padres and Red

Sox, but nothing had prepared him for Chiles. Robinson brought the manager a stack of index cards, explaining that Chiles wanted "formalized goal-setting." Robinson instructed Zimmer to set goals for the players during the next three weeks—hits, home runs, pitching victories—then sit down with each player and discuss the goals. Naturally, Zimmer's reaction was, "You've got to be kidding." The index cards lasted only a few days. Chiles posted nutrition charts in the clubhouse, advising players what to eat and drink to survive the Texas summer.[8] Presumably, beer was not part of the recommended diet.

The Rangers had achieved winning records in three of the previous four seasons, but the core of the team was aging. Robinson had unloaded forty-one-year-old Gaylord Perry and thirty-five-year-old Sparky Lyle in exchange for younger players. The staff ace, Ferguson Jenkins, was thirty-eight, and four other key pitchers were older than thirty. The leading hitter, outfielder/DH Al Oliver, was thirty-four. But the club started strongly and was in second place, just one and a half games behind Oakland, with a 33-22 record on June 12, 1981.

Then the players went on strike. The first midseason shutdown in history lasted fifty days, until the owners' strike insurance ran out and they settled on terms offered by the players months before. The strike wiped out more than one-third of the schedule. The season was split into two halves, with a new pennant race beginning on August 10. Zimmer thought he had the best team in baseball before the strike, but the Rangers tailed off to finish 24-26 in the second half.[9]

Robinson and Richards went looking for power in the off-season. They traded Oliver to Montreal for Larry Parrish, who had hit thirty homers two years earlier, and minor league slugger Dave Hostetler. They picked up Richards's White Sox first baseman, Lamar Johnson, and promoted twenty-three-year-old switch-hitting outfielder George Wright.

Their biggest deal was a costly mistake. They wanted Mets outfielder Lee Mazzilli as their lead-off hitter. Mazzilli, a New York native, was popular in his hometown but had never achieved the stardom predicted for him. In 1981 his average dropped to .228. Still, the Mets exacted a stiff price: pitching prospects Walt Terrell and Ron Darling. Richards was convinced that Terrell, a thirty-third-round draft choice, would never make it.[10] Terrell later won fifteen or more games in three straight seasons. Darling was the Rangers' number-one pick out of Yale the year before. He went on to 136 victories and was a mainstay of the Mets' strong 1980s clubs.

Robinson and Richards were delighted to be a team again. "We played golf together and things were like they used to be," Robinson remembered. But Richards had little influence in the organization. Coaches ignored the old man's suggestions. He doted on the young pitcher Danny Darwin and wanted to teach him the slip pitch, but Richards refused to suit up and go on the field during spring training, so it did not get done. Robinson said, "He didn't have the clout."[11]

In a move indicative of Richards's outsider status, he latched onto the front office's ultimate outsider as his spring companion. Robinson had hired a young schoolteacher, Craig Wright, to do statistical analyses. A few teams had employed statisticians earlier but kept them hidden in the attic like a crazy aunt, instructing the statheads not to acknowledge that they worked for the ball club. With the Rangers Wright attended meetings, carried a business card listing his title as "Sabermetrician," and offered advice on trades.[12]

Richards invited Wright to ride with him on several long drives to exhibition games. Richards once wrote that "well-kept statistics [can be] a method of disproving some old baseball assumptions."[13] That could have been a sabermetrician's creed, but he showed little interest in Wright's work. He did open the young man's eyes to the game as it was played on the field rather than in the stat books. Wright remarked on third baseman Carney Lansford's low assist rates, especially the fact that he started few around-the-horn double plays. Richards pointed out that Lansford played so shallow that his back was to second base, and he had to turn all the way around to throw there. "I liked it that he was secure enough in his standing and place in the organization that he didn't feel threatened by me or the perspective I was trying to bring into the game," Wright said. "But the truth is he wasn't real interested in it." He believed Richards "was essentially coasting," and some of his player evaluations "were pretty darn silly."[14]

The retooled Rangers fell to last place after losing eleven straight games in April and May 1982. Chiles brought in a motivational speaker to try to light a fire. When the owner met with players and staff on an off day, he posted armed guards to keep reporters away.[15] On June 9 the club had the second-worst record in the majors. Chiles said he didn't believe in firing people. Three weeks later he fired Eddie Robinson, even though he said Robinson "did a good job." Then why was he gone? "I don't have a reason." Chiles announced he would serve as his own general manager with advice from Zimmer and Richards.[16]

When the Rangers dropped twelve of fourteen games in July, it was Zimmer's turn to go. In one of the more bizarre firings in baseball history, Chiles summoned his "Mr. Manager" to his office on Monday, July 26, and dismissed him—effective Wednesday. Zimmer couldn't believe it: "The man says, 'You're fired, but you're going to manage Monday, Tuesday and Wednesday.'" Of course, word leaked to the press, but Chiles stuck to his timetable. When he announced the firing, he told the writers, "Don didn't do anything wrong." Then why was he gone? "It's a private problem. You are not entitled to know everything we do. This is not a publicly owned company. This is not the United States government."[17]

Randy Youngman of the *Dallas Times-Herald* revealed that Craig Wright had prepared a highly critical evaluation of Zimmer's handling of the club, and Richards had forwarded it to Chiles.[18] When Zimmer heard this, he exploded: "Craig Wright is the laughingstock of this organization and he is a disgrace to this organization. Mr. Chiles doesn't know anything about baseball and he has to listen to Craig Wright. That's a sad situation." Asked if he blamed Richards, he said: "I feel at this point, the less I say, the better things are. . . . But I don't think that Eddie Chiles is getting the right dope from his people upstairs. I think he's being misled." Zimmer's parting words were, "This place is a mess."[19] (Wright declined to discuss the matter in a 2005 e-mail exchange with me.)

The seventy-three-year-old Richards, the most prominent baseball man in the Rangers' front office, saw a chance to maneuver himself back into power. He engineered a trade that sent the unhappy Lee Mazzilli back to his beloved New York, this time to the Yankees, for shortstop Bucky Dent. It was a typical Richards deal, acquiring a player who had been with him before.

The Rangers did no better after Zimmer was fired. They finished next to last, twenty-nine games behind the division-leading Angels. Darrell Johnson, the eleventh manager in the franchise's eleven seasons in Texas, was let go. The search for the twelfth one embroiled Richards in his last controversy.

Chiles passed over Richards and promoted farm director Joe Klein to be general manager. Klein focused on three candidates for the managing job: Jim Leyland, the White Sox's third-base coach, who was recommended by his friend Tony La Russa; Bobby Valentine, a minor league coach in the Mets' system who was only thirty-two; and Doug Rader, a former Gold Glove third baseman who had managed San Diego's AAA team in Hawaii for three years. UPI reported that Leyland was the choice.[20] Instead, Rader got the job.

Now Eddie Chiles was really mad. He was paranoid about news leaks. He had been humiliated when Zimmer's secret firing became public knowledge within twenty-four hours. Craig Wright's report on Zimmer had gotten into the papers, Klein's appointment as GM was reported before Chiles made it official, and now this. UPI's mistaken "scoop" was written by Milton Richman, a former minor league infielder whose connection with Richards went back twenty-five years. The once-standoffish Richards had become cozy with many writers. Dallas sports columnist Blackie Sherrod thought Richards enjoyed the company of writers more than baseball men.[21] Chiles wrote Richards an angry, insulting letter blaming him for the leaks:

> If you had not been my close long time friend, I would have fired you immediately after the Zimmer incident.
>
> All of that is behind us now, and I will forgive, but I will not forget. From this point forward, if there is ever one thing—and I emphasize one thing that is leaked to the press which can be traced back to you, or even something that I think can be traced to you, it will bring about your immediate termination from the Rangers' organization.
>
> My advice to you henceforth is to keep your lips sealed.[22]

Chiles's letter alarmed Richards. In a contrite reply he denied the leaks and insisted he had not known in advance that Zimmer would be fired, so he couldn't have told anyone. Begging to keep his job, he wrote: "I know I can help the Rangers and Joe Klein. . . . The Rangers also need more constructive training of minor league players, and this is something I do better than anybody in baseball." He concluded, "I certainly personally hope that such inconsequential interests as newspaper reporters and other leaches [*sic*], nor even baseball itself, will ever affect our close relationship."[23]

Richards stayed on the Rangers' payroll as a "special assistant" for the rest of his life. He received regular reports on the team's minor leaguers, but he was no longer a decision maker or even a close adviser. He had, in effect, been pensioned off.

By the fall of 1982 Margie had been diagnosed with liver cancer. Her husband and daughter took her to a specialist in Houston for tests. After the doctor delivered the bleak prognosis—it was a death sentence—Margie returned to her hospital room. Paula found it odd that her parents did not discuss what they had been told. She and her father drove back to their hotel. As soon as he walked into his room, Paul called Margie, and they had a long talk about what would happen next. To Paula the moment was a revelation of the price of a baseball life:

> I realized that so much of their relationship had been over the phone when he was traveling on out-of-town games or spring training, that talking on the phone and making decisions was easier for them than face to face. Daddy always called home a great deal when he was traveling, and he and Mother would have long conversations. Next day at the hospital they were happy as could be over their decision. But the decision had been made over the phone. Prior to this I had never thought about how many decisions they had made over the years over the phone, so that was their comfort level in a dire situation. Then, when they were together, the hard decisions had been made and they could move on to other things.[24]

Margie's sister, Lucille Williams, moved in to care for her with the help of friends. Eventually, Margie went to a nursing home. She died on June 2, 1983, at seventy-one.[25] The couple had been married for fifty-one years. Recalling their courtship, Richards said, "She had long hair hanging down almost to her waist." He paused and sighed deeply, cleared his throat, and shifted to less emotional ground: "She could eat in those days. I know she almost broke me."[26]

Less than three months later Richards traveled to Cooperstown to see two of his favorites inducted into the National Baseball Hall of Fame. Sportswriters elected Brooks Robinson, a sixteen-time Gold Glove winner, in his first year of eligibility. He called Richards the biggest influence on his career.[27] George Kell had been passed over by the writers but was voted in by the Veterans Committee.

Tony La Russa led the 1983 White Sox to the AL West title before losing to Baltimore in the playoffs. Richards told him, "You're doing all right." La Russa commented, "When he said 'all right,' that was pretty strong."[28]

Chiles named Mike Stone, an executive from his Western Company, to be president of the Rangers. Richards escorted Stone to the winter meeting in December 1983 and introduced him to baseball people. Other front-office neophytes listened when the sage spoke. Wayne Krivsky was an assistant in the Rangers' farm system. More than twenty years later, as general manager of the Cincinnati Reds, he recalled: "Paul Richards once told me the purpose of player development is to get players to the major leagues healthy. That was one of his credos." Former outfielder Tom Grieve was also beginning his front-office career, and would become the Rangers' GM. "I always pumped him, every chance I could," he said. "How could you not listen to someone who had 60 years in baseball? One thing he always said: 'Don't be afraid to go with your young players if you believe in them. Don't be afraid to make a mistake.'" Bobby Valentine, the Rangers' rookie manager in 1985, talked with Richards for hours and invited him to join the team on a road trip, but Richards never went. He survived colon cancer and another surgery to repair an aneurysm. Blackie Sherrod wrote, "He was skin and bones, but he could go through a platter of babyback ribs like a liberated POW."[29]

Richards spent time with old friends, but his circle was shrinking. Jimmy Adair, Frank Gabler, Clint Courtney, Nellie Fox, and Archie Wise were dead. Eddie Robinson, who lived nearby in Fort Worth, said: "He never exhibited how he felt really close to you, you know, but you just knew he did. Never threw his arm around you, like some people will grab you and all that shit. That wasn't Richards at all."[30] Both Robinson and Waxahachie business leader Buck Jordan, once Richards's Sunday school student, considered him a surrogate father, but he was reluctant to give them advice. Jordan said, "You seldom ever got him to talk about anything other than baseball or golf." Richards would work out local teenagers who believed they had baseball talent—or their fathers did—but would never tell them they had no chance. Instead, he preached the value of practice.[31]

The widowed Richards settled into a retirement routine. Most mornings he left home, drove downhill to Highway 287, and made his first stop across the two-lane road at the Giles Monument Company. Perry Giles, who crafts gravestones, had a telephone line with a Dallas metro number so Richards could save a long-distance charge when he called the Rangers' office.[32] He checked in to see if the club had an assignment for him; the answer was usually no. Back in his Lincoln Town Car, he turned left and rolled on a few hundred feet to the driveway of the Waxahachie Country Club to play a round of golf, bumming a few cigarettes along the way.

He picked up whatever partners were available. Although he was still a skilled player, he did not shun the club's sorriest duffers. He'd play with anybody. And hustle them. One member—notoriously inept—joined him on a morning when there was a long line at the first tee. Richards suggested they start their round on the tenth hole. The man whispered, "Paul, I don't do too well when I start on number ten." Richards delighted in repeating the story.

He took pride in his game. When he butchered a hole, he would return there after completing his round and replay it, hitting the shots over and over, littering the fairway with balls.[33] There is no such thing as too much practice on the fundamentals. That's what he was doing on the afternoon of May 4, 1986. Texas's blast-furnace summer had not yet taken hold; it was a sunny, pleasant Sunday with temperatures in the mideighties.

Waxahachie's new fire chief, David Hudgins, heard the dispatcher's radio call: "Paul Richards is down on the golf course." The medics had to drive their ambulance across the grass to reach him. He was slumped in his cart beside the thirteenth fairway. No pulse. They sped to the hospital with siren blaring, but that was a formality.[34]

It was, of course, a fitting way for him to go. Best of all, he had finished his round.

The newspaper obituaries were perfunctory, pasted together from clip files, shot through with errors. Most of the writers who had jousted with him were retired or dead. The *Daily Light* put him on the front page: "Waxahachie's most famous baseball player, manager and authority."[35]

Several writers got it right: they called him a baseball man.

S. L. Price, "Dark Times for a Baseball Man," *Sports Illustrated*, June 4, 2007, online archive.

1. *Sporting News* (hereafter *TSN*), December 1, 1979, 50; January 3, 1981, 40.
2. Charles P. Korr, *The End of Baseball as We Knew It* (Urbana: University of Illinois Press, 2002), 211–13.
3. Paul Richards, interview by Clark Nealon, February 5, 1981.
4. *TSN*, February 28, 1981, 38; Eddie Robinson, interview by author, August 18, 2006, Fort Worth, Texas.
5. "Mad Eddie," *Time*, May 26, 1980, online archive.
6. *Dallas Morning News*, May 7, 1986, online archive.
7. Eddie Robinson interview.
8. Don Zimmer, with Bill Madden, *Zim: A Baseball Life* (Kingston, N.Y.: Total Sports, 2001), 148–49.
9. Ibid., 149.
10. Ibid., 153.
11. Eddie Robinson interview.
12. Alan Schwarz, *The Numbers Game: Baseball's Lifelong Fascination with Statistics* (New York: Thomas Dunne Books/St. Martin's, 2004), 222–24.
13. Paul Richards, *Modern Baseball Strategy* (Englewood Cliffs, N.J.: Prentice-Hall, 1955), 7–8.
14. Craig Wright, e-mail to author, December 30, 2005.
15. Mike Shropshire, *Seasons in Hell* (New York: Avon, 1996), 235; *TSN*, June 20, 1983, 22.
16. Herm Weiskopf, "The Week," *Sports Illustrated*, June 21, 1982, online archive; AP, *New York Times*, June 11, 1982, A26; Zimmer, *Zim*, 157.
17. AP, *Gettysburg (Pa.) Times*, July 30, 1982, 12.
18. Randy Youngman, "To Whom It May Concern," undated (1982) letter in Paul Richards Papers, in the personal collection of Paula Richards.
19. *TSN*, August 9, 1982, 29.
20. UPI, *Syracuse (N.Y.) Herald Journal*, October 14, 1982, D-8.
21. Blackie Sherrod, e-mail to author, August 3, 2006.
22. H. E. Chiles, letter to Paul Richards, October 20, 1982, in Richards papers.
23. Richards to Chiles, October 26, 1982, in Richards papers.

24. Paula Richards, interviews by author, 2006–2008.
25. Ibid.; Mike Hastings, interviews by author, August–September 2006, Waxahachie, Texas; *Waxahachie (Texas) Daily Light*, June 3, 1983, 8-A.
26. Paul Richards, taped reminiscences (undated; 1983 or later), in the author's files.
27. *TSN*, January 24, 1983, 38, 47; August 8, 1983, 25; Connie Robinson, undated letter to Paul Richards (1983), in Richards papers. She is married to Brooks Robinson and wrote to Richards to thank him for attending the ceremony.
28. Tony La Russa, telephone interview by author, November 16, 2007.
29. Michael Stone, letter to Paul Richards, December 20, 1983, Richards papers; *Cincinnati Enquirer*, February 12, 2006, online archive; Henry Hecht, "A Fond Farewell to a Baseball Man Who Wasn't Afraid to Take Chances," *Sports Illustrated*, May 25, 1986, online archive; *Dallas Times-Herald*, May 7, 1986, online archive; Paula Richards interviews; *Dallas Times-Herald*, May 7, 1986, online archive.
30. Eddie Robinson interview.
31. Buck Jordan, interviews by author, August 16–17, 2006, Waxahachie, Texas.
32. Perry Giles, interview by author, August 17, 2006, Waxahachie, Texas.
33. Jordan interviews.
34. David Hudgins, interviews by author, August 16–17, 2006, Waxahachie, Texas.
35. *Waxahachie Daily Light*, May 5, 1986, 1-A.

The Beauty of the Competition

The Fox Network television crew spotted it first: a brown stain on the pitching hand of Kenny Rogers, the Detroit Tigers' starting pitcher in the second game of the 2006 World Series against Tony La Russa's St. Louis Cardinals. Broadcaster Tim McCarver identified the stain as pine tar, an "illegal substance"—legal on a player's bat but illegal on a pitcher's hand. Several Cardinals saw the close-ups on the clubhouse TV and alerted their manager.

Before Rogers came out to pitch the second inning, La Russa told Randy Marsh, chief of the umpiring crew, "Get him to clean it off and let's play baseball." When Rogers returned to the mound, only a faint discoloration remained visible. The forty-one-year-old left-hander allowed the Cardinals just two hits that Sunday night, completing a streak of twenty-three consecutive scoreless innings in postseason play.

What happened next brought the teachings of Paul Richards into the spotlight twenty years after his death. When Fox's Joe Buck interviewed La Russa on live television in the fourth inning, he asked what La Russa had said to the umpires about Rogers's hand. La Russa refused to talk about it. McCarver commented, "I guess the big question is, if it wasn't illegal, why was it washed off?" After the game the yowling media horde wanted to know what was on Rogers's hand. "A big clump of dirt," the pitcher said. He had wiped it off. Umpiring supervisor Steve Palermo said the same. The media wanted to know what La Russa did about it. He replied, "It's not important to talk about."

Columnists stoked what one called the "smoldering controversy." Angry Cardinals fans buried La Russa on talk radio. If he had asked the umpires to examine Rogers's hand, and they found an illegal substance, Rogers would have been ejected and probably suspended for the rest of the Series. Even some Cardinals players thought La Russa had pulled his punches because the Detroit manager, Jim Leyland, was his closest friend in baseball. La Russa's wife, Elaine, told him, "I can't believe how much you're getting killed." A few friendly commentators suggested he was playing mind games with Rogers, who would be in line to start a sixth game if the Series went that far.

La Russa decided to address the controversy when he met the media the next day, an off-day in the Series. "I don't believe it was dirt. Didn't look like dirt." He thought Rogers was using something "to get a grip" on the ball in the forty-degree chill, but he would not utter the words *pine tar*. He never asked the umpires to search Rogers: "I said, 'I don't like the stuff. Let's get it fixed.' It got fixed, in my opinion, and we never hit the guy." He added, "If he didn't get rid of it, I would have challenged it."

Was La Russa treading softly because Leyland was in the other dugout? "If somebody raises it as a question, hey, you can see where it makes some sense. But if somebody tells me that's what I was thinking, it's really a personal insult. . . . And if somebody seriously accused me of that, I would get very upset and confrontational."

Then he shocked the audience of hardened sportswriters: "It's not the way we want to win. . . . I believe in the beauty of the competition."[1]

The Cardinals won the Series in five games, giving La Russa his second championship. After the victory parade *St. Louis Post-Dispatch* columnist Bernie Miklasz revisited the Rogers game. "I have absolutely no regrets," La Russa told him. ". . . I feel better because we won, but to me winning the right way was winning within the integrity of the competition." He said he learned this philosophy from Sparky Anderson and Paul Richards.[2]

More than a year later I asked La Russa what he meant by the beauty and integrity of the competition. In his clipped monotone he explained: "Competition is really a beautiful concept. The pure form—get your team to do the very best they can. The other team does the very best they can. You get a result that shows how you measured up. It's beautiful. And in baseball it happens 162 times [every season]. You do your best. They do their best."

When his players called his attention to Rogers's hand, "It was one of the most difficult decisions." He had only three or four minutes to consider: "If I undress this guy [have him searched], every day for the rest of the Series that's going to be the story." He did not think Rogers's transgression was worth a media firestorm like the one that erupted in the 2000 World Series, when Roger Clemens threw a piece of a broken bat in the direction of Mike Piazza. "Unless it's flagrant or abusive, you don't want a distraction to take away from the competition. There's a line there." In refusing to win on a technicality, "I was relying on my baseball upbringing. . . . It comes from Sparky and Paul. Sparky called me and said, 'You did the right thing.'"[3]

La Russa's willingness to experiment is another Richards legacy. La Russa sometimes batted his pitchers eighth to get more men on base in front of sluggers Mark McGwire and Albert Pujols. La Russa tried a three-man starting rotation, with each starter pitching only three or four innings. He shuttled relievers in and out even more than Richards did.

Sixteen men who played for Richards went on to manage in the majors. Dick Williams called him "my mentor," but others—no doubt including Joe Torre—would not say that.[4] Richards also influenced Earl Weaver, a minor league manager in the Orioles' system in Richards's time and a pioneer in the use of detailed statistical breakdowns.

While Weaver was one of the last managers to stick to a four-man starting rotation, most teams followed Richards to a five-man rotation by the 1970s (though Richards did not originate it). Baseball's Book did not catch up with him until long after he died, when on-base percentage was accepted as a measure of a hitter's worth and pitch counts became not just a strategy but a religion.

Richards was one of seventeen managers, executives, and umpires on the 2003 Veterans Committee ballot for the Hall of Fame. No one was elected. In 2007 he received ten votes from the committee of eighty-one Hall of Fame members and writers and broadcasters who had been honored by the hall. (Joe Morgan said he voted for Richards.)[5] After the voting structure was changed, Richards was dropped from the 2008 ballot.

Twenty years after Richards's death, nearly half of Americans described themselves as baseball fans, though football was the most popular sport.[6] The majors' revenues reached a record $6.5 billion in 2008 as attendance climbed toward eighty million. The old game was on a new high, despite the caustic fallout from the steroids era.

La Russa started managing just after Richards stopped. La Russa cited two sea changes that had transformed the job in his three decades: the new relationship with players after free agency and the influence of the pervasive, sensation-seeking media.

Players now listen to their agents and their posses rather than their manager. "If I pinch-hit Tony for Warren, they'll tell Warren, 'You should have been up there.'" The manager's "huge challenge" is to motivate men to play for the team, putting aside the individual statistics that determine how many millions each will be paid. When La Russa talked with coaches in other sports, they asked each other, "What are you doing to get their attention?"

The media lusted for conflict. "If it bleeds, it leads." The media no longer consisted of a handful of newspaper beat writers and columnists. TV, radio, and Internet reporters from national, regional, and local outlets swarm the clubhouse, relentlessly stirring the pot. Bloggers throw cyberbombs from behind the protection of anonymity. I was surprised that La Russa considered how the media would react if he raised a stink about Rogers's tarred hand. "You have to," he replied.[7]

Richards would not recognize baseball as Tony La Russa knows it. But he would recognize the game between the white lines—"a simple game. You throw the ball, you hit it, you catch it." The beauty of the competition is unchanging.

Paul Richards said it himself: "It starts over every spring, with you or without you."[8]

---

1. Accounts of the game and its aftermath come from the *St. Louis Post-Dispatch*, October 24, 2006, special section, 1–2; *New York Daily News*, October 24, 2006, 74; *Hartford Courant*, October 24, 2006, C1; *Tacoma News Tribune*, October 24, 2006, online edition; *Sports Illustrated*, October 30, 2006, p. 42.
2. *St. Louis Post-Dispatch*, October 30, 2006, online edition.
3. Tony La Russa, telephone interview by author, November 16, 2007.
4. Dick Williams, and Bill Plaschke, *No More Mr. Nice Guy* (San Diego: Harcourt Brace Jovanovich, 1990), 192.
5. *New York Times*, February 28, 2007, online edition.
6. Jeffrey M. Jones, "Nearly Half of Americans Are Baseball Fans," Gallup, April 4, 2006, www.gallup.com/poll/22240/nearly-half-americans-baseball-fans.aspx.
7. La Russa interview.
8. "Springing for the Check," *Time*, March 23, 1987, online archive.

Acknowledgments

This book would not exist without Paul Richards's daughter Paula. She and her husband, Bill McQuatters, welcomed me to their home and let me spend several days examining her parents' papers and scrapbooks, which had been in storage for twenty years. She generously shared memories of her daddy and put up with my endless questions without trying to censor what I wrote.

Two skilled baseball researchers and writers, Jan Finkel and Steve Treder, read the manuscript and left it bleeding on the floor, improving it with every cut. They deserve Gold Gloves for their many catches that saved me from embarrassment.

In Waxahachie, Texas, Buck Jordan was my guide to Richards's hometown and to Richards's life away from baseball. Waxahachie fire chief David Hudgins, an accomplished local historian, and Richards family friend Mike Hastings provided unpublished archival material. Eddie Robinson, the only surviving member of Richards's inner circle, gave me an intimate picture of the man he calls "my father figure." I got my postgraduate education in baseball in a conversation with Tony La Russa, hearing Richards's voice in La Russa's taut monotone. Brooks Robinson was generous with his time and insights.

I am a member of the Society for American Baseball Research—think of it as the board of deacons of Annie Savoy's Church of Baseball. The most important perk of membership is access to other members who share their research.

There are not enough pages to mention all those who contributed their time, knowledge, and insight.

Because golf was such an important part of Richards's life, I leaned on my brother-in-law, David Beacham, for his expertise. It seems unsporting to hit a ball that is sitting helplessly on a tee, but David and I will debate that over another of his bloody Marys.

At Southern Methodist University Press, director Keith Gregory was an enthusiastic supporter of the book. Kathryn Lang masterfully shaped the manuscript with patience, kindness, and good cheer. Polly Kummel copyedited it with a deft but light hand.

All these people helped. Any errors are mine. To paraphrase Huckleberry Finn, I hope I got it right, mainly.

Bibliography

ARCHIVES

A. Bartlett Giamatti Research Center. National Baseball Hall of Fame and Museum, Cooperstown, N.Y.
>   Paul, Gabriel. Untitled Cincinnati Reds press release, January 1939, in the Harry Craft file.
>   Player files for Paul Richards, Clint Courtney, Harry Craft, Tony La Russa, Eddie Robinson, and Harry Breechen.
>   Texas Rangers press release, February 1981. In the Paul Richards file.
Buffalo and Erie County Historical Society Research Library, Buffalo, N.Y.
>   Joseph M. Overfield Papers.
Ellis County Museum, Waxahachie, Texas.
>   Paul Richards. Untitled diary of the Seattle Rainiers' 1950 season.
Society for American Baseball Research. The Baseball Biography Project. Society for American Baseball Research, Cleveland, Ohio. These articles are available online at http://bioproj.sabr.org.
>   Borowy, Hank, by Lyle Spatz.
>   Culler, Dick, by Hank Utley and Warren Corbett.
>   Dyer, Eddie, by Warren Corbett.
>   Hemond, Roland, by Bill Nowlin.
>   Houtteman, Art, by Warren Corbett.
>   Mancuso, Gus, by Warren Corbett.
>   Ott, Mel, by Fred Stein.
>   Rogovin, Saul, by Ralph Berger.
>   Rucker, Nap, by Eric Enders.
>   Stevens, Chuck, by Mark Armour.
>   Tebbetts, Birdie, by Tom Simon.
>   Wilhelm, Hoyt, by Mark Armour.
>   Williams, Earl, by Jeffrey Katz.
>   Zernial, Gus, by Marc Aaron.
Society for American Baseball Research. Oral History Committee. Society for American Baseball Research, Cleveland, Ohio. These interviews are available only to SABR members.
>   Berres, Ray. Interview by Norman Macht. March 8, 1996.
>   Boyd, Bob. Interview by Brent Kelley. February 15, 1991.
>   Brecheen, Harry. Interview by Rick Bradley. October 26, 1992.
>   Brown, Harold. Interview by Brent Kelley. July 29, 1991.
>   Causey, Wayne. Undated interview by Brent Kelley.
>   Ferrarese, Don. Interview by Brent Kelley. February 19, 1991.

Gentile, Jim. Interview by Jim Sanders. Undated interview, ca. 2002.

Hansen, Ron. Interview by David Paulson. October 18, 2006.

Hinton, Chuck. Interview by David Paulson. February 6, 2000.

Hubbell, Carl. Interview by Walter Langford. June 15, 1982.

Pierce, Billy. Interview by Thomas Liley. February 24, 1992.

Pyburn, Jim. Interview by Brent Kelley. September 19, 1991.

Shetrone, Barry. Interview by Brent Kelley. August 10, 1992.

Woodling, Gene. Interview by Jim Sargent. May 6, 1997.

Texas Sports Hall of Fame, Waco.

Mancuso, Gus. Interview by Clark Nealon. ca. 1980.

Richards, Paul. Interview by Clark Nealon. February 5, 1981.

PUBLISHED WORKS

A Memorial and Biographical History of Ellis County, Texas. Chicago: Lewis, 1892.

Aaron, Hank, with Lonnie Wheeler. *I Had a Hammer: The Hank Aaron Story.* New York: Harper-Collins, 1991.

Aaron, Marc. "Gus Zernial." *The Baseball Biography Project.* Society for American Baseball Research, Cleveland, Ohio. Available online at http://bioproj.sabr.org.

Addie, Bob. *Sportswriter.* Lanham, Md.: Accent, 1980.

Adelson, Bruce. *Brushing Back Jim Crow: The Integration of Minor League Baseball in the American South.* Charlottesville: University Press of Virginia, 1999.

Alexander, Charles C. *Breaking the Slump.* New York: Oxford University Press, 2002.

———. *Our Game.* New York: Henry Holt, 1991.

———. *Ty Cobb.* New York: Columbia University Press, 1984.

Angell, Roger. *The Summer Game.* Lincoln: University of Nebraska Press, 2004. First published 1972 by Viking.

Armour, Mark. "Chuck Stevens." *The Baseball Biography Project.* Society for American Baseball Research, Cleveland, Ohio. Available online at http://bioproj.sabr.org.

———. "Hoyt Wilhelm." *The Baseball Biography Project.* Society for American Baseball Research, Cleveland, Ohio. Available online at http://bioproj.sabr.org.

———. "Hoyt Wilhelm, Starting Pitcher." *Articles Related to Rob Neyer's Big Book of Baseball Lineups.* 2003. www.robneyer.com/book_03_BAL.html.

———, ed. *Rain Check: Baseball in the Pacific Northwest.* Cleveland: Society for American Baseball Research, 2006.

Asinof, Eliot. *Eight Men Out.* New York: Henry Holt, 1963.

Baseball Reference. www.Baseball-Reference.com and www.Baseball-Reference.com/play-index.

Belth, Alex. *Stepping Up: The Story of Curt Flood and His Fight for Baseball Players' Rights.* New York: Persea Books, 2006.

Berger, Ralph. "Saul Rogovin." *The Baseball Biography Project.* Society for American Baseball Research, Cleveland, Ohio. Available online at http://bioproj.sabr.org.

Berney, Louis. *Tales from the Orioles Dugout.* Champaign, Ill.: Sports Publishing, 2004.

Bisher, Furman. "The Richards System." *Baseball Digest,* December–January 1966–1967.

Bissinger, Buzz. "My Right Arm." *Play,* online magazine published by the *New York Times,* June 3, 2007.www.nytimes.com/2007/06/03/sports/playmagazine/0603play-wood.html.

———. *Three Nights in August.* Boston: Houghton Mifflin, 2005.

Blake, Mike. *Baseball Chronicles: An Oral History of Baseball through the Decades.* Cincinnati: Betterway Books, 1994.

Blount, Roy Jr. "Atlanta, Tranquillity Base Here." *Sports Illustrated,* August 4, 1969, online archive.

Blundell, Jonathan. "From Dallas to Waco Via Waxahachie." *W—The Magazine of Ellis County (Texas),* July 2006, 14–19.

Brandon, Dave. "Then and Now: RC Q&A with Charlie Metro." Royals Corner, May 28, 2007, http://royals.scout.com/2/647130.html.

"Brave New Season," *Time*, April 5, 1943, online archive.

Briley, Ron. "The Houston Colt .45's: The Other Expansion Team of 1962." *East Texas Historical Journal* 32, no. 2 (1994), online archive.

———. "Roman Mejias: Houston's First Major League Latin Star and the Troubled Legacy of Race Relations in the Lone Star State." *Nine: A Journal of Baseball History and Culture*, 2001, online archive.

Brinkley, David. *Washington Goes to War*. New York: Alfred A. Knopf, 1988.

Brown, Warren. *The Chicago Cubs*. New York: G. P. Putnam, 1946.

Bryan, Mike. "Reflections on the Game." *Sports Illustrated*, April 24, 1989, online archive.

Burk, Robert F. *Much More Than a Game*. Chapel Hill: University of North Carolina Press, 2001.

———. *Never Just a Game*. Chapel Hill: University of North Carolina Press, 1994.

Cahan, Richard, and Mark Jacob, eds. *The Game That Was: The George Brace Baseball Photo Collection*. Chicago: Contemporary Books, 1996.

Cairns, Bob. *Pen Men*. New York: St. Martin's, 1992.

Callahan, Tom. *Johnny U: The Life and Times of John Unitas*. New York: Crown, 2006.

Carney, Gene. *Burying the Black Sox*. Washington, D.C.: Potomac Books, 2006.

Carroll, Dink. "When the Astros Tried to Trade Entire Team!" *Baseball Digest*, March 1983, 51.

Carruth, Gorton. *What Happened When*. New York: Signet, 1991.

Carry, Peter. "Mad Scramble East and West." *Sports Illustrated*, September 8, 1969.

Complete Baseball Encyclopedia. Electronic database available at www.baseball-encyclopedia.com.

Conn, Stetson. *Highlights of Mobilization, World War II, 1938–1942*. Washington, D.C.: Office of the Chief of Military History, Department of the Army, 1959.

Corbett, Warren. "Art Houtteman." The Baseball Biography Project. Society for American Baseball Research, Cleveland, Ohio. Available online at http://bioproj.sabr.org.

———. "Eddie Dyer." The Baseball Biography Project. Society for American Baseball Research, Cleveland, Ohio. Available online at http://bioproj.sabr.org.

———. "Gus Mancuso." The Baseball Biography Project. Society for American Baseball Research, Cleveland, Ohio. Available online at http://bioproj.sabr.org.

Cramer, Richard Ben. *Joe DiMaggio: The Hero's Life*. New York: Simon and Schuster, 2000.

Creamer, Robert. "Boot a Few, Bat a Million." *Sports Illustrated*, July 15, 1963, online archive.

———. *Stengel: His Life and Times*. 1984. Reprint, Lincoln: University of Nebraska Press, 1996.

———, ed. "They Said It." *Sports Illustrated*, March 5, 1973, online archive.

Darnell, Tim. *The Crackers: Early Years of Atlanta Baseball*. Athens, Ga.: Hill Street Press, 2003.

———. "Ponce de Leon Ballpark." *New Georgia Encyclopedia*, January 22, 2004. www.georgiaencyclopedia.com/nge/Article.jsp?path=/SportsRecreation/IndividualandTeamSports/Baseball&id=h-2475.

Deadball Era Committee of the Society for American Baseball Research. *Deadball Stars of the National League*. Edited by Tom Simon. Washington, D.C.: Brassey's, 2004.

Deford, Frank. "The Professional Opinion Is Mixed." *Sports Illustrated*, March 23, 1964, online archive.

Dethloff, Henry C. "Suddenly Tomorrow Came . . . A History of the Johnson Space Center." 1993. Johnson Space Center. National Aeronautics and Space Administration. www11.jsc.nasa.gov/history/suddenly_tomorrow/suddenly.htm.

Dierker, Larry. *This Ain't Brain Surgery*. New York: Simon and Schuster, 2003.

Doust, Dudley. "Bonus Baby Blues." *Sports Illustrated*, July 14, 1958, online archive.

Eisenberg, John. *From 33rd Street to Camden Yards: An Oral History of the Baltimore Orioles*. New York: Contemporary Books, 2001.

Elston, Gene, Harry Kalas, and Loel Passe. Play-by-play broadcast, Houston Astros v. New York Yankees, April 9, 1965. Exhibition game (first game in the Astrodome). Astros Baseball Network, Miley Collection.

Enders, Eric. "Nap Rucker." The Baseball Biography Project. Society for American Baseball Research, Cleveland, Ohio. Available online at http://bioproj.sabr.org.

Eskenazi, Gerald. *Bill Veeck: A Baseball Legend*. New York: McGraw-Hill, 1988.

———. *The Lip*. New York: William Morrow, 1997.

Faske, Frank. "Help from Home." *Baseball*, September 1946, 353, 356.

Feinstein, John. *Play Ball*. New York: Villard, 1993.

Feller, Bob, and Bill Gilbert. *Now Pitching: Bob Feller*. New York: Birch Lane Press/Carol Publishing Group, 1990.

Fetter, Henry D. *Taking on the Yankees*. New York: W.W. Norton, 2003.

Fox, Stephen. *Big Leagues: Professional Baseball, Football, and Basketball in National Memory*. New York: William Morrow, 1994.

Frick, Ford C. *Games, Asterisks, and People: Memoirs of a Lucky Fan*. New York: Crown, 1973.

Furlong, William Barry, and Fred Russell. "He Put the White Sox Back in the League." *Saturday Evening Post*, July 21, 1951, 25, 90–92.

Gazel, Neal R. "Nellie Does Right by the White Sox." *Baseball Digest*, August 1951, 5–10.

Gerlach, Larry R. *The Men in Blue*. 1980. Reprint, Lincoln: University of Nebraska Press, 1994.

Gilbert, Bill. *They Also Served: Baseball and the Home Front, 1941–1945*. New York: Crown, 1992.

Giles, Bill, with Doug Myers. *Pouring Six Beers at a Time and Other Stories from a Lifetime in Baseball*. Chicago: Triumph Books, 2007.

Goldman, Steven. *Forging Genius*. Washington, D.C.: Potomac Books, 2005.

Goldstein, Richard. *Spartan Seasons*. New York: Macmillan, 1980.

Golenbock, Peter. *Dynasty*. Englewood Cliffs, N.J.: Prentice-Hall, 1975.

———. *The Spirit of St. Louis*. New York: Harper Entertainment, 2001.

———. *Wrigleyville*. New York: St. Martin's, 1996.

Gough, David, and Jim Bard. *Little Nel: The Nellie Fox Story*. Alexandria, Va.: D. L. Megbeck, 2000.

Graham, Katharine. *Katharine Graham's Washington*. New York: Alfred A. Knopf, 2002.

Greenberg, Hank. *The Story of My Life*. Edited by Ira Berkow. New York: Times Books, 1989.

Greene, Lee. "Suddenly Wilhelm's a Mystery." *Sport*, September 1959, 74–79.

Gregory, Robert. *Diz*. New York: Viking, 1992.

Gutkind, Lee. *The Best Seat in Baseball, but You Have to Stand*. New York: Dial, 1975.

Halberstam, David. *The Fifties*. New York: Villard, 1993.

Hancock, Billy R. *A Story of Paul Richards Park and Waxahachie High School Baseball*. Waxahachie, Texas: Waxahachie High School RBI Club, 2008.

Hancock, Ted. "Hot Wells Natatorium Company." *This Was Ellis County*, a publication of the junior historians of Waxahachie High School, Waxahachie, Texas, 1977.

Hardy-Heck-Moore, Inc. *Historic Resources of Waxahachie, Texas*. July 1985. www.rootsweb.com/~txecm/waxahach.htm.

Harvey, Randy. "From Waxahachie to the White Sox." *Dallas Times-Herald Sunday* magazine, August 29, 1976, 20–24.

Harwell, Ernie. "Baseball Wizard." *Parade*, March 16, 1958, 24–25.

Hawkins, Edna Davis, Ruth Stone, Ida M. Brookshire, and Lillie Tolleson. *History of Ellis County, Texas*. Waco: Texian Press, 1972.

Hecht, Henry. "A Fond Farewell to a Baseball Man Who Wasn't Afraid to Take Chances." *Sports Illustrated*, May 25, 1986, online archive.

Helyar, John. *Lords of the Realm*. New York: Villard, 1994.

Herskowitz, Mickey. "The Land of the Nonbreaking Curveball." *Sports Illustrated*, March 11, 1963, online archive.

———. *The Mickey Herskowitz Collection*. Dallas: Taylor, 1989.

Herzog, Whitey, and Jonathan Pitts. *You're Missin' a Great Game*. New York: Simon and Schuster, 1999.

Hofstadter, Richard. *The Age of Reform*. New York: Vintage, 1955.

Hoke, Travis. "The Base in Baseball." *Esquire*, October 1935. www.baseballthinkfactory.org/btf/pages/essays/rickey/hoke.htm.

Holtzman, Jerome. "Pitch Counts Changing the Development Strategies of Starters." *Baseball Digest*, September 2002, online archive.

———. "Why Do Few Champions Repeat?" *Baseball Digest*, April 1961, 29–34.

Holtzman, Jerome, and George Vass. *Baseball Chicago Style*. Chicago: Bonus Books, 2001.

Honig, Donald. *A Donald Honig Reader*. New York: Fireside/Simon and Schuster, 1988.

———. *The Man in the Dugout*. Chicago: Follett, 1977.

Houk, Ralph, with Robert W. Creamer. *Season of Glory*. New York: G. P. Putnam, 1988.

Jackson, Frank. "Crossing Red River: Spring Training in Texas," 85–91. In Society for American Baseball Research, *The National Pastime*. Vol. 26. Cleveland, Ohio: SABR, 2006.

Jaffe, Chris. "Evaluating Managers." *Baseball Think Factory*, June 12 and July 17, 2006. www.baseballthinkfactory.org.

James, Bill. *The Bill James Baseball Abstract 1986*. New York: Ballantine, 1986.

———. *The Bill James Guide to Baseball Managers*. New York: Scribner's, 1997.

———. *The Bill James Historical Baseball Abstract*. New York: Villard, 1986.

———. *The New Bill James Historical Baseball Abstract*. New York: Free Press, 2001.

———. *This Time Let's Not Eat the Bones*. New York: Villard, 1989.

James, Bill, and Jim Henzler. *Win Shares*. Morton Grove, Ill.: STATS, 2002.

James, Bill, and Rob Neyer. *The Neyer/James Guide to Pitchers*. New York: Fireside/Simon and Schuster, 2004.

James, Bill, John Dewan, Neil Munro, and Don Zminda, eds. *Bill James Presents STATS All-Time Baseball Sourcebook*. Skokie, Ill.: STATS, 1998.

Jares, Joe. "The Big Screen Is Watching." *Sports Illustrated*, May 31, 1965, online archive.

———. "The Mets Find a Young Phenom." *Sports Illustrated*, June 26, 1967, online archive.

Jeffries, John W. *Wartime America*. Chicago: Ivan R. Dee, 1996.

Jordan, David M. *A Tiger in His Time: Hal Newhouser and the Burden of Wartime Baseball*. South Bend, Ind.: Diamond Communications, 1990.

Katz, Jeffrey. "Earl Williams." *The Baseball Biography Project*. Society for American Baseball Research, Cleveland, Ohio. Available online at http://bioproj.sabr.org.

Kavanagh, Jack, and Norman Macht. *Uncle Robbie*. Cleveland: Society for American Baseball Research, 1999.

Keegan, Tom. *Ernie Harwell: My Sixty Years in Baseball*. Chicago: Triumph, 2002.

Kelley, Brent. "Ben Hogan." About.com: Golf. n.d. http://golf.about.com/od/golfersmen/p/ben_hogan.htm.

Keri, Jonah, ed. *Baseball Between the Numbers*. New York: Basic, 2006.

Kerr, Jon. *Calvin: Baseball's Last Dinosaur*. Dubuque, Iowa: Wm. C. Brown, 1990.

Kerrane, Kevin. *Dollar Sign on the Muscle*. New York: Fireside/Simon and Schuster, 1989.

Koppett, Leonard. *A Thinking Man's Guide to Baseball*. New York: E. P. Dutton, 1967.

———. *Koppett's Concise History of Major League Baseball*. New York: Carroll and Graf, 2004.

———. *The Man in the Dugout*. New York: Crown, 1993.

Korr, Charles P. *The End of Baseball as We Knew It*. Urbana: University of Illinois Press, 2002.

Kurkjian, Tim. *Is This a Great Game, or What?* New York: St. Martin's Griffin, 2007.

Leggett, William. "Can the Pitchers Stay on Top?" *Sports Illustrated*, April 13, 1964, online archive.

———. "Some Brilliant Pitching in the New Corral." *Sports Illustrated*, May 7, 1962, online archive.

Lieb, Frederick G. *The Detroit Tigers*. New York: G. P. Putnam, 1946.

Linn, Ed. "The Double Life of Paul Richards." *Sport*, August 1955, 49–58.

Lowenfish, Lee. *Branch Rickey: Baseball's Ferocious Gentleman*. Lincoln: University of Nebraska Press, 2007.

Lowry, Philip J. *Green Cathedrals*. New York: Walker, 2006.

McCullough, David. *Truman.* New York: Simon and Schuster, 1992.

MacDonnell, Leo. "That Texas Tiger, Paul Richards." *Baseball,* November 1944, 407–8.

Macht, Norman L. "Turn Back the Clock: Memories from Former SS Joe DeMaestri." *Baseball Digest,* September 2003, 74–77.

MacPhail, Lee. *My Nine Innings.* Westport, Conn.: Meckler Books, 1989.

Marshall, William. *Baseball's Pivotal Era: 1946–1951.* Lexington: University Press of Kentucky, 1999.

Mead, William B. *Baseball Goes to War.* Washington, D.C.: Broadcast Interview Source, 1998. First published 1978 as *Even the Browns* by Contemporary Books.

Meany, Tom. "The Orioles Are Coming." *Sport,* February 1958, 23–27.

Miller, James Edward. *The Baseball Business: Pursuing Pennants and Profits in Baltimore.* Chapel Hill: University of North Carolina Press, 1990.

Miller, Marvin. *A Whole Different Ball Game.* New York: Carol, 1991.

Millikin, Mark R. *Jimmie Foxx: The Pride of Sudlersville.* Lanham, Md.: Scarecrow, 1998.

Minoso, Minnie, with Herb Fagen. *Just Call Me Minnie.* Champaign, Ill.: Sagamore, 1994.

Moffi, Larry. *This Side of Cooperstown.* Iowa City: University of Iowa Press, 1996.

Moffi, Larry, and Jonathan Kronstadt. *Crossing the Line: Black Major Leaguers, 1947–1959.* Iowa City: University of Iowa Press, 1994.

Montville, Leigh. *The Big Bam: The Life and Times of Babe Ruth.* New York: Doubleday, 2006.

———. *Ted Williams: The Biography of an American Hero.* New York: Doubleday, 2004.

Morgan, Joe, and David Falkner. *Joe Morgan: A Life in Baseball.* New York: W. W. Norton, 1993.

Morris, Peter. *The Game on the Field.* Vol. 1, *A Game of Inches.* Chicago: Ivan R. Dee, 2006.

———. *The Game behind the Scenes.* Vol. 2, *A Game of Inches.* Chicago: Ivan R. Dee, 2006.

Mowbray, William W. *The Eastern Shore Baseball League.* Centreville, Md.: Tidewater, 1989.

Mulvoy, Mark. "Things Are Different in Atlanta." *Sports Illustrated,* March 27, 1967, online archive.

Musial, Stan, as told to Bob Broeg. *Stan Musial: "The Man's" Own Story.* New York: Doubleday, 1964.

Nash, Ogden. "Behind Umpires' Backs Stars Relax." *Life,* September 19, 1955, 85.

Neft, David S., Richard M. Cohen, and Michael L. Neft. *The Sports Encyclopedia: Baseball.* New York: St. Martin's Griffin, 2001.

Nemec, David. *The Official Rules of Baseball.* New York: Barnes and Noble, 1999.

Neyer, Rob. *Rob Neyer's Big Book of Baseball Blunders.* New York: Fireside/Simon and Schuster, 2006.

———. *Rob Neyer's Big Book of Baseball Legends.* New York: Fireside/Simon and Schuster, 2008.

———. *Rob Neyer's Big Book of Baseball Lineups.* New York: Fireside/Simon and Schuster, 2003.

Niekro, Phil, and Tom Bird. *Knuckle Balls.* New York: Freundlich, 1986.

Nowlin, Bill. "Roland Hemond." *The Baseball Biography Project.* Society for American Baseball Research, Cleveland, Ohio. Available online at http://bioproj.sabr.org.

O'Neill, William L. *A Democracy at War.* New York: Free Press, 1993.

Outlar, Jesse. "The Reunion of Richards and Harris." *Atlanta Journal-Constitution Magazine,* April 7, 1968.

Overfield, Joseph M. *The One Hundred Years of Buffalo Baseball.* Kenmore, N.Y.: Partners' Press, 1985.

———. "The Richards-Jethroe Caper: Fact or Fiction?" *Baseball Research Journal* (1987): 33–35.

Parrott, Harold. *The Lords of Baseball.* 1976. Reprint, Atlanta: Longstreet, 2001.

Peary, Danny, ed. *We Played the Game.* New York: Black Dog and Laventhol, 1994.

Pepe, Phil. *Talkin' Baseball: An Oral History of Baseball in the 1970s.* New York: Ballantine, 1998.

Perry, Jim. "If You Build It . . ." *W—The Magazine of Ellis County (Texas),* May 2005, 8–13.

Pietrusza, David. *Judge and Jury: The Life and Times of Judge Kenesaw Mountain Landis.* South Bend, Ind.: Diamond Communications, 1998.

———. *Lights On! The Wild Century-Long Saga of Night Baseball.* Lanham, Md.: Scarecrow, 1997.
Pluto, Terry. *The Earl of Baltimore.* New York: New Century, 1982.
Polner, Murray. *Branch Rickey.* New York: Atheneum, 1982.
Prager, Joshua. *The Echoing Green: The Untold Story of Bobby Thomson, Ralph Branca, and the Shot Heard Round the World.* New York: Pantheon, 2006.
Price, S. L. "Dark Times for a Baseball Man." *Sports Illustrated,* June 4, 2007, online archive.
The Professional Baseball Player Database 5.0. Shawnee Mission, Kansas: Old Time Data, 2002.
Ray, Edgar W. *The Grand Huckster: Houston's Judge Roy Hofheinz, Genius of the Astrodome.* Memphis, Tenn.: Memphis State University Press, 1980.
Reed, Robert. *Colt .45s: A Six-Gun Salute.* Houston: Gulf, 1999.
Retrosheet. www.retrosheet.org.
Richards, Paul. *Modern Baseball Strategy.* Englewood Cliffs, N.J.: Prentice-Hall, 1955.
———. "Orestes Minoso: Minnie by a Mile!" *1952 Baseball Stars,* 60–63. Annual published by Dell.
———. "Paul Richards Looks at Baseball." *Atlanta Braves Scorebook,* 1972.
———. "Secrets of a Baseball Manager." *Collier's,* August 7, 1953, 40–45.
Richards, Paul, as told to Arthur and Milton Richman. "The Orioles Will Win the Pennant." *Saturday Evening Post,* April 15, 1961, 31, 124–26.
Richards, Paul, with Tim Cohane. "The American League Is Dying." *Look,* February 17, 1959, 41–47.
Richman, Milton. "The Ballplayers Give the Lowdown on A.L. Managers." *Sport,* October 1956, 80–83.
Rickey, Branch. "Goodby [*sic*] to Some Old Baseball Ideas." *Life,* August 2, 1954, 78–89.
Ripken, Cal Sr., with Larry Burke. *The Ripken Way.* New York: Pocket Books, 1999.
Ritter, Lawrence. *The Glory of Their Times.* New York: Macmillan, 1966.
Ronberg, Gary. "Felix Is One Sweet Ballplayer." *Sports Illustrated,* July 22, 1968, online archive.
———. "Houston's Boy Is Now a Man." *Sports Illustrated,* August 14, 1967, online archive.
Russo, Jim, with Bob Hammel. *SuperScout.* Chicago: Bonus Books, 1992.
Schwarz, Alan. *The Numbers Game: Baseball's Lifelong Fascination with Statistics.* New York: Thomas Dunne Books/St. Martin's, 2004.
Seymour, Harold. *Baseball: The Golden Age.* New York: Oxford University Press, 1971.
Shanks, Bill. *Scout's Honor: The Bravest Way to Build a Winning Team.* New York: Sterling and Ross, 2005.
Shapiro, Michael. *The Last Good Season: Brooklyn, the Dodgers, and Their Final Pennant Race Together.* New York: Doubleday, 2003.
Shatzkin, Mike, ed. *The Ballplayers.* New York: Arbor House/William Morrow, 1990.
Shaw, Bob. *Pitching: The Basic Fundamentals and Mechanics of Successful Pitching.* New York: Viking, 1972.
Sherwood, Robert E. *Roosevelt and Hopkins: An Intimate History.* New York: Harper, 1948.
Shropshire, Mike. *Seasons in Hell.* New York: Avon, 1996.
Sickels, John. *Bob Feller: Ace of the Greatest Generation.* Washington, D.C.: Brassey's, 2004.
Simon, Tom. "Birdie Tebbetts." *The Baseball Biography Project.* Society for American Baseball Research, Cleveland, Ohio. Available online at http://bioproj.sabr.org.
Smith, Tal. Interview by Maury Brown. 2005. www.businessofbaseball.com/smith_interview.htm.
Spatz, Lyle. "Hank Borowy." *The Baseball Biography Project.* Society for American Baseball Research, Cleveland, Ohio. Available online at http://bioproj.sabr.org.
"Stan Bolton Returns to Waxahachie." Home video. November 1993. In the personal collection of Michelle Bolton-Foster.
Stanton, Tom. *Hank Aaron and the Home Run That Changed America.* New York: William Morrow, 2004.
Staten, Vince. *Ol' Diz.* New York: HarperCollins, 1992.

Stein, Fred. "Mel Ott." *The Baseball Biography Project.* Society for American Baseball Research, Cleveland, Ohio. Available online at http://bioproj.sabr.org.

Stephan, C. David. "Allan Roth's True Discovery of Sabermetrics Revealed, with Others' 'Bells 'n' Whistles.'" *Grandstand Baseball Annual* (1994).

Stewart, Mark, and Mike Kennedy. *Hammering Hank: How the Media Made Hank Aaron.* Guilford, Conn.: Lyons Press, 2007.

Stewart, Richard W., general ed. *The United States Army in a Global Era, 1917–2003.* Vol. 2, *American Military History.* Washington, D.C.: Center for Military History, U.S. Army, 2005.

Stine, Whitney, with Bette Davis. *Mother Goddam: The Story of the Career of Bette Davis.* New York: Berkeley Medallion, 1975.

Stott, Kelly McMichael. *Waxahachie: Where Cotton Reigned King.* Charleston, S.C.: Arcadia, 2002.

Sullivan, Neil J. *The Minors.* New York: St. Martin's, 1990.

Terrell, Roy. "Baltimore's Bubble Bursts." *Sports Illustrated,* September 26, 1960, online archive.

———. "'The Damndest Mess Baseball Has Ever Seen,'" *Sports Illustrated,* December 19, 1960, online archive.

———. "Fast Man with a .45." *Sports Illustrated,* March 26, 1962, online archive.

———. "Hawkeye and His Boy Scouts." *Sports Illustrated,* April 17, 1961, 68–84.

Thorn, John, Pete Palmer, Michael Girshman, and David Pietrusza, eds. *Total Baseball.* 5th ed. New York: Viking Penguin, 1997.

Thornley, Stew, comp. "Minneapolis Millers." n.d. http://stewthornley.net/millers.

Titchener, Campbell B. *The George Kirksey Story: Bringing Major League Baseball to Houston.* Austin: Eakin Press, 1989.

Torre, Joe, with Tom Verducci. *Chasing the Dream.* New York: Bantam, 1997.

Treder, Steve. "Dig the 1950s." *Hardball Times,* March 23, 2004. www.hardballtimes.com.

———. "Eddie, Eddie, Eddie and the American League Walkathon." *Hardball Times,* September 1, 2004. www.hardballtimes.com.

———. "Franchises at Birth: The Colt .45s and the Mets (Part One)." *Hardball Times,* August 8, 2005. www.hardballtimes.com.

———. "Franchises at Birth: The Colt .45s/Astros and the Mets (Part Two)." *Hardball Times,* August 16, 2005. www.hardballtimes.com.

———. "The Persistent Color Line: Specific Instances of Racial Preference in Major League Player Evaluation Decisions after 1947." *Nine: A Journal of Baseball History and Culture,* Fall 2001, 1–30.

———. "The Value Production Standings: 1951–1955." *Hardball Times,* September 19, 2006. www.hardballtimes.com.

———. "The Wizard of Waxahachie." *Nine: A Journal of Baseball History and Culture,* Spring 2007, 1–31.

Turner, Frederick. *When the Boys Came Back.* New York: Henry Holt, 1996.

Tygiel, Jules. *Baseball's Great Experiment: Jackie Robinson and His Legacy.* New York: Vintage, 1984.

———. *Past Time.* New York: Oxford University Press, 2000.

Utley, Hank, and Warren Corbett. "Dick Culler." *The Baseball Biography Project.* Society for American Baseball Research, Cleveland, Ohio. Available online at http://bioproj.sabr.org.

Vass, George. "Juggling the Lineup." *Baseball Digest,* January 2001, online edition.

Veeck, Bill, with Ed Linn. *The Hustler's Handbook.* New York: Fireside/Simon and Schuster, 1989. First published 1965 by Putnam.

———. *Veeck as in Wreck: The Autobiography of Bill Veeck.* Chicago: University of Chicago Press, 2001. First published 1962 by Putnam..

Vincent, David. *Home Run: The Definitive History of Baseball's Ultimate Weapon.* Washington, D.C.: Potomac Books, 2007.

———. "Q&A." *Parade,* October 16, 2005, 14.

Viva Baseball! DVD. Documentary directed by Dan Klores. Shoot the Moon Productions. 2005.

Voigt, David. *American Baseball*. Vol. 1. University Park: Pennsylvania State University Press, 1983.

———. *From the Commissioners to Continental Expansion*. Vol. 2, *American Baseball*. University Park: Pennsylvania State University Press, 1983.

Ward, John Montgomery. *Baseball: How to Become a Player*. 1888. Reprint, Cleveland, Ohio: Society for American Baseball Research, 1993.

Weaver, Earl, with Berry Stainback. *It's What You Learn after You Know It All That Counts*. New York: Doubleday, 1982.

Weaver, Earl, with Terry Pluto. *Weaver on Strategy*. 1984. Reprint, Washington, D.C.: Brassey's, 2002.

Weiskopf, Herm. "The Week." *Sports Illustrated*, June 21, 1982, online archive.

Weiss, Bill, and Marshall Wright. "Team #8 1937 Salisbury Indians (80–16)." In the series "Top One Hundred Teams." *MiLM.com*. n.d. www.minorleaguebaseball.com/app/milb/history/top100.jsp?idx=8.

White, G. Edward. *Creating the National Pastime*. Princeton, N.J.: Princeton University Press, 1996.

Will, George F. "Fielder of Dreams." *New York Times Book Review*, May 7, 2006, online edition.

———. *Men at Work: The Craft of Baseball*. New York: Macmillan, 1990.

Williams, Dick, and Bill Plaschke. *No More Mr. Nice Guy*. San Diego: Harcourt Brace Jovanovich, 1990.

Williams, Peter. *When the Giants Were Giants*. Chapel Hill, N.C.: Algonquin, 1994.

———, ed. *The Joe Williams Baseball Reader*. Chapel Hill, N.C.: Algonquin, 1989.

Williams, Roger. "Baseball's Week." *Sports Illustrated*, May 9, 1960, online archive.

Williams, Ted, with John Underwood. *My Turn at Bat*. 1969. Reprint, New York: Fireside/Simon and Schuster, 1988.

Wright, Craig, and Tom House. *The Diamond Appraised*. New York: Simon and Schuster, 1989.

Zimbalist, Andrew. *Baseball and Billions*. New York: Basic, 1992.

Zimmer, Don, with Bill Madden. *Zim: A Baseball Life*. Kingston, N.Y.: Total Sports, 2001.

INTERVIEWS AND PERSONAL CORRESPONDENCE

Bolton, Paul. E-mails to author. September 2006.

Bolton-Foster, Michelle. E-mails to author. September 2006.

Columbo, Nelda Williams. E-mail to author. November 30, 2007.

Davenport, Clay. E-mail to author. March 19, 2007.

Dyson, Paul. E-mails to author. September–October, 2006.

Giles, Perry. Interview by author. August 17, 2006. Waxahachie, Texas.

Harrington, Olivia. E-mail to author. July 19, 2006.

Hastings, Mike. Interviews by author. August–September 2006. Waxahachie, Texas.

Hemond, Roland. Interview by author. October 18, 2006. Phoenix.

Hudgins, David. Interviews by author. August 16–17, 2006. Waxahachie, Texas,

Jordan, Nicholas "Buck." Interviews by author. August 16–17, 2006. Waxahachie, Texas.

La Russa, Tony. Interview by author. November 16, 2007. Telephone.

Mancuso, August R. III. E-mails to author. April 14, 18, and 23, 2005.

Mann, Earl. "Great Teams." Undated interview for Georgia Sports Hall of Fame, *The New Georgia Encyclopedia*. www.georgiaencyclopedia.com/nge/Multimedia.jsp?id=m-3850.

McQuatters, Bill. Interview by author. August 18, 2007. Fernley, Nev.

Meyer, Edward, Ripley Entertainment. E-mail to author. November 12, 2007.

Mooney, Bill. E-mail to author. December 6, 2006.

Richards, Paul. Taped reminiscences (undated; 1983 or later) of no known provenance, provided by David Hudgins. In the author's files (cited as "Richards Waxahachie tape").

Richards, Paula. E-mails to author. 2006–2008.
Richards, Paula. Interviews by author. May 17–19, 2007. Wadsworth, Nev.
Robinson, Betty. Interview by author. August 18, 2006. Fort Worth, Texas.
Robinson, Eddie. Interview by author. August 18, 2006. Fort Worth, Texas.
Rogers, Kim, Texas University Interscholastic League. Interview by author. January 24, 2007.
Sherrod, Blackie. E-mails to author. July–August 2006.
Wright, Craig. E-mail to author. December 30, 2005.
Wynn, Jimmy. Interview by author. February 28, 2007. Rosharon, Texas.

NEWSPAPERS AND MAGAZINES

I would like to thank the sportswriters of the following publications and wire services, without whose work this book would not have been possible: *Asheville (N.C.) Citizen-Times;* Associated Press; *Atlanta Constitution; Atlanta Georgian; Atlanta Journal; Atlanta Journal-Constitution; Austin (Texas) Statesman; Baltimore Afro-American; Baltimore News American; Baltimore Evening Sun; Baltimore Sun; Boston Sunday Globe; Brooklyn Eagle; Buffalo Courier-Express; Buffalo Evening News; Chicago Daily News; Chicago Defender; Chicago Sun-Times; Chicago Tribune; Christian Science Monitor; Cincinnati Enquirer; Dallas Morning News; Dallas Times-Herald; Decatur (Ala.) Daily; Everett (Wash.) Herald; Hartford Courant;; Houston Chronicle; Houston Post;* International News Service; *Jewish Daily Forward* (New York); *Joplin (Mo.) Globe; Long Beach (Calif.) Independent; Los Angeles Times; Macon (Ga.) News; Macon (Ga.) Telegraph; Minneapolis Star-Tribune;* Newspaper Enterprise Association; *New York Daily News; New York Evening Journal; New York Herald-Tribune; New York Journal-American; New York Sun; New York Times; New York World-Telegram; Oakland (Calif.) Tribune; Salisbury (Md.) Times; St. Louis Daily Star; St. Louis Post-Dispatch; Seattle Post-Intelligencer; Seattle Times; Sporting News; Springfield (Mo.) News and Leader; Syracuse (N.Y.) Herald Journal; Syracuse (N.Y.) Post-Standard; Tacoma News Tribune; Tucson Daily Citizen; USA Today;* United Press and United Press International; *Washington Post;* Washington Post News Service; *Waxahachie (Texas) Daily Light.*

I would also like to acknowledge useful unbylined stories from the following publications:

Life
"Chicago's White Sox Are White Hot." June 18, 1951, 27–31.

Time (from the online archive)
"After Byrnes, Baseball?" January 8, 1945.
"Amber Light." February 12, 1945.
"The Chicago Idea." April 13, 1953.
"Climbing into Orbit." July 8, 1966.
"Daymares in the Dome." April 16, 1965.
"Deep Trouble." June 28, 1943.
"The Longest Season." April 21, 1961.
"Mad Eddie." May 26, 1980.
"Outspoken Broadcast." August 9, 1943.
"The Penalties." January 1, 1945.
"Pennant Parade." September 11, 1944.
"Springing for the Check." March 23, 1987.
"Streetcar Series." October 9, 1944.
"Two for the Money?" September 26, 1960.
"Wanted: Rain." June 9, 1941.
"War & Baseball." July 20, 1942.
"Young Orioles." June 6, 1960.

Sports Illustrated (from the online archive)
  "Any One of Five Can Do." April 10, 1972.
  "Astros in Orbit." June 6, 1966.
  "Baseball Candor Via Air Vent." September 22, 1958.
  "Events and Discoveries of the Week." July 4, 1960.
  "Houston Colt .45s." April 13, 1964.

Index

The initials PR indicate Paul Richards.

Howard Lansat

WARREN CORBETT served briefly as a minor league play-by-play broadcaster before turning to news reporting. A past winner of the Aviation/Space Writers Association award for his writing on the space program, he is now the editor of a trade publication in Washington, D.C. His baseball writing has been published in the Society for American Baseball Research's Baseball Biography Project; the *Diamond*; *National Pastime*; *Go-Go to Glory: The 1959 Chicago White Sox*; and *Lefty, Double-X, and the Kid: The 1939 Red Sox*.